# CONQUEST
## BY
## MAN

* Paul Herrmann *

# CONQUEST
# BY MAN

*Translated from the German by*
MICHAEL BULLOCK

I L L U S T R A T E D

HARPER & BROTHERS · PUBLISHERS
NEW YORK

This book is published in Germany under the title
*Sieben Vorbei Und Acht Verweht*

*Library of Congress catalog card number: 54-10080*

# CONTENTS

*Across the Indian Ocean without a compass · Pilots and lighthouses · Antique sailing manuals · How long is an hour? · 2,000-ton freighters in antiquity · Roman anchorage directions for Indian ports · The Sinhalese are surprised in Rome · Have the Chinese got blue eyes? · Roman merchants in Peking · Empress Si-li-shi and the Bombyx mori worm · Mrs. Marcus Aurelius has no money for a silk dress · The vicious women of the island of Cos · Routes to China · Who sails to Singapore? · With folding-boat across the Atlantic · What did the ancient world know of America? · Red Indians land in Europe.*

## PART EIGHT

## WINELAND

### Page 267

## PART NINE

## FROM JOTUNHEIMAR AND SVALBARD TO BAGDAD AND CANTON

### Page 301

PART TEN

## THE CRUSADES,
## PRESTER JOHN AND THE GREAT KHAN

*Page* 341

*The inscribed stone of Singanfu · Father Trigault is no forger · Is Mary the Mother of God? · The history of the silk road · Professor Lactantius on the amorality of geography · Bias in early travel-narratives · Who were the 'Three Wise Men from the East'? · St. Thomas's Christians · Why Napoleon did not build the Suez Canal · Emperor Justinian practises economic espionage, but the Persians beat him to it · Medieval 'Baedeker' for the journey to the Holy Land · Who is Prester John · Prester John's open letter forgery or fantasy? · The story of the* sidicus *· An embassy from the Great Khan · Papal legates in Caracorum · Transylvanian experts in the Altai Mountains · 'Visum fuit mihi, quod evasissem de manibus dæmonum' · Two monks desert · 'If you can work magic, I'll become a Christian,' says the Emperor of China · Marco Polo freezes on the 'Roof of the World' · Chinese paper money · The magic island of Chipangu · John of Monte Corvino becomes Archbishop of China · Report from the land where pepper grows · Hanns Schiltberger among the heathen · Franciscans in Astrakhan.*

PART ELEVEN

## THE PORTUGUESE AND AFRICA

*Page* 399

*The first German menu card and old German recipes · Salt meat every day · Cold war against the West · Is Paradise in Abyssinia? · Europe's trade deficit with the East · Who were the Guanches and where did they come from? · Gold from Sofala · Malays discover Madagascar · Prince Henry the Navigator and Africa · Jean Mermoz flies through the Pot-au-Noir · Negro slaves, a sensation in Europe · Is the Senegal a tributary of the Nile? · The Portuguese and Prester John · Diego Cão stakes everything · Martin Behaim and the astrolabe · New directions for the voyage to Africa · Benedetto Dei in Timbuctoo · European inflation, the Centurione bank, and the gold standard · Antonio Malfante in the Sahara · Portugal plays two aces · The* Cabo Tormentoso *and Pedro de Covilhao's expedition · From the* Ploughman of Saaz *to the new era.*

# ILLUSTRATIONS IN THE TEXT

# MAPS

# HALFTONE PLATES

# FOREWORD

THE success this book has enjoyed on the continent of Europe seems to suggest that its subject matter, although long familiar to workers in the particular fields involved, has nevertheless provoked a lively interest even in readers with scholarly pursuits. Indeed, it has emerged that the specialists themselves were not always as well acquainted with the matters treated of here as might have been supposed. This is not due to the author's erudition, but merely indicates how wide is the no-man's-land, how deep the moats and how high the barriers which today divide the various branches of science and scholarship. Under the pressure of circumstances we are all well on the way to becoming specialists, specialists who, though they may be capable of some slight achievement in their own sector, have a much smaller share in their period's total body of knowledge than that possessed by their parents and forefathers.

This is a most regrettable fact, and it is one of the aims of my book to counteract this tendency by making a modest contribution to the broadening of our field of experience. It lays no claim, therefore, to being a work of original research; it is not aimed at the professional scholar or scientist, but rather at the harassed and overworked man in the street whom the struggle to earn a living and advance in his profession deprives of the time he would like to devote to increasing his general knowledge. For this reason I have tried, without any sacrifice of factual accuracy, to make the book rather more entertaining than is usual in works dealing with such a forbidding subject as ancient history, at least in Europe. Mr. Michael Bullock, who undertook the difficult task of translating my book, has carried out this wish to the full, and I must express my grateful admiration for the way in which he has entered into the spirit of the work.

A further aim in writing this book was to weaken the very widespread conviction that our progress in the technological aspects of civilization represents, in any *real* sense, a greater achievement than those of our forebears. The liberation of atomic energy probably means no more and no less than did the invention of the firedrill or the wheel in their day. Both discoveries were of immense importance to early man. But whether they wrought any change in his inmost being, whether they rendered him better or even happier, appears extremely doubtful.

The author's scepticism towards the dogmatists of technical progress is, however, no greater than his repudiation of those schools of thought which hold the end of our world to be imminent and draw existentialist and other conclusions from this belief. Spiritual situations similar to those of today must also have arisen during the transition from the Stone to the Bronze Age; and at the turn from the Middle Ages to the Modern Era, about 500 years ago, very much the same thing was being thought, said and written as is being thought, said and written at the present time.

It is, of course, entirely possible that man will destroy himself and that he will vanish from the earth as completely as the saurians and the mammoth. But this is no justification for seeing oneself as a tragic figure and making a new intellectual fashion out of it. Hence, throughout this book, an appeal is repeatedly made to common sense and to that vital optimism which destiny has bestowed upon every living creature, even the frailest and most transient.

There is no new thing under the sun. But every sunrise is the same great and glorious miracle as on the first day of creation!

*Berlin, June* 1954                                    PAUL HERRMANN

# ACKNOWLEDGMENTS

Permission to reproduce the illustrations in the text of this book was kindly given as follows: Nos. 2 and 3 by Verlag Eberhard Brockhaus, Wiesbaden, from Herbert Kühn: *Auf den Spuren des Eiszeitmenschen*; Nos. 45, 46 and 48 by Verlag Hoffmann und Campe, Hamburg, from A. W. Brögger: *Winlandfahrten*; No. 17 by *Passat 1*, Hamburg 1950; No. 1 by Prehistoric Museum, St. Germain-en-Laye, Paris; Nos. 4, 5, 7, 13, 14, 19, 20, 42, 44, 57 by Ullstein Bilderdienst, Berlin; all other numbers from archives.

The maps were drawn by Dr. W. Eggers and G. Lohr. Maps V, VII, IX, XXX and XXXI were drawn after Egmont Zechlin: *Martime Weltgeschichte*, Hamburg 1947; map XXVI after *Passat 3*, Hamburg 1949; map I after A. Schulten: *Tartessos*, Hamburg 1951; maps XI and XII after Albert Herrmann: *Die alten Seidenstrassen zwischen China und Syrien*, Berlin 1910; maps XIX and XXI after E. F. Gray: *Leif Eriksson, discoverer of America*, New York 1930; map XXI after Ullstein Bilderdienst, Berlin; the rest from the author's sketches.

The plates were kindly supplied by the following: No. 32 by the American Museum of Natural History, New York; Nos. 3 to 7 by Deutscher Kunstverlag, Berlin; Nos. 26 and 27 by Thor Heyerdahl from *Kon-tiki. Ein Floss trebt über den Pazifik*, Ullstein Verlag, Vienna 1949; Nos. 31, 33, 34 by Lateinamerikanische Bibliothek, Berlin; Nos. 46–8 by Lechler-Gray from *Die Entdecker Amerikas vor Kolumbus*, Curt Kabitzsch Verlag, Leipzig 1939; No. 36 by the Bishop Museum, Honolulu from Peter H. Buck: *Vikings of the Sunrise*, J. B. Lippincott Co., Philadelphia 1938; Nos. 40–3 by the National Museum, Copenhagen; Nos. 50 and 51 by the former State Museum for Prehistory and Ancient History, Berlin; No. 57 from archives; all others from Ullstein Bilderdienst, Berlin.

CAREFULLY the kneeling man raked armful after armful of gravel over the mouth of the shaft, which he had covered with biggish stones and camouflaged with branches of birch and fir. Now it was no longer visible, and not even the sharp-eyed hunters of the horde of primitive men from the ravine below would be able to find the cave.

It would be disastrous if they did. For then they would break the spell and appropriate it to themselves, the spell which he had cast for the benefit of his own horde. And it was so very necessary that his horde should at last find game again; they needed food and furs, and also fat for their lamps. The horde was hungry.

Satisfied with his work, the man sat back on his heels. Now he had finished. For days he had stood down there in the cave, painting on the rock wall the bison they were going to hunt tomorrow. He had taken the best ochre and fresh animal fat, and then he had carefully blown the coloured powder over the greasy surface by means of a thin hollow bone. Black manganese earth provided the contours and the shadows, giving the picture depth and, with depth, life. Ochre ground to a fine powder in the mortar and made lighter with chalk, or reddened and darkened with iron oxide, filled in the planes. Now the bison stood there as though it were alive; in the flickering torchlight its eye seemed to glow, its muscles seemed to tense beneath the glistening hide and its tail to lash to and fro in excitement: exactly like the gigantic beasts that were to be seen grazing on the grassy hillsides.

As an artist, as the principal and teacher of a great school of painting with many young people in it, our friend had really passed beyond realistic representations of this sort. The Old Ones had painted in this way, even at times and at places where there was no question of hunting-magic or the casting of spells. That could be seen everywhere in the caves, in El Castillo and La Pasiega, in Pindal and Corvalanas. It originated from early, naive, simple days, from the times when the ice came creeping down from the mountains, when rain fell unceasingly from the skies and men were happy if occasionally the sun shone. Then people had painted in this plain, straightforward manner.

Now they knew more. The mists had long since evaporated, ice clung only to the high mountain ridges, the light of heaven shone many days in the year, and now men *saw*, now for the first time they were *able* to see, that nature consisted of a rapid series of momentary images. *This* was what had to be painted. The swift herd of reindeer, for example: the first two animals one saw clearly, consequently they must also be clearly drawn, with antlers, long-shanked legs, and bodies.

*1. Bison. Stone Age engraving from a cave in the Dordogne.*

The last members of the herd were clear too, and therefore must also be portrayed clearly. But everything that stampeded along between the beginning and the end was no more than a wave of lines, shadows, and scratches all going in the same direction. So there was no other way of rendering this than by a cursory outline.

*This* was what the artist drew, *this* was what he had to paint. What he had been doing down there in the sacred cave the whole of the past week was artistically indefensible, and he really wondered whether, next time, he should not send his assistants instead.

His father had still been able to believe that success in the chase and the accurate flight of the arrow depended upon the verisimilitude of the picture, that a spell went forth from the image in the cave and worked upon the living animal somewhere over yonder, behind the mountains. Now no one believed this but the hunters, those delightfully old-fashioned simpletons. One had no wish to deprive them of their illusion. After all, what was there to set in its place in this enlightened century? Besides, it did nobody any harm to have painted the bison in the manner of his forefathers, as had been the custom since time immemorial. This was what the sacred usage of the cave demanded. As long as the young hunters hit their mark! . . .

*2. Passing reindeer herd. The first and last animals are clearly depicted. Those between are sketched in with a series of brief strokes suggesting rushing movement, a technique reminiscent of the modern impressionists. Drawing on bone, from the cave of Teyjat, Dordogne.*

With this the unknown man vanishes for ever from our ken. Thirty thousand years pass like a single day and disappear like a handful of chaff blown by the wind. It is 1868. There is a fox-hunt at the castle of Santillana del Mar, not far from Santander in Spain. And as one of the hounds suddenly vanishes into the earth, as a crack in the ground opens up at a kick from the huntsman, and ice-cold air blows up from it into the warm Spanish November day, the entrance is opened to those self-same sacred caves, which the magician-painter of the Late Ice Age had so carefully sealed.

Soon afterwards the huntsmen enter the caves with lanterns and torches. The first things they find are tools, such as had already been discovered in the Ice Age caves of France: bodkins, awls, harpoons, scrapers, rasps, sewing needles, in a word, all the implements proper to a well-appointed Ice Age home. Deeper into the earth nothing of this sort is to be found. Here men have never lived, here is the place of magic, here is holy ground. And here are the pictures.

Pictures, hundreds of pictures on all the walls and ceilings, which have remained, through thousands of years, as fresh and glowing as on the day they came into being. Pictures whose colours still adhere to the finger-tips that touch them, pictures upon which no human eye has looked from the time of their genesis till this day at the end of the year of Our Lord 1868. There is a wonderful, delicate hind, there is the bison upon which our magician-painter cast his spell, there he stands snorting and savage, there he falls to his knees wounded in the entrails —so replete with life and primeval power, so authentic, that the full force of this spellbinding can still be felt.

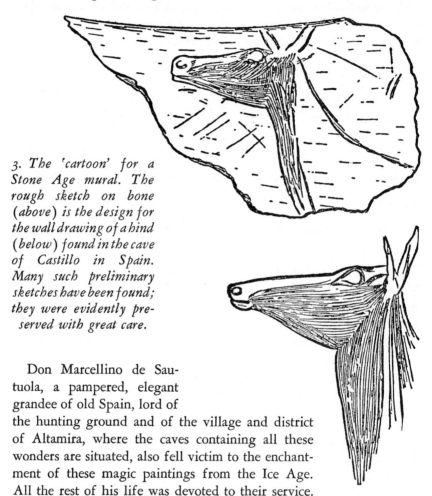

*3. The 'cartoon' for a Stone Age mural. The rough sketch on bone (above) is the design for the wall drawing of a hind (below) found in the cave of Castillo in Spain. Many such preliminary sketches have been found; they were evidently preserved with great care.*

Don Marcellino de Sautuola, a pampered, elegant grandee of old Spain, lord of the hunting ground and of the village and district of Altamira, where the caves containing all these wonders are situated, also fell victim to the enchantment of these magic paintings from the Ice Age. All the rest of his life was devoted to their service.

For many years he reaped nothing but scorn, mockery and searing contempt. He cared nothing for that. In 1880 the Congress of Prehistorians at Lisbon wholeheartedly condemned him. Old Virchow from Germany, the originator of cellular pathology, who enjoyed equal fame as a medical man, an archæologist, a physicist, an anthropologist and a liberal politician, after Goethe the last truly universally cultured spirit the earth brought forth; Undset, representing the Norwegian prehistorians;

the great Montelius from Sweden, and with him the best men from England, Italy, Portugal and the rest, all said No. They were all of the opinion that it was a swindle, a forgery, a lying fake. They were all so completely agreed that they did not even take the trouble to visit Altamira. Of course, up to then they were acquainted only with the fragments of primitive human skeleton unearthed by the Elberfeld grammar-school teacher, Dr. Fuhlrott, at Neanderthal near Düsseldorf in 1856: that weighty skull-cap with the heavy eyebrow ridges, reminiscent of a gorilla, and those thick, clumsy thigh bones, which the quarry workers threw carelessly aside because they did not consider them human at all. It was impossible to attribute to such a bestial creature the glorious paintings of Altamira.

4. *When people still went swimming in the Sahara . . . These thousands-of-years-old rock drawings were found 125 miles from the last thin trickle of water. The drawing seems to suggest that the former Sahara swimmers had mastered the 'crawl'.*

Today we know better. We know that before the end of the Ice Age a new race migrated into Europe from outside, presumably from the east; this was the tall, slender Aurignac man with the beautifully domed skull and the narrow, sharply cut face, a human being very similar to ourselves and regarded as the first representative of *homo sapiens*. Even the prehistorians of the Lisbon Congress would have had more faith in his capacities. But the first skeleton of Aurignac man was unearthed in 1909. Then it became finally certain that Don Marcellino had been right and that the pictures in his caves were genuine: paintings of the Ice Age, the works of a man who had been contemporary with the European bison. In the meantime we have discovered the 'cartoon' for one of the Altamira pictures—a very lively representation of hinds —a slab of stone engraved with a rough draft or sketch of the wall picture. The sketch of a bison which decorated the wall of another Ice Age cave was discovered long ago. And we long ago learnt how these wall paintings began and developed. The first stage consisted of scratches made by human nails in the soft walls of the cave, like those made by the claws of the cave-bear; then came coloured impressions of human hands; after this, brief outlines of animals, laboriously engraved in the wall, first with experimental touches of colour here and there and then coloured all over, with protracted conflicts ranging round the question of light and shade in the picture, round depth and perspective. Epochs of impressionistic concentration on movement in the picture, and on the fleeting moment of vision, followed; upon them ensued expressionistic eras, in which the painted object was simplified and taken apart, split up into the triangles, cubes, segments of a circle, rhombuses and rectangles familiar to us in the art of our own day. This phase was an essential link in the long line of development that culminated in the stylization and symbolism of early picture-writing.

Perhaps all these Ice Age pictures are connected with sorcery and possessed of magical significance. Where they are straightforwardly realistic and immediately and entirely recognizable to the mass of beholders, they are no doubt to be understood in this light. But at the point where impressionistic simplification and snatching at the ephemeral moment—as, for instance, in the beautiful bone rod of Teyjat, whose herd of reindeer consists of two minutely drawn animals at the beginning of the row, the rest of which is indicated by a cloudy wave of dashes, a symbol of lightning movement, an instantaneous image snatched from time—at this point an art may have commenced that was no longer dependent upon

5. *It was not Picasso, but an unknown Stone Age artist, who drew this archer on the wall of the Valltorta Canyon near Abocacer in Spain. Just as in contemporary art, the movement of the bent bow and flying arrow is transferred to the body of the archer.*

magical religion, no longer utilitarian. For this kind of symbolic representation was no longer universally intelligible, and hence can scarcely have still been magical. Representation through drawing and painting had become a private matter, an affair of the ego-conscious individual, the concern of a movement, a fashion, a school. And this may have been the beginning of the path that led, in the end, to picture-writing.

In 1903 prehistorians found at Font-de-Gaume in the Dordogne in

. The battle for the holy cow. The 'One Feathers' are defending their sacred possession gainst the 'Three Feathers'. Arrows hiss, bowstrings twang, blood flows. This wall painting rom the desert region of North Africa was executed many thousands of years ago, but it is bsolutely 'modern' in its stylisation.

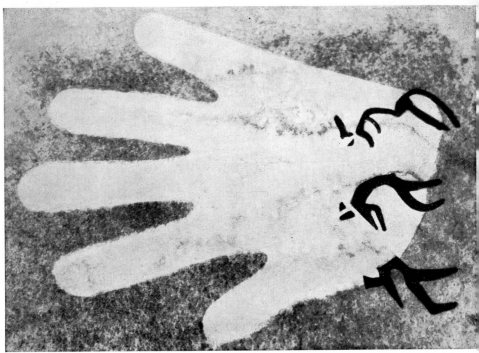

2. Art as magical conjuration. In the white area left by stencilling round his hand this Stone Age artist has drawn stylised human figures. Was he seeking to bring them under his protection —or to gain magical power over them? A rock drawing from North Africa.

3. North German flint implements from c.2000 B.C. These Neolithic weapons and tools (axe, sickle, saw, two daggers) are so skilfully worked as to suggest that they were produced by experts at a manufacturing centre.

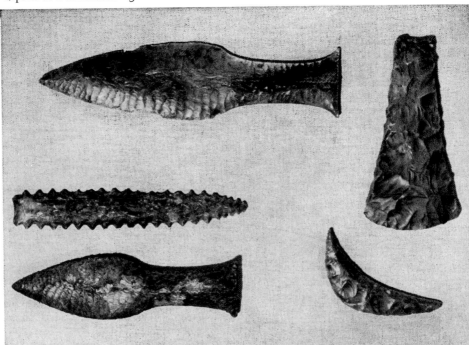

France, the wall picture of a mighty old bison, a gigantic beast, drawn with great individuality. Twenty-three years later, in summer 1926, a slab of slate was found 188 miles away in the prehistoric dwellings of Genière-Ain in the *département* of Ain, bearing the sketch from which the wall picture of Font-de-Gaume had been painted. This is an amazing fact, indeed it is almost more astonishing than the discovery of this Ice Age picture itself. For we must conclude from it that the mere sketch, only suggested in outline and still devoid of colour, which could have no magical significance in view of the absence of any serious attempt at realism, was so highly prized that some Stone Age art lover preserved it in his home—preserved it with such care that it survived ten or maybe even twenty thousand years.

Was there already an art trade in those days? This question has been asked by the Mainz prehistorian, Herbert Kühn, whose recently published book, *On the Tracks of Ice Age Man,* we have up to now been following. It is unlikely that we shall ever be able to answer it. But what can be deduced from the distance travelled by this materially quite worthless slab of stone is the fact that tens of thousands of years ago long journeys were undertaken in Europe. It is astonishing and moving that this journey was made not merely for the sake of some such immediately valuable objects as weapons, tools and ornaments, but for the sake of an insignificant-looking slab of stone covered in scratches.

Even if we honestly strive to be entirely unprejudiced and to rid ourselves of the pious superstition of our grandfathers that we have made splendid progress and that the pitiful early centuries lie, to their misfortune, in the dense fog of their own imperfection, it will still be difficult for us to believe that these far-off ancestors of ours possessed such enthusiasm for art, and even more difficult to credit them with having been able to travel such great distances. For if prehistorical research declares that occasional long journeys, even at a very early period, are not to be ruled out entirely, it nonetheless feels more at ease when it can explain the incontestable distant wanderings of particular objects by a local exchange from place to place and from hand to hand.

Whether this is correct is an open question. During the few dozen centuries we can see back, possession and the defence of possessions have provided the most powerful incentives. Nothing is more natural than to suppose that earlier epochs were subject to exactly the same laws, and that long journeys were undertaken for the sake of profit. And since the earth was then far more sparsely peopled than it is now, the traveller might certainly have covered great distances before so much as catching sight of another man. This same fact, however, reduced the danger of hostile attacks, and it seems quite possible that the peregrinations of which we are about to speak were made not only in the shuttle traffic from locality to locality, from resting place to resting place and from ford to ford, but also in long journeys.

2

No doubt it all began with the tool. Though the rough club may have sufficed at the outset, the wish to be able to cut and saw, to split, scrape and stab brought with it the need to find a suitable primary material. Such a material was stone, from which arrow- and lance-heads, knives, daggers and borers could as easily be produced as ornaments and household utensils. And furthermore stone concealed within it the divine spark of fire—reason enough for it to become, for a period of many thousands of years, man's favourite raw material.

This epoch is known as the Stone Age, though it had, of course, no precise beginning and end. Even at the present day the hands of the world's clock stand, for numerous human beings and over wide areas of the earth, at these early hours before sunrise. The Australian aborigines, the Bushmen of South Africa, the Indians of the South American jungle are repeatedly stated to be living under Stone Age conditions. Even our own existence cannot be imagined without stone, and if we think it over, the great value attached to iron and steel as a basic raw material, and the undervaluation of the part still played by stone in our world, are merely signs that this new primary material for the manufacture of essential tools, utensils, etc., has been known for only a few thousand years, that is to say, for only a very short time.

On the other hand, this recognition of the importance of stone causes us to wonder how the early men, whom chance had cast into vast regions of forest or desert, managed to get hold of tools. As a rule these localities, which appear so forbidding to the twentieth-century city dweller, are no more inimical to life than are lonely coral islands in the eternal ocean. Man can live tolerably well almost anywhere. As starting points for civilization and culture, however, stoneless districts are out of the question. If there are no stones and no possibility of stealing them or acquiring them by trade, the great clock remains for a long time almost stationary.

Wide areas of the land occupied by primitive man were, however, stoneless prairie, dense stoneless forest, reed-bed and marsh. And even where there were stones, there were not always obsidian and flint, lapis lazuli, agate, malachite, nephrite, not always hornblende, quartzite and diorite—the types of stone which flake easily, were therefore easy to work, and which it was necessary to possess if one wanted to emerge victorious in the struggle for existence. Hence anyone who could not pick up stones in his immediate vicinity was compelled to journey afar in search of them, compelled to acquire them by trade and purchase. So began the discovery of the earth.

In ancient Europe flint was the most costly raw material in those distant, early days. Men soon learnt too that flints still buried in the earth, which were still 'quarry fresh', were considerably lighter, and could be more quickly worked, than the weathered material, baked and dried by wind and sun, that lay on the surface.

Thus at a very early stage organized flint-mining developed, whose beginnings date from twelve to fourteen thousand years ago and which was carried on for several millennia. The main centres of this prehistoric flint-mining were southern England, where hundreds of old mine shafts have been discovered, and Belgium, where these primeval mining sites cover scores of acres. Later, around 4000 B.C., Sweden was added. These 'mining enterprises' were not, of course, the work of individual men. It is clear that undertakings of this sort could only have been carried out by a whole group of workers and an extensive division of labour. We know nothing for certain, but probably it all developed on exactly the same lines as early coal-mining in historical times.

Characteristically, around these mining areas, precisely as in our own day, industry developed, a flint-working industry that 'set the hammer' to the raw materials obtained from the mines right on the spot. These industrial undertakings produced for *trade*, for circles of purchasers who were often resident at great distances and must certainly have paid high prices for the valuable flint tools.

On the other hand, it seems as though flint itself was also exported as a raw material, and transported to the districts of the manufacturing industry. There was an industrial district of this kind in Thuringia, for instance, and its axes, hammers and hatchets obviously for a time enjoyed 'world renown'. In East Prussia and on the River Main, in Brandenburg and on Lüneburg Heath tools have been found which originated from these industrial districts of Thuringia. Another group of the ancient European tool industry appears to have been situated on the banks of Lake Constance. Whether it was connected with the

Thuringian 'concerns' we do not know, since our knowledge of the organization behind the rise of this early industry is nil.

But naturally it took place just as haphazardly as in our own day. There is some Stone Age trapper or hunter, pitching his tent, his yourta of thick hair blankets and skins, or his simple wind shelter. He has looked carefully around, this solitary man in the lifeless wilderness. Nearby is a stream with fresh water. Not far away lie the haunts of game. Lofty crags shelter the rear of the site. Now all he needs is to set a circle of fire round him and he is safe for the night. This is the place for the tent!

The soil must first be hollowed out a little, then a circle of stones piled up round the hollow to weigh down the walls of the tent and pull them taut; after that he can lie down.

Night is falling fast. Our Stone Age trapper is working busily. His axe is crashing into the soil—when suddenly a cloud of sparks flies up! Instead of recoiling in fear the man flings himself to the ground, scratches feverishly with his hands, and then lifts up to the departing light what he has found—flint, the most costly thing in the whole world!

No sooner does the first light of morning begin to break than our man is at work again. Drunk with joy, he burrows into the earth, and to his amazement sees that there is also flint deep down. So now he has staked a claim. Of course, he cannot do a great deal with it on his own, and from this point on the flint-digger of long ago ceases to bear any true resemblance to the gold-digger and prospector of the present. Nonetheless, his find is of inestimable value. The horde to which he belongs sets to work at once to deepen the shaft. Lump after lump of flint is brought to the surface, and for a time our hunter is the most respected man of his tribe. This does not last long, of course. After a while the old and important men of the horde take the matter in hand; they organize the flint-mining, put captives into the pits, cause the village specialists, those who were always particularly skilful in the manufacture of flint implements, to settle in the immediate vicinity of the excavation site; and when commission agents from neighbouring tribes and hordes arrive bearing venison, skins, fat, rare ornaments, etc., the wise old men realize that they are rich and that their people is one of the first in the world.

Naturally, the first things to be manufactured are weapons: arrow-heads, lance-heads, axes, daggers, harpoons and the like, and the articles that have been found all over the world are of wonderful workmanship. In order to preserve the technical superiority in weapon production of the horde at the site of the flint-quarry, an embargo on the export of weapons must very soon have been introduced. After the first successful attacks by other, less wealthy hordes, however, they must have come to realize that the spread of technical innovations could not be prevented. Thereupon a period of economic penetration must have ensued, an endeavour to pacify alien tribes and render them dependent by peaceful means, by supplying them with sewing needles, for example, whose smooth, sharp points easily pierced any skin, but whose finely bored and polished eyes were not so apt to cut the thread as bone needles, sewing needles that did not bend and very rarely broke. Ornaments were also manufactured, but above all axes, borers and hammers for working wood, and then rasps and scrapers for the preparation of skins. And such an immense impression did this gift make, so immeasurably miraculous was it, that philologists conjecture that words like sickle, hammer and Saxon—the latter derived from *sax,* the short dagger—have come down to us from the Stone Age.

Since it is very difficult to lower one's living standards and renounce technical achievements that facilitate the struggle for existence, it was natural for the lords of the flint-mines to make every effort to arouse needs in the neighbouring hordes and thereby place them in a position of dependence. Any neighbour who did not toe the line, who upset the established order and spread unrest, was no longer supplied. If he revolted, if it came to war, his technical inferiority again and again proved decisive. For even if he captured the flint-mines and the tool industry, he possessed neither the knowledge nor the experienced specialists essential to both the mining and the working of the flint. Thus ages that opened with turmoil and bloodshed were followed by long peaceful epochs, during which trade and commerce flourished.

There is a great deal of very ancient evidence to suggest that the great trade routes, which were first travelled at this period and which ran in all directions across Europe and Asia, were the subject of a universally respected taboo according to which the person of any man travelling them was sacrosanct. The object of this taboo was clearly to encourage the travelling merchant by protecting him from violence —not out of ethical considerations (even in those days a human life was very cheap), but solely because the fear of attack would inevitably have led to a cessation in the supply of urgently needed goods.

Hence it is in no way surprising that Stone Age industrial products and raw materials often travelled very great distances. Flints from the island of Rügen in the Baltic, easily recognizable by their special chemical composition, have, for example, been unearthed by the Lake of Neuchâtel in Switzerland; stone axes of obviously Finnish origin and workmanship found their way into central Russia; liparites, stones which were dug on the Lipari Islands and nowhere else, have been discovered in ancient Egyptian graves of the fourth millennium; and flint tools of a kind made only in Thuringia went, as we have already heard, as far as East Prussia.

This naturally caused the prehistorians of the last century much heart-searching. Since all of them at that time, often without really knowing it, were influenced by Darwin's theory of evolution, they believed that one had only to go to the still extant primitive peoples of central Africa and Australia to see a living demonstration of what the whole world looked like twelve to fourteen thousand years before. And since it was observed that European trade goods taken by natives on the west African coast made their way in quite a short time, in the shuttle traffic from kraal to kraal and from village to village, right across the whole African continent, till they reappeared again on the east African coast, they felt justified in assuming that things had been no different in Stone Age Europe, and that early trade must likewise have passed over short distances only.

This is possible, of course. And if we hear that cowrie shells have not infrequently been found in north German, Swedish, and English graves from the Middle Stone Age to about the tenth century B.C.—shells which occur only in the Indian Ocean and the Red Sea and which, till quite recently, possessed monetary value and served as coinage over wide areas of the earth—we shall scarcely be so rash as to assert that some Indian or Arab merchant travelled in primordial times from Bombay to London in order to sell his cowrie shells there. Here we shall indeed have to assume that the road was travelled in stages. On the other hand, however, we must not forget that the Late Stone (or Neolithic) Age was already capable of transporting enormous loads over very great distances. The gigantic monoliths of Stonehenge in England, that enigmatic holy place of the Celts, were conveyed from stone-quarries 190 miles away. The blocks of stone in the pyramid of Cheops come from a rock on the other side of the Nile; thus as long ago as 4000 B.C. men knew how to carry weights of thousands of tons across great rivers. How it was done remains to this day more or less unexplained. Even the modern engineer would scratch his head in perplexity when confronted by such a task.

Journeys of very great length were indisputably made in early times. In Mesopotamia of the fourth millennium B.C., for instance, teak from Further India was well known, and the rich merchants of Yemen, the ancient metropolis of the incense trade, preferred the indestructible foreign wood for the door-posts and architraves of their villas and counting-houses. But teak *can* only have come to Mesopotamia and Yemen via the sea route, and not by caravan through the impassable deserts of Baluchistan. It was just the same on the African shore of the Indian Ocean. Round 1500 B.C. many Indian trade articles were in circulation there which had been transported 1,250 miles across the open sea by utilizing the monsoon. The possibility of this was long doubted, because it seemed inconceivable that early man was already acquainted with the secret of the monsoon. But this must have been the case, and it is difficult to get round the fact that neolithic man already ventured on immense voyages across the open sea.

Manifestly then, the world has been since early times almost as great and wide as in our own day. And clearly nothing hindered early man from setting sail from his European or Asiatic homeland to regions as remote as America and Australia. *How* that happened, *when* it happened, what prehistoric races took part in these migrations, we have not the slightest idea. This is a romance that remains to be written when archæologists have finally sifted every square foot of the tundras of Siberia, the jungles of south-east Asia, and the icy wastes of Alaska. Till then we shall have to keep to the study of ancient legends, to comparative research on the tales of different tribes and peoples with their ubiquitous themes of creation, dragons, and the Flood—a task on which, as yet, only fragmentary beginnings have been made. How much lies behind many of these old stories we shall hear later.

3

Next to weapons and utensils, it was above all foodstuffs and delicacies, together with jewellery and ornaments, which impelled early man to undertake long journeys and so forced him to explore his immediate and more distant environment. As in the historical Middle Ages, spices and above all salt occupied the foreground. Just as the crusades might never have taken place, and the great voyages of discovery at the beginning of the modern era have been made much, much later, if pepper and cardamom, ginger, nutmeg, etc., could have been grown in Europe itself, so important prehistoric cultures would never have developed, or at any rate have developed much later, if they had not found salt in their territory.

There are wide areas of the world where this mineral does not occur, and long ago bloody battles were fought for the sources of salt, as they are today for oilfields. Then the same thing seems to have re-occurred here that we conjectured about the flint-mines and their industrial districts; the groups owning the salt-mines, with their 'strong capital position', were clever enough to persuade the hungry 'have-nots' around them that wars and violence were far less remunerative than sensible acceptance of the inevitable, and peaceful trade. Again Augustan ages of non-violent stability seem to have ensued upon epochs of unbridled warfare. The villages of the Hallstatt district, from which early Europe drew its salt supply, were no longer tucked away in inaccessible ravines, but situated in open valleys; a similar confidence in their safety must have determined the position of many of the settlements in central Germany, which was one of the main regions from which northern Europe imported its salt at that time.

Another important salt-producing district was Hall in Upper Austria, with its Salzkammergut (salt crown land). And as long, undisturbed possession of wealth tends to render people conservative, to produce collectors rather than artists, so this area came to fulfil the purpose of a prehistoric and proto-historic museum, though it created little of its own. It appears that at one time every peasant in the region prided himself on collecting and accumulating old bronzes, Egyptian glass beads, beautiful ivory carvings from Africa, exquisite and costly amber, expensive pottery, magnificent golden ornaments, enchanting pieces of wrought or hammered silver work, rare shells—in a word, everything in any way valuable. Many of these objects he hid in his stocking or under his bed; there they either went up in fire and smoke or are still lying in the earth—it is no coincidence that the Salzkammergut between the Watzmann and the Dachstein is full of old tales of buried treasure. At the same time, valuables of this kind were often placed alongside the dead in their graves. Here they were safely preserved and now address us in eloquent language: the bracelets, the marvellously beautiful garment fibulas of gold and iron, the armour and swords inlaid with bronze and amber.

The Hallstatt salt-mines were opened up around 2500 B.C. To begin with this region was approached along the age-old trade routes running from west to east between the southern fringes of European glaciation and the long glacier-tongues of the Alps; but now there developed a close network of roads whose crossings lay, almost without exception, in the vicinity of the old salt-pits. There was the road running from north to south from the Bay of Heligoland, across the River Elbe, the Brenner Pass and the River Adige to the Adriatic. There was a trade route that went up the Rhone and then along the Rhine to the north, or parallel to the foothills of the Alps on the Danube to the east. A much-used road led from Samland on the East Prussian coast, with its amber-laden 'Blue Earth', over the Vistula and the Oder, diagonally through the primeval forests of eastern Germany to the Moravian Gate and across the Semmering Pass to Italy and Dalmatia. Of these roads Aristotle subsequently stated that they were 'sacred', that he who travelled on them was under the protection of the gods and considered invulnerable.

In all probability these roads, which remained important for intra-European traffic till well into the Middle Ages, were definite long-distance trade routes. At the same period in which, for Homer and his contemporaries, countries like Egypt, Italy and Babylonia were far-away lands on the edge of the world seen through a haze of myth and legend, men from all the lands of the earth must have met in the Salzkammergut: north Italian Etruscans with broad-skulled, short-statured pedlars from western Europe; tall, long-legged strangers from the East, dark-haired, brown and handsome, with blond, blue-eyed Scandinavians; fat Cretan merchants with broad-faced Samlanders. And yet neither song nor story tells of Hallstatt as the little Paris of prehistory, and even the bones taken from the graves in the Hallstatt region do not permit any definite conclusions as to the race, origin and culture of the men who were once laid to rest here, often with grave-trappings that were positively ostentatious.

Here too the trade of the ancient world may have begun with game and skins, with salt and weapons. But then two valuable substances came pouring into the mountains from the north and from the south, almost as though they had been sent on purpose to accelerate the too tranquil pace of events. Southern bronze and northern amber made their appearance in the peaceful valleys almost simultaneously; and without a doubt the whole witches' sabbath of speculation and profiteering, boom and depression began that same instant.

Finds of amber from the Early Stone (or Palæolithic) Age have, it is true, been made in many Moravian, French, and Spanish caves, and it is generally supposed, with reason, that what we see here are the amber possessions of individual hordes migrating to the south. Almost without exception, however, it was worked amber that was diffused through Europe in this manner. The time when the yellow resin would be exported as a raw material from the shores of the North Sea and the Baltic was still a long way off. Then, towards the end of the Stone Age, amber seems all at once to have become 'fashionable'. Admittedly, it has frequently been found in Cretan graves from *circa* 2500 B.C., and

a few centuries later it appears in Egypt as well; but now it flows down
in broad waves from Samland and Jutland to the south. Graves of the
Mycenæan culture between 1700 and 1300 B.C. almost invariably contain amber—from which it has been deduced, with reason, that the
Mycenæans were of Nordic origin—and the Hallstatt epoch seems to
have been positively swamped by this gold of the north. The sweet-
smelling, lustrous golden-yellow, sometimes crystal clear and sometimes milkily opaque resin, which is so easy and so agreeable to work,
appears in bead form, in necklaces, as a head to bronze pins, as an inlay
in sword handles, as buttons, as pendants and brooches, and finally
as rings. And amber has been discovered in immense quantities along
the old trunk roads carefully hidden in the earth, in caves and clefts in
the rock! It has been conjectured—probably correctly—that these
finds are not so much the treasures of some wealthy man, as the depots
and warehouses of great merchants, which were drawn upon at need
in response to customers' orders.

Amber, the famous *electron* of the Greeks, is wrapped in mystery.
In ancient Greece its beads were deemed to be the petrified tears wept
by Phæthon's sister when her brother was hurled dead to the ground
by Zeus, after his flight to the sun. And on account of this divine com-
passion, magic powers of healing and aid were ascribed to the yellow
tear-drops. This is a poetic, pious, naive explanation. But even the
Stone Age mountain-people of Samland, the Pomeranian and Jutland
amber-fishers, can hardly have known, and probably did not much care,
where the sea-gold came from. All the same, it cannot have escaped the
observation of these children of nature that the many tiny creatures,
the flies, gnats, and ants, which were so frequently to be found enclosed
in amber, suggested its origin from the resin of a tree. To have come
out with such a prosaic explanation, however, would have spoilt their
business prospects in the south. *Mundus vult decipi,* the world *wants*
to be deceived: this ironic maxim was a widespread conviction long
before the Latin language existed, and so they may not have contradicted the story that amber was a kind of congealed sea-foam, or perhaps even the sweat of the sun.

Now, as everyone knows who has been to the Baltic, there is not a
great deal of sunshine there. And even on very hot days it would never
occur to anybody that bright sweat was pouring down the cheeks of
the great primal luminary in the sky. This idea *can* only have arisen
in much more southerly regions, where men fiercely hated the scorching shafts of the sun and naively inferred from their own dripping
sweat that the heavenly light must be sweating likewise.

With these ideas in his head, the short-legged, plump Sarmatian agent of an honourable Adriatic import and export firm may, long, long ago, have entered the workshop of a fisher and dealer in Cranz or Kolberg. Reverently he weighed in his hand the pieces of amber, weighing a pound or more each, which his Pomeranian or East Prussian opposite numbers fetched from the barrel in the corner. And mentally he quickly calculated what wealth these northern barbarians possessed according to the latest exchange rates at Aquileia. Then he set his wine on the table and watched delightedly as the gruff, long-bearded sea-dogs, with whom he would have to do business next day, lapsed into a state of felicity. He himself will have drunk mead or fermented, quickly-intoxicating mare's milk, or better still perhaps that homicidal drink of fermented honey which has borne locally, since time immemorial, the name 'bear-trap' and right down to our own day has put many a valiant toper on his back in next to no time.

And then our wily trader, burning with curiosity to know where amber really came from, will have started to talk about the sweating sun and his supposition that this sweet-smelling golden stone could be nothing else than drops of heavenly sweat. Pliny passed on the story later as it must once have been told at the mouths of the Persante in Kolberg, in Cranz, Rauschen or Palmnicken. 'Nikias', he reports of an ancient Greek scientist, 'considered amber to be a kind of juice from the sunbeams. In his opinion, these struck the earth with greater force in the west and deposited upon it a greasy sweat. This was then cast up by the waves of the Ocean on the shores of Germany.'

Our Pomeranian and East Prussian fishermen will have listened with the greatest delight when their southern business friend came to them with such tales. At last they had an explanation for the origin of amber which, although they were perfectly well aware that it in no way corresponded to the facts, obviously seemed to satisfy these crazy southerners. We can see them before us, those great, heavy figures with their weather-beaten faces creased by a thousand wrinkles, grinning candidly and nodding sententiously as they confirmed these notions thought up by the Greek know-alls, and reeled off a pack of lies in their support. So truly were these lies aimed at the mentality of 'scientific specialists', that some two thousand years later a statement was issued from the study of one such, a German, to the effect that 'amber is water-foam, mixed with a great deal of salt and compressed, which is dried by the air and the heat of the sun and attains an exceptional hardness'. Friedrich Samuel Bock, a member of the consistorial court at Königsberg in Prussia, had to write a big book in 1767, his *Attempt at a Natural History of Prussian Amber,* to prove that amber is a fossilized tree resin.

Events followed the same course with amber as they had in the case of the other treasures of the soil: salt and flint. In the immediate vicinity of the source, next door to the actual mine, was established the manufacturing industry, which in this case produced first and foremost amber beads. Of this too there is no documentary evidence, no historical proof. We have to confine ourselves to interpreting the finds. And these finds are so numerous and so extensive as to rule out the assumption that amber was cut and polished to satisfy the demand within the country of origin only; everything points to the probability that a brisk trade with the south began towards the end of the Stone Age. And since early Etruscan wares have been found in a few graves in eastern Germany, it must be assumed that the Etruscans were the final purchasers of the northern gold. Manifestly they too travelled the great amber route which began in Aquileia in the province of Udine and ended in Samland, that trunk road along which imperial Rome later drew its supply of amber.

From this we must conclude that the European trunk roads by no means served a one-way traffic from north to south. From the south, too, a dense stream of goods and travellers was in motion by the end of the Stone Age. It goes without saying that goods from the north, whether amber or salt, were not paid for in money, but in kind, in other words, through the medium of barter. In this exchange of goods, the principal commodity supplied by the south was ivory, which in ancient times was as 'fashionable' in northern Europe and as greatly sought after as amber in the south. In many cases it may have been fossil ivory, that is to say, the tusks of mammoths or elephants taken by the lucky finder from some 'graveyard', one of those mysterious places which these colossal, intelligent beasts used to seek out when they felt their end approaching. On the other hand, the elephant was still very common in the Mediterranean zone in prehistoric times. In 500 B.C. Herodotus reported that at the time elephants were eagerly hunted in the coastal districts of Morocco, and in the ninth century B.C. there were still many of these primeval creatures in Syria and Palestine. The bulk of the numerous ivory implements which were used in Europe from 2000 B.C. onwards must, therefore, have been made from ivory acquired in the chase and not from fossil ivory that had been found. It was a considerable feat of transport to carry this material to northern Europe and Scandinavia.

At the same time it must be remembered that at least ivory and amber, and in a certain sense also salt and flint tools, were not mass, but luxury articles. The great profit that was clearly to be made on them may be supposed to have resulted, already in very early times, in a whole series of great individual journeys. But it is hardly to be imagined that long caravans of pack-animals now crossed the Alpine passes head to tail, and there is little reason to suppose that innumerable bands of merchants trekked along the highways that criss-crossed central and northern Europe. This was left for later centuries, those which, with the discovery of gold, invented the dealer.

This measure of value, this internationally valid medium of exchange, was entirely unknown to the ancient world. Hence our long-travelling merchant from these early centuries knew no office and no counting-house, he knew no bill of exchange and no cheque, he knew no agents and representatives, he had to do everything himself. To begin with he did not even know the wheel or the cart. Everything he had to offer, salt, ivory, stone tools and stone weapons, was immensely heavy. It had to be carried, either by slaves or by asses and horses. There were no roads in our sense. Now and again, in particularly impassable areas, we find log roads constructed by the people of the district, so that the travelling merchant should not be frightened off, but should come to them as well.

And he came, patient, unflinching. In his right hand he bore his naked sword, in his left his shield. Only the bravest men, the most intrepid, the best swordsmen and fighters, became traders. Very often trade was conducted by 'dumb barter', as it still is in central Africa today and as so many myths and stories from prehistoric times describe it. At the strangers' frontier, watched by a myriad eyes though he can see and hear no one, the travelling merchant lays down his goods. They still lie there untouched the following morning. But beside them are piled the things which the people of the district offer in return for the strange goods. If it seems to the merchant sufficient, he packs it all into the saddle-bags and panniers of his beasts. If it is too little, he leaves it lying exactly as it is. Perhaps the local people give more. If they do not, he picks up his goods again and moves on.

Then an idea occurs to him. Is it sensible to go on travelling with such a heavy load? Rivers run to right and left. Where there are rivers there are men. Where there are men there is lucrative trade. Wouldn't it be best to bury the major portion of his stone axes, daggers, and needles here, in this district? Wouldn't it be better to branch off to left and right with a light pack, to show samples, take orders and only deliver once the order has been received? And couldn't he also, to speed up business, send out his servant, his first slave?

That things could have happened like this has been again and again disputed. But again and again extensive hoards have been unearthed, which can only be construed as the depots and warehouses of travelling merchants. If that is so, if the quantities of similar axes, daggers, and wedges, if the piles of foreign shells, the vast heaps of semi-precious stones such as nephrite, jadeite, chloromelanite, are to be regarded as storehouses, as a kind of primitive forerunner of latter-day foreign agencies and branches abroad, then we must get used to the idea that the merchant of the Stone Age had already learnt how to organize his business. From here to the invention of the sample-case and the travelling salesman is but a short step. We shall hear more about it in the next chapter.

## PART TWO

# THE ROYAL METAL

*Berzelius and catalysis · The metal of royal crowns · 'The time is ripe' · Unholy Tarshish · Atlantis, America and the moon · The wholesale dealers of Crete · Did the Greeks eat fish? · The invention of money · Lawyer Lysias and big capital · Ox-heads, the dollars of the Bronze Age · Tin from the Cassiterides · The discovery of Malta · The dye-works of Tyre · Isaiah's prophecy and the downfall of Tartessus · Sand in the eyes of the competitors · Gold-smuggling in Gaul · Branches, commercial travellers, sample cases · Virchow says No again · Intra-European highroads · Land-portage tackle by the Adriatic and the North Sea · Odysseus in Danzig · Truso, the prehistoric Elbing · The Black Sea– Baltic road · The Scandinavian metal industry.*

IT was well over a hundred years ago that a brilliant idea came to the Swedish chemist, Berzelius, as he stood one evening in front of his retorts. He had been occupied for nearly a decade on the chemistry of plants, and again and again he had observed that certain chemical processes were speeded up in a manner that seemed almost magical in its suddenness. Some unknown force or agent must be at work. And as he pondered this miracle the solution came to him: 'Certain bodies,' he wrote in his notebook, 'on coming into contact with others, exercise such an influence on the latter that a chemical reaction takes place, combinations are destroyed or new ones formed, without the body whose presence causes the reaction taking the slightest part in it.'

This sounds like alchemy or witchcraft, and Berzelius himself, the child of an enlightened, rationalist century, did not pursue his ideas experimentally. It sufficed him to have formulated a concept for this mysterious process and this magical substance. He called the process catalysis and the substance whose presence he surmised a catalyst.

This is nothing new; it happened once before. When our age of coal and metal began, some four thousand years ago when bronze was discovered and swept victoriously across Europe, very similar phenomena occurred. Here too the purely technological advance was most in evidence. At last mankind had found a usable metal that was easy to forge and equally easy to cast, and on the other hand was hard enough to satisfy all the demands of life. But this was not the decisive factor. When we see how a cultural development, which was already existent in embryo, suddenly gained strength; how philosophy and fine arts blossomed; how social and economic life at once invented forms very like our own; how trade and commerce reached out across the sea and through unknown, wild lands to fresh shores; how the single ego, the individual, rose up out of the anonymous mass, and with him law and justice began to break free from custom rooted in magical obscurity— without the new metal playing any immediate causal role in it all—we recognize a catalytic process, as described and demonstrated chemically by Berzelius and Ostwald.

Quite manifestly, with bronze a royal era had commenced. First one by one and then in greater numbers, swords and bracelets, fibulas and shield bosses, daggers and belt buckles made of a wonderful new metal had come from the south and the far west. They gleamed like copper, which was already known, or like the red gold the great kept hidden in their coffers for feast days. What was copper, or even gold, against this new metal? This was really the metal of kings: like gold in its colour and its malleability, but harder, much, much harder. It rendered stone worthless as a tool, and even copper implements could now be laid aside. A new age had dawned.

Certainly, bronze did not emerge overnight and suddenly burst in upon the European cultural community. When people had once got to know the new metal, however, a rapid change took place, which was as clearly marked in the spiritual and artistic spheres as in the technological. Such a glorious burgeoning commenced that one cannot escape the impression that time and evolution had only been waiting for the moment when they could finally unburden themselves of age-old impediments. Iron, which, in a practical technological sense, has been of far greater importance to mankind, and which was already known at this time—the beginning of the second millennium—but was too expensive to be used for anything save ornaments, slipped in almost unnoticed. Indeed, it almost seems as though the entry of iron into the history of culture put a noticeable brake on the artistic upsurge let loose by bronze. From iron ploughs are made, from bronze the crowns of kings and the swords of heroes. Iron is the metal of a peasant, bronze of an aristocratic epoch. Hence everything that originated in this era acquired a noble, heroic mien.

2

No one knows where the classical mixture of 10 per cent tin and 90 per cent copper, of which bronze consists, was first discovered. We may guess that it happened in those regions of the earth which were rich in copper, that attempts had been made since early times somehow to harden the soft red metal, and that the new alloy had come about by chance in the process of casting copper. It must have been like this in England and Spain, the principal regions of European bronze production, and also in the centres of the ancient Indus culture, the famous 'industrial' cities of Mohenjo-daro and Harappā, which John Marshall began to excavate twenty-five years ago and where bronze has been found dating from about the same period as in the West. Is it not remarkable that the New World, apart from Peru, in spite of its plentiful supplies of copper, never succeeded in discovering bronze on its own account? Although tin is not very abundant, lead, silver, or antimony could have been used to harden the copper, as was done at first in Hungary, Babylonia, and Sumeria. Obviously, 'the time must be ripe' for it. In the New World, apparently, it never was.

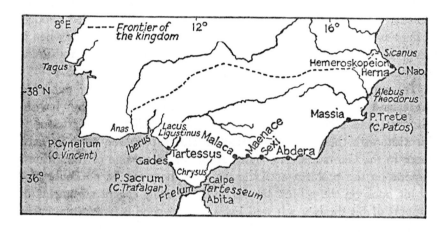

*1. The kingdom of Tartessus. While Gades, roughly on the site of the modern Cadiz, was founded by the Phœnicians to compete with Tartessus, Mænace, not far from the present Malaga, was an early Greek colonial outpost. It was connected by metalled roads with Tartessus and along the east coast of Spain with Italy.*

Thus it was mainly in Europe that the new tin and copper alloy long enjoyed absolute supremacy over other materials. And in a perfectly logical manner, during these times of revolutionary technological innovation those regions in which both tin and copper were to be found captured universal interest. These were Spain and England, and so it came about that these countries were of paramount importance for the early history of the Old World.

To begin with, the supplies of ore in the Iberian peninsula were manifestly sufficient to satisfy the need for bronze of metal-hungry Europe. On the Rio Tinto, copper and tin lie pretty close together, so the centre of the early Spanish bronze industry was probably here. To this must be added the goldfields of Ilipa and the thriving and abundant silver-mines of Almeria and Catula. They played their part in deepening the world's interest in the mineral wealth of Spain.

This interest found its most visible expression in the rise of the famous, fabulously wealthy city of Tartessus, the lascivious, sinful Tarshish of the Bible. Where Tartessus was actually situated, whether at the mouth of the Guadalquivir, in the vicinity of present-day Seville, or, as others have assumed, in the neighbourhood of the later Xeres de la Frontera, is an open question. We know equally little of the nationality or race of its founders and inhabitants, and the thesis that they can only have been Etruscans is by no means unassailable. Finally, we do not know when Tartessus was actually founded, though it must have been towards the end of the third millennium, nor when it declined. And yet, although so much is doubtful, unknown and uninvestigated, it is absolutely certain that Tartessus really existed.

The complete obscurity surrounding all the details of an indubitably great and immensely wealthy place, reliably attested by Jewish, Assyrian, and Greek evidence, has led to the belief that Tartessus is identical with the mysterious Atlantis. This supposition owes its existence to the German archæologist, Adolf Schulten, one of the greatest experts on the problem of Tartessus, and there can be no doubt that in his book on the subject he has adduced many cogent arguments in support of his thesis. As is well known, the legend of Atlantis is based on a report given by Plato in the dialogue *Critias*. He states there that, according to ancient Egyptian tradition, nine thousand years ago a great island lay in the Atlantic Ocean immediately west of the Straits of Gibraltar, 'larger than Asia and Libya together', an island whose kings ruled wide areas of Africa and Europe. When the potentates of Atlantis set out to subdue the rest of Europe as well, the Greek army, under Athenian leadership, successfully opposed them. And then began the great climax of this drama, its sudden change to calamity and destruction. 'But as earthquakes and floods broke out, the whole Greek army in one evil day and in one evil night sank into the earth, and the island of Atlantis likewise sank into the Ocean and was seen no more. And therefore the Ocean at this place became unnavigable and has remained unexplored, for the muddy shallows left by the submerged island made it too difficult . . .'

Since no other reference to Atlantis has been found in the whole of ancient literature, Plato's account has perpetually exercised the minds of geographers and historians. To begin with, many people believed that this enormous island was identical with America and that Plato's report related to a very early, but later forgotten, knowledge of the

New World. But just the most sensational part of the Atlantis legend, the sinking of the island 'in one evil day and in one evil night', would fall to the ground, because America still stands. Consequently the imaginative amateurs of geographic calamities had to seek for other hypotheses. And so they did. About sixty years ago, for example, it was asserted that in early millennia our moon had broken loose from the earth and that this trusty friend of all lovers and all poets was really the island of Atlantis and properly belonged not in the sky, but in its damp bed in the Atlantic Ocean. Conversely, supporters of glacial cosmogony in our own day have explained that the little planet Luna, our moon, approached the earth and exercised such a pull on the waters of the Ocean that Atlantis was submerged beneath their waves.

But this and other catastrophes, which must have taken place during the earth's most recent past, since otherwise Plato's account could not have been so clear, must be geologically demonstrable and have left some traces on the globe. With this in view, a close examination was made of the Atlantic Ocean. In the eastern part, that is to say, where Atlantis is supposed to have lain, the ocean bed consists of an 11,500-feet-thick layer of so-called pelagic red clay, a deposit composed mainly of the red shells of dead animal plankton. Since it is known that such a deposit takes a thousand years to reach a thickness of three-tenths of an inch, it follows that 500 million years would be needed to produce a sediment 11,500 feet thick. Unfortunately, therefore, there is no place for Atlantis here. And likewise, there is no place here for a moon that rose up out of the Ocean. For samples drawn up from the bed of the Ocean show irrefutably an alternation of plankton that requires cold water with plankton that only lives in warm water. In other words, these samples, which mirror the coming and going of the ice ages, show that the sediment strata have been entirely undisturbed. They could not have remained undisturbed, however, if the tremendous lunar spring tides of glacial cosmogony had really taken place during the prehistoric past. The sediment strata would show lasting traces of disturbance.

On the other hand, it was claimed in 1898, during repairs to one of the cables that run across the Atlantic Ridge—the submarine mountain range which runs from north to south through the Ocean between Europe and the New World—that rock brought up from the sea-bed was lava, a volcanic ejectum, which, by its structure, must have hardened not under water, but in the air. If this is correct, then at some time in the far distant past single volcanic peaks of the Atlantic's submarine mountain range must have projected above the surface and later sunk below it again. If this did happen, it must have been during the tertiary period of mountain foldings on the earth's crust: at a time when there were as yet no humans on the earth.

The conflict of opinions over the position of Atlantis is of no further concern to us here. Anyone who wishes to pursue the matter is referred to Högbom, Gattefosse and Bessmertny's bibliography of some twenty-five thousand publications devoted to the subject. It is sufficient for our purposes to know that for many long centuries Tartessus enjoyed a position of manifestly paramount importance in the bronze production, and above all in the bronze trade, of awakening Europe. At the outset it probably played a crucial role in the immediate production process, as a smelting and manufacturing centre. Then from about 1500 B.C., when the nearby Spanish tin-mines began to give out, it developed its specific importance: it became the metropolis of world trade and the main focus of the Atlantic traffic.


3


Yes, of the Atlantic traffic! For with the invention of bronze more had entered the life of man than merely a new raw material. The Neolithic Age, as we have heard, already had its mining concerns and its centres of industrial production. Now, under the assault of bronze, everything developed with impetuous speed: the dealer appeared, money was invented, and, closely linked to money, navigation on the high seas and long-distance traffic.

Little is yet known of the beginnings of this development. But it seems as though Egypt, Sumeria, and above all Crete saw the first wholesale dealers operating over long distances. From about 2000 to 1400 B.C., in any case, Crete, not Spain, not Rome, not Greece, was the leading sea power in the Mediterranean. And if the presence of Spanish silver can be demonstrated on Crete itself around 2500 B.C., and a little later in Troy, if a brisk goods traffic existed between the latter and Sicily, if Spanish bronze was used in Egypt round 2000 B.C., this can only be explained by the assumption that the major sea power of these centuries was also engaged in overseas trading.

Precisely how this Cretan sea traffic evolved is not yet known. In its earliest beginnings, however, Minoan Crete seems to have been just as hostile to the sea as another island—Britain—was many millennia after it. As is well known, England's sea traffic was originally carried on by the Hanseatic League; only when the hard hand of the virgin queen Elizabeth had forced the English people out onto the sea did the aid and representation of the Hanseatic League become more and more unnecessary—until the situation was completely reversed, until Britain alone ruled the waves and the descendants of the Hansas could think themselves lucky if they too were allowed to show their flag on the high seas.

The early history of the Mediterranean appears to have followed a rather similar pattern. To begin with, traffic with Crete manifestly lay in the hands of Egyptian shipowners and Egyptian seamen, who sailed under the Cretan flag. At the time of Thothmes III (1481–47 B.C.) a considerable proportion of the Egyptian fleet—the so-called Keftiu ships—were still set aside for the Crete run. And yet, as we shall hear, these Egyptian ships were not intended for sea voyages at all, but merely for river sailing.

6. *Seal stones with ancient Cretan hieroglyphics.*

When the Hyksos, a race of Asiatic nomads, whose interest in water was confined to whether it was drinkable or not, invaded Egypt around 1680 B.C., Egyptian power fell into decline. In the Mediterranean they gradually ceded their place to the Cretans, who finally took complete control of international traffic. By the time that happened, the commerce and technology of the Cretans were already adequate to the new task. The Cretan ship, of which we possess only a few meagre representations, was no longer rowed, but entirely under sail. It has been surmised that the form of its rigging was copied from Egyptian vessels. This is possible, but it does not apply to the much more important shape of the hull. With its keel, ribs, and planks it is definitely the product of an island in the open sea, not that of a country predominantly concerned with inland waterways.

The whole seaborne trade amongst the Greek islands was in Cretan hands from the outset, since the entirely continental Greek peasants and cattle-breeders, who had immigrated from the north, could, to begin with, make nothing of the sea. It has been claimed that originally they did not even have a word for the concept 'sea', but adopted one from the Carians, a pre-Indo-European people. Long after they had taken to fishing and could row and sail, it still did not occur to the Greeks to practise water sports, at the Olympic Games for instance, so alien to them had the watery element remained. And it is probably true that their city population regarded fish as a very unappetizing dish, to be eaten only at times of extreme shortage.

What inner process prepared the Cretans to assume the dominion of the seas for which they were destined, we do not know. But inevitably this island, with its always intractable population, did not for long remain content to transport whatever oil, wine, and corn happened to be on hand in the Greek ports, and to exchange them for bronze-ware, ornaments, and pottery. The Cretans must certainly, at an early period, have set sail for the open sea and landed upon distant shores. But then mere barter proved inadequate for long-distance international commerce. Ingots of Spanish silver, English tin, north German amber, and African ivory called irresistibly for an independent standard of value, a universally valid medium of payment, they called for money, and a money whose currency and mint value were in accord.

A full thousand years after the times of which we are speaking, Aristotle summed up these considerations in a few pregnant phrases. 'All the things which are exchanged', he taught, 'must be comparable to one another. This purpose is served by money, which in a certain respect has become a mediator. Money measures and compares; it states whether and by how much the value of one thing exceeds another —for instance, how many pairs of shoes are equal in value to one house. It indicates what relation the value of the work of a mason bears to the work of a shoemaker, and how many pairs of sandals must be given for a house.'

This was said in about 350 B.C., after money had already existed for a long time; it is carefully considered and cleverly expressed. But many, many generations had thought it before the great Greek philosopher put it into words. This formulation enables us to judge what an admirable intellectual achievement the invention of such a medium of payment was. It presupposes an absolutely new economic attitude, completely different to that of preceding eras. And these early times had long since taken the logically necessary and inevitable second step, going far beyond Aristotle. Though they may at first have looked upon money as a mere standard of value, an auxiliary to trade by barter, this auxiliary construction soon made itself independent in a manner that would greatly have surprised its inventors. Money, at least in its smaller units, which simultaneously served as weights, immediately became a commodity in itself; it became an international commercial value and, like any other possession, was subject to the rules of the market, the laws of supply and demand. And when the

Athenian arms manufacturer and lawyer, Lysias, in about 400 B.C., complained: 'Only by birth are these people citizens of our state. By conviction they consider any land their fatherland in which they find profit, because they do not regard their country, but possessions, as their fatherland', he would have had to put back the hands of the world's clock for more than a thousand years, in order to live once more in the good old days of up-right probity and contentment with one's place in the world.

Yet this trader, against whom Lysias so eloquently and so vainly inveighed, was anything but a cheapjack. He was a royal merchant in a royal age, he was one of the first great explorers and dis-coverers of the wide, wild world.

We see this trader going barefoot on his way, no longer exclusively with beasts of bur-den and enslaved bearers, like his early predecessors of the Stone Age. Covered waggons have long ago come into use, heavy, clumsy things with enormous disk-wheels, just like the vehicles drawn by

*7. Weighing gold. This wall draw-ing (circa 1380 B.C.) from the tomb of a sculptor at Thebes in Egypt shows a precision balance of great perfection. The right scale holds a weight in the shape of an ox-head, the left gold ingots.*

four oxen with which the Pulesata, the Philistines, invaded Egypt around 1200 B.C. and which the scribes and priests of the temple of Medinet Habu portrayed in their reliefs. Lumbering, infinitely slow, the trade carts jolt and sway over the rough tracks. But beneath their leather tilts are heaped all the treasures of the earth: bronze swords, daggers, razors, lance- and spear-heads, sewing-needles, garment fibulas, bangles, and mirrors. And carefully guarded in heavy casks with thick hoops rest special treasures: Cretan ox-heads, the 'dollars' of the Bronze Age.

They were simultaneously weights and units of payment, both the small silver pieces bearing a stamped device, which were clearly a kind of small change, and the larger golden ox-heads, which are por-trayed on many Cretan writing-tablets. This identity between measurement of weight and independent medium of payment was one of the prerequisites for the invention of the concept 'money'. For all the Cretan media of payment, the small change of silver, the golden ox-heads, and the large coins—heavy copper and bronze ingots weighing 64 lb., cast in the shape of an outspread ox-hide and stamped with the sign of the Cretan Mint—were ambassadors of their king, the great lord Minos in the magnificent palace of Cnossos on the island of Crete, who had already grown into a myth. *That* is why they were accepted as a medium of exchange as far as the *Oikoumene* (the area of the earth that was known and considered inhabitable) extended. For behind the mere unit of weight stood the myth of power.

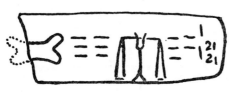

8. *Cretan writing-tablet with copper bars and balance.*

9. *Cretan writing-tablet with weights in the shape of ox-heads.*

Since the low melting point of bronze was soon universally known, bronze-casting very rapidly established itself. Hence discoveries of foundries and cast implements have been frequent. As a rule, the crude bronze that poured in from the south and west was worked up in the country itself. This was naturally an activity of exceptional importance, and the fearful respect for the smith evinced in most Indo-European legends probably stems from this early period.

When the Spanish tin deposits began to run out, the tin-veins of Brittany and Normandy, and above all the great tin-mines on the Scilly Isles off the coast of Cornwall, stepped to the fore. The voyages made with Spanish tin in the early Mediterranean were now replaced by much longer voyages with tin from Britain and France. Of course, the Tartessans did not themselves sail as far as England. They themselves probably travelled only as far as Uxisame, the modern Ushant, whence the further journey to the British Isles was undertaken by Celtic ships. We have very little detailed knowledge about all this. But it is certain that close cultural relations existed between south-west Spain and Britain, such as could only have been possible if there was very close, brisk commerce between them. No doubt, however, a few isolated voyages to England were made by Spaniards, just as Tartessans may also have sailed as far as the shores of the North Sea. The Cretans, who in any case sailed through the Straits of Gibraltar on their way to Tartessus, may even have got as far as England. We know that tin was already exported from the British Isles at a time when stone implements were still in use there. It must, therefore, have been extraordinarily cheap, much cheaper at all events than in Tartessus, where a trading

*10. Negroes with Cretan metal ingots in the shape of an ox-hide.*

profit of several hundred per cent was undoubtedly taken. And it is entirely possible that the Cretan trade barons' urge for gain was sufficiently great for them to have risked a voyage into the mysterious and perilous north. At all events, metal bars in the Cretan ox-hide shape dating from *circa* 1700 B.C. have been found at Falmouth in Cornwall, as well as pieces of jewellery exactly similar to those found by Schliemann at Troy.

They may, of course, have reached England via Spain. Nevertheless, it is very suggestive that the Greek for tin, *cassitéros,* is in all probability a Celtic loan word. It is thought to be derived from the description given by the Celts to the British Isles. *Cassiterides,* they called them, 'the very distant islands', and we might infer from the adoption and transformation of this Celtic word a direct connection between the Cretan sphere of culture and the far north of Europe.

Since the nautical and shipbuilding capacities of the ancient world were far higher than is often supposed, it is entirely possible that the Tartessans already discovered the Atlantic islands, or at least Madeira and the Canaries. This cannot be proved. But these groups of islands so close to the mainland *cannot* have escaped the much-voyaged Tartessan seafarers. People accustomed since days of old to cross the

Bay of Biscay, cannot have thought anything of a run along the west African coast, and there is every reason to suppose from later evidence that the Tartessans reached West Africa. In that case, they must have passed Madeira on their way. There is one indication that Tartessus had already discovered the coastal islands of the Atlantic Ocean and that Crete and the Greeks had also learnt of them—we shall hear later that Homer speaks in the *Odyssey* of the 'Isles of the Blessed'—which may also explain the riddle of the decline, the sudden disappearance without trace, of Tartessus.

When the Minoan 'thalassocracy', Crete's mastery of the seas, broke up, its place was taken by the Phœnicians. In the far west this task fell to the lot of the mighty Phœnician colony of Carthage, and when the rich city felt strong enough, it marched into southern Spain. Its first act was to forbid all but Punic ships to pass through the Straits on pain of death. This took place in about 530 B.C., at a time, that is to say, when there was a growing tendency to abandon bronze for iron. At this time British tin was no longer so much to the fore that the blockade of the Straits could have been instituted solely on its account; the blockade meant renouncing the huge profits to be so effortlessly gathered from the old centres of world trade in south-west Spain. If the Carthaginians prohibited vessels from sailing past Gibraltar, therefore, it must have been for other reasons. These reasons can only have been the Atlantic islands, of which the Phœnicians had long known and whose products they urgently required for the great dye-works of Tyre and Sidon. On the Atlantic islands was to be found a vegetable dye which, used in conjunction with their own local dyes, enabled them to give Phœnician purple fabrics that luminous red famed throughout the ancient world. To make quite sure that Tartessus should not impede them in this, the Phœnicians took the opportunity offered by their conquest of Spain to 'eradicate' the troublesome city. And as Carthage was thorough in everything it did, it was particularly thorough over this. Its soldiery indulged in a frenzy of murder and arson until there was nothing left of Tartessus but loose rubble, so that excavation has been quite unable to bring the prosperous city to light. 'For a day of the Lord shall come upon all the ships of Tarshish,' Isaiah had prophesied in 700 B.C., two hundred years before the downfall of Tartessus. Now this day had come. Tarshish vanished, and with it all the lore of the great western sea. Demons, eerie darkness, mudflats, immense fields of seaweed from which no ship could free itself, horrible monsters and a ghastly death awaiting the seafarer who ventured beyond Gibraltar was all the Phœnicians allowed to be glimpsed. They were believed.

And so competition was finally eliminated. Two thousand years later, when the Portuguese felt their way cautiously along Africa towards the south, these old wives' tales were still current, and Henry the Navigator, the real discoverer of the sea route to India, later had great difficulty all his life long in persuading the captains of the Portuguese navy, which he had created, to sail into that uncanny sea.

This is very remarkable. One would have thought that the broken coast of the Iberian Peninsula, with its many promontories running out into the sea, was perfectly calculated automatically to produce sailors, as though by a law of nature. Of course, there were always fishermen in Spain, even at the time of the Carthaginian occupation, but the *mare altum,* the high, open sea, which the Tartessans had sailed for a thousand years, right across the Bay of Biscay and often as far as the British Isles, subsequently passed entirely from memory. It was the Romans who later laboriously rediscovered the old routes of seaborne commerce. Yet these had once run like thick arteries through the Mediterranean, converged in the heartland of Spain, and stretched up into the far north: thronged with cargo ships carrying tin and gold, sailed regularly by thousands of seafarers, for many centuries the object of all the longings of the human heart and the theme of yard-long oaths in all the languages of the world of that day.

The voyage to England via Tartessus made by the early Mediterranean peoples was actually blocked by the Carthaginians. To this was added, of course, the fact that by now tin did not play nearly such an important role as it had done five hundred or a thousand years previously. But instead of tin, which was not required in the smelting of iron or in the preparation of steel, Irish gold was calling. To slip the Carthaginian barrier, a land route was now explored that led along the Rhone and the Loire, or the Rhone and the Seine, to the north. Early historical Burdisala, the modern Bordeaux at the mouth of the Garonne, was certainly drawn into this overland traffic. But naturally, those who used this route had as much reason to keep their discoveries to themselves, for fear of the Carthaginians, as the Carthaginians had to camouflage their own communications. Consequently, beyond the fact that both parties paid repeated visits to the Anglo-Irish paradise of gold and tin, it has so far been impossible to ascertain any details of this Gallic backdoor road to these metals. How far the secrecy of the rival economic groups, the south European group led by the Romans and the north African under the patronage of the Carthaginians, went and how international economic espionage flourished, can be gathered from an account given by the Roman chronicler, Strabo, who mentions amongst other things that a Carthaginian captain ran his ship aground to prevent the Roman trade vessel following him from learning his destination.

These are all highly capitalistic, and at the same time highly nationalistic, attitudes. And since they cannot have arisen overnight, there is reason to suppose that the Neolithic Age also had a hand in their development. These impulses only came fully to light in the Bronze Age, however; the new metal seems to have acted like a catalyst, accelerating the slowly simmering process of evolution as though by magic.

## 4

Of course, even in the ancient world, the entrepreneur could not do everything himself. Just as he engaged seamen and captains for his ships, although to begin with he frequently went on voyages himself, so he must certainly also have employed assistants in his overseas trade. Even the occupation of commercial representative seems to have grown up at an early stage, accompanied, as was logical, by purchase on order. Nothing could be more natural. The distances between production centre and purchaser were great, the roads bad, the risk of taking valuable wares round the country in vain considerable. It was preferable to establish branches and depots and send out one's representatives with cases of samples, to tender the commodities and take orders. One such Bronze Age sample case was found some decades ago in the Pomeranian peat bog of Koppenow near Lauenburg. It was a solid wooden box, 26 inches in length, containing in specially hollowed compartments various types of axe, sword blades, ornamental pendants, buttons, garment pins, etc., and perhaps intended to give the customer an idea of the merchant's wares, so that he could place his order.

It is not absolutely certain whether this wooden box from Koppenow is really the sample case of a travelling merchant. Virchow, who had already rejected the Ice Age cave-paintings in Spain as impossible, also vigorously opposed the supposition that the Koppenow find might be a sample case. But in view of the generally 'capitalist' economic trend of the Bronze Age and the fact that the logical counterpart of the sample case, the depot or branch from which the orders of a whole district were executed, has frequently been unearthed, the idea seems well-founded. When we think of the great length of time required to traverse the European mercantile highroads—if the merchant had to travel back to the production centres and fetch the goods ordered from there—it seems only natural that he should have scattered secret stores about the countryside, from which to satisfy his customers' requirements. Such Bronze Age storage depots, often with very considerable stocks of goods, have been unearthed in some numbers. Thus, for instance, a depot was discovered in 1880 near Homburg-vor-der-Höhe with several hundred lance-heads, sickles, hairpins, garment fibulas, rings, etc.—certainly the contents of a veritable Bronze Age emporium. Similar storehouses have been found by Lake Constance, in Switzerland, in Sweden and in England. Of course, it may be objected that these are all mere caches and their contents valuables that were hidden and then forgotten. On the other hand, there is no really cogent argument why the otherwise so capitalistically organized Bronze Age should *not* have had the obvious idea of the commercial depot and the travelling salesman. We must therefore assume that all this existed long before the Christian era.

The cross-country routes of early Europe, as was the case during the conquest of North America, must have run along the rivers, which were naturally more pleasant to travel than the narrow, almost uncleared tracks through forests and marshes. The latter will only have been used to traverse swamps, as for example on the plank road through Federseemoos in south Würtemberg, to pass round rapids and torrents, or to cross the watersheds between two river systems.

At such places roads were secured and differences of level overcome by methods which are surprising in their technical accomplishment: for instance, by tunnels, which were calculated and built with great precision as early as the third millennium B.C. In addition there was tackle for lifting ships overland, steps cut in the existing watershed with rollers over which vessels were raised or lowered by a complicated system of blocks and pulleys. One of these land-portage installations was situated on the Isthmus of Corinth, just about where the Corinth canal runs today. This mechanism, the so-called *diolkos* or 'pull-through', can still be clearly distinguished. Possibly it served as a prototype for another, equally famous, construction on the passes in the Nanos mountains in what is now Yugoslavia, through which the old Samland-Adriatic road ran. We know that this trunk route only attained its true importance in the time of the Roman Empire. But it was certainly discovered a great deal earlier, as is attested by the Etruscan objects found in so many graves in east German burial grounds. In any case, it may be presumed with certainty that on this great international road complicated technical arrangements were made, at a very early period, with the aim of prolonging to the limit the waterway along the south-eastern rivers of the Alps—a method of transporting goods doubly convenient in this mountainous region.

Another land-portage installation in use very early on ran right across the isthmus of Schleswig and constituted a sort of 'North Sea– Baltic Canal on rollers' linking the two seas. We are very well informed concerning this artificial connecting road, because it remained in use until well into the twelfth century A.D. Even at the height of the Middle Ages there was great reluctance to risk ships on the dangerous route through the Skagerrak and Kattegat from the North Sea to the Baltic. Instead they sailed up the Eider and along its tributary, the Treene, into the region of contemporary Hollingstedt. Here there were great marts; we know from tradition that the English possessed market rights in this district, but no doubt the Dutch, the merchants of the Lower and the Upper Rhine, and perhaps even traders from Marseilles, also had warehouses and branch establishments at Hollingstedt. From Hollingstedt, a solid road led to Schleswig, the wealthy old Sliesthorp on the Schlei, on which passengers and cargoes reached the Baltic in a few hours.

For nearly a thousand years and perhaps longer, a stream of travellers laden with all the precious things of the earth flowed through here from west to east and from the Baltic to the North Sea. Swedish merchants from Birca, the mercantile metropolis of Scandinavia standing on an island in Lake Mälar, tall, wrapped in costly garments trimmed with fur, generous and liberal. Short-legged Slavs from Truso, now called Elbing, with heavy loads of amber, with Sarmatian and Pontic embroideries and laces. Brown-skinned Arabs, journeying from distant Spain as traders and envoys to the kings of the Danes, with colourful turbans over wide, swinging burnouses, sparkling and flashing with gems. Flemish merchants with gigantic packs of woollen cloths and freize goods; dealers in earthenware from the Lower Rhine with pottery jars, pots, and bowls; sailmakers and ropemakers from Cologne, delivering hawsers of walrus skin and smelling of blubber oil. From Marseilles came spices and aromatics. The elegant, volatile men accompanying these wares smelt just as sweet as their bales and packages. The casks of wine that rumbled along the road on heavy carts came from the fertile plains around Worms and Speyer.

Not far from this motley and glittering throng, ships could be seen gliding up hill and down dale; up the last steep incline to the ridge of the watershed, on a kind of sledge so constructed that the vessel sliding down dragged that which was mounting the opposite slope and was

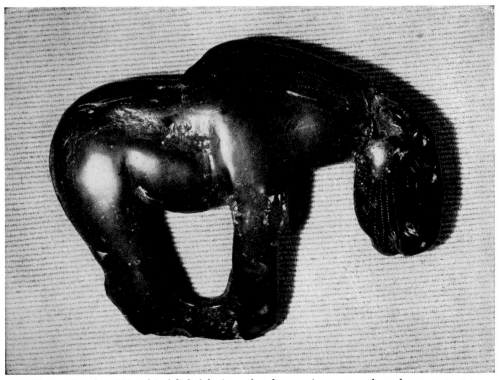

4. Horse of amber. Was this delightful piece of amber carving, executed nearly 5,000 years ago, a pendant on the necklace of some beautiful woman?

5. Bronze ornaments from northern Germany: a collar, a decorative pin and a garment fibula. These were the adornments of a great lady.

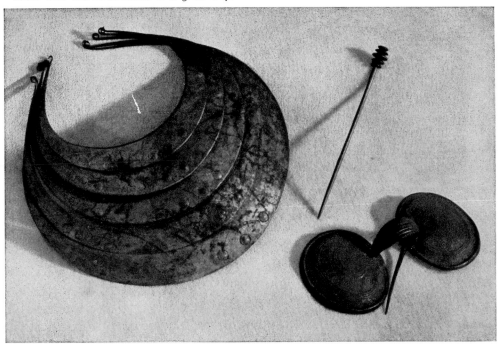

6. The Koppenow sample-case. This 2 foot 6 inch long oaken box found near Koppenow in Pomerania containing a sword, decorative fibulas, axe-heads, buttons, etc., was presumably the sample-case of an itinerant merchant of the Bronze Age. Circa 1000 B.C.

7. Decorative pottery of the Hallstatt period. These brightly painted bowls and vases from the 7th or 6th century B.C. are so thin that they can only have been intended for ornament, not for use.

at the same time braked by the latter. Before and behind them lay the rollers, so set that they revolved in spite of the immense weights resting on them, whose bearings, smouldering from the friction, had perpetually to be smeared with water and tar to render them resilient. To the right and left of the roller runway plodded teams of oxen, slaves tugged at the ropes, the long whips of the overseers whistled across bent backs, and rumbling, rattling, groaning and grating, the ships with their tall masts, shivering shrouds, and creaking ribs jerked slowly towards the water. Of course, all those journeying along the road had long ago heard of this miracle of technology. Nonetheless, now that they saw it, it took their breath away.

Sliesthorp itself, the forerunner of the equally wealthy Haithabu, was from A.D. 800 onwards the main seat of all the merchants of the Baltic, just as, a thousand years later, London was the first city of the North Sea and of world commerce. Since days of old the trade highroads going up towards Jutland and across the island bridges to Scandinavia had met at Sliesthorp the roads that ran along the southern littoral of the Baltic. Since days of old immense wealth had accumulated there. Since A.D. 800 too the Danish kings sat at Sliesthorp, and to the wealth of the merchants, their luxury, their superabundance of feasts and revels, was added the noble lustre of the court: a brilliant picture, some of whose fairy-tale radiance may have been transferred on to the legendary city of Vineta which, as local story has it, sank into the waters of the Baltic many long ages ago.

The mountain foldings of Europe, already so worn down in comparison with the wild Asiatic mountains, do not appear, on the whole, to have exercised such an inhibiting effect on travel as might have been expected. In the third millennium the Brenner was already frequently traversed; this was the lowest of all the Alpine passes, but the Great and Small St. Bernard, Mont Genèvre, Mont Cenis, etc., all had their importance. The main north–south connection from the amber lands to Italy ran first along the Elbe, the Moldau and the Inn, and then, after crossing the Brenner Pass, linked up with the Eisack–Adige system; the latter, however, on account of its torrents, serve more as a signpost than as a road.

At right-angles to this north–south connection lay an immensely old route, probably in use during the Ice Age, which no doubt followed the Danube and which led to the Black Sea. This east–west trade road acquired its maximum importance with the beginning of the Copper Age, since it linked the copper deposits and the later bronze industry of Hungary with the purchasers in south Germany, Italy, and Switzerland, as well as with those in Russia. Very large finds made along this route, with exceptionally rich golden ornaments and utensils, attest a high level of economic development in this region, the precondition for which was the extraordinarily fertile plains round the Danube estuary. But although this east–west road between the tundras of the north and the thrusting tongues of the Alpine glaciers had been in use for thousands of years, the course of the Danube remained unknown until very much later. Probably the commercial firms with an interest in this road kept their knowledge to themselves and surrounded the reports of their agents with as much secrecy as Tartessans and Carthaginians had once exercised concerning their trade routes. This is the only explanation for the wild stories related about the Danube in very early antiquity. It was said to be guarded by huge swarms of bees; the Alps and the Carpathians, which had been obscurely heard of and were thought to be mountain streams, were its tributaries; its source lay in Spain; and in addition to its estuary in the Black Sea it had another running into the Adriatic. These, in a slightly different form, are the same frightening and confusing fables as the Tartessans and the Carthago-Phœnicians told of the Atlantic. And here, as there, the object of these fairy tales was to throw sand in the eyes of commercial competitors.

When the Romans, five hundred years later, began to take an interest in Britain, exactly the same thing happened. Again the wildest rumours were circulated. And when the Romans refused to be frightened off, their competitors feigned ignorance. Even when Cæsar was on the very point of crossing to England, he could glean no information from the Gaulish fishermen and merchants. It is not difficult to imagine how the Celtic sea-dogs must have grinned inwardly when the almighty Roman general with his elegant, clever intelligence officers asked them the most fantastic questions about a country that lay a stone's throw across the sea.

If we regard the Danube route as the abscissa of the system of co-ordinate axes made up by the trade routes of Europe, then the Adriatic–Samland connection is the easterly, and the Rhone–Rhine path the westerly, ordinate. Of course, traffic up the Rhone only became really brisk with the founding of the Greek colony of Massilia, the present-day Marseilles, around 600 B.C. But the Rhone was always an important component in the west European network of trade roads. At one time it was part of the Irish-British gold and tin route running towards the north and north-west; at the same time, however, it formed a useful signpost for traffic with the north-east, the rich lands on the Rhine and the Main, and the far-off amber lands shrouded in the haze of distance.

Whether the great merchants of Massilia travelled thither themselves is questionable. The north, with its multitude of forests and swamps, was an eerie place to the men of the Mediterranean. But the astute Greek traders certainly came as far as Asciburgium, the Teutonic Eschenburg, that lay in the region of present-day Duisburg and was the main centre for commerce with the amber lands. This can be deduced from a piece of information given by Tacitus in his *Germania*. He states there that Odysseus is sometimes said to have drifted, in the course of his wanderings, into the North Sea and to have reached Asciburgium, 'Which lies on the banks of the Rhine, is still inhabited, and is said to have been founded by Odysseus'. Rome, therefore, deemed the manifestly celebrated and prosperous great port to be a Greek colony. It may at least have been a Massiliot colony, and this would make it probable that isolated journeys to the north were undertaken before the time of Pytheas, the great commercial expert and geographer from Marseilles, of whom we shall have more to say presently. Since amber cannot, for geological reasons, have been found in any quantities on the islands of the Rhine estuary, the 'gold of the sea' must have come from the Jutland and Baltic shores. Nothing could be more natural than for an enterprising Greek inhabitant of Eschenburg to go there himself. We do not know what route he followed to get there. Probably, however, he would have travelled via Soest and Paderborn to Porta Westfalica, crossed the Weser near Nienburg and, via Verden on the Aller and Stade near Hamburg, have reached an old Bronze Age trade road that led into the area of the present estuary of the Eider. But there is no record of any of the illustrious gentlemen of Asciburgium ever having reached the North Sea, and since Pytheas was clearly commissioned later on to carry out an investigation of the amber lands, we must fear that our Mr. Andropoulos, or whatever the Eschenburg merchant's name was, never attained his goal.

Egyptians and Hittites boarded their ships and sold their glass beads, their utensils and bronze figures in Crete. Cretan merchantmen carried the goods to Aquileia, the main port for the trade with the far north-east. With two-wheeled carts and draught animals—in the mountains with beasts of burden—the caravans wound their way to the Semmering. Here traders from the Balkans, who had crossed the passes over the Nanos mountains, may have joined the great convoy. Now it passed through the Moravian Gate and, making use of the

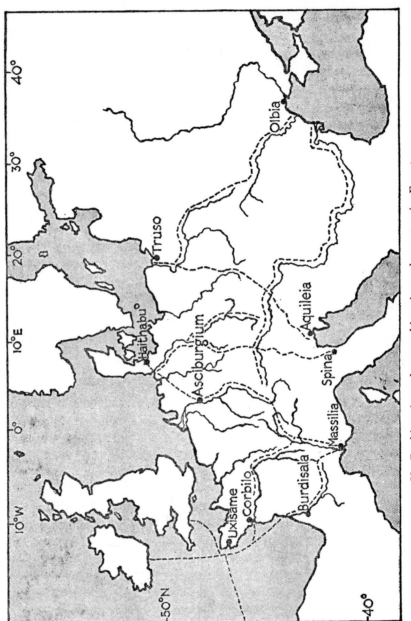

II. *Prehistoric and proto-historic trade routes in Europe.*

Oder or the Vistula, reached Truso to the north of present-day Elbing, the rich mart for the trade with Samland and the endless tracts of forest in the farthest north. No doubt the Etruscans, who were conveying bronze from Tuscany to the north, handed their goods over to the caravan leader, who knew his way about north-east Europe, at some point *en route*. And only during the centuries round the turn of the ages, when in Rome, as Pliny remarked regretfully, amber was so dear that 'the smallest figure made from it costs more than a living man'— and that was about £20 to £30 in our currency—only then did this 1,200 mile long road attain its true importance. But a thousand years before this the rich, the princes and lords, laid their dead wives, their ministers, and their faithful servants to rest in graves filled with Egyptian valuables and shining amber beads along the whole length of this road—an indication of its great antiquity.

Of course, not only salt, bronze, and amber were traded and transported along the great old roads. Costly furs, particularly valuable types of leather, and other luxury commodities must have played then the same role as in later millennia. This was especially evident on our north-eastern road after 700 B.C., when the colonies founded by the Greeks on the Black Sea littoral had overcome their initial difficulties. As in all young colonies, money must have been made here at a tremendous rate and spent equally fast. And so a demand for luxury articles arose which seemed to contemporaries unparalleled and a symptom of extreme decadence. The port of Olbia on the Dnieper estuary was outstanding for the immeasurable wealth it acquired. Under the influence of this port the Samland–Adriatic route developed a branch to the south-east which, utilizing the Vistula–Dnieper system, led straight to the Black Sea. Now, Olbia was founded by Miletus, the mercantile city of Asia Minor, and since early times had had a share in the widespread traffic with south Asia; at the same time, however, many of the communications running into the interior of Russia terminated at Olbia itself. Commercially, such an important place was naturally of the greatest interest, and we may presume that the wonderful gold treasure-trove unearthed at Eberswalde shortly before the first World War, whose heavy golden bracelets, diadems, necklaces, and drinking bowls are of south European-Greek origin, has some connection with the 'Paris' of the Black Sea, Olbia. Most of what streamed into Europe along this eastern route must have mouldered away: silks, carpets, precious stones, incense and the like. Other things have been preserved in the earth: coins, pottery, weapons and so on. And since the seventh century, these finds have been so numerous in the Vistula region that we can tell from them what a 'boom' this district must have enjoyed.

Our account may have given the impression that central and northern Europe had nothing with which to answer the wealth of metals in the south save amber and furs, as though they gave much less than they received. This is true enough of the early Bronze Age. It is true that it has recently been asserted that the northern ore mountains started very early to produce bronze, indeed that the classical proportion of tin to copper was actually discovered here. But it looks as though, to begin with, Spanish and Tuscan bronzes ruled the market unchallenged. This is very significant. For during this period the manufacture of bronze in both Spain and Italy was in the hands of that mysterious people, the Etruscans, who had manifestly long been acquainted with this new metal. We know a good deal about this remarkable nation, which must have emigrated from Asia Minor. But our knowledge is like a jumbled

*11. Three southern Etruscan alphabets from the eighth to seventh centuries B.C. Although the Etruscans used many written characters known from other Mediterranean cultures, their script has not yet been deciphered.*

and, in addition, not quite complete jigsaw puzzle. For although many definite pieces of knowledge are available, we simply cannot fit the numerous small pieces of this culturo-historical puzzle together in such a manner that they form a complete picture.

An immense quantity of most beautiful finds have, in any case, been made in Etruscan Italy between the Arno and the Tiber: urns, vases, swords, ornaments of gold, silver, ivory and amber, as well as many paintings in old burial chambers, and numerous statues of men and animals, all of them evincing a high and very impressive feeling for form. The picture of their neighbours drawn by the Romans, however, presents this artistic, undoubtedly highly gifted, people in a totally different light. The Etruscans, they said, were very wealthy, very capable in commerce and seafaring, much addicted to good living. But they were crass materialists, utterly devoted to the things of this world, and so entirely devoid of morals that they did not shrink from performing the sexual act in public. Their women were mere objects, belonging in common to all procreative men. This may be an exaggeration. But it is a fact that the phallus was regarded by the Etruscans with religious veneration, and that images of it were worshipped to the accompaniment of orgiastic debauches. It is also a fact that the whole of Etruscan art, despite the high level of its formal qualities, exhibits many grossly materialistic features.

Nothing, therefore, fits together in this blurred mosaic. It is certain, however, that the Etruscans emigrated from Asia Minor, perhaps set in motion by the great tide of nations that swept up against the Mediterranean from Asia at the beginning of the second millennium B.C. It is certain that when this happened they had a thorough mastery of ore-mining, bronze-manufacture, metal-casting, and the art of the smith. It is certain that after their expulsion from Asia Minor they tried to gain a foothold in Egypt. Egyptian records refer to them as the Turusca. But the Pharaohs were too powerful; they flung back the strangers. So they turned to the west and sailed round Malta and Sicily to Italy, where part of them settled. The rest seem to have sailed on via Sardinia and the Balearics till they reached Spain, where Tartessus, the ancient mercantile city on the Guadalquivir, rose to the full height of its wealth and power through this influx of new blood.

In any case, for a long time a tremendous stream of bronze flowed through Europe from Tartessus and also from Tuscany, the ancient Tuscia, that is, the land of the Tuscans or Etruscans, later called Etruria. When in *circa* 700 B.C., after five hundred years of ruthless exploitation, the Etruscan copper deposits began to give out, their northern neighbours had to set to and expand their own bronze industries. This happened in particular in Scandinavia, and soon splendid north European bronze goods—implements, ornaments, and weapons—were making their way down to southern Europe and Egypt. They have been unearthed at Mycenæ and also on the Nile, and the Egyptian chamberlains' love of order and precision has even supplied us with an exact date for a few very early pieces: the Pharaoh's sign of ownership has been hammered into three Nordic bronze swords from the state treasury of Setekhy II, towards the end of the thirteenth century B.C.

Ocean traffic at that time was mainly carried on by the Phœnicians, the Semitic people on the eastern littoral of the Mediterranean, which took the place of Crete after the latter's decline. Coastal traffic, however, and to begin with the Spanish run, remained for a long time in the hands of the Etruscans. From their port of Spina, situated in the vicinity of present-day Bologna on a branch of the Po estuary which is today dry land, vast quantities of goods were dispatched over a long period. Besides metals or costly tropical products such as cowrie shells, corals, and incense, corn and other foodstuffs, staple commodities of great value, later came to play an important role in overseas trading in the ancient world.

On the overland routes the transport risks for staple commodities would, of course, have been too great. In addition, the costs of lengthy journeys by land were out of all proportion to the profits, which were naturally far lower than in the case of luxury goods. But this did not rule out the transport of very considerable loads, and although there were hardly any roads suitable for vehicles, and in moutainous districts no made-up roads at all, although four-wheeled waggons were not yet universally known, the merchant of these remote centuries was entirely capable of moving bulky, heavy commodities. This is attested by the fact that there are to be found all over Europe, as far as Sweden and Norway, very early massive bronze vessels, or even tank-trucks, intended as outsize mobile wine-tureens to carry round the refreshing beverage to all the guests at festive gatherings. Their weight is usually so extraordinarily great that all sorts of guesses have been made as to how such huge loads could have been transported.

Once more we are confronted by an apparently incredible technological achievement, once more we ask ourselves in vain how early man can have accomplished this and other tasks. What are we to make of it? Are we to assume that our ancestors were gifted in one direction only? That they lived in a predominantly technological age and had not yet properly evolved their specifically spiritual potentialities? There is no convincing ground for this belief, especially as the artistic creations of this period are quite equal to the purely technological. One can only infer from this that those factors of early historical existence which are no longer visible were also fully developed. In form and content they must have corresponded very closely to similar elements in our own existence, so that the flashback technique occasionally employed in the course of our narrative must not be regarded as a cinematic trick, but as an attempt to draw parallels which will help to give us our bearings. And just as the parallels of geometry intersect at infinity, so our parallels cross in the unchangeability of man, to whom the gods early granted that he should be the measure of all things, their beginning and their end.

## PART THREE

# PUNT, LAND OF GOD, AND THE 'ISLES OF THE BLESSED'

# I

THIS chapter begins with a beautiful lady, or rather, with her powder box. Of course, we do not know who this lady actually was, nor what she looked like. And since some four thousand five hundred years have elapsed since her departure from this earthly world, it will not be possible to take down this lady's particulars with the exactitude desirable in the case of such an important witness. Probably she was a princess, or at any rate a relative, of the Sixth Dynasty Pharaohs, who are generally regarded as ending the Old Kingdom. But that is of no particular importance in our context. What interests us is solely the fact that there was still a little rouge in the make-up box which she had been given for her journey to the land of the dead, and that one of the constituents of this rouge was antimony.

The next link in the chain of proof being forged here is the inscription on the grave of helmsman Knemhotep from Elephantine, a small town near the first cataract of the Nile. Knemhotep died in *circa* 2300 B.C., perhaps a few decades later than our princess with the rouge box, and he was buried with great pomp. He must have been a very famous man. We know little of him either, and he would be of no importance to us were it not that his grave tablet reverently records the fact that, with his captain Khui, he eleven times undertook the long voyage to Punt, the Land of God, completing the journey both ways without mishap.

That was the second link. The third is a queen in person, namely Princess Hatshepsut of Egypt, who came to power in 1501 B.C. and was violently done to death, probably by her husband, a bare twenty years later. James H. Breasted, the celebrated historian of Egypt, admiringly terms Princess Hatshepsut 'the first great lady in world history'. And so she probably was. But it is of no concern to us here. For she is important solely as the point of intersection between the lines that lead respectively from the lady with the powder box and helmsman Knemhotep. Nevertheless, we shall have to devote a little more attention to the princess.

Hatshepsut was the daughter and the only legitimate heir of Thothmes I, that great man by whom Egypt was restored to her old position as a world power, after the devastating attack by the Asiatic Hyksos. For almost a hundred and fifty years, from 1700 to 1555 B.C., this alien people had held Egypt in thrall, and during this century and a half everything had been turned topsy-turvy. 'Leader of the young martial generation' the Hyksos kings had styled themselves. We know what that means; it must have been a pretty turbulent period. It is highly significant that, after the expulsion of the Hyksos, the Egyptian people desired nothing more fervently than a return to law and order. As a ruler, therefore, Thothmes I was certainly the right man in the right place—but, although the Pharaoh, he was only a prince consort. For the blood of the founder of the dynasty, the real and genuine blood of the Pharaohs, flowed exclusively in the veins of his wife, Queen Aahmes. *She* was the bearer of tradition, of those powers of order not to be apprehended with the understanding, and believed— as always in times of unrest—to be god-given, which alone could preserve Egypt from a relapse into epochs of lawlessness.

The Egyptians must have noted with concern that no male heir, but only a daughter, sprang from the Prince Consort's marriage. When Aahmes died, the rights of the Prince Consort, Thothmes I, would lapse, and be transferred *in toto* to his daughter, Hatshepsut. What would happen then? Another prince consort? And what guarantee was there that the new holder of power, who would, after all, have risen from below, would not stir up trouble to compensate his inferiority complex?

Hatshepsut herself cut this Gordian knot after the death of her mother. Since a woman could not become queen in Egypt, she was only entitled by law to the position of a 'Great Wife of the King', and when she married the considerably younger Thothmes III, a man of unknown origin, she was at first content with this. Nonetheless, the whole machinery of the State was in her hands from the beginning, and a few years later, supported by her chancellor and favourite, Senmut, she also arrogated to herself the titles of the Pharaohs. Now she was 'King of the North and South, Son of the Sun, Golden Horus, Giver of the Years, Goddess of the Ascents, Mistress of the World, Lady of the Two Lands, Animatress of Hearts, she, the Mighty'—in a word, *she* was the Pharaoh; and accordingly she had herself portrayed with a chin-beard and short loin-cloth, that is to say, in the traditional garb of the Egyptian kings.

Her husband, who, after Hatshepsut's apparently violent death, led

Egypt to the most brilliant position of power, bitterly hated the highly gifted woman at his side throughout his life. When she was finally out of the way, all pictures of her were as completely as possible destroyed, at his command. So we do not know what she looked like. All that remained of her were the scratched and scraped contours of her reliefs on the temple walls. This is symbolic. For little more than her outline was preserved to written history.

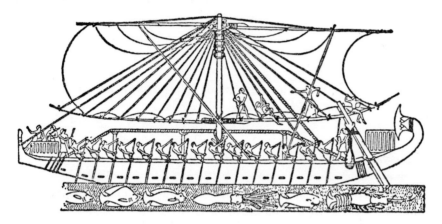

*12. One of Queen Hatshepsut's expedition ships. In 1493 B.C. the Egyptians made a voyage of discovery to the God's Land of Punt. This is reported in an inscription in the temple of Dehr el Bahri, from which this drawing is taken.*

We ourselves must fill in the disembodied outline of this lady who succeeded in changing her sex. The obvious question is: What would an energetic and intelligent woman do, who, being the legitimate heir to the throne, is striving for power against the prevailing law of the State? She would do what is always done in such cases. She would ally herself with the legitimists, to whom tradition is more important than reasons of State. That is the first thing. The second: she would endeavour to make herself popular by some widely visible, striking successes.

Then Senmut, her chancellor and friend, would have advised her to establish a link with the ancient tradition of the Pharaohs by a great expedition to Punt, the Land of God, far down in the southern seas. This would be a deed in the authentic spirit of the old Pharaohs and would create a profound impression. Furthermore, the priests would be on her side, and, finally, it would be easy to achieve the military successes that so affect the public, in an attack on Punt, a primitive country defenceless against the modern arms of the Egyptians. This was clear enough. Whether Senmut's suggestions were decisive for Hatshepsut is an open question. As a rule, women have little regard for purely theoretical reasoning, and since God has set a calculating and practical head on their delicate shoulders, they like to look round for realistic arguments. These were not far to seek. According to ancient reports, during all earlier expeditions—the last was more than five hundred years ago—large quantities of incense had been plundered in Punt. Why should that not be possible now? In this event, Senmut's project could be put into execution without any financial outlay. For incense was expensive, more expensive than gold, and the needs of the priests in the temples were immense. Perhaps this expedition might even bring in money!

Let us begin with this incidental, but possibly decisive, idea of Hatshepsut's. Since time immemorial, Egypt had purchased the huge amounts of incense she needed for the worship of the gods, for the preparation of mummies, and as a medicament, with gold, and goods to the value of gold, from her eastern neighbours beyond the Red Sea. To quote figures: round 1200 B.C. 2,189 jars and 304,093 bushels a year of this precious substance were delivered to the temple of Amon at Thebes alone—such an exorbitant quantity that one hesitates to translate it into contemporary values. But it was just the same amongst other ancient peoples. Year by year, for instance, the Chaldean priests burnt incense to the value of ten thousand talents before the altar of Baal. The Arabs paid a thousand talents of incense as a fixed tribute to Darius, the King of the Persians, and gigantic holy garners were set aside for the storage of this gift of God in the Temple at Jerusalem. The smoke of incense rose skywards in honour of Olympian Zeus all over Greece, and later it reached Rome in an endless stream of cargo boats.

This incense had come, since ancient times, from Hadramat in southern Arabia, the Hatzar Ha-Mavet (Heb. 'Courtyard of Death') of the Bible, a miserable wilderness made rich and world famous by its scented resin. Three thousand aristocratic families were entitled by hereditary right to tap the incense trees. All sorts of religious prescriptions had to be observed in the process, and anyone who possessed the right to participate in the harvest, which lasted from March to August, was looked upon as holy. After the harvest, the incense made its way in heavily armed, carefully guarded caravans to the consuming countries, from oasis to oasis, from royal city to royal city. To begin with, the route taken by these caravans—a definite incense road, just as there were silk roads in Asia, and salt and amber roads in Europe—ran along the coast of southern Arabia to the west. In the eastern

Yemen, probably not far from the modern Aden, the road swung north
and followed the coast of the Red Sea. Here it split into a western
branch, that went to Egypt, and an eastern route that led to Babylon
or to silver Syria. Pliny has described this road in some detail and also
reported the cost per camel load from Hadramat to the Mediterranean
—688 denarii, about £100.

For many millennia, incense was accompanied along this road by
the precious things and luxury commodities of India and the Far East.
For these parts of the earth also derived their supplies of incense from
Hadramat. With the monsoons, Indian traders arrived from the port
of Barygaza, the modern Broach at the mouth of the River Narbada on
the west coast of India. They purchased incense with teak from Further
India, which was built into the palaces of the rich merchants of the
Yemen, with sweet-smelling nards from the Ganges and aromatic
malabathrum (cinnamon leaves) from the Himalayas, muslin-like fabrics
from Taprobane (Ceylon), and silk from Çin (China), tortoise-shell
from Malacca, indigo, pepper, diamonds, emeralds, sapphires, and
lapis lazuli from India. From Hadramat or Aden these costly foreign
things now accompanied the incense on its journey to the north, to
Europe. When it finally reached its destination, it bore a 500 per cent
profit. And so sterile Arabia, suffocated by sand, became immeasurably
wealthy; it became the *Arabia felix* of the Romans; it became the gor-
geous dreamland of the Thousand and One Nights.

The Egyptians, since time immemorial, had been customers of the
Hadramat Arabs for incense; the proud lords of the Land of the Nile
must have resented having to pay numberless pounds of gold year
after year for the lumps of resin that were so important to their priests.
Naturally, the Pharaoh's officials bought only the best quality and did
not permit themselves to be fobbed off with inferior wares, like the
foreigners in Syria and beyond the sea. It is laid down as a criterion of
quality in the mercantile specifications of Rameses III, dated about
1200 B.C., that the colour of incense may vary from a cloudy amber
yellow to a jade green as pale as moonlight. Everything else is worthless. But precisely these qualities were particularly dear, and it is quite
possible that at an early stage the Egyptian government conceived
the wish to get the supply of incense into its own hands. There was no
other source open than the coast of East Africa, where incense occurred
at certain points.

The first incense expedition to the distant land of Punt was undertaken in *circa* 3000 B.C. under Pharaoh Sahu-Rê, the second ruler of
the V-th dynasty. Unfortunately, little knowledge of this expedition

has come down to us. It may have set out from Kosseir on the north of the Red Sea; we know neither how long it took, nor whether there was more than one. Even the actual whereabouts of Punt is not stated in the ancient reports. On the other hand, the great success of Sahu-Rê's venture is announced with pride: 80,000 measures of myrrh, 6,200 weights of electrum (a gold-silver alloy), and 2,600 pieces of costly woods were brought from Punt to Egypt. Punt also provided dwarfs, which for a long time played an important part in the religious dances of the Egyptians. This is stated in an inscription from the reign of the Pharaoh Ysesi, the penultimate ruler of the V-th dnyasty, dated about 2400 B.C. Now ancient Egypt seems to have developed a taste for expeditions to Punt. They were manifestly more frequent during ensuing centuries and apparently became a regular institution. This, at least, is the inescapable inference from the grave-inscription of the good helmsman Knemhotep from Elephantine, whom we introduced at the beginning of the chapter.

But then all that was forgotten. The regular traffic with Punt lapsed, and only under Mentu-hotep IV, in about 2000 B.C., is a journey to the Land of God mentioned once more. During this time, the Egyptians obviously turned away from the sea and towards the land—following a still uninvestigated law according to which periods when a nation delights in the sea and is open to the world seem to alternate with periods when it turns away from the outside world. Not until after the defeat of the invading Hyksos under the energetic Thothmes I (1555–1501 B.C.) did the period of decline give place to a period of advance.

This brings us back to Hatshepsut, to the advice of her chancellor, and to her own cogitations. Naturally she knew more about Punt than we do. Although about three-quarters of a millennium had passed since the cessation of regular voyages to Punt, the actual position of Punt must still have been known. In this Hatshepsut and her chancellor have the adavantage of us. The fact is, we do *not* know exactly where it was; consequently its position has become the subject of a scholarly guessing game, with the constant production of fresh pros and cons. For a long time it was sought in India. This proved mistaken, because it did not tally with the dates of the Hatshepsut expedition as they have come down to us. Then Eritrea, the narrow coastal land on the southern littoral of the Red Sea, was considered. But this did not fit either, for a variety of reasons.

Then, in his thirst for knowledge, a German professor examined more closely the rouge of that Egyptian beauty, whom we mentioned at the outset; suddenly he was able to tell us where Punt must have

lain. We have already heard that this charming unknown lived in the
middle of the VI-th dynasty, at about the same time or slightly earlier
than helmsman Knemhotep, who sailed to Punt. In addition, we learnt
that antimony was one of the constituents of our witness's cosmetic.
Now, we know that the great sources of antimony in Persia and Asia
Minor were not discovered till much later. And the deposits of antimony
in north and west Africa were likewise brought to light at a period
when our Egyptian beauty had long since fallen into dust. The only
other places in Africa where there is antimony are the Transvaal and
Southern Rhodesia, particularly on the lower reaches of the Zambesi.
Therefore, if antimony was used in Egypt four thousand five hundred
years ago, at the same period as that in which Knemhotep sailed to
Punt, then it can only have come from the Zambesi.

At first sight this sounds a tall story. For the distance from north
Egypt to the Zambesi is 5,000 miles along the coast. This is such a vast
stretch that there is every reason to ask how it could possibly have been
travelled in those early times. Moreover, antimony is not found on the
coast, but 300 miles inland in Mashonaland and around the little
mining hutment of Gwelo. Are we to suppose that the Egyptians
travelled half-way round the world merely to dig antimony? It is true
that this mineral can be used to harden copper and produce bronze.
To a small extent this was actually done in Egypt. The crucial reason
for the expeditions to the Zambesi was not antimony, however, but
gold. From time immemorial gold was washed and mined in Mashonaland, and when the famous *Harris Papyrus* had been found and
deciphered, a document from the reign of Rameses III that told how
the Pharaoh had established a great Egyptian mining-colony round
1180 B.C. in a far-off gold land to the south, the gold-mines of the
Zambesi immediately, and no doubt correctly, sprang to mind. Probably numerous Egyptian prospectors, early in the V-th dynasty and
before Sahu-Rê's expedition to Punt, had combed the coasts of East
Africa and, either by chance or at a hint from the natives, had washed
the gold placers of the Zambesi and so provided the incentive for the
expeditions of the V-th and VI-th dynasties—and also for Hatshepsut's
venture.

That events took place on these lines seems quite evident. As we
shall see later, the ship-building technique of the Egyptians was
sufficiently advanced to enable them to make long voyages very early
on in their history. But we do not wish to strain the reader's credulity
at the very outset of this book; for the sake of completeness we will
mention a compromise solution that has been proposed for the historico-

geographical tug-of-war concerning the position of the enigmatic Land of Punt. We are asked to suppose that Punt was a geographical concept that varied through the millennia, so that the rich 'Land of God' had no fixed location and may as well be sought in Eritrea as in Arabia or elsewhere.

*13. Bearers with myrrh trees from Hatshepsut's Punt expedition. From the temple of Dehr el Bahri.*

There is something to be said for this argument, but it would not have commended itself to Hatshepsut if put forward by her experts. Naturally, she knew exactly where Punt lay. She also knew exactly what was to be got there. And if she spoke of frankincense, myrrhs, and other holy things, she meant gold—just as later on there were those who talked of Christ and meant the dry-goods trade. By her own account, the proceeds of her Punt expedition were earmarked for the erection and sumptuous appointment of her temple at Dehr el Bahri, whither she proposed to transfer the remains of her father, Thothmes I, and where she herself wished one day to rest. No doubt her plans were partly inspired by feelings of love and admiration for the great man who was her father. When we read in Dehr el Bahri: 'I have made him a Punt in his garden, as he commanded me . . . It is big enough for him to walk abroad in', genuine filial affection can be detected in this delighted reference to the thirty-one myrrh trees in wooden tubs brought by Hatshepsut's ships from the African south. But the princess was a clever woman; she certainly knew that the magnificent pyramids of the Old Kingdom could never have been erected without the vast wealth of gold in the eastern desert of Upper Egypt. Now, it was particularly necessary for her, precisely because she was following in so much the example of the ancients, to create grandiose religious tombs.

Since the XII-th dynasty, however, from about 2000 B.C. onwards, the gold deposits of Upper Egypt had been completely worked out. With the forty-odd tons of gold which her father had extracted from his mines he had dug the last ounce. If she was really to build on a royal scale, she must obtain gold for the purpose from distant foreign lands.

In this connection, we must recall Hatshepsut's difficult situation. That the law of the State was against her was manifest to all. That her husband, Thothmes III, whom history later surnamed 'the Great', was waiting silently and full of hate for his hour to come, was no secret. The queen herself must have been profoundly conscious of the fact that, because her exercise of power contradicted all traditional usage, she needed a dramatic success as much as she needed her daily bread.

So in 1493 B.C. Hatshepsut dispatched the five great galleys of thirty rowers each to Punt from Kosseir. The navigational peculiarities of the Red Sea, in which, from the end of June on, northerly winds begin to blow, suggest the summer as the date of departure. By late autumn the ships must have reached Cape Guardafui—a distance of 180 miles; then the north-east monsoon set in, whose outrunners drove the fleet on a steady course to the south. There is absolutely no documentary evidence that the secret of the monsoons was known so early. But the regular voyages to Punt during the VI-th dynasty must necessarily have led to utilization of the monsoons. And Hatshepsut's seamen would hardly have been able to reach the Zambesi if the monsoon had not come to their aid.

When the queen's great expedition returned we do not know—scarcely before 1491 B.C. But *how* the sailors landed at Kosseir again, bursting with success and no doubt proudly conscious of having proved themselves worthy successors to their world-sailing forebears, is reported. Hatshepsut herself has informed us in lengthy inscriptions on the walls of the temple at Dehr el Bahri: 'The ships were laden full with the costly products of the Land of Punt and with its many valuable woods, with very much sweet-smelling resin and fresh frankincense, with quantities of ebony and ivory, set in pure gold from the land of Aamu, sweet-smelling resin, *ahem* incense, holy resin, painted with dog-headed apes as a delight to the eyes, with long-tailed apes and greyhounds, furthermore leopard skins and natives of the country with their children . . .'

The queen's artist immortalized this homecoming in a picture in the temple of Dehr el Bahri, with the ships of the fleet, with the potted myrrh saplings, with sacks and boxes, with apes and dogs, and with the portraits of the prince and princess of Punt, whom Hatshepsut's people had taken captive. As was right and proper for south African natives, the huge fat buttocks of Her Highness the Princess of Punt were included in the picture, clear and unmistakable. This, as the German geographer and zoologist, Eberhard Stechow, has recently explained, is one more argument for the belief that the Egyptians who sailed to Punt penetrated quite deep into the south of Africa. The princess of Punt was manifestly a Hottentot lady, and no doubt a very beautiful woman by Hottentot standards.

*14. The Prince and Princess of Punt receive the Egyptian ambassador.*

Whether Hatshepsut achieved with her great expedition to Punt the political aims she undoubtedly set herself, we do not know. At all events, there is nothing to show that she repeated it. Yet that would have been the natural thing to do if the first expedition had enjoyed the success claimed by her State propaganda. But perhaps her attempt to win popularity by repeating the deeds of the ancients was doomed from the outset, because the old-style Egyptian, to whom she was appealing, no longer existed. We therefore have no need to inquire further why the voyages to Punt were not repeated, nor what caused the great lady, whom we have discussed at such length here, to meet her death on the scaffold, by the poisoned cup, or by the sharp-pointed dagger. Perhaps love for her friend Senmut had overcome her and made her weak. Let us hope so, for this would lend a touch of tragic humanity to the stern, imperious features of the god-queen.

The strict sequence of our account compels us to leave Hatshepsut behind. All that remains for us is to quote the words with which she concluded the commemoration of the Punt expedition in her temple: 'Exact and correct were the gifts from Tehuti, which the queen had prepared for her father, the Amon of Thebes, with the injunction to weigh silver, gold, blue stones, green stones, and all other costly gems . . .'

It is clear that these 'costly gems' were Indian emeralds and turquoises, lapis lazuli and sapphires, the same precious stones, most of them originating from Ceylon, which had been reaching Egypt via the land route from Hadramat and Aden. Since this is the first mention of the presence of Indian commercial products on the east African coast, we should do well not to derive too far-reaching conclusions from it. Nevertheless, it is quite possible that knowledge of the monsoons, those steady winds that fill the expanse of ocean between India and Africa in tireless alternation, is much older than history relates. The fact that the name of the island of Socotra, east of the Somali peninsula, stems from the Sanskrit—it has been derived from the Sanskrit *Dvípa-Sukhádhára*, 'the Island Abode of Bliss'—and that the port of Sofala, south of the Zambesi delta, comes from the Sanskrit word *Supara*, 'Land of the Beautiful Shore', lends support to this view. The early history of navigation on the Indian Ocean is still so obscure, however, that we must leave its discussion to specialists in this field of research.

2

Another subject now briefly claims our attention: the question of whether early Egypt really possessed vessels capable of weathering the high seas and sailing long distances. This question is all the more justified because, on the one hand, voyages to the Zambesi presuppose considerable shipbuilding technique and seamanship, while, on the other, Egypt was a land without forests and hence without long timber for beams and planks. How could such a country produce ocean-going vessels, how could such a people go to sea? And yet this is what happened. There is no doubt that the Egyptians went to sea thousands of years before the Christian era. Innumerable vase paintings and mural reliefs from pre-dynastic times, that is, before 3500 B.C.—in particular the lively representations of Hierakonpolis, which depict a great variety of vessels—prove the important role played by the ship in the Land of the Nile. The Egyptians' first voyages must certainly have been on the river. But the Nile is not always calm, gentle and slow-flowing; in its lower reaches especially it can be extremely rough and boisterous; at many points it presents dangers equal to those of the sea.

The transition from river sailing to sea voyages proper probably took place as early as the second half of the fourth millennium B.C. The Egyptians were very urgently impelled to this by the great lack of timber in the sandy country round the pyramids, and it may be surmised that the mountain country of Sinai, with its copper deposits

and forests, was one of the first destinations of the ancient Egyptian
ocean-going ships. Then Phœnicia was discovered, whose cedars of
Lebanon provided excellent building timber; with the introduction of
this timber, Egypt began to develop those tough, seaworthy vessels
she needed for her world-wide voyages.

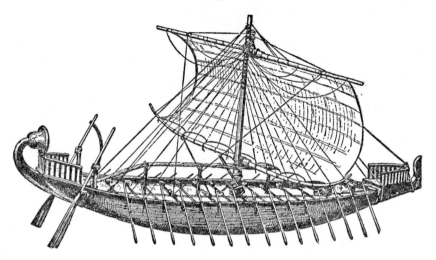

*15. Egyptian ship, 1700–1400 B.C.*

While the Nile freighters attained great dimensions at an early
period—vase paintings from the fifth millennium show gigantic
galleys with more than fifty rowers on either side, that is to say, ships
of 200 to 260 feet in length—the later Egyptian ocean-going ship
remained within reasonable bounds. It was about 100 feet from stem to
stern, with a beam of 21 feet and a draught of about 4 feet; its displacement must, therefore, have been from 80 to 85 tons. It was constructed
as a rowing or sailing ship and built to move on an even keel. Under
oars or with wind astern, it must have reached very considerable speeds.
Square-rigged as it was, it is hardly likely to have been capable of
tacking against the wind. But antique navigation is not to be judged by
our standards. The captains of the ancient 'windjammers' were altogether devoid of sporting ambition. If the wind was favourable they
sailed, if it was unfavourable they stayed at anchor in port.

The original Egyptian ship, which, under the necessity of doing
without timber of any length, was built of short planks, must have
suffered a great deal in the wave-troughs on the high seas. When
vessels of this type enter rough sea, their joints invariably prove
inadequate to the strain exerted when they are lifted up by two lines

of waves at the same time. Even the Viking dragon ships, which were built with long timber, frequently got into difficulties. The latest

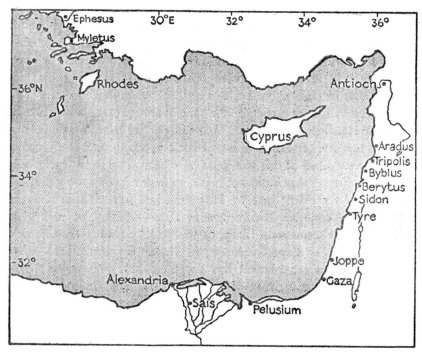

III. *The Phœnician seaboard. Aradus represented the northern and Gaza the southern limit of Phœnician influence. Byblus and Gaza were the main centres of trade with Egypt, Tyre and Sidon of long-distance trade. Tyre (really Tshor, rocks) owed its name to the low cliffs that ran out 100 yards from the shore and were later incorporated into the harbour by means of great moles. Its rise was due not only to its value as a port, but also to its metal industry and purple-dye works. Joppe stood on gleaming white chalk cliffs (the word means 'the white' or 'gleaming one') and had dyeworks and glass factories; it belonged within the Tyrian sphere of power. Berytus (from beêroth, the fountains) belonged to Sidon; as a flourishing town and the port for Damascus it was called under Augustus: Colonia Julia Augusta Felix Berytus. Byblus, probably founded at the same date as Sidon, was called after the city-god Gebâl, Arabic Jebêl. In consequence of its proximity to the Lebanon it was the chief mart for the Egyptian import of shipbuilding timber. Through the founding of a new city by Sidon, Tyre and Aradus—Tripolis, 'Three-city'—it subsequently declined in economic importance. Aradus (from Phœnician arvâd, sanctuary) was the only haven on a long stretch of sandy coast.*

example of this was afforded by the total loss of that Swedish Viking ship, ostensibly an exact replica of the old longships, which broke up during a storm in the North Sea and went down with all hands in the summer of 1950.

The seafarer of today has no need to bother his head with things of this kind. It would never occur to him that antique marine engineers had to cope with such problems. Nonetheless, many of their achievements are still completely incomprehensible. Thus we know, for instance, that in *circa* 1500 B.C. two obelisks weighing 700 tons each, and 100 feet tall, were carried up the Nile in a huge cargo boat from the temple of Hatshepsut at Karnak. Accordingly, we have to assume that this boat had a water displacement of some 1,500 tons. It is altogether obscure how a vessel of this size could have been constructed exclusively of wood, so strong that it did not break up under its own weight alone.

It is not by accident that we have launched into this excursus on shipbuilding technique. The voyages to Punt—whether we seek it on the Zambesi, as seems most likely, or whether we tend to the old view that it lay south of Cape Guardafui, in present-day Somaliland—were such a prodigious achievement that they absolutely presuppose highly evolved sea-going craft. Nor do these voyages stand alone as isolated *tours de force*. We have long known that round the middle of the third millennium B.C. the Egyptians sailed to Spain, under their own flag as well as under the flag of Crete, to take part in the tin and bronze trade. Egyptian ships likewise landed repeatedly on the shores of Greece and Phœnicia. The run to the Asia Minor coast offered itself spontaneously, so to speak, and we are well acquainted with its conditions. As is well known, the prevailing winds on the Egyptian littoral in summer are south and south-west, which more or less automatically bear ships to Phœnicia and Syria. In addition, a rather powerful current runs along the Syrian coast to the north, so that it was not difficult to traverse the 300 nautical miles or so from the Nile delta to the port of Byblus in central Phœnicia in four times twenty-four hours, a voyage time that corresponds to a speed of three to four knots. Since there was perpetual contact between Egypt and Phœnicia on land as well, chiefly in connection with military expeditions, the history of Egyptian and Phœnician exploration very soon became so completely intermingled that the two peoples often appear at sea together, and it is no longer possible to distinguish who was the initiator of an expedition and who carried it out. The next two voyages which we have to name here, before we turn to the truly classical period of Phœnician maritime supremacy, were executed by the Phœnicians, certainly with the connivance and foreknowledge of the Egyptians and possibly on their direct instructions.

At first, the highly civilized Egyptians spoke most slightingly of their Phœnician neighbours, who were clearly a quite primitive tribe of desert nomads, entirely incapable, on their own account, of dealing with the sea. We repeatedly find the Phœnicians referred to as 'miserable Asiatics' in ancient Egyptian records. 'Evil is the place in which he lives, inaccessible because of the many trees and with bad water. The roads there are also wretched because of the mountains. He never dwells in one place and his feet wander . . .' But the fine cedar wood brought from Byblus to build ships, and coffins for Egyptians of rank; the cedar oil which served so excellently for embalming the dead; and finally habituation to the Phœnician's mode of life, led the Egyptian mariners and merchants to adopt a less critical attitude. On the other hand, the Semitic nomads, who had been thrust against the eastern littoral of the Mediterranean by unknown migrations inside Asia, rapidly became acclimatized. They may originally have stood at a cultural level not much higher than that of Punt. The first Phœnician ships, which we know from Egyptian portrayals, were constructed entirely on the pattern of their much admired Egyptian models. Gradually, however, they broke away, and the point was soon reached when the 'Byblus vessels', built by Phœnician shipbuilders to Egyptian order, differed considerably from the Egyptian ship.

These vessels are manifestly built for the sea and not for river sailing. A great deal more compact than the long, narrow Egyptian ships, they were not nearly so susceptible to the strain of being lifted up by two lines of waves simultaneously, which caused the marine engineers of the Pharaohs such headaches. Broad and tubby, these craft slipped into the wave troughs and rode like corks. A high, stockade-like bulwark sheltered the crew from inundation by the breakers; fore and aft there seems to have been, at a very early stage, the rudiments of a deck; and if the high stem, the manner in which the rudder was attached, the form of rigging, and the deck beams penetrating the outer skin were unmistakably adopted from Egyptian prototypes, the Phœnician shipbuilders had taken careful note of the drawbacks of the Egyptian type of ship and had avoided them in their own.

The Phœnician shipwrights must soon have engaged in the construction of fully-decked craft. Naturally, such ships offered only limited opportunities for rowing, and it is easy to imagine what conflicts must have raged in the construction offices of Phœnicia between the advocates of the combined rowing and sailing ship and the partisans of the pure sailer. In any case, the modern trend triumphed, and the ships that made the voyages we are about to hear of were primarily sailers: 100 to 130 feet long, 26 to 33 feet across, with a draught of 8 feet and a corresponding displacement of up to 400 tons, rigged with a square-sail of about 380 square yards, and manned by a crew of some thirty men. The building of larger craft was always rejected in the Phœnician-Babylonian cultural sphere, apart from Noah's ark, whose

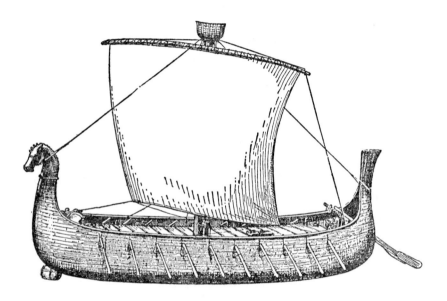

*16. Phœnician warship, eleventh to eighth century B.C.*

length is given in Babylonian texts as approximately 480 feet. Contrary to the Egyptians, whose kings liked building extremely large river boats with several decks, with kitchens, baths, sports grounds, sleeping, living, and dining rooms on board—prodigiously luxurious wonders of shipbuilding technique, even by our standards—the Phœnicians always confined themselves to vessels of manageable and practical proportions. To this intelligent moderation they owe the right, which is still theirs today after thousands of years, to a paramount place amongst the great explorers and discoverers of our earth.

Their historical role was, of course, primarily commercial. It is clear that, for the most part, the Phœnicians showed their sails in seas that were already known. They did not simply sail into the blue, and the unbounded admiration for this seafaring people which prevailed in our grandfathers' time was undoubtedly exaggerated. Yet what they achieved as seamen in their efforts to pursue trade, establish monopolies, and acquire wealth, was magnificent in itself.

3

The Phœnicians took their place in the story of discovery five hundred years after Hatshepsut—first along the routes already travelled regularly by the Egyptians, and obviously on the basis of knowledge which they owed to the lords of the Land of the Nile. This time the Bible is our witness. It is written of Solomon's famous voyage to Ophir in I Kings 9:

'And king Solomon made a navy of ships in Ezion-geber, which is beside Eloth, on the shore of the Red Sea, in the land of Edom. And Hiram [king of Tyre in Phœnicia] sent in the navy his servants, shipmen that had knowledge of the sea, with the servants of Solomon. And they came to Ophir, and fetched from thence gold, four hundred and twenty talents, and brought it to king Solomon . . . For the king had at sea a navy of Tharshish, with the navy of Hiram: once in three years came the navy of Tharshish, bringing gold, and silver, ivory, and apes, and peacocks.'

If this Biblical report, which is repeated almost word for word in II Chronicles 8 ff., is correct, then Jews and Phœnicians set sail from the Israelite Red Sea port of Ezion-geber, the modern Akaba, for the southern gold land in *circa* 945 B.C. From there they are said to have brought apes and peacocks—according to another rendering, apes and slaves—together with ivory and silver, and finally 413 cwt. of gold, about £3–4 million worth at its present value. The voyage is said to have taken three years there and back.

Unfortunately that is all the Bible has to tell us, and to our regret it is not much. Above all, nothing whatever is said as to the position of Ophir; consequently, as with Punt, it has been sought all over the place: in the South Seas and in India, in Peru and on San Domingo. At first the most likely interpretation seemed to be the one which placed Ophir in the region of Massawa on the Red Sea, where very ancient gold-mines were found in the hinterland near Keren. When it began to appear that Punt was to be sought on the Zambesi, fresh light was cast on the problem of Ophir. Solomon's land of gold, as Kant already surmised, is likewise to be looked for on the coast of south-east Africa; especially as this would tally with the three years the voyage is stated in the Bible to have taken. At all events, Massawa could have been reached in far less time. An expedition to Massawa would not have excited the universal attention spoken of in the Old Testament in connection with the visit of the Queen of Sheba.

So far so good. But there is one highly remarkable fact about this ancient adventure story: the report that Phœnicians and Jews made common cause in Solomon's expedition to Ophir. This runs entirely counter to the normal business practices of the great mercantile houses of Tyre and Sidon, which made every effort to conceal and monopolize important discoveries. What can have caused the Phœnicians to vary their custom in this case?

There seems to be quite a simple explanation. It is well known that King Solomon (972–939 B.C.) married a daughter of the Egyptian Pharaoh, Sheshank II, seeking to form an alliance with the Land of the Nile, which was growing slowly stronger. In so doing, he had clearly opted against the great power of Assyria, just established by Tiglath-pileser (1116–1090 B.C.). Naturally, Solomon was aware of the dangers inherent in his position between the world empires of Assyria to the east and Egypt to the west. Egypt alone was not enough; he needed further friends, and pursuing entirely the same foreign policy as his predecessor, King David, he turned to the Phœnicians. The wealthy international trading concerns of this small neighbouring country were also acutely conscious of their precarious situation between the great millstones of the eastern and western hemispheres. They were already on friendly terms with David, as with the Greeks and Tartessans. But fundamentally, David, who had only just compelled Judah and Israel to unite in one kingdom, was not yet to be taken seriously as an ally.

Was the picture different now that Solomon had mounted the throne? Well, as Pharaoh's son-in-law, he was naturally *persona grata* in Egypt. In addition, Sheshank II had conquered the Canaanite city of Gezer for him, presenting it to him with his daughter as a kind of dowry. But there must have been more to it than that. Solomon was a clever man; if he intended to form a 'Third Force' between east and west, he must have had some further trump card up his sleeve.

The Phœnicians were only mildly encouraging in this diplomatic game. Their policy was 'wait and see'. Hiram, their king, wrote cordial letters, sent occasional emissaries with gold and purple, dispatched masons and architects for the building of the Temple at Jerusalem— and then it came out! Solomon played his trump card: he knew, so he let it be rumoured, where Egyptian Punt lay and whence the Pharaohs had obtained the immense quantities of gold which, since time immemorial, had constituted the true basis of their eminence in the world.

He also possessed a port, Ezion-geber on the Red Sea, from which an expedition could be launched unobtrusively. He had no ships and no sailors either. So he proposed to the gentlemen in Tyre and Sidon a fifty-fifty partnership. He would invest his knowledge in the enterprise, indeed he could give a guarantee of success, since the gold-mines established in Punt by Rameses III some two hundred years ago were still in regular operation. In return the Phœnicians must furnish the necessary ships and the naval personnel.

Of course, we have no record of these discussions and negotiations. But they must have taken place along these or similar lines. The Phœnicians were obviously quite clear in their minds that they need take their Palestinian cousins with them on the first trip only. After that, things would look quite different, for the landlubbers of Canaan would never get to Punt by themselves!

If they really calculated like this in Tyre and Sidon—and no doubt they did, since man has not changed one jot since the beginning of time—they were absolutely correct. For when the Israelites tried, a hundred years after Solomon, to reach Ophir without the co-operation of the Phœnicians, the ships which King Jehosaphat had had built broke apart as soon as they were launched. If this was the situation, it explains why no further voyages to Ophir by the Jews are recorded. Once the Phœnicians had learned what they wanted, they no longer had the slightest reason to share the east Africa trade with their cousins from Canaan. They must have continued to sail to Ophir themselves for many more centuries; hence it is always assumed that they were the builders of those mighty towers and ramparts whose ruins have been found in Mashonaland, particularly in the mining area of Gwelo, Que-Que and Selukwe, the central point of which is probably the colossal fortification of Zimbabwe.

Zimbabwe lies seventeen miles south-east of Victoria in Southern Rhodesia, 280 miles from the sea in the valley of the Upper Mtetkwe, a tributary of the Sabi which leads into the vicinity of the goldfields. It seems to be the centre of a zone of approximately 385,000 square miles within which it is surrounded by the remains of some five hundred enigmatic constructions, mostly conical defence towers, that are without direct parallel except in the Balearics and Peru. Here, as in East Africa, these strange edifices still stand, built of rock split into separate blocks by some unknown method and so wonderfully hewn that these Cyclopean blocks lock into a firm and gapless structure without mortar. Similar buildings in Sardinia, known as *nuraghi*, in all probability go back to the Etruscans. It is quite possible that Etruscan influences, passed on by the Egyptians, were at work at Zimbabwe. Any connection with Peru, however, seems at first glance out of the question. Whether this is really so is another matter. For towers of like construction to the *nuraghi* also rise in the Shetland and Orkney Islands,

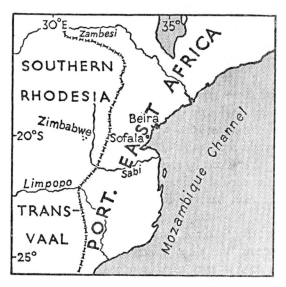

*IV. The position of Zimbabwe.*

the Hebrides, and the north of Scotland—a fact of considerable interest, as we shall see later!

The Portuguese came to Zimbabwe in the middle of the eighteenth century. The German explorer, Carl Mauch, visited this region in 1871, and a little later Carl Peters also stayed at Zimbabwe. Both of them fully agreed in the opinion that these ruins were of ancient Phœnician origin and might possibly be the Ophir of the Bible. Convincing proof could not, however, be found. After them came Englishmen, Italians, Americans, and more Germans; amongst the latter above all Leo Frobenius.

All these archæologists and geographers were profoundly impressed by the Cyclopean ramparts they encountered, and even the thoroughly matter-of-fact *South and East African Year Book and Guide*, almost the official handbook of the Union of South Africa, betrays a tinge of excitement between the lines when it says:

There is no doubt that they were known to the Portuguese some century or more ago. No burial ground or inscriptions have yet been discovered which adds to the difficulty of assigning a date to the ruins.

The main wall was in some places upwards of 30 feet in height and was about 10 feet thick at the base and 7 feet at the summit. The chief building, at some little distance from a granite kopje, was however included within the walls and seems to have served as a citadel or refuge.

In their present condition the ruins appear to stand in three groups, but it is probable that they all formed part of one settlement, of which the so-called citadel formed the centre. The total extent traced so far covers an area of about 2 by 1¼ miles, but remains of walls, some deeply buried, have been found in the secluded valleys and on the hillsides to a distance of a mile or two beyond this area.

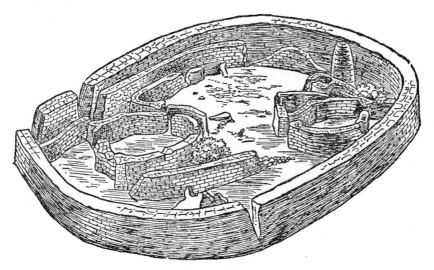

*17. Reconstructed model of the Zimbabwe fortifications. In the right background is one of the characteristic conical defence towers.*

As is so often the case in ruins found in the east, the measurements of the various buildings bear a mathematical relationship to each other. By means of calculations it has been possible to trace the greater part of the original design and to fill up many of the gaps now existing.

No mortar was employed, but the stone was dressed and squared by the hammer. Amongst the ruins numbers of relics have been discovered, including statuettes of Astarte or Venus in the hawk form; Phallic symbols of various dimensions; bowls, trinkets, etc., the best collections being those in the Museums of Bulawayo and of Capetown.

So much for the *S. & E. A. Year Book* for 1938. It is clear that its authors had an Egypto-Phœnician origin of the Zimbabwe ruins in mind, an assumption rendered very natural by the great buildings erected without mortar and the finding of falcon-headed statues of gods. The individual finds do not, however, appear sufficiently conclusive to permit the identity of the builders to be unequivocally deduced; German archæologists in particular have established that all the alleged Egyptian or Phœnician finds are fakes. There has not yet been enough systematic spade-work in the area. Yet the district of Zimbabwe is easily reached along good motoring roads and the Great Zimbabwe Hotel directly overlooks the ruins.

To unprejudiced listeners like ourselves, who can follow the conflict of opinions over Zimbabwe with an open mind, it sounds reasonable to suppose that the lords of the thousands-of-years-old Mashonaland mines established a system of strategically placed outer forts round a gigantic central citadel. Gold was such a very alluring substance, and it would have been easy enough for a band of robbers skilled in navigation to swoop down on the gold-mines along the rivers Sabi and Mtetkwe. Such reflections may already have occurred to the Egyptians; they will undoubtedly have occupied the minds of the Phœnicians, who certainly did not rest content with the single gold expedition carried out jointly with the Jews. The question of how they could most effectively bar the African gold monopoly against alien incursors must have struck them all the more forcibly since they themselves were reaping what others had searched out. This natural inference does not, of course, prove anything, and for the time being Zimbabwe remains one of those riddles to which archæology has not yet found the answer.

4

If we draw up a balance sheet of the items so far enumerated in this chapter, they amount once more to a demonstration that world-wide travel was not initiated by the modern era. Men sailed from Crete to Tartessus and thence to Britain; they journeyed from the Black Sea to Samland; a network of communications extended between the estuaries of the Rhone and the Elbe and between Jutland and the Adriatic. It was the same in other parts of the world and over still greater distances. At the dawn of history, men were clearly far less inhibited than, say, in classical antiquity; they were unafraid of long journeys, because they had no idea how big the world really was; they did not yet know the fear that comes with understanding, which seems to be a concomitant of culture and a punishment of the gods for man's meddlesome curiosity.

All this explains how one of the greatest feats of discovery in early

8. Etruscan woman's head from a wall painting in the Tomba dell' Orco in Tarquinia. Decked in jewels, her hair artistically dressed and with plucked eyebrows, this is how an unknown painter has portrayed for us this young Etruscan woman. 4th century B.C.

9. Etruscan couple from a sarcophagus at Cerveteri, 6th century B.C. The almond eyes, sharply cut faces and straight, narrow noses indicate the Etruscans' origin in Asia Minor.

10. Tombstone of a Roman couple, 1st century B.C. This is how we have always imagined the old Romans: on the left the domina, the mistress of the house, on the right the man, with full lips but with the corners of his mouth somewhat drawn down. Is this an idealised picture of a later date, or a genuine portrait?

history, the circumnavigation of Africa by an Egypto-Phœnician expedition during the reign of Necho II of Egypt (609–594 B.C.), later slipped into oblivion. Yet this voyage, which Herodotus recorded a hundred and fifty years after it was made, does not seem to have been the first voyage round the Dark Continent. It is possible that the mariners of Hatshepsut had already accomplished this prodigious feat. We do not know for sure, but there are certain grounds for the supposition. It is not likely that the sea-going vessels of the ancient world were capable of sailing against the strong northerly currents in the Mozambique Channel between Madagascar and East Africa. Once having sailed through this channel immediately south of the Zambesi, they could not have returned by the same route. Hence there was no other alternative but to follow the approximately 9,400 miles of coast round Africa and back to the Nile delta.

Much doubt has been cast on Herodotus's account of the expedition organized by Necho II. Here are some extracts from it:

The shape of Libya [Africa] shows that, save for the part that borders on Asia, it is surrounded on all sides by sea. The first to bring proof of this, as far as I know, was Pharaoh Necho of Egypt. When he ceased the digging of the canal which was to link the Nile with the Red Sea, he equipped an expedition and commanded it to sail round Libya through the Pillars of Hercules [Straits of Gibraltar], back into the Mediterranean, and so return to Egypt. Therefore the Phœnicians left port and sailed out of the Indian Ocean into the southern sea. When autumn fell, they landed, tilled the fields, and waited for the harvest, in whatever part of Libya they happened to be. When they had harvested the corn they sailed on, until, after two years, they sailed through the Pillars of Hercules, and so returned to Egypt again in the third year. They related, which I cannot myself believe, though perhaps some other may, that as they rounded Libya they beheld the sun on their right hand.

The two most striking passages in this account are at the beginning and the end and concern Africa's geographical position. The first reveals Herodotus's clear knowledge that Africa is surrounded by the ocean. Soon after him, this knowledge was lost, so utterly lost that Claudius Ptolemy, the greatest geographer and astronomer of classical antiquity, could teach in *circa* A.D. 150 that the Indian Ocean was an inland sea, since Africa curved round to the east and was directly connected by land to the Far East. And yet Ptolemy had lived in Alexandria, that is to say, in the very country whose rulers, not so long ago, had established that their continent was circumnavigable. Nonetheless no information, no hint reached him that might have taught him

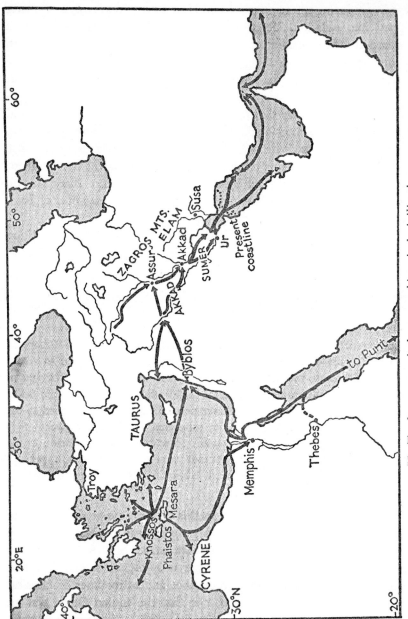

V. Trade routes of the proto-historical civilizations.

better; and only when the Portuguese came to the Cape of Good Hope in 1487 did it transpire that Ptolemy was wrong.

The fault for this, however, lies less with Ptolemy than with Herodotus himself, for retailing in his concluding sentence the statement that, on circumnavigating Africa, Necho's expedition had the sun on their right. To people living north of the equator, this must have sounded like blatant humbug, and Herodotus himself, as emerges clearly from his report, felt thoroughly ashamed of having to pass on such arrant nonsense. But he took his profession of historiographer and travel journalist very seriously. As a rule, therefore, he faithfully noted even those things which he considered nonsensical. He did so in this case, and the very remark which rendered his report so incredible to the antique world proves that some bold captain did in fact sail round the African continent at a very early period. For if this were done in a westerly direction, that is, along the course taken by Necho's expedition, then south of the equator the sun would appear on the right, i.e. in the north. The very thing that caused antique geography to regard Herodotus's report as nonsensical, therefore, points unequivocally to its accuracy.

This voyage, like so many others, took place too early to be deemed important by its own period. It is difficult to see what Necho's purpose was in ordering it to be carried out. He was an enterprising man; this is shown by his attempt to cut a canal to the Red Sea near Bubastis on the Upper Nile delta. He abandoned the work unfinished, not because of the hundred and twenty thousand human lives this stupendous undertaking is supposed to have cost, but because he was informed by an oracle that he was merely assisting the Persians—who, a century later, under Darius I, did in fact complete the canal. Here we must interpolate that the bloody history of the Suez Canal did not begin with Necho. A water communication between the Nile and the Red Sea was already established during the Middle Kingdom—we shall describe the forerunners of the Suez Canal later—so that Necho was only following older models. This makes it psychologically probable that his Africa expedition was also a repetition of much older enterprises, that it merely pursued an ancient tradition, and that its sole purpose was to enhance the Pharaoh's prestige. Herodotus's statement that Necho commanded his captains to sail round Africa and through the Pillars of Hercules, as the Straits of Gibraltar were known in classical times, sounds as though Egypt already knew of the connection between the Indian Ocean and the Atlantic, and as though the Egypto-Phœnician reconnaissance expedition was undertaken to confirm its existence. At all events, the wording of Herodotus's report implies certainty on Necho's part that his ships would return from the *west*.

5

With the Biblical testimony to Solomon's Ophir expedition and Herodotus's report of Necho's African venture, we have the first documentary evidence of the important position in seafaring and world commerce meanwhile acquired by the Semitic Phœnicians. Of their gradual rise to the status of a great mercantile power we know next to nothing. Somewhere round the fifteenth century B.C. they took over the role of the Cretans, who suddenly disappeared from the stage. Why this happened, why the grandiose Cretan empire of the Mediterranean vanished without trace, and without any signs of hostile attack, by the Egyptians for instance, is an absolute mystery. It looks as though oceanography may recently have furnished a clue. When a Swedish research society took samples of the bed of the eastern Mediterranean in 1947, they ascertained the presence in the undersea sediments of deep layers of volcanic ash. Chemical examination established that this ash could only have emanated from the Santorin volcano on the island of Thera in the Ægean and that it must have been deposited between 1500 and 1400 B.C.

These ash deposits were so vast that they clearly indicated an eruption of catastrophic proportions. And although Thera is some sixty miles from Crete, it was obvious that this eruption must have had disastrous consequences for the wealthy and flourishing island State. Probably it was so weakened thereby that it finally lost its position of dominance to the rising Phœnicians.

With the extinction of Crete the way was clear for the rise of new seafaring peoples. And since the Hittites, who till then had dominated Syria, receded from their proud pre-eminence at about the same time, whilst Egypt had her hands full with the Hyksos wars, Phœnicia's hour had come, and she flung herself into the gap.

Via the Greek islands, which they occupied with mercantile *entrepôts,* via Malta, Sicily and Sardinia, which they colonized, the Phœnicians slowly felt their way towards the west, towards the centre of the bronze trade. In the twelfth century B.C., very shortly after the founding of Tartessus, they established the city of Gades, the present-day Cadiz, in the immediate vicinity of golden Tarshish. They picked the site of Gades with consciously competitive intent, and so well that it still stands today—one of the oldest cities in Europe. Not long after, they built Tingas (Tangier) on the African coast, as a base for their ships on the north African and Atlantic runs, and Lixus on the Atlantic coast of Morocco. In about 1000 B.C. Utica, the present-day Hanchir Bou Chateur, was founded not far from Tunis; and two hundred years later, a little to the south-east of Utica, the most illustrious and power-ful Phœnician colony, Carthage (New City), the date of whose founda-tion is assumed to be 814 B.C. With these numerous and strong colonial stations the Phœnicians had created points of departure for an attack on the eastern half of the Atlantic Ocean.

The main blow, as we have heard, fell in *circa* 530 B.C. with Carthage's lightning conquest of southern Spain. One of their aims was, of course, to gain control of the trade with Britain. This goal of foreign policy was particularly underlined by Cathaginian diplomats when, a little later, round about 525 B.C., they sent one of their most competent men, Admiral Himilco, with a majestic fleet to the northern Tin Islands. Any information which they may have allowed to seep through after Himilco's return from this voyage has not reached us. All we have is a late Roman travel poem, written nine hundred years later, which is probably based on the original report and makes highly sensational play with horror stories of loathsome monsters, everlasting calms, masses of seaweed, and so forth. This enables us to infer what the Carthaginians *did* make public, and that it was obviously important to them to frighten off other potential voyagers to Britain. The expedi-tion seems to have been a success, for the Carthaginians continued their trips to Britain into the second century B.C.

The real reason for the occupation of southern Spain and the blockade of the straits must, however, as was stated in the previous chapter, have lain in the south and in the fact that there were valuable dyestuffs on Madeira and the Canary Islands, which did not occur in the Mediterranean zone. Alongside glass manufacture and a highly evolved goldsmith's art, Phœnician and, later, Puno-Carthaginian industry rested on the production of the famous Tyrian purple, which had a particularly warm, rich lustre. It is highly significant that the Greek word *phoinix* means both Phœnician and purple-coloured.

To begin with, the dye chemists of Tyre used mainly the juice of the purple-fish (*Murex*), which the Hellenes also employed in dyeing their fabrics. For large-scale production, however, this method was much too expensive and much too complicated. Each shellfish yielded only a few drops of dye fluid. This fluid had to be condensed to a six-teenth of its volume by hot steam. In addition, the dyeing process demanded constant supervision to ensure that the desired colour was obtained. For the juice of the purple-fish is originally milky white. Under the influence of light it takes on a lemon-yellow shade; longer exposure to light renders it greenish yellow, green, violet, and red. The most various colours can be obtained according to the duration of exposure, down to a purple that looks almost black. It is understandable that Phœnician purple was prodigiously expensive. By A.D. 300, at the beginning of a period of inflation it is true, a pound of purple silk, the celebrated *metaxablatta*, cost the stupendous sum of about £10,000. But since in Rome and the rest of the world all badges of rank were made of purple materials, these huge sums were paid. However, the methods of production outlined above were naturally only successful in the hands of small craftsmen or family businesses, where the experience of generations was handed down from father to son. For manufacturing enterprises such as the Phœnicians established, this complicated process was out of the question. Each one of them needed millions of purple-fish for a single dyeing, and there was no certainty of obtaining the same shade next time. Since great value was attached in Tyre to the exact repetition of shades, a new and practical dyestuff was of national importance.

It is not difficult to imagine that excitement aroused in Phœnicia by the discovery of the Atlantic islands. These islands produced the dyestuffs for which Tyre had long been seeking: the *Roccella tinctoria*, litmus or dyer's lichen, as well as the dragon tree (*Dracæna draco*), whose deep red resin, known as dragon's blood, also yielded an excellent purple dye and whose mightiest representative, the famous dragon tree of Orotava on Teneriffe, which was blown down in 1868, is reputed to have been six thousand years old. Those two raw materials of the dye trade were naturally of the utmost industrial and commercial importance to the Phœnicians, and it was doubtless this which later induced Carthage to incorporate Madeira and the Canaries in its sphere of power.

A few simple aniline derivatives suffice to enable modern chemistry to produce lustrous purple dyes, and beneath our grey skies ancient man's passionate liking for these violent tones is utterly incomprehensible. But when the Phœnicians first brought out their Canary Islands purple, it must have been a severe shock to the Greek manufacturers. No doubt they racked their brains again and again, yet the whole antique world was baffled by the riddle of Tyrian purple until much later. Nevertheless, obscure rumours of the rich, fertile islands in the Atlantic Ocean did get as far as Hellas. We shall have more to say about this presently, and will confine ourselves here to mentioning a thesis propounded by geographers decades ago to the effect that the famous Isles of the Blessed, the *Nêsoi Makáron* of Greek mythology, were nothing else than a verbal distortion of the ancient Phœnician 'Isles of Makar', the favourite Tyrian city-god, Melkart. Geographical discoveries as important as these simply cannot be hushed up completely.

At roughly the same time as the dispatch of Himilco to Britain, round about 530 B.C., a second and even larger Carthaginian mariner expedition was undertaken under the command of Admiral Hanno, a close relative of Himilco; this expedition proves how immensely important the Atlantic islands were to the Carthaginians. In the words of the original report, which is extant in a Greek translation—admittedly inaccurate and moreover incomplete—the purpose of this carefully planned voyage was to set up colonial stations along the west African littoral as far as the Canary Islands. The function of these coastal stations was undoubtedly to safeguard the seaway to the Atlantic islands against attack from land, which was thus firmly in Carthaginian hands, and to give assistance to the Atlantic ships. Hanno's enterprise was equipped with sixty galleys of fifty rowers each, carrying some three thousand men and women, together with stores and everything needed for the planting of colonies.

This first aim of Hanno's expedition seems to have been accomplished in full. Six named settlements were created, the most southerly being situated on Cape Juby roughly level with the Canary Islands. Strangely enough, however, Hanno did not rest content with this, but, instead of turning round, sailed on to the south. It has been conjectured that he was stimulated by the circumnavigation of Africa under Pharaoh Necho only two generations earlier, to sail round the Dark Continent on his own account. This is not to be ruled out, but cannot be proved. It is not possible to identify all the points at which he cast anchor, but it is certain that he got as far as Mount Cameroon. Here the voyage was broken off because provisions had run out. Hanno makes the following report:

We had now been sailing for four days and throughout each night we saw the land full of flames; in the midst of them was a very tall flame that towered above the other flames and seemed to reach up to the stars. By day we saw that it was a very high mountain. We named it the Chariot of the Gods [Mount Cameroon]. When we had sailed along beside streams of fire for three days, we came to a gulf called the Southern Horn. In the depths of this bay lay an island. Upon it was a lake and in the lake an island peopled by crowds of savages. Most of them were women with rough, hairy bodies.

Our interpreter called them gorillas. We pursued them. We could not catch the males; they escaped by flight. They were able to leap away over the rocks and kept us at bay with stones. Three of the females, who absolutely refused to follow, defended themselves against our men so violently by biting and scratching when we captured them, that we killed them. We then flayed them and brought back their skins with us to Carthage. As we had come to an end of our provisions, we did not continue our journey any farther.

It may safely be inferred that the fire issuing from a high mountain and towering to the stars, in the first sentence of the quotation, is a volcano. And since there is no other volcano along the whole west African coast which is active or has been active in geologically recent times, indeed since there is no other really high mountain at all, the Phœnicians' Chariot of the Gods *must* have been the 13,500-feet-high volcanic peak of the Cameroons. So Hanno went almost as far as the Equator and, with all the detours and by-ways, covered a distance of about 6,250 miles: a remarkable achievement, which it took the Portuguese, two thousand years later, nearly seven decades to accomplish!

If this can now be looked upon as certain, the report of the meeting with 'gorillas' is less easy to understand. For a long time, this part of Hanno's narrative was regarded as a fable. It was not until 1847, when the Gaboon gorilla, an anthropoid ape exactly corresponding to Hanno's 'savages', was discovered that the ancient Carthaginian accounts were realized to have been correct. The statement that these creatures had rough, hairy bodies proves beyond doubt that they were, in fact, apes, since negroes have very little body-hair. If they were really gorillas that the Carthaginians slew and stuffed, however, one is inclined to deduce from this that Hanno and his Carthaginians had a much lower consciousness of their individuality, a much lower capacity to differentiate between man and beast, and a much more unstable conception of the exceptional position of human existence than ourselves. For it is absolutely clear from their report that they took the gorillas to be savages, natives, and that they did not instinctively feel that the creatures which bounded away across stones and rocks into the undergrowth were animals. What can have been the cause of Hanno's uncertainty? And, to put the question differently, were men like Pythagoras or Æschylus, contemporaries of Hanno, no more certain of their human dignity than the Carthaginians? Might they not have recognized the gorillas as an apparition which, though man-like, was in fact animal?

No, they too would probably have thought, as almost all European explorers still thought two thousand years later, that they were 'wild men of the woods' or 'savages'. As such, anyway, the Dutch army doctor, Willem Bontius, addressed the orang-outang which he dis-

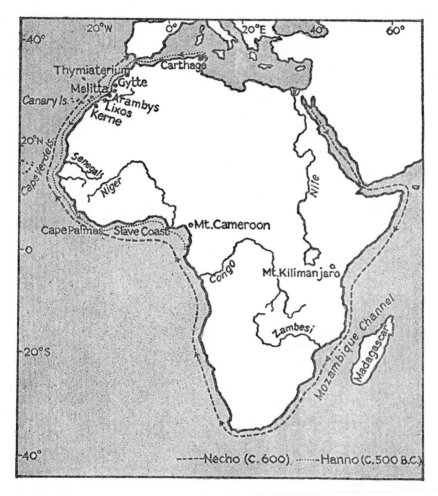

*VI. The African expeditions of Necho and Hanno.*

covered in the primeval forests of Borneo in the middle of the seventeenth century. And Linnæus, the great Swedish systematist, was not one whit more sure of his business a hundred years later. He classified the orang-outang as a 'wild man of the woods, that is, a second species of man, also called night man', and the chimpanzee he deemed a close relation to the pygmies. And this despite the fact that Linnæus had plenty of opportunity to observe both animals in the private zoo of the Prince of Orange during his stay in Holland! There is not much sign here of the consciousness of human dignity!

Before we leave the Carthaginians and Phœnicians, we must recall one more voyage that they made, a heroic voyage and a heroic deed: the discovery of the Azores.

No epic recounts it, no half-mouldered old document such as historians always demand, even from ancient history, and to which they ascribe magic validity merely because it is in black and white, records it. A smoke-blackened old pot with a handful of coins, Carthaginian coins from the beginning of the fourth century B.C., is the only relic. In the middle of the eighteenth century, this earthenware pot was found after a severe storm-tide on the island of Corvo in the Azores amongst the foundations of a ruin on the beach. Since the coins, some of which were from Carthage and some from Cyrenaica, vanished after passing through many hands, there has been no lack of doubt and incredulity. But the report of the circumstances of this find is so unambiguous and definite that, for better or for worse, it must be believed, although the Azores lie in total isolation and far, far out in the ocean. The German geographer, Richard Hennig, mentioned above, who studied this remarkable case fifteen years ago, propounded an argument, authoritatively confirmed by numismatics, which irrefutably guaranteed the eighteenth-century report. It would have been quite impossible in 1750, stated the numismatists, to have got together an almost complete set of Carthaginian coins from the decade 330 to 320 B.C. Hence there can be no question of fake or fraud.

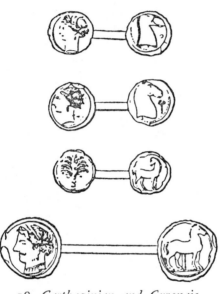

*18. Carthaginian and Cyrenaic coins from the fourth century B.C., found on the Azores.*

So the specialists no longer doubt the early discovery of the Azores by the Phœnicians. For since the ocean currents round these islands everywhere flow away from them, there can be no recourse to the supposition that the coins found on Corvo were carried thither on pieces of flotsam. They must have reached the Azores on manned vessels—in other words, men really discovered this group of islands some 940 miles from the coast of Europe. This may, of course, have been the result of ships being blown off course by persistent easterly gales, and it is quite conceivable that not one man from those Punic ships which at last saw land rising from the stormy waters of the Atlantic in *circa* 320 B.C. ever got back to Europe. Since nothing grows or is produced on the Azores which might attract merchants, they would not have become a distant goal of Punic mariners even if the unknown crews of unknown ships really did return to their homeland. For this reason also, no reference to the remote islands is to be found in antique literature, and till the fifteenth century, when the Portuguese discovered them, they lay outside the *Oikoumene*.

Thus their discovery may not have been a deed of heroism, as asserted earlier, or at least not one undertaken voluntarily and consciously. But just as something begins to stir in Hanno's remarkable advance to the Equator, exceeding his immediate task and perhaps prompted by a joy in new things, by the call of adventure, by delight in exploration and discovery, so the very spirit of the age seems to have been at work in the Punic voyage into the immense distances of the ocean, announcing the dawn of a new epoch: the Age of Heroes. To this age we shall now turn.

PART FOUR

# GREEK LEGENDS
# AND WHAT LIES BEHIND THEM

*The downfall of the chariot · Schliemann and the ostrich egg · Princess Medea, model for tragedies · Hercules steals apples · Stonehenge and the singing swans · Priam blockades the Dardanelles · Only barbarians wear long trousers · The Scythian boozers · 30 per cent interest on Greek capital · Who ever goes to Ogygia? · Herodotus earns £5,000 · The trunk road to Urga, Mongolia · Professor Pytheas from Marseilles · Where was Thule? · Pytheas solves the riddle of amber · The problem of the Erythræan Sea · How did crocodiles get into the Indus? · Alexander the Great sails on a torrent · The discovery of the Ocean · Gold-digging ants · Brief instructions for the catching of elephants.*

THE battle had ended in disaster. The king had fallen, all the officers were slain or captured, the chariots lost and their crews transfixed by arrows and dead. The chariot horses were gone too: dead, wounded, or roaming terrified about the steppe. Much worse than this loss of men, weapons, and equipment, however, must have been the knowledge that henceforth the chariot was utterly outmoded as a tactical weapon. This brilliant invention of the ancients, a kind of fortress on wheels, had hitherto ensured the supremacy of its users. Lightning onslaughts and equally rapid withdrawals, instantaneous concentration of forces: these possibilities had again and again lent the chariot squadrons an immense advantage over the unmanoeuvrable mass of infantry with its vulnerable flanks.

That was all over. The method employed by these slit-eyed, little yellow fellows, with whom this was the first encounter, their brilliant plan of mounting their warriors and sending them into battle on horse-back, had proved far more effective than the use of chariots. The latter were no match for cavalry. There was nothing for it but to adopt this new method of warfare.

We do not know when this battle was fought, nor where. We only know that it took place somewhere on the broad steppes of southern Eurasia, round about the middle of the second millennium B.C.; that much we can safely assume. We know too that Mongolian pastoral peoples, accustomed to the saddle since time immemorial and used to fighting and hunting on horseback, finally halted the irresistible advance of the Indo-European chariot armies before they could break through to central Asia. Perhaps the centaur legend of the Greeks is an obscure recollection of this first encounter with enemy cavalry.

For at this early period the Indo-European was no horseman. He knew the horse only as a draught animal to the light chariot. He had nothing to oppose to the swift Mongolian cavalry. Not until much later did he himself mount the horse, and later still did he evolve methods of dealing with massed atacks by huge mounted armies.

Disappointed and discouraged, the nameless Indo-European hordes broke off their advance into the interior of Asia. They pressed back to the west and south-west and, in the thirteenth century B.C., came up against the thickly-populated areas of the eastern Mediterranean. In 1227 B.C. King Mer-en-Ptah of Egypt repulsed the 'Northern Peoples' in the western delta of the Nile. Under Rameses III (1198–1167 B.C.), however, they returned. In 1190, in the eighth year of his reign, the Pharaoh had the following inscription written on the walls of his sanctuary at Medinet near Thebes:

> The northern peoples on their islands were in turmoil, torn away by the storm, all at the same time. No country stood firm before their hands—they wiped out its people as though they had never been—they came at Egypt as if a fire blazed up in front of them . . .

The Land of the Nile escaped destruction, but the Hittite Kingdom collapsed; and at about the same time the royal castles of Mycenæ and Tiryns fell into the hands of the Dorians, who broke off to the south in the wake of the great migration.

The ancient masters of the country certainly did not go down in silence. Murder and arson raged; their strongholds were razed to the ground; thick layers of ash, dust, and lime lay over the ruins of their magnificent houses, piled up in the luxurious bathrooms, covered the wide halls, the treasure-houses filled with precious things from all over the world, and the gold-studded mausoleums. Goats and cows grazed on the overgrown mounds of rubble.

For three thousand years time stood still here. Then the hands of the world's clock sprang at one stroke to 7th August 1876. Heinrich Schliemann, who had just discovered and excavated Troy, began to dig at the foot of the ruin-mounds of Mycenæ. With great labour his men shovelled their way through immense mountains of rubble, till finally the Cyclopean walls of Agamemnon's stronghold emerged from the depths. Amongst the innumerable finds, no particular attention was paid to an oval object, about eight inches long, which Schliemann took to be an alabaster vase. The find was recorded and laid aside. There was so much else, more valuable, more brilliant.

By chance the supposed alabaster vase came into Schliemann's hands again some time later. And then it transpired that the whitely shimmering, smooth material that showed here and there beneath the incrustations was not alabaster and that the whole thing was not a vase, but—an ostrich egg.

Schliemann realized the importance of this discovery. There had never been ostriches in the countryside of Argolis on the Peloponnese. So Agamemnon's ostrich egg must have been imported from Asia or Egypt, and preserved in the subterranean treasure-chambers of the fortress because of its rarity. More objects of the same kind came to light: a delicate little ape of blue glass bearing on one shoulder the ownership stamp of Amonhotep II, the Pharaoh of the XVII-th dynasty who succeeded Thothmes III and reigned from 1448 to 1420 B.C.; an exquisite scarab, which had belonged to Queen Tyi, the wife of Amonhotep III (1411–1375 B.C.). Since Mycenæ is four hours' journey from the sea, however, it never occurred to Schliemann that these articles might have been imported on Mycenæan ships. He therefore construed a cultural relationship which originally linked Egypt with Asia Minor and later included Mycenæ as well. At this time, of course, he knew nothing of the collection of Mycenæan pottery which was found later in the treasure chambers of Thothmes III, the consort and successor of Queen Hatshepsut. Nor did he know anything of the Mycenæan earthenware widely exported from early Greece, fine examples of which have been found in Cyprus, Syria and Palestine, Sicily, Malta, Sardinia, and Spain. He knew nothing of the Spanish silver, northern amber, and Nubian ivory that crammed Mycenæan tombs. He could not have guessed, as we do now, that the Mycenæan Greeks, like the Cretans, ventured onto the high seas at a very early period.

Archæology cannot tell us anything more about the subject, however, and classical philology is even more reticent. It advances the view that the early Hellenes never went beyond Sicily in the west and Troy in the east. This is certainly a fallacy. Since we want to proceed with our story, we must look round for more communicative sources of information than excavation and the study of languages. We shall devote our attention to subjects at which these two august and illustrious sciences would look askance: such dubious matters as sagas, fables, and legends, whose content, however, yields information not easily accessible through either archæology or philology.

To begin with, there are all those innumerable collections of the legends of classical antiquity which we read as children, but which, if we look at them afresh today, will appear to us in quite a new light. For these ancient fables and legends conceal, as though in code, a great deal of maritime lore and commercial knowledge. We only need to read these venerable tales correctly.

No one knows how old the themes of these legends really are, nor to what remote ages they go back. Most of them, however, probably belong to the Mycenæan sphere of culture, to the world of those Bronze-

Age Indo-European clans of princes and lords whose impregnable fortresses and heavily fortified castles reached the magnificent apex of their development around 1400 B.C. in the Cyclopean edifices of Mycenæ and Tiryns. For these lords and demigods were manifestly not only clever masons, but also splendid seamen, whose ensign contested the seas with that of Crete and who journeyed far and wide through the world. Mycenæan finds have been unearthed in Asia Minor as well as in Egypt and the western Mediterranean; and Mycenæan seafarers may be assumed also to have entered the Black Sea on rapid voyages of plunder and reconnaissance.

This is corroborated by the famous legend of the *Argosy*, the audacious expedition of the pirate captain Jason, who set sail for Colchis in the southern corner of the Black Sea in his swift fifty-oared long-ship *Argo* with all the recognized heroes of his day on board, to steal the Golden Fleece. This Golden Fleece was the pure gold hide of a winged ram, which was believed to have once belonged to Hermes, the Greek god of merchants, travellers, and thieves, and later to have come into the possession of the king of Colchis. The fleece was regarded throughout the world as a great treasure, and its fame had spread to Greece.

After many adventures, Jason and his crew reached Phasis, the river of the Colchians, in whose estuary the *Argo* cast anchor. Things started off tolerably well, but then they took a rather nasty turn. Aëtes, the king of Colchis, had a plough entirely of iron, and Jason inspected this valuable object with the interest due from a man of the Bronze Age. But the bulls with which Aëtes ploughed were thoroughly unruly brutes, who belched forth pitch and sulphur from their subterranean stall and were enveloped in smoke and flames when the hero Jason had to do a turn behind the plough for honour's sake. Now, the Golden Fleece, the expedition's main objective, was guarded by a similar monster, a fiery dragon, with whom it is evident that Jason, despite his divine ancestry, was not anxious to try conclusions. However, Medea, Aëtes's blonde-tressed daughter, saved him the trouble. She stole the State treasure of Colchis, the Golden Fleece, and went with it to Jason aboard the *Argo,* leaving the hero with nothing to do but sail home victorious with his double booty.

For safety's sake they did not follow the route they had come by, which had proved somewhat perilous, but sailed up the Danube. Some member of Jason's team of heroes was in possession of old manuscripts showing that the Danube, far above its estuary in the Black Sea, sent out a branch to the 'Sicilian Sea' (the Adriatic). By good fortune, our Colchis expedition succeeded in finding this branch, sailed down it to the Adriatic, and after many further adventures landed again one fine day in Greece.

So much for the legend as such. We might take it at its face value, as an indication that ancient Greek Jack Tars liked spinning far-fetched sailors' yarns. But clever professors of geography have subtly dissected the innocent seaman's jargon and, in so doing, have come across all sorts of remarkable facts.

The keyword from which they set to work spinning up the coiled yarn was Phasis, a city and river in Colchis. We know from later records, particularly the travel diaries of Herodotus, that this city and river really did exist, and that the Greeks there encountered an unusual, brilliant-plumaged and very pleasant-flavoured bird, the *phasianos*, our pheasant. Modern research has revealed the River Phasis to be identical with the Caucasian river Rion and that the Colchian metropolis of the same name corresponds to present-day Poti, an oil and petrol town somewhat to the north of Batum.

In the opinion of geographers, oil, the second keyword, affords the answer to the riddle of the bulls enveloped in smoke and flame, with which Jason had to plough, as though he were the captain of a fire brigade clad from head to foot in asbestos. They believe it was burning petroleum that so terrified the fair-haired, blue-eyed heroes from Mycenæan Hellas. Herodotus, whom we must once more quote here, knew nothing about oil, of course, since Messrs. Benz and Diesel did not make their appearance till three millennia later. But he is acquainted with pitch, and he does in fact record that Phasis, the city built on piles amidst iridescent swamps, was the principal centre for the export of pitch.

The Golden Fleece itself is open to a not improbable interpretation. The Greek geographer Strabo, who lived round the period of the birth of Christ, recorded that the natives of Phasis had been accustomed, since time immemorial, to place the hide of a wether in the gold-bearing river to catch the particles of gold swept onto it by the stream. Nowadays the same purpose is served by carefully constructed sieves. If there is enough gold, however, a sheepskin may do just as well.

Even the figure of Medea, who has served poets and dramatists as a model for tragedies from Euripides to the contemporary American dramatist, Robinson Jeffers, is shown up in a strange light by the ancient stories. It is true that she is as blonde and blue-eyed as Jason himself, as was only right for a princess and ruler's daughter of the Mycenæan world. Nevertheless, she is an evil witch, a sorceress and mixer of poisons, in close touch with the inhabitants of the nether regions, who, right from the start of her acquaintance with Jason, is perpetually engaged in thoroughly suspect activities. Now, we know from early accounts that the south coast of the Black Sea had long been the goal of Phœnician and Assyrian merchants, that the archaic inhabitants of the land of Colchis were Egyptian in appearance, and that they possessed many cultural traits reminiscent of the Land of the Nile. If that is true, it is clear why Medea must have appeared to the peasant lads of Mycenæ a dangerous sorceress. Anyone as cultivated as the Assyrians and Egyptians, anyone so adroit in their dealings with death, with bygone ages, and with subterranean powers as the ancient peoples at the feet of the pyramids and the Tower of Babel, *must* be able to cast spells, even if his home were barbarian Colchis and his origins otherwise quite reputable!

We meet the same thing in the much later Germanic world of heroes and legends. There, instead of Egypt or Colchis, 'Welshland' (not Wales, but any far-off country, particularly the region of France and Italy) is invariably spoken of when one of the great chooses a beautiful foreigner as his bride. But at least these legends made a point of portraying this alien sorceress, who usually comes to a sticky end, as a dark beauty. And if nothing happens in the way of witchcraft that can be laid at her door, no foot-and-mouth disease in the cattle, no influenza epidemic or other misfortune among men, then at least she is an ill-famed 'Lady Venus'. It is always the same.

Modern scholarship, however, has not rested content with talking away Medea's capacity for magic; it has also put Jason's fabulous return journey via the Danube and the Adriatic under the microscope. As a result, it has come to the conclusion that the supposed branch of the Danube leading to the 'Sicilian Sea' is nothing else than the ancient trade route that once led from the Danube to the Semmering Pass, across the River Sava and the Nanos Mountains to the Mediterranean; the southern part of this route, from the old land-portage installations on, could in fact have been travelled by water. This strange detour made by the Argonauts must be deemed an obscure recollection from more remote days, and it would be wrong to dismiss it as a mere fairy-tale.

Unfortunately we have not the space to sift the whole *corpus* of Greek legend for hidden records of exploration, but must confine ourselves to a few brief indications.

In addition to the saga of the Argonauts, we have the many myths of Hercules, culminating in his heroic labours. One of these—the eleventh—was to obtain for King Eurystheus of Mycenæ the Apples of the Hesperides. The story of these apples was as follows: when Zeus and Hera wed, untold ages ago, the goddess Gæa, the Earth-Mother, brought to the wedding table as a dessert a few specimens of a golden apple, which, as she divulged at the time, grew on a myriad-branched tree on the infinitely remote western shores of the Ocean. Either because she knew the liking of the gods for such delicacies, or because she feared vandalism by inquisitive humans, she had her apple-tree guarded by four beautiful virgins, the Hesperides. And in case thieves should not feel afraid of the four beautiful virgins, but perhaps just the reverse . . . she gave the four young ladies, as protector, aid, and chaperon, a hundred-headed dragon. We are not told what these hundred heads were supposed to defend—the apples or the virtue of the four Hesperides.

Despite these five guards, then, Hercules was to steal golden apples. But just like Jason, the divine hero had no wish to start a quarrel with a dragon, and, as is well known, he was not interested in women either. He finally succeeded in persuading the giant Atlas, who happened to be standing nearby with the firmament on his shoulders, to settle the matter of the dragon. Once that was done—Hercules did not, we must sadly admit, behave with great fairness towards Atlas over the affair—the divine hero stuffed the apples in his pocket and hurried back to his king.

This too sounds like a tale for children. But the German geographer, Richard Hennig, was not prepared to leave it at that and discovered all sorts of surprising facts behind this legend as well. Here the keyword is Atlas. For it is evident from Homer's *Odyssey,* and also from other ancient records, that it is not the Atlas Mountains in Morocco which are referred to here. Although some obscure rumour of the existence of this mighty elevation does seem to have reached Herodotus, the Atlas Mountains did not become known to the antique world till Roman times; so that the 'lofty pillars that divide the heavens from the earth', as Homer puts it, can only be taken to mean the gigantic snow-capped Peak of Teneriffe on the Canary Islands, which rises straight up to 12,200 feet above sea level. This was already known to Alexander von Humboldt, and many other scholars have since concurred with his view. If the helpful giant Atlas of the Hercules legend is the Peak of Teneriffe, then the fruitful garden of the Earth-Mother, Gæa, cannot be far away: the land of the Hesperides can only be sought on the Canaries. Then the golden apples must have grown there; perhaps, as Hennig surmised, they were really the golden-yellow fruit of the *Arbutus canariensis,* the Canary strawberry-tree.

In other words, the eleventh labour of Hercules may conceal an early intimation concerning the Atlantic islands in the Ocean beyond Gibraltar, those 'Islands of the Blessed' discussed above. Whence the Mycenæan Greeks had this knowledge, whether from the Cretans, to whose families of heroes they were frequently related by marriage, or from the Phœnicians, with whom they carried on a brisk trade, or whether they themselves sailed the Ocean west of the Pillars of Hercules, we do not know and probably never shall know.

But there are more of these ancient riddles. For example, there is an old Hellenic tale about the land of the 'Hyperboreans', a far-off region in the dim north, no doubt Britain. Here, the legend states, there existed in ancient times a great circular sanctuary, into which singing swans sometimes entered to give praise to the deity. This sounds like a very poetic, but quite unreal fairy story. Yet prehistorians and geographers are of the opinion that this circular sanctuary is the ancient Celtic temple of Stonehenge on Salisbury Plain, where great religious festivals were held at the summer solstice. In the view of these scholars the singing swans, which, according to Greek documents, did homage to their god 'like feathered choristers', are themselves a sign of the authenticity of the ancient legend. For the singing swan, the *Cygnus cygnus* or *Cygnus musicus,* is to be found in northern Europe and especially in England, whereas it is unknown in central and southern Europe. Brehm has given a detailed description of this now rare bird. 'Its voice sounds like a silver bell,' he says at one point. And elsewhere: 'When they rise up into the air in small flocks their melancholy voices sound like distant trumpets . . . At one moment the . listener compares their singing call to the notes of a bell, at the next to those of some wind instrument; but it is not the same as either, surpassing both for the very reason that it issues from a living creature and is more akin to our own voices than to the sounds of inert metal. This strange singing makes a real fact of the legend of the swan-song, which is regarded as fiction . . .'

Possibly the singing swan was sacred to the Celtic god Borvon, the deity of Stonehenge, and protected at the ancient cult places of the Celts. This would explain its presence at the great summer solstice festivals. That the legend tells of it, although the singing swan is unknown in southern Europe, proves that the supposed seaman's yarn once more contains a hard core of genuine knowledge. From whom can the Mycenæan Greeks have acquired it? From the Cretans on the Tartessus run, from the Phœnicians, or from their own experience?

We cannot answer this question either. We know nothing about it;

we know very little about the times of the great migration in Europe at all. But the little we do know enables us to feel that in Hellas quite different incentives were at work to those operating in Egypt or amongst the Phœnicians and Carthaginians. A Viking wind is blowing; seafaring and exploration are man's work, lord's work, hero's work. Hercules the demigod, the obviously unattainable ideal of every Greek voyager, roams hither and thither through the *Oikoumene*, not to make trade and do business, but in quest of adventure. It is for the sake of this adventure, for the sake of heroic love and heroic combat in distant lands, that Odysseus, the Greek national hero, strives with the myriad adversities to which the mariner is exposed. If Homer's listeners and admirers had not had complete understanding for the king of Ithaca's desire to wander in far-off lands, instead of virtuously pursuing the business of government at Penelope's side, none of those unfavourable winds in the *Odyssey* that blew the poor 'divine sufferer' to and fro across the Ocean would have arisen. But to experience that sort of thing themselves was exactly what Homer's public yearned and dreamed.

Since at all times the poet, not the merchant, has been the hero's herald, we shall henceforth increasingly call upon poets, journalists, and scholars to appear as our witnesses. The first of this long succession of men mighty with words and skilled in writing is Homer—or more correctly, that sequence of unknown singers, extending over several generations, which we describe by the collective term Homer, and whose work is known to us as the *Iliad* and the *Odyssey*. The multiple components of the two epics render it extremely difficult to reduce them to one common geographic and historical denominator. For the images are in perpetual metamorphosis, the world is perpetually expanding.

The archaic Homer, if we may so describe the manifestly oldest stratum of this literary 'sediment', depicts the world of *circa* 1200 B.C. To be sure, nothing was further from the mind of the supposed blind poet than to furnish a geography in verse. His interest was focused on men of flesh and blood: heroic wanderers like Odysseus, or fearless champions like the heroes of the *Iliad*. To describe the peregrinations of the traveller from Ithaca, or the vicissitudes of the Trojan war, however, demanded considerable knowledge of the world. This Homer certainly possessed. How much of the grippingly presented wealth of geographical information he knew from his own experience is an open question. That he rendered accurately the current picture of the world as his contemporaries saw it is, however, certain. With this in mind we must vigorously oppose the view recently advanced by Egon Friedell in his excellent *History of Greek Culture* (see bibliography), where he emphatically states that there was only *one* Homer. Friedell sees his friend, and ours, in terms of the early Teutonic bards: as a singer and declaimer, who sang of ancient times to the 'noble heroes' of his day in an artistically and artificially archaic mode. This is very unlikely. For a Homer living in 800 B.C. would under no circumstances have let slip the magnificent adventures that 'befell' about this time as the

*19. Stonehenge on Salisbury Plain, erected 2000–1500 B.C. (Early Bronze Age.) Reconstruction with the stones in their original positions.*

outcome of the Greek expeditions to the Black Sea, nor the dark tales of the wonders of the distant East, which was now beginning to thrust its way into the European sphere of culture.

Yet he did let them slip. To be sure, he knows the name of Jason and that of Aëtes, he has also heard of the swift long-ship *Argo* and of the frightful Symplegades: more than that he does not know. He tells neither of the Golden Fleece nor of Medea, and he misplaces the Symplegades to the west of the Mediterranean. In other words, the Homer who let this grand story slip through his fingers lived at a period that was really old, really archaic. To return to our starting point: Homer's works are in fact a literary sediment, a precipitate of very early, very ancient mariners' experiences poured into appropriate moulds by unknown poets and bards; they are a knightly romance of adventure told by the very aristocratic and very ragged bards of the glorious past to the sensation-hungry Dorian peasants who were trampling, full of awe and wonder, about the ruins of Mycenæ, Tiryns, Argos, Asine, Mideia and other half or totally destroyed castles of the Mycenæan Greeks, after their victorious invasion.

The centre of the world of which Homer tells, a world whose supports were the lofty prominences of Teneriffe in the west and of the Caucasus in the east, was the 9,900 feet high Mount Olympus in Thessaly, the Home of the Gods. The Mediterranean thus became the central ocean of the *Oikoumene,* cutting it into two parts, the nocturnal with the huge mountain chain of the Rhipæans in the extreme north, the diurnal in the south. Of the cold, rainy, and dismal nocturnal side little was known. In the south lay Ethiopia, Libya, and Egypt, which were already tolerably well known as the result of numerous voyages. The only regions about which really certain knowledge existed, however, were the area round Troy, the Cyclades, Crete, the Peloponnese, the central and southern parts of Greece, and the Mediterranean roughly as far as Sicily. This confined space is all the more astonishing because we have just seen a much more comprehensive knowledge distilled from the old Hellenic legends. It appears that a great deal of this knowledge was lost in the turmoil that followed the invasion of Greece by the Dorians, so that it vanished from the bright light of day into the semi-darkness of legend.

By the middle of the eighth century B.C., however, the new lords of Hellas had reached the point of going to sea in their turn. We even know the name of one of the most successful shipowners and captains of this period: Colæus of Samos, who, apparently driven off course by persistent high winds, reached Tartessus. Whether, as tradition avers, he was the first Greek to land in the happy country of the 'Phæaceans' seems dubious. But Colæus must have been the most successful captain on the Spain run; that is why his name has been so well remembered.

About the east, the Black Sea, Homer had little information either. He knew of its existence, of course, and was fairly well acquainted with the coasts nearest to the Bosphorus. But on the Dardanelles lay Troy. Powerful princes ruled the prosperous great city, whose connections stretched as far as Egypt and Babylon, as well as to Hellas, but whose specific domain must have been the trade with the fertile lands round the Black Sea: a seaport as thriving as the more or less contemporary Tartessus, as splendid and powerful as the seaports of Flanders and Italy were later. And just as the Carthaginians a thousand years later closed the straits of Gibraltar, so the Trojans denied foreign ships entry to the Black Sea. It has been conjectured that the legend of the Symplegades, those fearful rocks of the Dardanelles which clapped together at short intervals, crushing any ships that happened to be between them, refers in legendary guise to the naked political fact that no Hellenic ship could pass through the straits unmolested. It has been surmised further that the whole Trojan war was, in reality, nothing else than the forcible elimination of the Trojan blockade of the straits. This may or may not be so. There is no doubt, however, that the early Greeks were already very much concerned to ensure passage through the Dardanelles. By the time of the Greek settlement of the Black Sea littoral at the latest, forts and strongholds were built along the straits in evident recognition of the fact that a blockade of the Dardanelles would cut off corn supplies from southern Russia. There are a number of records of reckless speculation on the antique Corn Exchange at Athens, in connection with which the 'bulls', in order to drive up the price, circulated the rumour that the straits were being blockaded. Hence we may well suppose that the Greek expedition to Troy had nothing whatsoever to do with the rape of a beautiful woman, but was a bare-faced economic war particularly prettily decked out by propaganda.

However that may be, the Black Sea did not become accessible to the Hellenes till towards the end of the eighth century B.C. Then they flung themselves vigorously into the new area. They did not go in blindly of course. By this time the Black Sea had ceased to be virgin territory. The Assyrians and Phœnicians had reconnoitred it long ago, as well as the Greeks living in Asia Minor; in particular, the shippers and merchants of Miletus, the Ionian seaport and metropolis on the Mæander, were thoroughly well informed as to all the commodities obtainable along the coast of the *Pontos Axeinos,* the inhospitable sea, as they called it. But only when Sennacherib of Assur brought Phœnicia under his sway was entry to the Black Sea opened to the Greeks. In quite a short time the coastlands of the Black Sea were Greek colonial territory. The *Pontos Axeinos* became the *Pontos Euxeinos,* the friendly, hospitable sea.

Greek colonization proceeded in such an admirably planned sequence that one might almost think it based on careful preliminary bank inquiries in the modern manner. They first occupied Sinope, roughly in the middle of the Pontus coast, an ancient Phœnician mercantile centre with extremely profitable tunny fishing and vast smoking-works: an extensive preserving industry, as we should say.

The next blows were struck from the magnificent double harbour

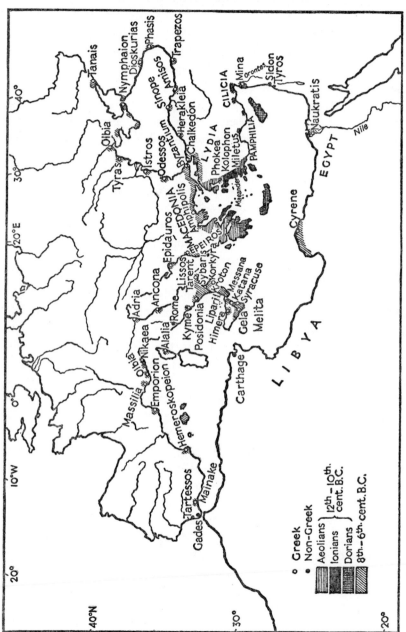

VII. *Greek colonization.*

of this city, which afforded protection from both the easterly gales that
tore down from Asis, and from the equally feared west winds. Trapezus
(Trebizond) was founded as a harbour for the dispatch of Anatolian
ores and as a port of reshipment for old trade routes to the countries
on the Euphrates and the Tigris. At almost the same time they took
possession of the ancient Phasis on the Rion, of which we have heard
quite a lot already—not so much on account of the gold which was
still washed down from the mountains, as because a much-used Indian
caravan route terminated here. The rate of interest on loan capital, on
the so-called 'sea-loans' made available by financially strong mercantile
houses to efficient captains, amounted in Hellas at this period to 30 per
cent; the import duty placed by the mother country on Pontic goods
ranged between 15 and 17 per cent. But this was easily earned in
Sinope, in Trapezus, and in the Greek colonial towns on the Caucasus.
Hence they were all enormously wealthy and—as far as the Greek
tongue reached—a byword for their barbaric display of magnificence
and their unbridled luxury.

Scarcely a century passed before the Black Sea Greeks found out
that there was a second caravan route leading from the interior of
Asia. It ended on the River Don; here too an unending stream of precious
stones, gold, silk, and furs poured into the hands of the merchants.
This was reason enough to bring the north coast of the Black Sea under
Greek influence as well. Thus the town of Tanais arose, midway
between Rostov and Taganrog, a vast caravanserai in which all the
languages of Asia mingled with the elegant Greek. Almost simultaneously, the biggest Greek city on the northern littoral of the Black
Sea was developing at the Dniester estuary: wide-stretching Olbia,
which had become prosperous and powerful through the corn trade.
Both Hellas herself and the Greek coastlands of Asia Minor gradually
became so over-populated that they were no longer capable of feeding
themselves. In the fourth century fertile Attica was drawing some
963,000 bushels of wheat annually from the Black Sea zone, more than
50 per cent of its consumption. In other parts of the Greek countryside
the situation was worse still. There the population had turned exclusively
to olive planting or pure market gardening, so that in fifth-century
Athens fresh figs, grapes, violets, etc., could be bought in midwinter,
all from hothouses, but not an ounce of corn. The northern Pontic
coast soon became the granary of the Hellenic world, and immediately
all those features of a monopoly position developed which are known
to us from the present. It produced solely for export—*epi presi* was
the technical expression—which meant that the Scythian husbandman

grew wheat alone and nothing else. He planted a few acres with cheap crops adequate for his own use. The wheat to which he devoted the major portion of his land was for the foreigners; it went to dealers at Olbia, and what the Scythian obtained for it he spent on all sorts of luxury commodities.

Greek wine was first amongst these. To be sure, the Scythians themselves had an alcoholic beverage which they brewed from mare's milk; but the sweet, heavy Greek wine was better. To dilute this gift from god with water, after the western custom, was a crime! For his part, the Greek landing on the Pontic coast from Attica observed with a shudder that wine was here drunk neat. Thereafter the expression 'Scythian boozing' was used throughout the whole Greek world to describe barbaric immoderation.

Apart from this, Greece had nothing against the barbarians, and Plato as well as Isocrates and Eratosthenes expressly declared that it was unjust to divided mankind into Greeks and Barbarians, and that the designation Greek was an indication only of a man's culture, not of his racial origin.

All the same, they too were thoroughly disgusted by the fact that the Black Sea Greeks wore long trousers, just like the Scythian or Persian barbarians. It is well known that this article of clothing was regarded as extremely objectionable in antique Europe, and again and again we find very disapproving references to it in Greek literature. Of course, the Greeks of the mother country lived in a more clement climate than their cousins in Asia Minor and on the Black Sea, with their frequent icy winter gales. To this is added the fact that long trousers were an invention of equestrian peoples, those very equestrian peoples with whom the forefathers of the highly cultured Hellenes had undergone such painful experiences in the early war-chariot period. The Greek aversion to trousers was, therefore, manifestly a kind of hereditary instinct. For the bow and arrow were as much despised and proscribed as trousers. Euripides still put into the mouth of the hero of one of his tragedies the words: 'No one yet evinced manly courage as an archer, cowardly arrows are his weapons and his art is flight.' Alexander the Great was the first to employ archers. Bows and arrows were weapons of his cavalry as well, and naturally all the mounted sections of his army wore long trousers.

The Greeks also settled very early in the western Mediterranean. The first town to rise, in *circa* 725 B.C., was Kyme, later Cumæ, the mother-city of Naples. This was followed in *circa* 600 B.C. by Massilia on the Rhone estuary, the modern Marseilles, and the Mediterranean littoral was trimmed with a border of flourishing Greek settlements right down to the Straits of Gibraltar. Nice, formerly Nicæa, and Antibes, called Antipolis by the Greeks, are of Hellenic origin; so are Ampurias and Rosas in Spain, Reggio, Taranto, Sybaris and Croton in south Italy, and Syracuse in Sicily. The Greeks even crossed to Africa. Sailing from Thera, they established themselves in Barca, the capital of Cyrenaica and terminus of the old African trade roads. For nearly half a millennium the Mediterranean was a *mare græcum,* a Greek sea, and throughout the whole of this period the spiritual link between the colonies and the home country remained unbroken.

Of course, there had been trade with these countries long before it came to the planting of official colonies. There can be no doubt that the western basin of the Mediterranean was at an early stage as familiar to the Greek mariner as its eastern section. Hence there can be no question of Corfu, where many writers have placed the Homeric land of the Phæacians, having been the western limit of the Greeks' geographical horizon. It is equally nonsensical to assert that Scylla and Charybdis, those two terrible monsters of the deep—probably dangerous whirlpools—which Odysseus escaped by the skin of his teeth, were situated in the Straits of Messina. They are to be sought, rather, by the Straits of Gibraltar, and it is highly significant that Strabo already declared: 'Homer portrays the voyages of Odysseus in such fashion as to make the majority of them take place in the Atlantic Ocean.'

Numerous thick tomes have been written on this question. Whereas modern geography, starting with Alexander von Humboldt, who deems the island of Ogygia to be Madeira, takes the view that a great part of Odysseus's adventures occurred in the ocean, classical philology is a great deal more hesitant. But even Wilamowitz-Moellendorff has emphasized that the Ogygian isle of Calypso must undoubtedly have lain in the open ocean, since its un-Greek name, derived from the Semitic *ogeg,* a circle, i.e. a circular current, denotes an oceanic island. If we agree with this derivation, however, then the land of the Phæacians must also be sought beyond the Pillars of Hercules, probably in the Hispano-British bronze paradise of Tartessus, of which we have already spoken. Then there is no need to ask where the mist-enshrouded, sunless land of the Cimmerians lay. It *can* only have lain in the north, under the same skies beneath which the costly tin was found: somewhere in Brittany, on the way to the *Cassiterides,* to the tin-mines of Cornwall.

2

Some four hundred years have passed since the last hand was put to the fashioning of the Homeric epics. Homer has long since become a Greek classic, whose works are publicly declaimed every four years at the Panathenæa by order of the State and read by school-children as textbooks in religion and history. Quotations from Homer are in every mouth; he has become an integral part of public and private life.

Then one fine day in the year 445 B.C. there appears in the Athens of Pericles which, with its hundred thousand inhabitants, has become the largest city of Greece, a very elegant foreigner in his fifties, a colonial Greek from Halicarnassus in Asia Minor, one whom arrogant Athens regards as 'half-Greek', a semi-barbarian with Carian blood in his veins from his father's side. This man, a certain Herodotus, who is, after all, not entirely a nonentity, for he comes of a good family and has travelled widely—being personally acquainted with Egypt, Persia, Arabia, Cyrene, the Black Sea lands, Sicily, and Italy—boldly demands permission to give a public reading on the Agora, the official meeting place of Athens, of a few chapters from his recently completed historical work. Public readings of this kind have taken place frequently during the last few decades. But they have always been of poetic, or at least dramatic, works; and it has often happened that such a little thing as a clumsy fold of the cloak, and even more an odd word or unsatisfactory delivery, has set the crowd laughing.

Herodotus knows what he is about, however. The main theme of his historical work, which covers the last three hundred years, is the Persian war—in the eyes of Hellas a tyrannical attempt by Persia to swallow up the Greek fatherland. This attempt came to naught. The whole affair, including Thermopylæ, Salamis, and Platæa, took place some forty years ago. But every man's heart still beats faster when someone speaks of these heroic events.

And Herodotus speaks of them: very elegantly, very wittily, with a hint of irony. He does not simply denigrate the adversary and foreign ways and customs. Such a naive approach would not have satisfied the Athenians. He begins with the declaration: 'My task is to recount legends.' True to his avowed aim and taking full account of his au- dience, he presents exotic adventures, character sketches, anecdotes— and from the narration of historic happenings there emerges a romance of geography, so grippingly told that the Athenians hold their breath and finally give vent to a boundless enthusiasm. As honorarium for his recitation they fix the immense sum of sixty thousand drachmas—no mean emolument for a time in which a whole family could live comfortably on one drachma a day and a one-family house cost approximately five thousand drachmas!

But, as we moderns can confirm if we forget the dismal experiences of our school days and take a fresh look at old Herodotus after all these years, it was well-earned money! For this magnificent travel journalist can still serve as a model, and the standard he set is not always reached today. Homer and his age already thought it worthwhile to spice their historical narratives with geographic and ethnographic comments. But for Herodotus geography became the very kernel of world history and historical writing. For the first time in the West, the earth and its discovery were described for their own sake. For the first time, a European journeyed across land and sea, over distances that astonish us, for no other reason than to explore the world. For most of what Herodotus reports he had seen for himself; where that was not possible he used the reports of picked authorities, after sifting them critically. He travelled personally through wide areas of Asia and north Africa. His gaze to the east reached as far as the Caspian Sea; in the west he looked out a considerable distance beyond the Pillars of Hercules. Sarmatia and Scythia, which a little while before had been legendary names in stories, were solid concepts to him. He tells of the Tin Islands in the dim north as vividly as of Africa and its circumnavigation by Necho. He stands thrilled at the foot of the huge ruins of the Tower of Babel, which were still extant in his day. In amazement he tells posterity of the colossal pyramids of the Egyptian Pharaohs, of the infinite breadth of the world; he was a vigorous supporter of Pythagoras's teaching that the earth is a sphere. His discoveries and voyages of exploration definitively completed the world picture of the ancients and it was he who conveyed this world picture to us. All later explorers have, in one way or another, started from his findings. Herodotus, upon whom Aristotle also leaned, remained an undisputed authority until far into the Middle Ages; and our own day has only succeeded in endorsing most of his statements.

How reliably informed Herodotus was, even as to details, despite the occasionally legend-like tone of his reports, is shown by the following example, the elucidation of which we owe to the scholarship and acumen of the German geographer, Richard Hennig. Herodotus speaks at length of a trade route from the Black Sea to the north. It led, he reports, from Pontus in a north-easterly direction across the

11. Rowing vessels on the Nile. Wall relief in the tomb of Ti, an official of the V-th dynasty, at Sakkara, 2500 B.C.

12. Hittite war-chariot in the battle against the Egyptians under Rameses at Kadesh. Relief on a wall of the Ramesseum at Abydos. 13th century B.C.

13. Princess Kavit having her hair done. Relief on the Princess's coffin.

14. The erased picture of Queen Hatshepsut in the temple of Dehr el Bahri.

Don to the Volga and along this river to Selonus, a town of fur traders and trappers at the junction of the Kama.

From here the road continued in a north-easterly direction through desolate country across the Urals to Siberia and through the Dzungarian Gate to the central Asian plateau. Up to this point land and people were fairly well known. 'For in part Scythians go to this place, from whom it is easy to obtain information concerning it, in part Greeks from Olbia and the various trading places on the Pontus.' A little farther to the east lay the Northern Ocean. The winter there lasted for eight months, during six of which the people hibernated. There was much gold in this region, but the gold was guarded by griffins, which were reputed to scratch it up out of the ground 'and to watch over it with the same strange cupidity with which men steal it'.

At first sight it does not look as though much could be made of this story, which presumably goes back to some ancient and long-vanished tradition; for a long time Herodotus's account of this eastern Asiatic trunk road was considered pure fable. Only gradually did it transpire that the route he described really did exist. Indeed, it was travelled till far into the Middle Ages. But even at an early period it is unlikely that Pontic merchants normally crossed the Urals. Most probably it happened on rare occasions only that one or two of them pressed on beyond their usual stopping point and so came to hear stories of the goldfields on the Northern Ocean, in which truth and fiction were interwoven. Von Humboldt put forward the conjecture that Herodotus's strange tale referred to the goldfields on the upper Yenisei and in the Altai Mountains; at the time, however, this was pure guesswork totally unsupported by factual evidence. Only today do we know that Humboldt's hypothesis was correct and that Herodotus must really have received some vague information concerning Siberia.

Excavation has now disclosed that the auriferous regions of western Siberia were once the centre of an astonishingly highly evolved archaic culture. In particular, the existence of manifold and lively commercial relations between the Pontus region and western Siberia in 1000 B.C. has been incontestably established. So Herodotus's obscure report of an ancient north-easterly trade route rests upon facts. Numerous finds have confirmed it. In 1922 some forty very valuable pieces of silver work of ancient Pontic origin, which had probably come to Siberia in exchange for furs, were unearthed near Yekaterinograd-Sverdlovsk. These investigations were crowned some years later by a further early historical find in the vicinity of Urga, the capital of Mongolia. The opening of some old tombs revealed, alongside costly silk garments of the Han dynasty (*circa* 200 B.C.), various Scythian woven fabrics in an excellent state of preservation, which could only have been manufactured on the Black Sea and demonstrated how world-wide were the trade routes which—so long ago—girdled the earth.

## 3

Herodotus too we must unfortunately leave behind us, although there is much more to tell of him and his gripping survey of world events, which is as thrilling as any news-reel. For round the edge of the screen peeps the powerful figure of the Marseilles explorer and economic expert, Pytheas—the first southerner of whom we know for certain that he visited the remote, eerie seas of the north, the desolate lands of misty darkness, the jungles of mouldering primeval forest, at his own resolve and for the sake of exploration.

We have already heard that the Straits of Gibraltar were closed from about 530 B.C. by north African trading groups and the Carthaginian navy acting on their behalf. We learnt further that this was done less on account of Carthage's mercantile interests in Britain than to protect the seaway to the Atlantic islands. Nonetheless, the northern Tin Islands were of considerable interest because of their gold deposits. For the southern European mercantile concerns there was the added consideration that the north was also the home of amber. Massilia had established outposts as far as Asciburgium on the lower Rhine, and it is not impossible that a good deal of information about the countries round the Bay of Heligoland had filtered back through these channels. But this will not have been enough for the Massiliot big businessmen. People who go to the colonies are usually distinguished by practical abilities, rather than by scientific knowledge. The former were good enough to plant colonies and run them profitably; the latter were now needed in order to exploit their resources on a more ambitious scale. Not only today but at all periods times have arisen when the captains of industry thanked God for scientists whom, if occasion arose, they could send through hell and high water.

The acute competition between the rising port on the Rhone and the long-established power of Carthage rendered it imperative to obtain more detailed information about the gold and amber lands of the north. In 325 B.C., therefore, Pytheas, a geographer who had already made a name by his voyages to the Atlantic Ocean and his numerous books on astronomy, was put at the head of this enterprise, the main aim of

which may have been to reconnoitre Britain and the amber districts
of the Gulf of Metuonis (Bay of Heligoland).

The Carthaginian blockade of the Straits of Gibraltar made it
impossible to start out on the sea route, which, with a little luck in the
Bay of Biscay, represented a more agreeable and, for born seamen like
the Massiliots, more accustomed way of making the journey. The land
route through Gaul was handy enough, however; it had been used by
the metal convoys of Marseilles firms ever since the sea route had been

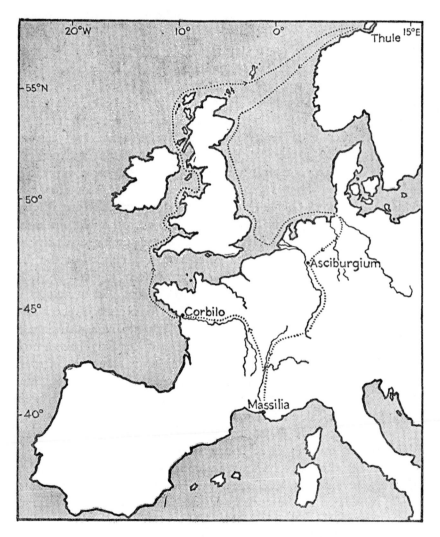

*VIII. Pytheas's voyage to Thule.*

blocked. It led first along the Rhone, turned off in the region of the present-day St. Etienne sur Loire, and ran from there, in about thirty days' march, to Corbilo, the embarkation harbour on the Atlantic coast, which had already disappeared in Cæsar's time and may have lain in the vicinity of present-day St. Nazaire. There the real task began.

A very great task and an equally great solution! Pytheas's prime concern was no doubt to ascertain whether Britain, or Albion as the remote country of mists was called by the Massiliots, was an island or a part of the mainland that jutted out to the north. Further, the home of northern gold was to be explored in greater detail, while an excursion to the completely unknown amber country that must lie somewhat farther east was also on the programme. Finally, Pytheas seems also to have intended to continue the study of the tide problem, which he had commenced years ago on the oceanic coast of Spain. The accomplishment of all these tasks demanded considerable time. Thus the circumnavigation of Britain took a full forty days. Three hundred years later Strabo stated that Pytheas had roamed England on foot. Since the latter's own records have unfortunately not come down to us and only about a dozen sources are known which go back directly to Pytheas's great work *On the Ocean,* there is no means of telling whether he ever set foot in Britain. Nevertheless, it is very probable; the whole of Cæsar's knowledge of Britain was probably acquired and transmitted by the Greek explorer. The tide phenomenon, unfamiliar to the sons of the Mediterranean, must certainly have been studied afresh by Pytheas in the deep estuaries of the English rivers. The movement of ebb and flow is particularly strong on the whole coast of the British Isles. In the Bristol Channel it quite regularly attains a difference of height of 53 feet, a phenomenon that must certainly have caught Pytheas's attention. It is noteworthy that it already occurred to Pytheas to link the alternation of the tides with the moon. At all events, Ætius of Antioch states: 'Pytheas asserts that the flood tide is caused by the waxing, the ebb tide by the waning moon.'

There can be little doubt that Pytheas also included the Shetland Islands in his investigations. It may be surmised that it was here he added to his altogether brilliant enterprise a particularly outstanding achievement: a six-days' sail across the open North Sea to the land of Thule, considered by the ancients *ultima Thule,* the northern termination of the world. Of this highly venturesome journey there exist a whole series of later accounts, which doubtless go back to Pytheas's own reports. Thus Pliny states in the first century A.D.:

The outermost of all known lands is Thule. At the time of the solstice, when the sun passes through the sign of the crab, there are no nights there. In winter the day lasts only a short time, whereas the nights are very long. Many people even assert that this is the case for six months without interruption.

And two hundred years later the geographer Solinus adds, obviously from even greater knowledge:

From the Orcades to Thule is five days' and five nights' sail. Despite its northerly position, Thule is fertile and rich in late-ripening fruits. From the beginning of spring onward the inhabitants live with their cattle. They feed on milk and vegetables, but store up the fruits for the winter.

It is impossible to be absolutely certain, from the few indications extant, which of our modern countries was Thule. Fritjof Nansen, however, has proved with a probability bordering on certainty that Pytheas's statements can only apply to Norway, and to central Norway at approximately 64° N., roughly in the area of the Trondhjem Fjord. The fact that Norway is joined to the mainland, whereas Thule was deemed an island, is of no significance, since Scandinavia was held to be an island long after the beginning of the Christian era.

The texts cited cannot, unfortunately, afford any idea of the full extent of the information furnished by Pytheas. The lasting effect of his book on the Ocean can, however, be inferred *a posteriori*. Thus, for instance, Tacitus reports in his *Germania*:

Beyond the Guiones [Teutons?] lies another sea, a sluggish mass, almost motionless. That the terrestrial disk is encircled and enclosed by this sea is confirmed by the fact that the last gleam of the setting sun endures with such brightness till the following sunrise that it causes the stars to pale . . . The world—on his point rumour speaks the truth—reaches so far and no farther.

This is a first vague report of the Arctic Ocean mingled with seamen's tales of the ice-gleam, that strange light which shines over the wide expanse of the ice-fields, repeatedly described by Arctic voyagers. All these pieces of information undoubtedly go back to Pytheas. Only through him, it may be assumed, did the knowledge of an ice-bound northern sea reach southern Europe.

We have no idea how long Pytheas remained in Thule. Probably he returned from there to Britain, continuing the circumnavigation of the latter in a southerly direction. Passing through the Straits of Dover, he pushed on eastwards to the amber lands. At this point his enterprise assumed its special significance. Pytheas is the first southerner known to have reached Germany by sea. He is also the first to have left a detailed account of the voyage.

We have already mentioned that for many centuries amber was one of the most sought-after commodities imported from the countries of the Hyperboreans. Known as *elektron* by the Greeks, the easily worked, warmly lustrous, sweet-smelling stone rapidly acquired a vogue as the most highly-prized raw material for the manufacture of all kinds of *objets d'art*. Regarding the genesis of amber, however, the ancients, as we have already heard, yielded to the most bizarre notions. To test and, if necessary, correct these notions was patently one of Pytheas's chief commercial tasks. It seems already to have been known that amber occurred principally on the North Friesian Islands and the west coast of Schleswig-Holstein. That it was also to be obtained from the Baltic appears to have remained unknown in western Europe for several more centuries. Pytheas certainly succeeded in reaching the amber districts. He probably did not get any farther, however; in particular he cannot have gone beyond Cape Skagen.

All the same, that was quite enough to elucidate the problem of the genesis of amber, and we may suppose that Pytheas's report was of the greatest interest to his contemporaries. Pliny says on the subject:

Pytheas reports that the Guiones [Teutons?], a people of Germany, lived on an *æstuarium*—a stretch of tidal coast—named Metuonis reaching 6,000 stades from the ocean: from here the island of Abalus [Heligoland] was a day offshore. In spring amber was washed up by the sea on this island. It was an ejectum of the curdled sea, which the natives used in place of firewood or sold to their neighbours, the Teutons . . . It is certain that it is formed on the islands of the North Sea and is called *glæsum* by the Germans . . . But it is formed by pith oozing out of pine trees; just as rubber forms on cherry trees, so resin forms on pines. It wells forth from the trees in consequence of their excess of sap, is condensed by the cold or by the effect of the sea-water, when the rising spring tide sweeps it away from the islands. In any case, it is washed ashore and is so light that it seems to float in the water and not to sink to the bottom. That it is a tree-sap was also believed by our forefathers . . . That it really comes from a tree of the pine family is proved by the resinous odour which arises when it is rubbed and the fact that, when ignited, it burns and smells exactly like a torch . . . That it is indeed originally exuded in a fluid state, is attested by certain objects contained in its interior and visible through its transparent substance, such as ants, gnats, and lizards; for there is no doubt that these adhere to the resin whilst it is still fresh and remain enclosed within it after it has set hard.

As can be seen, Pliny's information was substantially correct; he may be forgiven for not having heard of either the Yoldia Sea *circa*

12,000 B.C., nor the Ancylus Sea *circa* 8000 B.C., nor yet of the Litorina Period to about 500 B.C., which played a part in the development of amber, since all these seas, which contained the petrified resin in their depths, have only been rediscovered and cartographically reconstructed by contemporary geologists.

By what route Pytheas returned from the amber lands to Massilia we do not know. Probably he took the land route again because of the Carthaginian blockade—most likely to the great north-east amber road leading from the Hamburg region via the valleys of the Rhine and the Moselle to the Rhone and thence to Massilia; since 600 B.C. this road had begun to take the place of the one leading to the northern Adriatic, at least for travellers heading for the western Mediterranean. But evidence is totally lacking. Since, in our terms, Pytheas was a commercial spy, who would have had short shrift if the Carthaginians had got hold of him, the Council of Massilia undoubtedly took great pains to prevent his life and work from attracting public attention. This no doubt explains why we know practically nothing about him, and it must have been the dim half-light cast upon him by this official reticence that caused Greek antiquity to brand him an arch-liar and braggart, an *'anér pseudéstatos'* as Strabo put it. Certainly very unjustly! For there is no doubt that he was one of the most important geographers of all time. The loss of his book *On the Ocean,* which must have lain for many years in the secret archives of Massilia, is therefore extremely regrettable. For many centuries passed before explorers were again found in whom ability, information, and desire for knowledge were combined with such favourable external conditions. Pytheas seems to have been no merchant, but a scholar living in poor circumstances. Nonetheless, as the son of a distinctly mercantile city, he was sufficiently conversant with the commercial outlook to be capable of solving economic problems. On the other hand, he did not expend his energy on purely material considerations. His voyage to Thule, whose immediate commercial significance to the ancient world is quite unknown, seems to have been undertaken primarily for scientific purposes. This is suggested by the frequency with which Pytheas took bearings in order to ascertain his geographical position. But however that may be, it is certain that he considerably expanded the world-picture of classical antiquity. He rendered the world services for which it owes him more thanks than he ever received.

4

At roughly the same time as this immense expansion of the geographical horizon to the north was taking place from the western
Mediterranean, a deep penetration into the mysterious obscurity of the
Orient was being made from its eastern basin: India was added to the
geographical knowledge of the West. The first mention of the far-away
wonderland in classical literature is to be found in Hecatæus *circa*
500 B.C. Since, as a Hither Asian Ionian, he cannot pronounce an 'h',
he calls the Hindus *Indoi;* and this Ionian expression has found its way
into every European language. It is to this peculiarity of an ancient
Greek dialect, and to Columbus's geographic error, that the American
Indians also owe the name later bestowed on them by the Old World.

Homer has manifestly never heard of India, although right at the
beginning of the *Odyssey* he speaks of the Ethiopians of the sunset and
those of the sunrise: the Dravidians of India it has been conjectured,
though not very convincingly. Strabo remarks ironically that if Homer
had known of India he would never have omitted to have the heroes of
his *Odyssey* sail thither. The world known by hearsay to Homer did
not extend farther to the south-east than the Red Sea and the beginning
of the Indian Ocean. Even the Arabs he only mentions briefly along
with Libyans and Phœnicians. Many centuries later, a man like Herodotus still knew only the extreme north-west of India, and even that only
from secondhand reports. It remained for Alexander the Great to
initiate the conquest of India by the white man with his audacious
march to the Hindu Kush and the Indus.

Alexander's basic purpose is clear. Though the primary aim of his
attack on the Persians—Europe's first great blow against the Asian
threat in the east after the long defensive struggles of the Greeks—
was to destroy the Persian naval base in Phœnicia, he must have felt
compelled to advance beyond this and strike the heart of the Persian
Achæmenid Empire. This he did when, in the autumn of 331 B.C.,
after the victory of Gaugamela, he occupied the Persian administrative
centres of Babylon and Susa. Perhaps Alexander hoped this would lay
the whole of Asia at his feet. But he who fights against the East fights
against space. It avails him nothing to get a few nodal points of trade,
travel, or industrial production into his hands. He must subjugate space
itself.

But what did the space into which Alexander now had to advance
look like?

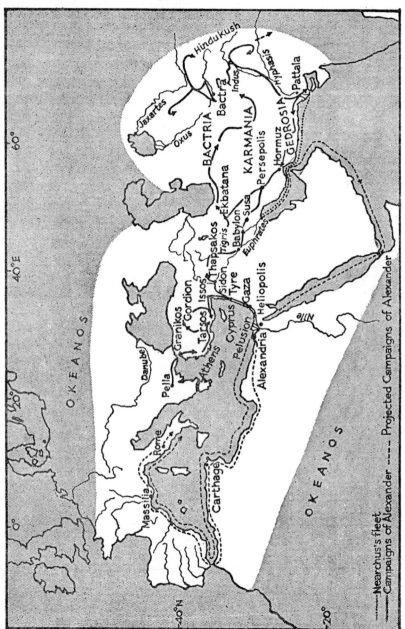

IX. *Alexander's plan for a world empire.*

Nearchus's fleet
Campaigns of Alexander
Projected Campaigns of Alexander

No one had the slightest inkling. No one could give Alexander a picture of India that was even half true. This must be made abundantly clear, because we are all inclined to succumb to the seduction of maps and tacitly to assume that, by and large, Alexander had exactly the same notions of Asia as ourselves. There is no question of this however.

When the great king launched his campaign against the Persians in 334 B.C., he was operating at the outset in districts well known to the Greeks. Their geographic knowledge even extended as far as Arbela and Gaugamela, where the decisive battles were fought. They were regions known of old and much sung, and the 'Bematists'—the scientific detachments of his general staff: historians, surveyors, cartographers, engineers, and army doctors—had little to do at first.

With the invasion of the tableland of Iran the problems began. No one could answer even the prime questions of how land and sea were distributed in these unknown eastern regions and whether they would come to the end of the world. It was known in Greece at this period that there was a sea somewhere to the south of Persia, which had been perfunctorily designated the 'Erythræan Sea'. The Euphrates and Tigris were also known of course, and that these two ancient rivers flowed out into the Persian Gulf. The latter's northern bays were known and also a hint of the Red Sea, called by the ancient world the Arabian Gulf. It was further conjectured that these two areas of water joined somewhere in the deep south. But whether the Erythræan Sea was an inland sea, because Africa and Asia curved round and combined in one immense land mass far south of the equator—or whether it was in fact the Ocean, which the ancients believed to form a closed circle round the *Oikoumene*—was unknown. Alexander himself, as we know, assumed the Erythræan Sea to be a relatively insignificant depression, similar to the Caspian Sea. A large proportion of his decisions rested on this conviction.

The exact truth about the Caspian was equally doubtful to Alexander and his age. The ancient Greek geographers had unanimously assumed that this remarkable stretch of water was the extreme southern tip of a vast bay thrust into Asia by the Northern Ocean. This conception was vigorously contradicted by Herodotus and Aristotle. Both held the opinion that the Caspian could only be an inland sea. Alexander also inclined to this view, though he supposed that this largest inland water of the earth extended as far as the region of the Sea of Azov. He did not obtain certitude until 330 B.C., when he stood on the southern shore of the Caspian in Hyrcania, the present Mazanderan. Here he ascertained that, although there were seals—a clear proof that this huge lake had once been joined to the open sea—sea-fish proper did not occur in it; from this he quite rightly deduced that a link with the Northern Ocean had existed at some very early period, but that it had long ceased to be—a conclusion not disputed by modern science.

There was an additional factor to be considered. According to the universal opinion, the Don, which flowed into the Sea of Azov at the old Greek colony of Tanais, constituted the boundary between Europe and Asia. The broad plains and the many nomadic tribes on the right bank of this river belonged to the West; everything to the left was Asia. No one knew the true course of the Don nor where it came from: perhaps from the north, perhaps from the east, or even in a wide arc from the south. When Alexander crossed the mountains of the northern Iranian border in 329 B.C., when he forded the Amu-Darya, the Oxus of the ancients, at Khojend and reached the Syr-Darya (Jaxartes), he believed that he was on the hitherto unknown upper course of the Don, which patently flowed in a great curve round the Caspian, thereby proving this water to be an inland sea and not an inlet of the Ocean.

Up to this point we can follow the reasoning of the great king of the Macedonians. But it becomes incomprehensible to us when—from his angle quite logically—he deduces that on the Syr-Darya he has reached the frontier of Asia. To understand Alexander we must forget the modern Atlas. We must simply hold fast to the fact that everything to the left of the Don was Asia, everything to the right of it ascribed to Europe. It follows that anyone who reached the Syr-Darya and saw the heaven-scraping mountains from which it flowed, believing it to be the Don which divided Europe from Asia, was inevitably convinced that everything to the left of this river was Asia and that on the other side of its flowing waters lay Europe.

This is unintelligible to us, yet that was what happened. When Alexander of Macedon reached the Syr-Darya he believed, and he had *reason* to believe, that he was on the utmost borders of Asia. India alone remained to be overcome, then he had won his battle with space!

India alone: as unshakably systematic as a chess-player, Alexander sets his troops marching from Bokhara to India in the year 327 B.C. He follows old caravan roads, at whose junctions the Greeks establish towns, of which Herat and Kandahar stand today. He marches down the Kabul Valley to the Indus. Delightedly his divisions throw themselves into the cold, clear stream. All Macedonians can swim. They enjoy swimming and they don't care two hoots, especially here in Asia, what the Athenian intellectuals say about it! Suddenly ear-splitting death screams ring out across the untilled river lands. Horrible demons drag their comrades beneath the water, blood reddens the stream, and the loathsome sound of snapping jaws and cracking bones violates the evening peace.

Crocodiles? They *can't* be! Crocodiles are only found in the Nile, the holy river of Egypt. These beasts occur nowhere else. Crocodiles?

But it is true; there they are! That half-submerged log over there, shimmering green and yellow, utterly motionless, utterly dead, suddenly moves! Crocodiles in India! Has this foreign river some connection with the Nile? Might it even be one of the sources of the great ancient river? Does not the occurrence of crocodiles furnish conclusive evidence that Africa and Asia really are linked somewhere in the south?

That was how Alexander and his army took it. A few weeks later they came to the Hydaspes, the modern Jhelum. This river too was seething with crocodiles. Could there be any doubt, with these monsters here as well? Now it was clear: the Indus and the Hydaspes were the secret sources of the Nile. There could be no doubt about it: the melting snows of the titanic mountains from which these two rivers flowed emitted the enormous masses of water which Old Father Nile poured out over his banks year after year.

This was so patent that the problem of the Erythræan Sea appeared to have been solved. It *could* only be an inland sea, scarcely larger than the Caspian. The Nile flowed round it somewhere to the south, and if one sailed down the Hydaspes and the Indus one would be bound to come to the Nile. If this were correct it would be an easy route by which to return with the whole army to Egypt and the Mediterranean.

At first this was just a passing thought. But when Alexander learnt that a bare lifetime before him Artaxerxes III (358–337), the last great ruler in Persia, had planned to divert the Indus, which he too deemed to be the true source-river of the Nile, and so dry out the rebellious Egyptians and bring them once and for all to their knees, the Greek king commanded his admiral, Nearchus, to set about building a fleet forthwith; he also wrote home to his mother that he had discovered the sources of the Nile.

As chance would have it, this proud victory bulletin lay for a few days in the tent of his staff orderly officer. During these few days reports from his scouts, information from the natives, and statements by Indian prisoners of war mounted up, from which it emerged that none of the rivers of the Punjab, neither the Indus, the Hydaspes, the Acesines (Chenab), nor the Hyphasis had anything to do with the Nile, but that

all of them flowed into the 'Great Sea', as the natives called the unknown expanse of water to the south. Alexander rapidly grasped his
mistake. The letter to his mother came back into the chancery, and the
king's proud boast of having discovered the sources of the Nile was
erased.

Alexander did not, however, revoke his order to Admiral Nearchus
immediately to build a fleet. Fortunately not! For a few weeks later he
was to need those ships more urgently than daily bread. This transpired
at the moment when he reached the Hyphasis and his troops mutinied
and refused to follow their idolized king any farther. They had endured
appalling hardships during the last few weeks' march. The tropical
rains had set in, the matted primeval forest had changed into a tangled
morass; it was impossible to light a fire, to dry one's things or to eat
in a manner even half befitting humans. But this was not the real reason
for the mutiny: all this they could have borne. A little later they bore
the frightful torment of the thirst-march through the Gedrosian desert.
Then, however, they were going westwards, towards home. Here on
the Hyphasis they were to go farther to the south and to the east,
towards the edge of the world. That was too uncanny, and the army
knew what it was that drew their king! Beyond this river, said the
natives, lived a people that possessed an extraordinary number of
elephants.

The Macedonians made the acquaintance of the elephant when they
had to fight these forerunners of our tanks at Arbela and Gaugamela.
They finally succeeded in bringing down these colossal beasts. But fear
of them was still in the army's bones. Whereas their king and leader
was burning to find out more about this new, tactically so important
weapon, they were in a blue funk. Were they to advance once more
against the trampling monsters? Must they once more hear their
comrades screaming in agony as they bled to death, transfixed by the
beasts' tusks? Watch them picked up by the jerkin by sinewy trunks,
hurled through the air like weightless dolls, and dashed to pieces on
the nearest rock?

No, no and no again! And the king had to give way.

Bitterly hurt, as though he had been betrayed, Alexander ordered
an about-turn. A bunch of desperate Macedonian peasants had made
world history. After the vast distances already covered by the King
of the Pan-Hellenes only a short stretch separated him from the realm
of King Chandragupta in the Ganges lands, which soon after rose to
magnificent heights and attained one of the pinnacles of Indian cultural
achievement. What a different course history might have taken if

Hellenic and Indian culture had come at that early point into the fruitful contact which was established soon after Alexander's death in the Bactrian kingdom of Seleucus, one of the generals of Alexander who made themselves 'independent' after their chief's demise.

But this was manifestly not intended to be. By forced marches the Greeks returned to the Hydaspes. The king was full of gloomy thoughts and for the most part kept with the rearguard. One morning, however, the army found him at the head of the mobile units which skirmished and reconnoitred ahead of the main body. He had remembered the fleet which Nearchus was to build. If there was no Nile for him to sail down, if the Hydaspes and the Indus did not issue in the Erythræan Sea, if the natives' 'Great Sea' were the Ocean itself, then at least by sea he would reach the edge of the world!

His head buzzing with new plans, feverish with impatience, the king whipped his trusty followers forward. For eight years they had marched with him this way and that across the world. For the first time in all these years they were going westward, towards home. Now with a last supreme effort the whole company advanced, in an incredibly short time, to the Hydaspes.

And sure enough, Nearchus had kept his word. There rode the fleet: galleys for thirty oarsmen, one-and-a-half-deckers, and cargo ships. Good old Nearchus! Reliable as ever! But now to the boats! Man the oars! And downstream with flashing bow-wave and wind-swelled sails.

Alexander's 'Bematists' took careful notes of this section of the Asian campaign. And some five hundred years later these notes lay on the desk of a Roman general, Flavius Arrianus (Arrian) of Nicomedia in Bithynia, who occupied his leisure with military history and had become an Alexander specialist. Naturally, the fact that his great colleague had managed to get the whole of his army on board ship greatly interested him. His report of this extravagant undertaking, which is extant and doubtless goes back to sources from Alexander's own day, shows this very clearly.

When Alexander had made ready on the shore a great number of thirty-oared galleys, one-and-a-half-deckers, and cargo ships with all the stores necessary for the army's voyage, he resolved to sail down the Hydaspes to the Ocean. Along the whole of the stretch travelled by Alexander the Hydaspes is about 20 stades [2 miles] wide. But where the Hydaspes joins the Acesines the river narrows greatly. It becomes a torrent full of unpleasant rapids. The water roars and rages so loudly that the thunder of its waves can be heard a great way off . . .

When Alexander reached the Indus he pressed on at even greater speed. He resolved to sail to the point at which this river issued into the sea, and selected for this purpose his swiftest ships. Since those who dwelt on the banks had all fled, he lacked guides, which made the voyage extremely difficult. For this reason Alexander sent mobile patrols of infantry into the interior to capture Indians who might serve as guides for the rest of the journey. When they came to a place at which the river widened to a breadth of 200 stades a strong sea wind suddenly arose. The water became so rough that it was almost impossible to raise the lower oars out of the waves. Therefore the Greeks anchored in a calm branch of the Indus. While they were waiting here for an improvement in the weather, the tide ebbed and left all the ships high and dry. This was something Alexander's companions had never seen, and it filled them with terror, which naturally increased still further when the river rose with the flow and set the ships afloat again. The following day Alexander sailed out through the estuary of the Indus on to the open sea, ostensibly to ascertain whether more land would emerge anywhere, but in reality, I believe, so that he could say he had sailed the Indian Ocean.

Arrian's concluding remark to the effect that pure ambition caused Alexander to sail out on to the high seas is, of course, only partially justified. For undoubtedly the Macedonian intended to ascertain whether this vast sea, with its huge sand dunes and enormous tides, was really the *Okeanos,* or whether land would appear somewhere after all. It is possible that this voyage on the high seas aroused in him those ideas of suzerainty of which Plutarch later wrote. Perhaps it was here that Alexander conceived the plan of subjugating the whole world encircled by the Ocean. At all events, Plutarch held the opinion that this was the reason for the king's command to Nearchus to reconnoitre the seaway from India to the Persian Gulf.

Sending the head of his navy back to Persia by sea, Alexander himself marched home along the coast, following a waterless desert track on which his army suffered agonies of thirst and heat. Even Arrian, who paints this appalling march through the deserts of Baluchistan in the hardest colours, declares it to have been devoid of any military significance and undertaken solely out of a desire for knowledge.

Like this march through Baluchistan, Nearchus's expedition from the Indus to the Tigris was purely a voyage of exploration, with the sole purpose of acquiring further information about the Indian Ocean. It is possible that the idea of getting to know the seaway to India, as well as the landways reconnoitred by Alexander himself, may have had a background in power politics. But it is more probable that the urge to discovery was the primary motive. Plutarch explicitly states that Alexander considered this voyage of Nearchus merely a curtain-raiser to even more ambitious enterprises and intended, after his admiral's return, to circumnavigate Africa. Whichever was behind it, power politics or a thirst for knowledge, Nearchus's expedition remains a deed that forms a worthy appendage to Alexander's own enterprises.

Two centuries before Nearchus, another had sailed the same route: the Greek captain Scylax, who, at the command of the Persian king Darius I (521–486 B.C.), likewise pursued the aim of reconnoitring the coast from the Euphrates to the Indus and the northern part of the Red Sea. To be sure, men had been sailing across these seas for three thousand years; but official expeditions like those of Scylax or Nearchus, undertaken for purposes of exploration and with the avowed aim of acquiring a closer knowledge of the coast by occasional landings, had never been launched on this scale before.

Perhaps Nearchus, who seems to have been an exceptionally conscientious character, might have brought even more information home from his voyage if he had given freer rein to his venturesome helmsman, Onesicritus. On the other hand, Nearchus's reports are of exemplary reliability. He is the source for all his successors, and must be counted one of the most outstanding geographers of this epoch. Nearchus compiled a report of his voyage which has unfortunately been lost, but which must have been available to Arrian. It cannot be said from Arrian's presentation of them that Nearchus's experiences were as hugely exciting as might have been expected. The Greek seaman manifestly drew up his report to Alexander on the basis of his log; he confined himself to noting, with pedantic exactitude, the number of stades travelled each day, the anchorages, conformation of the coast, harbours, etc. Nevertheless, one of his experiences, an encounter with a shoal of whales, which were till then unknown to the Greeks, is worthy of note, because the frightful excitement about these 'monsters', which still sets Arrian's narrative atremble, makes it plain what a daring venture such a long sea voyage must have been, even for people as used to the sea as the Greeks. Their concern is, of course, nothing to the trepidation with which the Romans, confirmed landlubbers, went to sea. But of this presently. Arrian recounts:

In this foreign sea there live great whales and other large fish, much bigger than in our Mediterranean. Nearchus tells of his encounter with them as follows: As we set sail we observed that in the sea to the east of us water was blown aloft, as happens with a strong whirlwind. We were terrified and asked our pilots what it was and whence it came. They replied that it was caused by whales, which inhabit this sea. Our sailors were so horrified that the oars fell from their hands. I went and spoke to them encouragingly. Then I walked round the fleet and ordered every steersman I met to steer straight at the whales, exactly as if they were going into a naval battle. All the men were to row hard and with as much noise as possible, including yells. The sailors regained their courage, and at a signal we all set off together. When we had approached the beasts, everyone shouted as loudly as they could. On top of that, trumpets were blown and the noise of the oars echoed across the sea. The whales, which could be seen just in front of the ships, dived terrified into the depths. Not long after, they surfaced again behind the fleet, blowing water into the air as before. The sailors clapped their hands, rejoiced in their escape, and praised Nearchus for his courage and astuteness. Now and again a few of these whales come ashore, having been stranded on the flat beaches at ebb tide. Often, too, they are flung up on dry land by a violent storm. They then die and rot. When the flesh has mouldered away the skeletons are left, which the inhabitants of these shores use for building their houses. The large bones at the sides form the beams of their houses, the smaller ones the laths. From the jawbones they make doors. For many whales are twenty-five fathoms long.

This encounter, as may be imagined, made a great impression on all Nearchus's contemporaries and provided material for a multitude of fables. Four hundred years later, the 'enlightened' Pliny turns the harmless, and perhaps playful whales into giant sea serpents, and his successors follow him faithfully. It is therefore not surprising that the Middle Ages, which were in any case farther removed from nature than classical antiquity, should abound in frightful horror stories, which, apart from a few additions of their own, were taken over lock, stock and barrel from the tales of the ancients.

Amongst these horror stories is the dreadful account of the gold-digging Indian ants retailed by the Ionian Greek Megasthenes—who, from 302 till 291 B.C., was the accredited envoy to King Chandragupta from Seleucus of Bactria—and subsequently repeated by all classical and medieval travel reports. These 'ants', as big as foxes and with pretty skins like a panther's, dwelt, Megasthenes relates in one of his ambassadorial reports, in holes in the ground. Like moles, they piled up round the entrances to their dwellings the earth they had grubbed out in excavating them; the natives had only to sieve these heaps of earth to obtain possession of the gold contained in them. 'The people take this gold very secretly', Megasthenes concludes his report. 'For if the animals notice it they pursue the fugitives and kill them and their draught animals.'

An old wives' tale? Not entirely. For there really were gold-digging

ants, and still are. Thus, for instance, it is reported that the harvester
ants (*Pogonomyrmex occidentalis*) of Texas are in the habit of armouring
their fortress-mounds with a mosaic of tiny stones, for preference
grains of gold, so that the dismantling of these ant-heaps is an extremely
lucrative activity. Megasthenes's gold-digging ants must, of course,
have been marmots, which are common around the Brahmaputra and
on the Sutlej in the Punjab and riddle the top soil with innumerable
passages, cavities, and nests. If these animals, quite harmless herbivores,
happened to start digging in an area of auriferous sands and gravels
the earth they cast up might well have contained gold. The rest of
Megasthenes's account, the blood-thirstiness of these marmots, their
size and speed, is naturally pure fable, concocted by traders to frighten
away any competitors who might have contemplated washing and
sieving these valuable heaps of earth on their own account.

Gold-digging ants—that was something which really had to be
reported. And in absolute good faith. For it was also said that India
contained vast quantities of gold, copper, iron, tin, and precious stones;
that a reed grew there 'which yielded honey without bees'—sugar
cane; that the sun stood so high in the sky that shadows pointed to the
south. Each one of these reports sounded as marvellous as the rest,
and in such a country gold-digging ants were perfectly possible.

The prime interest of antique explorers was centred on quite a
different animal, however: the Indian elephant. We have already heard
how deeply Alexander himself regretted never having entered the real
elephant country. And General Flavius Arrianus, sitting peacefully at
his desk in Nicomedia in A.D. 150, seems to have felt just the same. It is
true that the Punic wars, during which the Romans too had learnt
terror of the elephant, were over long ago. And it is hardly to be supposed that the huge grey and sandy-brown trunk-wielders continued
to play any military role in Arrian's day. At most they may occasionally
have been thrown against Roman scouting patrols by natives on the
south-eastern confines of the *Imperium Romanum*. Nevertheless, the
general interest in elephants, which the Roman populace frequently saw
in their circuses, was as lively as ever. At all events, Arrian's elephant
stories were positively lapped up in the salons of Rome and Alexandria
—and no doubt with more than merely zoological interest.

The general presented the purely factual account of an expert, free
from fairy-tale ingredients. The Romans, who were well acquainted
with elephants, would not have believed him if he had spiced his stories
with details of his own invention. But this alone does not suffice to
explain the objectivity of his accounts. The fact is, they were probably

drawn almost verbatim from the reports of Alexander's 'Bematists', and we can be sure that Alexander insisted on these being absolutely factual and objective. Arrian's books therefore reveal precisely the information available to Alexander. His description of elephant-trapping in India tallies almost exactly with the method employed today:

Although the Indians hunt other wild beasts in the same fashion as the Greeks, their manner of hunting elephants is totally unlike any other kind of hunt. For the elephant itself is unlike any other kind of animal. Having found a flat, warm spot they dig a trench round it which is so wide that they could encamp a large army within it. This ditch is about five fathoms wide and four fathoms deep. The earth thrown up from the trench they heap on both sides of the trench. This embankment serves them as a kind of wall.

They then place three or four particularly tame she-elephants inside this enclosure, leaving only one entrance across the trench. This entrance they cover with earth and grass, so that the animals do not recognise this bridge as being the work of man and suspect no trap. During the day elephants do not approach inhabited areas; during the night, however, they roam every-where and feed in great herds, following the biggest and boldest amongst them as cows follow the bull. When they come within the proximity of the enclosure and hear the voices of the she-elephants within it, they run quickly towards it. Having followed the edge of the trench till they reach the afore-mentioned bridge, they press across it into the enclosure. As soon as the hunters see that the wild elephants are inside some of them remove the bridge, whilst others hasten to the nearest village to spread the joyful news that the wild elephants have been caught.

This detailed account is certainly taken from those military sources from Alexander's day, which were still accessible to Arrian and doubt-less came originally from the archives of the Macedonian army. Flavius Arrianus, however, felt that he owed it to his public to add a few touches of his own to this extract from his sources. He therefore appends some original experiences:

Elephants whose riders have been killed in battle have even been known to bear them to the grave themselves. Others have fought on for their riders although the latter already lay dead on the ground. Others again have braved dangers in defence of their fallen masters. One elephant that had killed his rider in a rage died of grief and remorse. I myself have seen an elephant playing cymbals, whilst others danced to the music. The player had a cymbal attached to each of his forelegs and another to his trunk. He rhythmically beat the cymbals on his legs, one after the other, with the cymbal on his trunk. The dancing elephants hopped round in a circle, following the rhythm played by the cymbal player by raising one foreleg after the other.

Alexander's achievement, slight as were its immediate political consequences, was nonetheless of immense significance. Not only in a geographical respect, though a fleeting comparison of Herodotus's world picture with a map of Alexander's discoveries renders his success and the tremendous extension of the Greek *Oikoumene* immediately apparent. Even more important was the psychological effect of his radiant figure. A whole literature arose in the Far East out of the myths of a brilliant, baneful hero from the West, which he engendered. Perhaps the ultimate significance of his life did not consist in the *palpable* effects which it necessarily exercised. Infinitely more important was the resulting imponderable increase in the white man's self-confidence which became apparent after his era and which may have been one of the psychological preconditions for the genesis of the Roman Empire. In contradistinction to the mere exercise of power, dominion is ultimately moral superiority. The thousands of street minstrels who, for centuries after Alexander's death, earned their living by singing his deeds to the best of their ability; the poets whose verses the cultured world recited when it recalled Alexander; all the immeasurable, imponderable influences which proceeded from that heroic life tended in one direction: to cause posterity to experience in retrospect the fact that it was a European, that it was the West, to which the world had bowed down. To the power held by Alexander was added in fortunate conjunction the splendour of a flourishing, highly evolved culture, one of the most magnificent to which the West ever gave birth. Thus the proud knowledge that he was a Greek gave Alexander the most powerful moral incentive to his achievement, and this knowledge lent his Indian campaign that cultural effectiveness of which we have spoken, and which so far outstripped the political significance of his enterprises.

## PART FIVE

# FROM ROME TO THE FAR EAST
# AND AMERICA

*The water-shy Romans · Did the Carthaginians know the secret of the trade wind? · Hotel Septumanus in Lyons · Roman amber experts in East Prussia · The François Vase and dwarfs and cranes from the marshes of the Nile · Across the Indian Ocean without a compass · Pilots and lighthouses · Antique sailing manuals · How long is an hour? · 2,000-ton freighters in antiquity · Roman anchorage directions for Indian ports · The Sinhalese are surprised in Rome · Have the Chinese got blue eyes? · Roman merchants in Peking · Empress Si-li-shi and the Bombyx mori worm · Mrs. Marcus Aurelius has no money for a silk dress · The vicious women of the island of Cos · Routes to China · Who sails to Singapore? · With folding-boat across the Atlantic · What did the ancient world know of America? · Red Indians land in Europe.*

WE have now to turn to the most exciting theme in ancient geography: the story of the truly world-wide Roman Empire as it existed at the beginning of the Christian era. Whatever we may have learnt at school about the ancient world, we were not usually told anything about its colorful, busy life, about its commercial connections, about its seafaring. We never met the wholesale merchant from Alexandria or Miletus, whose opposite number in western Europe traded from Massilia or Gades with Gaul and the British Isles, or even with the German amber lands, while he himself was in contact with Barygaza in Hither India, the modern Broach, or even with Cattigara, the great port in far-away China. Chinese silk was piled in his warehouses, spices and precious stones from the fabulously rich island of Taprobane (Ceylon) sped thousands of miles across the high seas on his Far East freight-ships as they scudded before the monsoon with billowing sails. Frankincense from Hadramat came from Adana, our Aden, ivory and gold from Nubia, glass from Phœnicia, silverware and wheat from the Black Sea; fat bags of Roman gold coins, skins of heavy Greek wine, and costly German amber ornaments went out in return. And while the merchant's buyers in Asia Minor waited for the trans-Himalayan caravans from inner Asia and the huge junks from China, Celtic stevedores unloaded from the giant cargo ships, which his west European business friends had dispatched to a British port, corals and cowry shells, Syrian purple stuffs and Roman weapons, and perhaps also the costly, gossamer-fine silk gauzes picked by the delicate-fingered factory slaves on the island of Cos in the Ægean from Far Eastern brocades.

We shall not meet this wholesale merchant personally either. He certainly already had an 'office', in which a host of more or less well-paid clerks—slaves they were called in those days—worked for him. There were no bills of exchange, and hence no bill-jobbing, no 'bouncing' bills, nor any of the other vexations which they can cause one to suffer and to inflict upon others. But credit existed, and conse-

quently a properly functioning banking system with a fully developed
clearance-house business; there were letters of credit for the travelling
merchant; there were cheques. Indeed, cheques were such a usual
method of payment in Rome that Ovid mentions them in his *Art of
Love,* where he deplores the avarice of women. If you tell them you
haven't got so much money as they are demanding in the house, they
answer pertly that they would be quite content with a cheque. In
detail all this can scarcely be proved of course. The debris that two
thousand years of destruction have heaped up over our Alexandrian
wholesale merchant; the fires that have sent his bills, his tax and customs
receipts, and his business correspondence up in flames; the plundering
to which his warehouses have been subjected, make that impossible.
But it is certain that he really lived. The *auri sacra fames,* the holy-
unholy hunger for gold, engendered him in the first place, caused him
to grow great and active, swallowed him, and smothered him beneath
the ooze and dust of innumerable later lives. But we shall come across
traces of him; from the Yangtse Kiang in the Far East to the western-
most tip of Spain. And perhaps some inkling already reached him, a
vague rumour, the merest hint of a report of a great land beyond the
western Ocean—America. We shall hear more of this.

It was a long, laborious path that led to these times of real world
intercourse. For at the outset the Romans were anything but seafarers
and explorers, and in comparison with the Greeks they achieved little
in the way of *conscious* geographic discovery; knowledge for them
possessed an inner justification only when it could be put to immediate
concrete use in the interests of the Roman power system. Consequently
Roman exploration offers little parallel with the world voyages made
by the Greeks. This is all the more surprising because their neighbors
and forerunners, the Etruscans, must have been magnificent seamen.
As inventors of the grappling-iron and as pirates they were for a long
time the terror of the seas; for many centuries the word 'Etruscan' was
synonymous with 'pirate'. Nonetheless, the Romans put to sea only
unwillingly and hesitantly, and not until much, much later did they
consider and call the Mediterranean *mare nostrum*, 'our sea'.

There is no visible reason for this delay. We must simply accept
it as a fact. If we reject mere chance as a determinant of historical evolution, we may gain the impression that some force consciously and
intentionally protected the Roman people from the risk of dispersion
for ever presented by the alluring breadth of the sea. Rome's historical
task seems to have been the consolidation, preservation and methodical
correlation of what her predecessors had acquired with effort, suffering

and struggle. This, if it is true, explains why the Romans were such late starters in exploration, and why they generally confined themselves to collecting, scrutinizing, and cataloguing existing knowledge.

Knowledge was plentifully available and pretty well delivered at the door of the city on the Tiber. The Roman Empire's well-organized news service made it possible to present an excellent over-all picture of information from all over the world. The advances of mathematics and astronomy—due, above all, to the Greeks—permitted a multitude of reliable individual observations. Land-registry offices and State archives saw to it that the material collected and filed was preserved to posterity. Particularly important in this connection was the guild of *agrimensores* or land-surveyors, which was responsible for the construction and surveying of the Roman road network. (A set of their mathematical instruments has been preserved and can be seen at the Romano-Teutonic Museum at Mainz. Surprisingly, it corresponds in every detail to the mathematical instruments of our modern surveyors and engineers.) Detailed itineraries were drawn up for each of these roads, containing not only the names, but also the dimensions of the various halting-places.

'Officially' Rome did not become aware until 150 B.C. that there were other human beings living beyond the mountains and seas which formed their geographical horizon. This discovery was made through a sea expedition to the north-west African coast, immediately after the annexation of Carthage, which seems strangely unmotivated in the context of Roman exploration as a whole. It was carried out under the direction of the Greek geographer Polybius, a friend of Scipio Æmilianus, the Romans' Africa general. We do not know the real aim and object of this reconnaissance expedition. It has therefore been surmised that, after the conquest of Carthage, the Romans had found in its archives the report of Hanno's magnificent Cameroon expedition and were now endeavouring to explore the western littoral of the Dark Continent on their own account. This cannot be proved, nor can it be altogether discounted, especially since Pliny, who reported this remarkable voyage two hundred years later, speaks of a mountain called the 'Chariot of the Gods'.

How did Pliny know this name, which is given in Hanno's report of his expedition? The knowledge can only have come from the Carthaginians, and we may assume that the Romans, with their cold-blooded attachment to palpable realities, will have taken a special interest in the archives and patent-offices of Carthage when they finally overcame the prosperous city. It is possible, we may infer, that the

astute Polybius utilized the proudly triumphant mood of his Roman
friends to provoke them into venturing forth onto the Ocean. It
remains surprising that the cold Romans should have proved susceptible to an appeal to their national vanity. Anyway, they sent out seven
ships on this Africa and Atlantic expedition, a large number in view of
the restricted size of the Roman fleet. Or was Scipio after something
quite different? Had parts of the Carthaginian armada escaped to the
Ocean, as some ancient sources aver? Had they sought aid from the
Punic coastal stations founded in north-west Africa by Hanno? We
do not know for sure how far Scipio went. He seems, however, to have
reached Senegal and Cape Verde around latitude 14° N.; a considerable
achievement, if we recall that it was not till some sixteen hundred years
later that European fleets once more pushed so far south. There were
no more Punic coastal stations here, however, as we know from Hanno.
Since their purpose was to guard the seaway to the Canary Islands, it
would have been senseless to plant colonies a full ten degrees farther
south—in that case, Scipio's voyage was equally senseless. Why, then,
did he extend his enterprise so far?

Now, this is roughly the latitude at which the north-east trade wind
starts, that regular current of air which, one and a half millennia later,
blew a certain Christopher Columbus from the Cape Verde Islands to
America in twenty-one days! Anyone pursued by merciless enemies
would be more disposed, if he were a good seaman, to trust himself to
the trade wind than to the clemency of the hereditary foe. Did the
Carthaginians know about the trade wind? Did they guess that there
was land across the Ocean? Did Scipio prolong his otherwise peculiarly
unmotivated voyage so far to the south in order to make certain that
the Carthaginians really had disappeared into the Ocean? When
Columbus accomplished his glorious feat on three miserable ships that
were scarcely larger than the Carthaginian warships, he knew nothing
of America. That is definite. Whether he had ever heard of the trade
wind is doubtful. Nevertheless, he risked the crossing. Did the Carthaginians do the same? But of all this presently!

Impressive as the voyage of Scipio's seven ships to Africa is—how
different from Carthage! When this city overran southern Spain in
*circa* 530 B.C., it did not hesitate for an instant to reconnoitre the
Atlantic Ocean to north and south with mighty fleets. Of course, its
mariners had not had to put up with a three-centuries' blockade of the
Straits like the Romans, who could venture no farther than eastern
Spain, and that only at times when there happened to be peace between
Carthage and Rome. Relations between the city on the Tiber and the

other great sea-power, Syracuse in Sicily, were also very strained as a rule, and wherever the giant dreadnoughts of the Sicilians caught the wretched Roman ships they shot them to pieces with catapult artillery. The unfavourable situation in the Mediterranean proved a serious handicap to Rome's maritime development and must be taken into account. Nevertheless, it does not serve of itself to explain the Romans' antipathy to the sea. The reasons for this were deeply imbedded in their nature.

The next undertakings we hear of that seem to contain the germ of voyages of discovery were mainly directed towards the north. Efforts were made to remove the veil of mystery enveloping the upper course of the Ister, our modern Danube. An advance was made into Germany, which was eventually quite thoroughly explored to the west of the Elbe; a large-scale naval expedition to Britain was launched in *circa* A.D. 80, since knowledge of this country had been lost in the intervening three hundred years since Pytheas—not least because of the conscious reticence of west European export firms, who had no interest in enabling outsiders to cut in on the lucrative trade with the British Isles. Finally, there was the colonization of Gaul, which was also closely attached by commercial ties to the Roman sphere of power.

Germany can never have been anything like so permeated with Roman, Spanish, Greek and Syrian traders as Gaul, and it certainly could not have been said of the land of mists on the Elbe and the North Sea, as it was of Gaul: 'It is swarming with merchants there; it is full of Roman citizens; no Gaul completes a transaction without a Roman, and every coin circulating in Gaul passes through the books of a Roman!' This quotation from Cicero's speech *pro M. Fonteio* may at first sound exaggerated, but it is emphatically endorsed by the numerous finds on French soil. These tell us that Spaniards were members of the Corporation of Winedealers of Lyons, where Syrians also lie buried. Seats at the theatre were permanently reserved by the sea and river transport companies at Nîmes for their captains, and the publicity manager of the Hotel Septumanus in Lyons, which was mainly used by travelling Roman merchants, inscribed on the hotel sign: 'Here Mercury promises profit, Apollo health, and Septumanus bed and breakfast. He who stops here will travel better thereafter. Stranger, take care where you stay!'

Economic penetration of Germany was confined to Cologne, Trier, Asciburgium and one or two other places. Only on the seaway from the Rhine estuary to the Weser and the Elbe, that is, in the proximity of the amber lands, was there an opening for stout-hearted men to do really profitable business. The name Copenhagen is significant in this connection: it is derived from the Latin *caupo*, a wine merchant, and the Scandinavian *havn*, a harbour. Copenhagen was probably at one time the favourite port of south-European wine merchants. This suggests that the Romans ultimately grew accustomed to the vagaries of the northern shallows and made contact with the coastland tribes of Batavians, Friesians and Chaucians, with whom they were able to do extensive business in wine jugs and glass, earthen and metal ware, which they traded for German export articles like amber, goose down, furs, women's hair, and animals' skins.

Nevertheless, the North Sea remained an uncanny region, and if the Romans are to be credited with discovering the Baltic during an amber expedition to Samland in *circa* A.D. 65, i.e. in Nero's day, this is a deed which cannot be rated too highly. For Tacitus's gruesome characterization of Germany as a whole—'If the outward appearance of the country exhibits some variations, it nonetheless presents a general impression that is eerie because of its forests and repellent because of its morasses'—refers particularly to eastern Germany and the Vistula region. Unfortunately there is no record of the specific incentive to this Samland expedition so we are rather in the dark as to its motive. The effort and dangers involved are more likely to have appeared necessary for economic than for military reasons, however, and we shall not be far wrong if we surmise that it was some boom in amber caused by a swing in fashion round the middle of the first century A.D. which inspired this voyage to Samland.

At all events, Pliny has told us that the Roman officer who carried out the expedition brought back so much amber 'that the net and the protective fences of the *podium* (at the circus) were beaded with amber; the land strewn in the arena likewise contained amber; and the stretchers of the dead were decorated with it, so that the whole festal apparatus of this one day everywhere abounded in amber. The largest of the pieces brought back by him weighed 13 lb. . . .' The great economic importance to Rome of this remote zone is also attested by the considerable flow of Roman coins to the Baltic littoral at that period. While coin finds from earlier decades are comparatively rare, excavations from this epoch have been very rewarding both in quantity and as to the quality of individual pieces. Hand in hand with all this goes the utilisation of news reaching Rome from the Baltic in poetry, which is such a striking feature of Roman literature from Nero's reign onward. Whereas Pomponius Mela in A.D. 50 had no knowledge whatsoever of the existence of the Baltic, Tacitus in A.D. 100 was thoroughly well informed even about individual Baltic tribes, and another five decades later Ptolemy drew a map of the southern Baltic coast which was remarkably complete and correct in many details.

But the expeditions of the Romans did not only go north. In fact their work of conquest and exploration was even more extensive in southern latitudes. Frequently, however, they merely rediscovered districts long ago regarded as belonging to the *Oikoumene* by older cultures, but of which all knowledge had been lost in the interim. Thus, for example, Ælius Gallus, who, in 25 B.C. under orders from Augustus, sought in vain to subjugate Arabia and bring its gold-mines into Roman possession, although he advanced almost as far as Hadramat, was only following in the footsteps of early, mostly equally unsuccessful enterprises, undertaken many, many years before by the Egyptians, Assyrians, and Persians. Almost simultaneously with him, another Roman general, Petronius, marched from Egypt into the region of the Upper Nile. Romans had never penetrated so deep into the interior of Africa before; but they got no farther than Cambyses with his Persian host had gone five hundred years previously. Elephantine, the modern Aswan, remained as before the southernmost border-town on Egypt's frontier with Ethiopia.

The incursion into the south by Cornelius Balbus, Roman governor of the Syrtes country, from Tripoli in the year 19 B.C., which carried him into the region of Phazania (Fezzan) and to Garama, capital of the Garamantes—somewhat north-east of Murzuq, where Heinrich Barth rediscovered its ruins some eighteen centuries later—was also not an expedition into completely unknown and unexplored territory. Herodotus already speaks of the Garamantes as one of the greatest and most active peoples of the well-watered lowlands south of the Sahara. Since time immemorial a much-travelled trade road ran here, roughly along the twentieth line of longitude, which crossed the Sahara from oasis to oasis and led far south into the Dark Continent. Hence it had long been known that south of the land of the Garamantes lived Ethiopians, but the distance had been greatly under-estimated. Thus Strabo supposed that the southern shores of the country of the Ethiopians were only ten days' journey from the territory of the Garamantes. The inaccuracy of this supposition was not revealed until years later, when Roman merchants accompanied the Garamantes on their raids to the south and so came as far as the Lake Chad region. The true position had, of course, long since slipped into oblivion by the time the Portuguese began sailing to Africa some fourteen centuries later.

Rome also turned her attention to the exploration of the Atlas

Mountains round about this time. Pomponius Mela and Pliny inform us that Suetonius Paulinus, governor of the north African colonial empire, carried out in the year A.D. 42, during the reign of the Emperor Claudius, an expedition to the Wady Ghir, in the course of which he crossed the Atlas Mountains, being probably the first European to do so. His expedition was not a success. But Pliny notes in his report that the highest peak of the Atlas Mountains is covered with perpetual snow, even in summer—a highly satisfactory confirmation of the ancient myth of snow-capped Atlas.

2

In *circa* A.D. 60 two officers of the Imperial Guard set out on a journey of exploration to the sources of the Nile. This journey led from Egypt to the vast Nile marshes round latitude 5° N., and brought one of the great world-riddles of antiquity, the sources of the Nile, a good deal nearer solution. We have several accounts of this audacious enterprise, of which that given by the philosopher, Lucius Annæus Seneca, in his *Quæstiones Naturales* is the most striking. It runs:

. . . I have had an opportunity of hearing the report of the two centurions sent by the Emperor Nero to the sources of the Nile . . . We came, they reported, to immense swamps, the area of which is unknown even to the natives and which no one can tell. For the water plants there are so closely intertwined that no one can measure this water, either on foot or in a boat. Even if it were only just big enough to carry a man it could not be propelled through the resistant bog. There we espied two rocks, between which the Nile gushed forth in mighty fullness. Whether this is an affluent of the Nile or its source, or whether it here breaks forth from the depths after running for a stretch underground, must it not be assumed that it springs from a great lake? Since it emerges between the rocks with such pressure, it can only come from a basin containing the water that has collected and flowed together from all over this region . . .

The journey here reported by Seneca was made by order of Emperor Nero. We have already referred to Nero's part in initiating an expedition to explore the amber coast of Samland. On that occasion there were undoubtedly solid material grounds for the undertaking: we may be sure that Nero ordered as much amber as possible to be brought back to him. There were, however, no conceivable mercantile motives for the second expedition. It may have been a reconnaissance carried out for military purposes by two officers of the Roman general staff;

or it may simply have been that Nero wished to shine as a discoverer. For the sources of the Nile and how to track them down were puzzles which had already exercised the minds of the Great Kings of Persia. Since the Roman conquest of Egypt, it had become the favourite topic of conversation in all the salons of the capital with an interest in geography. The prospect of celebrity as an explorer of the earth was bound to attract the dictator, and perhaps personal vanity was the incentive to this expedition.

However that may be, it is certain that the two Roman officers pushed forward to a region not reached again by white men for another eighteen centuries. In all probability they came to the Bahr el Ghazal, the Gazelle River, and its debouchment into the Nile marshes, an impassable region of swamp jungle.

Our two Romans did not, however, reach the real sources of the Nile. Yet it seems that they were moving on soil which had long been known to the ancients, at least by hearsay. Livingstone already indicated this, and his conjecture was patently correct. The Nile marshes on the Mokren el Bohur have been since time immemorial the home of the Akka negroes, whom Georg Schweinfurth discovered on his celebrated Nile expedition in 1870. These black dwarfs were known to Pliny, who tells of them in his *Historia Naturalis*—and obviously also to Homer, whose *Iliad* contains the following lines which long puzzled scholars:

The Trojans advanced with a shouting and a din like that of birds. They filled the air with clamour, like the cranes that fly from the onset of winter and the sudden rains and make for Ocean Stream with raucous cries to bring death and destruction to the Pigmies, launching their wicked onslaught from the morning sky. (Penguin Classics, trans. E. V. Rieu, p. 64.)

While Pliny's information may go back direct to those two Roman guard's officers, who undoubtedly ran into the Akkas, Homer must have had very much earlier sources which told him, first, that there were dwarfs dwelling in the far south, and second, that these regions were the migratory goal of numberless cranes. Homer's account evidently caused an immediate sensation amongst his contemporaries; perhaps it was supplemented later by more circumstantial Egyptian reports. Anyway, the foot of the world-famous François vase in Florence, which originated in sixth-century Attica, is decorated with a portrayal of this combat between dwarfs and cranes. The anecdote must, therefore, have been well known, otherwise the nameless artist would certainly not have thought it worthy of depiction.

In any case, it looks as though our two centurions were not the first white men to wade about the Nile swamps, and as though the Egyptians came to the reed-thickets of the Sudd Region thousands of years before them. All the same, they were the first to whom geography owes any detailed information concerning the fountain-head of the Nile. For the most bizarre notions were still current as to the sources of the Nile and the course of that sacred river. Whilst some averred that the Nile issued from the Ocean, others, as we have seen, held that it originated in India; yet others sought it in unknown West Africa, terming the Congo, as Stechow has explained, the 'other Nile'. Finally, a fourth group declared that the sources of the Nile lay among lofty peaks, and that one half, the Nile we know, flowed north, while the other half flowed east. Not until eighteen centuries later did Europeans enter this region for the second time; and only then was the secret of the sources of the Nile finally illuminated.

## 3

There was naturally a good reason for Rome's striking interest in Egypt and the countries bordering it. This reason was eastern Asia. It was mentioned in the previous chapter that ancient caravan roads led to the west from the Far East, from India and central Asia, whose northern branches debouched into the Black Sea zone. Besides these overland communications, however, there were distinct sea routes running from India to Hadramat and Adana, and linking East Africa with the wonderland on the Ganges. The Egyptian Pharaohs already knew and used these connections. True, knowledge of the monsoons, those winds which blow in summer from Africa to India and in late autumn reverse their direction and blow from India to Africa, is attested only for later ages. Classical sources inform us that the Greek helmsman, Hippalus, who lived somewhere round 100 B.C., was the first consciously to utilize the monsoons. They were certainly known long before this, however, and there is no doubt at all that Indian and Arab ships were sailing to and fro across the Indian Ocean many centuries earlier than Hippalus.

No doubt both sides in the India-Africa trade did all they could to keep their knowledge secret. And they were manifestly successful in concealing it from both the Persians of the Darian epoch and from the Greeks of Alexander the Great. Hence these two upstart and highly troublesome competitors in the India trade only saw small vessels that battled their way laboriously along the perilous coasts and finally cast

Gigantic triangular sails drive the vessels silently over the water from Cairo to Sofala and Zanzibar to Bombay. They are Arab dhows crossing the wide ocean with the monsoons. is a modern cargo boat on the Nile.

16. A tidal wave caused by a submarine earthquake. The wall of water thundering towards the land at 40 miles an hour is 40 feet high. Crete was probably destroyed by a tidal wave of this sort produced by the explosion of the Santorin volcano in c.1500 B.C.

anchor in India, if fortune was kind to them, after a year's voyage. This was no whit better than the endless caravan journeys by land, the accomplishment of which demanded an oriental patience and self-denial that neither the Persians nor the Greeks possessed.

Thus Europe cannot, in fact, have learnt till much later that it was possible to shorten the long journey to India from twelve months to two, if one had the courage to sail 1,250 miles across the open sea without sight of land, and trust oneself, there and back, to the monsoons. This was first tried by European ships around 100 B.C., and we know from Strabo that at this time some twenty freighters a year sailed to India. When Egypt was conquered by the Romans in *circa* 30 B.C., this number suddenly soared. A hundred ships were now dispatched to India yearly, and they were not only freighters and tramp ships that sailed when they had enough cargo; there was a proper liner service with passengers on board and fixed times of sailing.

This was a tremendous achievement, and when we recall that the stretch of open sea with which Columbus had to cope fifteen centuries later was not much greater, it is clear how much respect is due to the antique India captains. Their successors still put to sea today. Year after year, Arab dhows with high bows and richly decorated, broad sterns, like medieval caravels in appearance, set sail from Port Sudan for India with the arrival of summer. In late autumn they speed back to Africa under their gigantic triangular lateen sails before the north-east monsoon. Their *nakoudas*, their skippers, have never heard of a sextant. The compass is known to them, but they do not use it. The knowledge of where India is, and of their position at sea at any given moment, has been in their blood for generations. '*Ana baref*', 'I just know', they say if they are asked how and by what means they can possibly take their bearings in this waste of wild water. '*Ana baref*', 'I just know!'

All this did not, of course, take place from one day to the next; it can only have been the conclusion of a long and gradual process of development. In the beginning men doubtless confined themselves to coastal navigation, to cautious progress from place to place within continual sight of land. No doubt they soon discovered that sailing on the open sea, far from all rocks and shoals, far from any breakers, was in many respects less dangerous than inshore sailing. At first, however, they lacked the necessary nautical knowledge for deep-sea sailing, while a great deal was done to detract from the dangers of coastal sailing. Long before our era canals with locks were built, e.g. the Athos canal, which Xerxes had dug through Mount Athos in 480 B.C. to obviate the

wearisome voyage round the rocky headland during his attack on
Greece. At critical points piles were sunk to mark the channel. At the
approaches to the harbour, pilots or strong local vessels sailed out to
bring the foreign merchantman safely to land and anchorage. On
shallow coasts towers were erected as seamarks, and at night fires were
lit on them. Occasionally proper lighthouses were already built, e.g.
at Ravenna, Ostia, Piræus, Boulogne-sur-Mer, and Las Coruñas in

*20. The lighthouse of Alexandria, reconstruction. The lighthouse
stood on the island of Pharos at the entrance to the harbour of
Alexandria. It was built by the master-builder Sostratos circa 280
and stood until the fourteenth century A.D.*

Spain. The most famous of them, one of the Seven Wonders of the
World, was the 530-feet-high Pharos lighthouse built on a small island
of that name off Alexandria in *circa* 280 B.C.; its light was said to be
visible at a distance of thirty miles. Idrisi, the Arab cartographer of
King Roger II of Sicily, of whom we shall have more to say presently,
saw and described this colossal structure in 1153. The Pharos lighthouse,
the prototype for most later lighthouses, stood till the fourteenth
century, when it collapsed during an earthquake.

Sailing directions were also numerous. One of them, the *Periplous Pontou Euxeinou* (Voyage round the Black Sea), written in *circa* 90 B.C. by the Greek skipper Artemidorus, played an important part in the Crimean War and far into the nineteenth century. Since charts of the Black Sea, such as there were, proved highly unreliable, the commanders of the western fleets in the Black Sea during the Crimean War often steered according to the instructions of the approximately two thousand years old periplus. A sailing manual of the Mediterranean, the so-called *Stadiasmos* (stades indicator), is also extant. It consists of a series of paragraphs, each one indicating the distance in *paraplous* (i.e. inshore sailing) from one point on the coast to another. Only where larger bays or gulfs permit a considerable shortening of the voyage, or in the case of islands some way offshore, is the *diaplous* (crossing) also given. Few bearings are mentioned in this sailing manual; as a rule they were not necessary, since the mariner was in any case hugging the coast. On the other hand, it is regularly stated whether a place has a harbour or even an anchorage; whether there is protection against the wind; the depth of water; whether the shore slopes gradually or steeply; whether the sea-bed is sandy or rocky; whether shoals or rocks impede navigation; whether there are any landmarks on the coast; whether a city possesses fortifications or towers; whether there is drinking water; whether and where water can be obtained by digging on the beach, etc. Extracts from the *stadiasmos* for the African coast from Leptis towards Carthage exemplify the punctilious exactitude of antique sailing manuals:

93. Approaching from the sea you observe a low land with small islands lying in front of it. On drawing nearer you descry the town beside the sea, a white dune and a beach. The whole town also has a white appearance. It has no harbour. But you will lie safely at Hermaion. Incidentally the town is called Leptis.

95. From Hermaion to Gaphara is 200 stades. The cape offers anchorage on both sides. It has drinking water.

96. From Gaphara to Amaraia is 40 stades. The rampart offers a place of shelter. There is drinking water there. Ploughed fields can be seen beside the river. The river is called Oinalodon . . .

In navigation out of sight of land, the nautical science of the ancients confined itself to stating the direction and distance of the stretches travelled. There was no possibility of measuring speed at sea. There was no log, the mariner had to depend on mere estimation of speed by eye. The modern sailor does this with great accuracy, and one might suppose that the mariner of antiquity was at least his equal in this respect, since he was closer to nature and had more direct contact with the sea than the sailors of our great deep-sea sailing ships. This was not the case, however. For the seamen of antiquity lacked an important prerequisite, which today we take for granted, viz. an exact unit of time. The concept of the hour as the twenty-fourth part of a day was unknown to the ancients. Their day commenced with the rising of the

X. *The coast from Leptis to Carthage according to the* Stadiasmos.

sun and ended when the source of light sank below the dip of the horizon. This day, although its length varied considerably according to the season and the latitude, was stubbornly divided into twelve equal parts, the hours. In high summer their duration was a great deal longer than that of our own hour, in winter, conversely, a great deal shorter. At the end of June the hour in Rome contained approximately seventy-five minutes, but at the end of December only forty-five. And at various latitudes the hours varied even on the same day. On the longest day, for example, the hour in Massilia lasted seventy-six minutes, while in Rhodes it lasted seventy-two. Only when day and night were of equal length, i.e. at the spring and autumn equinoxes, were the hours equal too. That this kind of hour-reckoning, which was still employed in Rome in 1850, would not serve to measure a fixed and invariable period of time was, of course, known to the ancients. They therefore constructed special chronometers, sand or water clocks, in which a given quantity of water or sand flowed from one part to the other in a given time. Such chronometers were also widely used in civil life, as well as pocket sundials roughly the size of a modern pocket watch. Physicians employed these chronometers to calculate their patients' pulse-rate; school hours were measured by them; and courts of law determined with their aid the time allowed for the speeches of plaintiffs and defendants.

Whether such chronometers were also reliable on a ship in motion is questionable. In any case, it proved impossible to set up sundials. Water and sand clocks, though independent of the ship's angle to the sun, were subject in their flow to the motion of the vessel and were generally too inexact. The mariner of antiquity could therefore estimate the ship's speed only approximately; consequently all statements regarding sailing speeds in the ancient world, particularly those laying claim to records, must be treated with reserve. The ancient historians knew this; hence they quote only rough estimates of the over-all sailing speed. Thus Herodotus, for instance, reckons a day's sail in summer at 700 stades, and a night's sail at 600 stades. Scylax, the marine expert of Darius I, gives only 500 stades a day in 500 B.C., while Marinus at the same period reckons from 500 to 1,000 stades according to circumstances. We may take the average distance sailed in twenty-four hours to have been about 1,200 stades or 120 miles, which represents a speed of approximately 5 knots. From Gades to Ostia on a fast sailer and with a favourable wind took six to seven days, from the African coast to the same place about two days, a speed of 6 to 7.5 nautical miles per hour. From this we can see that the speed of antique ships was not much below that of our tramp steamers, though it is naturally far below that of modern liners.

The course was set by the sun during the day and by the stars at night. Since fine weather prevails almost throughout the summer in the Mediterranean zone, there was little need to evolve an instrument for taking bearings—as was to be expected, the discovery of magnetic energy and its importance in determining direction was made, as far as Europe is concerned, in the north. In winter such a direction-indicator would naturally have been eminently necessary in the Mediterranean too. Since the Mediterranean seamen did not possess one, however, they followed the only possible alternative and ceased navigation altogether from October to March. It was not the autumn and winter storms that frightened the antique mariner; he could usually cope with these. What he could not surmount was the difficulty of taking bearings during long overcast periods.

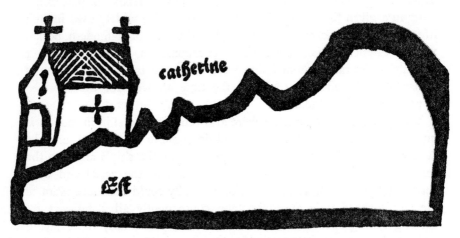

21. *From a sixteenth-century sailing manual. In these late sailing instructions, which were still modelled almost exactly on those of antiquity, little drawings like silhouettes were occasionally added to the descriptions of the run of the coast.*

To a certain extent, soundings could be used as a guide when visibility was poor. Already in antiquity plummets were hollowed out underneath and smeared with tallow, so that samples could be brought up from the seabed. Thus on a voyage to Egypt the skipper knew he was only one day's sail from the Nile delta if mud was drawn up by the plummet from a depth of eleven fathoms. Another means of estimating position is recorded from navigation on the Indian Ocean: when the ship had sailed so far south that the North Star sank below the horizon, birds were released. The ship then sailed in the direction of their flight, in the hope that it would lead to land. Changes in the colour of the sea-water were also used to estimate position. Thus one of the antique sailing manuals for the Indian Ocean contains the instruction to watch for the sudden appearance of light-coloured water in the proximity of the Indus: if followed it would lead to the Indus estuary. In connection with the approach to the port of Barygaza, it is stated that the ship is on the right course and nearing the harbour if it encounters first large black sea-serpents and immediately afterwards small green ones. Records show that this ancient recognition sign was still regarded as valuable in the eighteenth century.

As we see, the antique mariner's means of establishing his position were pitifully inadequate. They could not be developed until geography and astronomy as a whole had attained a certain degree of maturity. An advance was made once a fairly sound method had been evolved for ascertaining the altitude of the sun, and the mariner was able to establish his latitude with some degree of accuracy.

Eratosthenes employed in measuring the altitude of the sun a very ancient procedure, with which the Egyptians were already familiar. A rod pointed at the top, the *gnomon*—the Pharaohs used their obelisks for this—was set up on a flat and open piece of ground; taking its axis as centre, concentric circles were described on the ground; by means of these circles the points were observed at which the shadows of the stick cast by the sun were of the same length in the morning and in the afternoon. The arc between these two points was then bisected, giving the meridian. By measuring the length of the shadow at midday, the altitude of the sun could be calculated from the relation between the height of the gnomon and the length of the shadow. Some centuries later, the Vikings made use of a very similar procedure. It enabled them to find their way successfully, even when it was carried out on board ship. The skippers of the ancient long-distance ships were probably able to use it as well, although there are few or no records to this effect.

Whereas we have only a very superficial knowledge of what Egyptian, Cretan, and Phœnician ships were like, we know a little more about Græco-Roman vessels. In contradistinction to the Egyptian and the first Phœnician craft, Græco-Roman ships were intended from the outset for sea voyages. Built on stocks with slips and runways much like our own, these vessels were keel-boats with firm prow and stern posts, ribs, and planks. External and internal supports gave the keel and posts the firmness necessary for ramming, the principal tactic of naval warfare. All heavy craft were carvel-built, i.e. with their planks meeting flush, so that the outer skin was smooth and the loss of speed by friction reduced to a minimum. The seams were caulked, the whole hull tarred and then sheathed in a metal casing against ship-worm (*Teredo*). The larger ships, at least during the latter centuries B.C., were all built full-decked. This was not so in Homer's day. The very much smaller boats of that time had forecastles and quarterdecks only, and remained undecked amidships. In the later trade-sailers, the deck did not run from stem to stern in one plane. It was built lower amidships to accommodate the rowers, whose oars were supposed to break water as nearly as possible horizontally. Even sailing ships had occasionally to rely upon oar-power. On the poop or quarterdeck was the place for the captain and the privileged passengers, for whom small cabins were here erected. Below this deck was space for luggage and stores, while beneath the middle deck was stowed the ballast, usually heavy, squared stone, and the cargo proper. The forecastle was the crew's place; below deck were the sail-lockers and the cable-stage; the kegs of drinking water also stood here. Round the ship ran the rail, replaced in warships by a breastwork. Smaller vessels merely had fixtures for the attachment of a wash-board.

Although even big trade-ships patently derived their shape from rowing galleys and the occasional necessity of falling back on oar-power for their propulsion, they carried pretty heavy sail. A huge mast bore the enormous square-sail, which was criss crossed with strips of leather for greater strength. An auxiliary mast usually stood on the forecastle, with a smaller, likewise square-rigged, foresail; below the masthead, which in warships was naturally carved to represent Mars, the sailing ships of the imperial era often carried a topsail. It can be seen from their rig that antique ships were dependent upon a following wind. Of course, they could tack as well. But square-rigged ships are always somewhat clumsy in tacking. The hull-construction of the Mediterranean vessels also indicates that they were built to sail on an even keel. As a rule the mariner of antiquity waited for a favourable, i.e. a following, wind before weighing anchor.

Concerning the rowing apparatus of Græco-Roman craft we are not yet clear. We know that Greek and Roman shipwrights very soon endeavoured to avoid the increase in the ship's length necessitated by the greater number of oarsmen and resulting in a bad trim, by placing the rowers in several ranks one above the other and constructing ships that were very high in the water. The most useful vessel of this type was the trireme, a lightly built 'three-decker' 130 to 165 feet long and about 20 feet across, with a crew of some two hundred men. The 170 oarsmen of this ship sat on three decks one above the other. We do not know exactly how the seats were arranged. We hear only that very long oars were used by the top rank of rowers, and that the difficulty of moving these colossal beams, 30 feet or more in length, finally proved insuperable.

There is no doubt, however, that the ancients achieved great things in the field of shipbuilding. We will not discuss here the outright giant

17. Ladies of the Cretan Court. Mural painting from the Palace of Cnossus.

18. The island of Thera in the Aegean. The layer of ash deposited over the island by the Santorin during its eruption in the 15th century B.C. was up to 100 feet deep.

20. Bronze sacrificial vehicle. Heavy mobile 'mixing vessels' were constructed to facilitate the serving of drinks to guests at banquets. This one comes from Cyprus, c.1000 B.C. The winged beasts clearly indicate its Asian origin.

19. Dionysus in his ship. With its projecting ram and beautifully curved stern this early boat from the Exekias Plate (c.540 B.C.) shows how carefully the Greeks, who had advanced from the mainland to the sea, observed. Dionysus's ship is a kind of big brother of the dolphins round it.

ships, e.g. the armoured *Tessarakontere* of King Ptolemy Philopator *circa* 200 B.C., which is supposed to have had a length of 426 feet and 6,500 tons burden; or the *Alexandria* of Hiero II of Syracuse, which is alleged to have been constructed by Archimedes and whose tons burden has been estimated at 4,500. The normal passenger ship, the ordinary merchantman, was of no mean dimensions. Thus Lucian writes that the Alexandrian wheat-sailer, *Isis*, was 180 feet long, 45 feet wide, with a

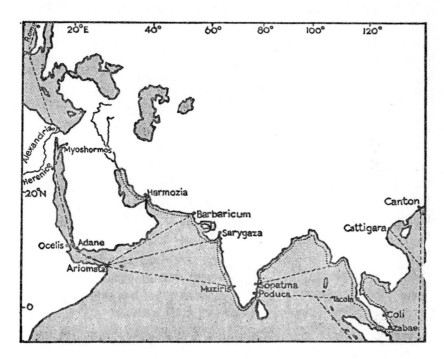

XI. *Routes for sea traffic between Rome and China in* circa *100 B.C.*

depth of 43 feet 6 inches. If we compute the tonnage from these figures, it gives a displacement of 2,672 tons. It is possible that the ship's carpenter from whom Lucian made his inquiries exaggerated a bit, and that the *Isis* did not exceed 2,000 tons. At that she would not have been exceptionally large. As is well known, Paul relates in the Apostles that there were 276 souls aboard the ship that took him to Rome, and the Jewish historian Josephus tells at about the same period of a passenger list of 600, and this on a vessel that also carried cargo: both ships must have been of a large type.

We are also exactly informed concerning the vessels on which the Roman emperors brought Egyptian obelisks across the Mediterranean.

Pliny tells us that the obelisk which stands today in front of St. Peter's in Rome and weighs about 500 tons, was borne on a wheat-ship that also had 1,300 tons of corn on board. Accordingly this vessel must have reached a displacement of approximately 2,500 tons. The ships that brought the Flaminian and Lateran obelisks to Rome must have been of an equal size.

The great mass of Græco-Roman ships, which were mostly confined to inshore sailing, were naturally appreciably smaller. Like the Phœnician ships, they must have had a displacement of 200 to 400 tons, doubtless quite sufficient for the Mediterranean. For the prime incentive to increasing a ship's dimensions, the desire to carry more cargo, was not operative for coastal sailing. Here the wares could easily be divided amongst a great number of ships. This brought with it a division of the risk, which was naturally greater than today. But for long-distance voyages, from Egypt to Italy for example, big ships were of course preferred. For purposes of international traffic it was no doubt more economic in the ancient world, as today, to use only such ships as could carry in one voyage all the goods accumulated in a port. If only half the goods to be transported were loaded, either the ship had to make the voyage twice, or a second ship had to be used. Thus either double the time or twice the crew was required to transport a single cargo. On top of this there were the losses incurred through longer ware-housing, taxes, rent, etc.—burdens as oppressive to the merchant of antiquity as to the modern freighter.

This was of little significance in the Mediterranean, but of great importance in traffic with the Far East, which, as we have seen, was tied to the monsoons. As a rule, ships sailing to India set off at the end of June on a south-easterly course from Myoshormos or Berenice on the north of the Red Sea. After a month they reached Ocelis near Bab el Mandeb; from there they sailed with the moonsoon across the open sea to India in about forty days. Thus they were at sea longer than Columbus on his voyage to America! They set out in December, with the north-east wind, on the homeward journey, which generally took longer than the voyage out. The length of time required for each of these journeys makes it probable that fairly large ships were employed on this run. Together with Sigerus, north of Bombay, and Muziris, the modern Cranganore, where pepper, drugs, dyes, and precious stones were taken on board, one of the principal ports for the Egypt–India run was Barygaza (probably from the Indian Bharukhatsha), the present-day Broach. The harbour on the River Narbada, which is now silted up, was in antiquity the main export centre for cotton, and the import harbour for Greek wine, *objets d'art,* and industrial products. In consequence of the silting of the Narbada, which began in the first century A.D., the sailing manual for India, mentioned above, gave very precise anchoring instructions.

It also contains precise instructions for other Indian ports. Attention is particularly drawn to the exceptional ebb and flow of the tide, which is still noticeable on parts of the Indian coast.

This exact knowledge shows how carefully the far-away land had been studied. And the many coins of the first imperial period found in India reveal that commerce between Europe and the eastern sun land must have been very brisk. Ceylon, called Taprobane after its capital Tambapanni and considered by the ancients to be the northern tip of a continent that stretched far to the south, was less well known. What little knowledge of Ceylon existed was derived from the brief reports of Alexander the Great's geographers; but its name was spoken with great respect in Rome, probably on account of the fabulous wealth it was stated in these reports to possess. Hence the envoys sent to Rome from Ceylon by the king of this dream island—*circa* A.D. 50–5—were received with lively interest and plied with questions.

This strange story began when a captain on the Arabia route in the pay of Annius Plocamus, a Roman millionaire, was blown off his course. Annius Plocamus had farmed the Indian Ocean customs of the Roman Empire, and his captain, a freed slave, who doubtless drew a percentage on his takings, clearly had the task, similar to that of a modern customs and excise patrol, of scouring the Indian Ocean for freighters that had slipped through the net of the seaport customs authorities. This was no doubt a very lucrative job. At all events, when a cyclone blew him to Ceylon he had on board a vast quantity of money coined at widely different places. Pliny, who recounts this adventure, relates that the Sultan of Taprobane was very surprised that all denarii 'were of the same weight, although the different images stamped on them made it evident that they were issued under various rulers'.

This continuity in matters of state was bound to interest an oriental ruler. Furthermore, there must long have been curiosity in Ceylon, the ancient outpost of the world silk-supply, the country of origin of magnificent gems and many precious spices, to learn more about the great realm in the far west from which so much minted gold had poured in for so many centuries. Hence the Sultan, without more ado, appointed four noble Rajahs from his immediate entourage to be his envoys to Rome, sent them aboard the ship of his Roman guest, and told them to head for Rome with all speed.

And they did indeed reach the capital of the world. At least the
report given by Pliny shows unequivocally that the four brown men
in splendid raiment must have come from regions close to the equator.
'Whilst they were amongst us they were astonished by the Pole Star
and the Pleiades, as though the sky were something quite new to
them', relates Pliny, manifestly very surprised himself. And then he
continues:

Most of all, however, they were amazed that in our country all shadows
fall to the north and not, as in theirs, to the south; and moreover that the
sun does not rise to the right and sink to the left, as in their country, but
exactly the reverse . . . Of India they recounted that beyond the Emodian
Mountains [Himalayas] lived the Seres, with whom they traded . . . These
latter were tall, with fair hair, blue eyes, and very rough voices not well
adapted to speech.

It is obvious that these blue-eyed, fair-haired, tall men with whom
the people of Taprobane traded were not Chinese, but members of
some Indo-European people—possibly the Yue-chi tribe, whose men-
folk had brought silk across the Himalayas to India since time immemorial. The name 'Seres', which is derived from the Chinese word
for silk and means in Greek and Latin 'Chinese', must be taken here
as a trade, rather than an ethnic, designation—something like 'silk
merchants'. For despite the undeniable dash of Indo-European blood
in both the Chinese and the Japanese ethnic groups, there are no fair-
haired, blue-eyed Chinamen! This proves that silk was brought to
India not only by sea, but also by land, however incredible this may
appear when we think of the enormous mountain barrier that shuts off
the north of India. This land route was patently of extreme antiquity.
Nearchus already comments on the presence of *serica dermata*, Chinese
silken garments, in India. We shall hear more of this presently.

From Barygaza and Muziris, the connection with the Far East was
extended by stages round the southern tip of India to Poducta (Pondi-
cherry) and Sopatma (Madras). From there the route went across the
Bay of Bengal to Further India (Burma) and then along the coasts of
Indo-China and China, or via the Sunda Strait and Borneo, to Canton
and Cattigara, probably the modern Hangchow. Oddly enough, these
first contacts between European and Chinese culture remained without
any visible consequences for the West. It is certain, however, that
Westerners reached the country of Çin, the home of the Seres, as early
as the beginning of the second century A.D. When south-east China
was united into an empire in 250 B.C. under the Ts'in (or Ch'in)

dynasty, Indian seafarers called it China, the Arabs Çin, and the Greeks Sinai. The Greeks already knew north China as the land from which silk came, through central-Asian trading peoples. The Greek words for silk, *serikon*, and for the Chinese, *Seres*, were both derived from *ser*, the Chinese for silk. Similarly, the Arabs distinguish South China, Çin, from North China, Cathay, a Mongolian loan word that probably goes back to the Tungusic Kitans, a tribe which invaded China at the beginning of the tenth century. This distinction appears to have been adopted by the Romans. Thus Ptolemy writes of Asia in the second century A.D.: 'The inhabited part of our earth borders in the east upon unknown land which is peopled by the eastern nations of Asia Minor, the Sinæ and the nations of Serica.'

It is significant that the first extant reports of direct contact between the West and the Far East are of Chinese origin. They occur in the *Hou-han-shu*, the official annals of the Later Han dynasty compiled in the fifth century A.D. Here it states:

The ruler of the land of Shan in the first year of Yungning [A.D. 120] once more sent an envoy, who brought with him musicians and jugglers when he was received by the Emperor. The latter were able to swallow fire and could cast spells; they could bind their limbs fast and then free them without help from others. They were able to interchange the heads of cows and horses, and possessed such skill that they danced with a thousand balls. They said of themselves: 'We are men of the Western Sea. That is the same as Ta-ts'in [the Roman Empire, particularly Syria]. Ta-ts'in is reached by travelling through the south-west of the land of Shan.'

We may consider this nothing but a curiosity. The second record, however, is in the form of an official communiqué describing what purported—not quite truthfully, as we shall see—to be a solemn embassy from the Emperor Marcus Aurelius to the Emperor of China. It also comes from the *Hou-han-shu* and runs:

The land of Ta-ts'in is very great. It has many cities and embraces a large number of subject countries. The houses are of stone, and there are numerous inns in the streets. The inhabitants of Ta-ts'in cut their hair and wear fine clothes. In war they take with them drummers, banners and tents. Their capital is 100 *li* in circumference and contains ten palaces, each one 10 *li* from the next. The people of Ta-ts'in possess many gems and much gold and silver. They have grown very rich, in particular through trade with the Parthians and Indians. Hence all the costly things and all the rare things which are in other countries originate from this realm. The people of Ta-ts'in are open and staunch by nature. Their merchants are upright men and never have two prices. Corn is always cheap. The State possesses a well-filled treasury.

The embassies of neighbouring countries are brought from the frontier posts to the capital; they receive gifts of gold coins. The kings of Ta-ts'in are supposed always to have wished to send embassies to China. But the Parthians wanted to keep the silk trade to themselves, and therefore Ta-ts'in did not succeed in establishing contact with us. This lasted till the ninth year of the Yenshi Period, when King An-tun sent envoys bringing ivory, rhinoceros horn and tortoise shell as gifts. Since this time direct intercourse has existed with Ta-ts'in. Amongst the gifts which the envoys brought there were no gems, in spite of the wealth of Ta-ts'in, which leads us to suppose that the envoys appropriated these to themselves.

The chronicler's astonishment, and the humorous surmise which he adds to his account of the poverty of the gifts from the Emperor of Rome, probably hold the key to this remarkable story: the visitors were obviously not envoys from the Emperor Marcus Aurelius—whose cognomen was, in fact, Antoninus—but Roman merchants, who gave themselves out to be envoys from the neighbouring and friendly power, Ta-ts'in, in order to be received and so have the opportunity of making the contacts necessary for the better discharge of their business. A trick that was hardly likely to be found out and must frequently have been employed! This is the only possible explanation for the poverty of the gifts brought to the Chinese Emperor. In view of the immense efforts made by official envoys during these centuries to do justice to their countries, it is quite unthinkable that an Imperial Roman embassy should really have been sent to China with such wretched gifts.

Furthermore, there is no mention of any such embassy in any Western source, and there is no reason why Marcus Aurelius should have sent to the Emperor of China confidential emissaries whose visit was not recorded in the State annals. All the same, this embassy may not be entirely a fraud. The Chinese annalist's report was not made out till several centuries after the event, and we must make allowances for some obscurity having crept in. At all events, whether this embassy was genuine or false, it is certain that Roman merchants really did reach China as early as the beginning of the second century A.D. It is equally certain, however, that geographical knowledge was not greatly enriched thereby. Although fairly lively trade relations may have existed between the Roman Empire and the Far East until the end of the third century —attested by the frequent finds of Roman coins in China—these connections were broken off again before any close spiritual contact could take place between the world empires of the West and the Far East.

4

The real reason for these relations, for these efforts to make contact with the remote and enigmatic land in the east, which were started long before the Christian era, lay forty-seven centuries back in a sudden flash of insight that struck the Empress Si-li-shi, the head wife of Hwang-ti, the 'Yellow Lord' and the emperor whom Chinese legend credits with initiating the cultivation of silk in the Middle Kingdom. One 'fortunate day', as the ancient annalists of the Sons of Heaven write, while she was walking with the ladies of the court in the imperial gardens, her glance happened to fall upon a mulberry tree beside the path, whose fruits were gently moving. Suddenly a beautiful, iridescent butterfly rose from one of the little balls, which Si-li-shi had taken to be the fruit of the mulberry tree, and flew away. Curiously, the empress examined this remarkable phenomenon more closely, and to her amazement she observed that these 'fruits' were balls of the finest animal fibre. With her sensitive fingers she soon found the beginning of the web; cool and silvery it wound round her hands, and soon they were entirely wrapped in the 4,400 yards of silk thread which the horned silkworms spin round themselves in their cocoons.

This happened at a time when the Chinese were still without clothes. Instead they wore leaves or bird-skins, and in the ancient temple of the 'Three Majesties' at Shantung, one could formerly see for oneself how badly off for clothes they were in the Middle Kingdom prior to Si-li-shi. Whereas Hwang-ti stood proudly in splendid silken apparel befitting his high rank, his two predecessors were still clad in grass kilts and a few miserable leaves.

How they must have frozen, poor fellows! What a good thing it straight away occurred to Si-li-shi to have the cocoon thread wound onto a bobbin and taken to a weaver's loom. And what a good thing that Hwang-ti did not stand in the way, but issued an imperial edict ordering the people to learn the art of silk spinning and weaving, 'so that they should have clothes and no one need any longer suffer from chilblains and cracked hands'.

Although it has long been established that the invention of silk weaving in China is much older and may go as far back as the fourth millennium, the Chinese stuck to their legend, elevated Si-li-shi amongst the gods as the 'Ancestress of the Thread' and revered her as one of the stars of the Scorpion.

In the period that followed, the new fabric was popularized by all
the means of imperial propaganda, and even today the breeding of
silkworms and the manufacture of silk does not only mean bread and
livelihood for twenty to thirty million people: it is almost a cult. Was
not silk a gift from the gods? Was not its fabrication from the bodily
product of the dirty-white, yellowish-brown striped worm *Bombyx
mori* therefore a sacred activity? So sacred that it was permissible only
to the chosen people of the Middle Kingdom, but not to the barbarians
all round, from whom the miracle of its genesis must at all costs be
concealed!

But this intense secrecy itself—the punishment for espionage or
betrayal was death—caught men's interest, almost more than the silk
itself. And so caravan after caravan came from the West, men and beasts
in a long, unbroken chain. They came with ivory and Tyrian purple,
with frankincense and spice, with gold and amber, with rare delicacies
and costly furs. They fought their way for six months through the
Tarim basin; faced the combat with death from thirst as they passed
through sand deserts and salt marshes; they surmounted the high passes
of the Pamirs with racing pulses and agonizing shortness of breath;
they came by ship, thousands of miles across the open sea; they paid
any price—for silk. The trans-Asian trade route mentioned by Herodotus, which Alexander the Great sought to bring under his dominion,
along which Marco Polo travelled, now rustled, crinkled and sparkled
along all its 6,000 miles with silk on its way to Europe. This began
around 300 B.C.—at least this is the approximate date of the earliest
written records of the import of silk into Europe. But it continued only
so long as was permitted by the Parthians, an Iranian equestrian people
who held the territory between the Caspian and the Persian Gulf.
When the Bactrian kingdom of the Seleucids collapsed in *circa* 150 B.C.,
the Parthians blockaded the land communication between Europe and
Asia which had been established by the Persians and kept open by
Alexander the Great; Seleucia on the Tigris and Antioch in Syria grew
rich on silk; the Parthians, immediate neighbours of the sacred silk
land, considered themselves for a space the lords of the world, because
they were the middlemen in the silk trade—to their immense profit,
for Rome had been wearing silk since the century before Augustus.
A pound of this material costs £200, moans Caligula later, and Marcus
Aurelius refuses his wife the coveted silk dress—because he cannot
afford it!

European artifice now further 'refined' silk. The isle of Cos in the
Ægean produced fabulously beautiful women, women who liked to

wear silk, and silk that did not conceal its wearer's form as did the closely-woven Chinese silk, but simply veiled it. So the material imported from China was picked apart into its individual threads and re-woven into a gossamer-thin gauze, as light and transparent as a spider's web. This was worn on Cos in the Ægean, it was worn in Rome, and very soon it was exported to the Orient. The men of the West, for their part, wore brocade interwoven with gold and dyed purple in Tyre if they could afford it. 'Thus continual pilgrimages have to be made to the end of the world', writes Pliny, 'that our ladies may envelop their beauty in transparent veils, and the men expend their possessions for brocade.' And as a fervent advocate of 'Buy Roman' propaganda, he adds in another passage: 'At a conservative estimate our imports from India, China and Arabia cost a hundred million sesterces per annum. This is what we pay for our luxury and for our ladies.' He overlooks the fact that this is only the *monetary* loss suffered by the Roman Empire. Amber, metals, glass, wool, linen, etc., in brief a large proportion of Rome's exports, were given in exchange for Chinese silk and must be added to the debit side, increasing Europe's adverse balance of trade.

Finally the inevitable happened: the State went bankrupt, as it was bound to do if it spent more than it earned. It reached this point in A.D. 300 under Diocletian. But whereas the private individual calls a meeting of creditors in such circumstances, the State employs other means. It cancels its obligations by bringing about inflation. We hear the most pitiable accounts of despairing fathers, whose laboriously accumulated capital, intended as an insurance for wife and children, vanished like a puff of smoke. We hear amazed statements that the chicken which cost a drachma a day or two ago had suddenly risen to thirty thousand drachmas or more; or that a mortgage of three million eight hundred thousand drachmas could be obtained in A.D. 307 on a house which was worth two thousand drachmas in A.D. 267. Just as some countries during modern inflations have reckoned in billions, so the Diocletian era reckoned in thousands and millions of drachmas. As was to be expected, the State had recourse to laying down maximum prices. The famous *edictum de rerum venalium pretiis* (edict concerning purchasable commodities)—which has served as a model for all later price regulations, which was buttressed by threats of severe punishment, and remained as fruitless as modern regulations of the same sort —fixed to a fraction the price of every conceivable commodity and service: provisions and slaves, wages, doctors' fees, hire of vehicles, including the *dormitoria*—the *wagons lit* of the ancient world—the bills of shoemakers and tailors; in short, nothing escaped the Argus eyes of the State.

The fact that trade with eastern Asia was carried out not only with chinking coins, but also with barter goods, undermined the Middle Kingdom's traditional policy of seclusion from the rest of the world. To be sure, traders from the west and south did not often set foot on Chinese soil, not in these early times at any rate; but trade by barter presupposed on both sides an exact knowledge of each other's wares. If Chinese customs officials and dealers entered thirteen different qualities and types of incense in their registers, from the inferior East-African incense, through the low sandy-brown qualities of Arabia to the select product of the incense trees of Hadramat, they *must* have possessed at least some rough idea of the countries of origin.

There was nothing in that distant, early world that was not exported to China. From India came gems, diamonds, pearls, attar of roses, hemp and sandalwood; from Persia and the Parthians caravans bore quicksilver, beeswax, rock-crystal, corals and storax; the Spice Islands (Moluccas) sent pepper, so dear that it was worth its weight in rubies, camphor, nutmeg, cinnamon and benzoin, together with parrots and coconuts; finally, the Arabs brought ivory, rhinoceros horn and, above all, negro slaves. Amongst the wealthy Chinese these 'devil slaves' were especially sought after, and the Arabs did such good business with these 'wares' that they maintained their own settlement in Canton from A.D. 300. It is true that China adopted a very reserved attitude towards all foreigners. But some degree of knowledge of the lands of the 'barbarians' cannot have failed to spread gradually amongst the Sons of Heaven.

Despite these long-maintained and lively connections with the rich silk land in the Far East, the latter lay as though behind a curtain as far as antiquity's geographical knowledge was concerned. Hence the description given below from the *Periplus Maris Erythræi*, a sailing manual compiled in A.D. 80 by a Greek merchant-skipper resident in Berenice on the Red Sea, which also dealt with India and China, remained unchallenged in all its vagueness until the time of Marco Polo. There we read:

Beyond India the sea ends somewhere at a land. And in the interior of this land there is a large city called Thinae. From there wool [cotton], silk embroideries, and silken fabrics come to Barygaza through Bactria. It is, however, not easy to reach Thin; and but few people come thence. The country lies immediately beneath the Little Bear. This means that these regions lie amongst the most remote areas on the Black and Caspian Seas . . .

This vagueness makes it difficult to trace with precision the route to China followed in the ancient world. In part, at least during the period round A.D. 100 when the Chinese Emperor Ho-ti reopened the old silk road, travellers must have used the ancient land route, which, as we know, had been opened up countless ages ago. Of course, the hostility

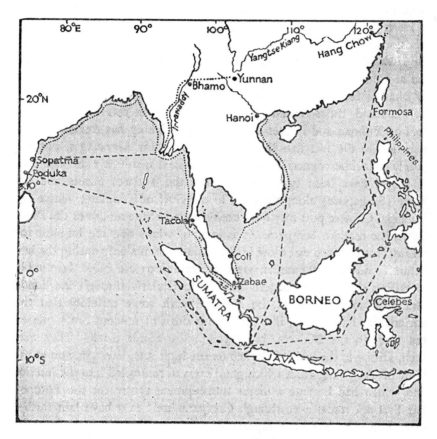

XII. *Sea traffic between India and China. Because of wind conditions it was only in late autumn and winter that sea traffic from India to China passed through the Malacca Straits. As a rule it went through the Sunda Straits. If Cattigara is located roughly on the site of modern Hangchow, ships to China would mostly have sailed east of Borneo along the Philippines to the north. To get to Hanoi, on the other hand, they would have sailed west of Borneo. A shorter route to the Chinese interior was along the Irrawaddy to Bhamo, whence a caravan road, roughly in the tracks of the modern Burma Road, led into the Yunnan region. It is a reasonable conjecture that the Yangtse Kiang was also used at an early period for Chinese trade.*

of the Parthians rendered this route extremely difficult and costly for the Greeks and Romans, and when access to the Orient was ultimately rendered easier at the beginning of the second century A.D. by the successful conclusion of the Parthian War, the Tarim Basin had ceased to be passable owing to the attacks of savage Mongolian horsemen. From now on preference was probably given to the sea route.

Here there were two alternatives. The quicker, but doubtless very laborious and strenuous way went first across the sea to the mouth of the Irrawaddy in Burma. Here the traveller changed to river boats and the arduous way led up the Irrawaddy through mountainous districts to Bhamo; from here, roughly along the route taken by the modern Burma Road, there existed a very ancient caravan connection into the area of Yunnan and farther north. Richard Hennig has recently drawn attention to the fact that this route offered many advantages. For the purely maritime connection with the Far East manifestly did not run, as might have been supposed, through the Malacca Straits and via Zabæ (Singapore) along the coast to the Gulf of Tongking, where the principal Chinese port may have been situated at the mouth of the River Serus, the modern Song-koi. As is known, winds that can be used for sailing from west to east blow in the Malacca Straits only during the late autumn and winter months; weather conditions are more favourable to sailing through the eastern islands, particularly through the Sunda Straits. It may, therefore, be assumed with some certainty that the ancient Far East sailers, like the sailing ships of modern times, passed not through the Malacca, but through the Sunda Straits. They may then, sailing to the west of Borneo on the high seas, have gone on to the Gulf of Tongking, from which good caravan routes led into the interior and which had become a major transhipment centre for the Europe–Far East sea trade, even though Cattigara itself may have lain farther east. The view has been repeatedly advanced that Cattigara must be sought on the Hang Chow Bay, into which a branch of the Yangtse Kiang flowed until the third century. If this is correct, our antique mariners may have come through the Sunda Straits, round the east of Borneo, and along the Philippines—an impressive achievement that inspires deep respect.

## 5

We have greatly anticipated in our narrative and skipped several centuries. This was not by accident. For if we now turn to the West and to the question of whether voyages on the same immense scale as

were already made on the eastern seas in early historical times may also
have been carried out on the Atlantic, we must first discuss the preliminary question of whether the necessary technical prerequisites
existed for such long-range enterprises on this stormy and unpredic-

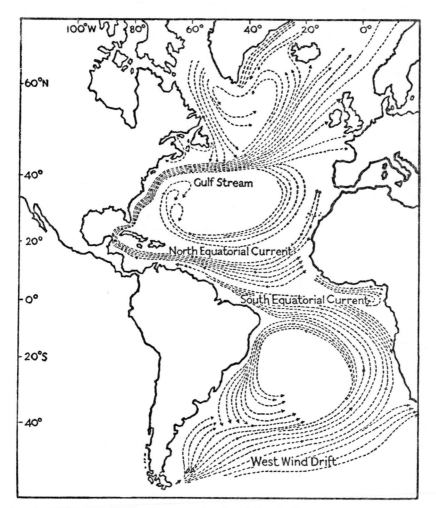

*XIII. Currents in the Atlantic Ocean.*

table ocean, i.e. whether the ancients possessed ships capable of braving
the western seas. In view of what was achieved on the Indian Ocean,
this question must be answered in the affirmative even for very early
times; everything suggests that classical antiquity was technically
capable of sailing far out into the Atlantic, and perhaps even crossing

it. Such distant voyages may well have taken place more than once involuntarily, as a result of ships being blown off course by persistent heavy gales. The crossing of the Atlantic in a folding-boat in 1930, the voyage across this ocean in an open rowing-boat fifty years ago, the recent conquest of the Pacific on a raft clearly prove what is possible to an experienced and courageous seaman, and that enormous distances can be traversed even with such tiny craft. During the last few decades the Atlantic has several times been crossed in one-man yachts. Since they can be made nowadays, it is clear that these crossings were not impossible in ancient times and no doubt they were frequent long before the beginning of the Christian era. There is no reliable documentary evidence of this, however, and at present we do not know of any firmly attested discovery of America prior to Columbus other than by the Norsemen.

A glance at a map of the winds and currents of the Atlantic makes this appear surprising. The trade winds and the drift impart to the water masses of this sea a current that moves in one direction for thousands of miles at a speed often exceeding 1¼ knots, constituting a kind of moving bridge from continent to continent. Once entrusted to it the mariner would be carried across the desolate waters of the Atlantic. He would first have to know of its existence, and secondly be convinced that he would find land on the other side of the Ocean.

This conviction, however, was undoubtedly very widespread throughout the ancient world. On the one hand, there were physical reasons for holding this belief. As long as the world was deemed to be a disc encircled by the waters of the *Okeanos*, it was logically necessary to suppose a shore beyond the *Okeanos*, whose slopes enclosed its waters like an embankment. Hence there *must* be land beyond the turbulent expanse of this enormous river.

On the other hand, it accorded perfectly with the notions of the afterworld current among Mediterranean peoples since time immemorial. Somewhere in the west, beyond the sea, where the sun sank to rest each evening, must lie the Kingdom of the Dead, the home of departed souls. Ancient Egypt let its dead voyage in a ferry of the gods across the still river of the Last Things into the Beyond. Gilgamesh, the legendary king of Uruk, crossed the waters of death; and Circe informed Odysseus that beyond the Ocean spread the realm of Persephone, the goddess of death.

When the Greeks thrust forward from their ancient continental home to the Mediterranean, the notion of an afterworld beyond the western seas was manifestly unknown to them. They thought of the Kingdom of the Dead as situated in subterranean realms. For a time the two concepts seem to have existed side by side: the dark Kingdom of the Dead beneath the earth, and the other world beyond the Ocean waves. Then vague rumours began to reach Hellas to the effect that the islands discovered by bold mariners outside the Pillars of Hercules were by no means spectral lands, overcast and grey, but smiling, peaceful and fertile; so that the ancient oriental notion was now overlaid by beautiful tales of Elysium, the Fields of the Blessed. Hence Proteus promises Menelaus:

You will not meet your fate and die in Argos where the horses graze. Instead, the immortals will send you to the Elysian plain at the world's end, to join red-haired Rhadamanthus in the land where living is made easiest for mankind, where no snow falls, no strong winds blow and there is never any rain, but day after day the West Wind's tuneful breeze comes in from Ocean to refresh its folk. (Penguin Classics. Trans. E. V. Rieu, p. 78.)

Henceforth the 'Blessed Isles' are a recurrent theme in classical poetry, and it is probable that the many more or less veiled references in Greek literature to far-away lands of the west beyond the Ocean all go back, in the last analysis, to this ancient belief in the Elysian Fields.

This is patently still so with Plato, who, in *Timaius*, makes the priests of Sais relate, after a lengthy account of Atlantis, that beyond this island, 'at the edge of the Ocean, lay a great continent'. This great continent is not, of course, America: it is the outcome of the reasoning referred to above according to which there must be land round the Ocean to hold its waters in place like an embankment. The notion of Elysium was also involved, and later the perspectives opened up by the Pythagorean hypothesis, which was naturally known to Plato, that the world was not a disc, but a sphere.

His pupil Aristotle (384–322 B.C.) expressed the unequivocal opinion that the earth was a sphere, and that a single sea extended from the Pillars of Hercules to India. From the new notion of the earth as a sphere it was immediately deduced that the 'embankment' surrounding the Ocean, the old Elysian Fields, was the east coast of Asia.

A few decades after Aristotle, Eratosthenes (275–195 B.C.) added an eminently modern touch to this already very up-to-date conception of the world. He states: 'Only that area of the earth in which we ourselves live and which is known to us is called by us *Oikoumene*, inhabited world. But there may well be another, or even several more inhabited continents in the temperate zone.' And supported by his measurement of the number of degrees between Alexandria and Syene (Aswan), Eratosthenes calculates that the continent of the Old World comprises about a third of the circumference of the earth; so that the distance between the eastern Asiatic coast and Spain is approximately 240° longitude, which is not far from the truth.

An astonishing fact. How did Eratosthenes come to this opinion? How did he manage to shake himself free from the authority of Aristotle, which was unconditionally accepted until well on into the Middle Ages? For Plato's great pupil, Europe was and remained the world; precisely Western man was and remained the centre and measure of all things. Consequently, Aristotle expressly declared the existence of other continents to be impossible. What prompted Eratosthenes to undertake this geographical secularization of the *Oikoumene*?

We find it hard to imagine that there was nothing more behind it than a mere hypothesis. We feel inclined to believe that knowledge of some sort had reached the great Greek scholar concerning the New World, which, in his day as in ours, was linked to Europe by the ocean bridge of the Atlantic and continually sent the Old World fresh signs of its existence.

Did some hint of America really reach Eratosthenes? Oskar Peschel, one of the founders of modern geography, once said that since time immemorial 'the two banks of the Atlantic valley announced their presence to one another'. A study of the biography of Columbus will show us what a quantity of solid proofs of the existence of a not too distant continent to the west of the Ocean were available to the Genoese discoverer, and convince us that Oskar Peschel was right. There is no doubt that America did everything in its power to acquaint the far-away easterners of its corporeal existence.

Naturally, this was also the case in antiquity. Hence we come across passages in classical literature from which we may infer the arrival in Europe of such envoys from the New World in very ancient times. In his interesting, if not always convincing book on Atlantis, A. Braghine draws attention to an important report dating back to the historian Pausanias (*circa* A.D. 150). Pausanias states that far west of the Ocean there lies a group of islands whose inhabitants are red-skinned and whose hair is like that of the horse. Unless we assume that both details, the red skin and the lank horse's hair, are the products of Pausanias's imagination, this report cannot be explained otherwise than as referring to American Indians.

Could Pausanias really have had any knowledge of the inhabitants of America? Is there any way of proving it?

**21.** Alexander the Great. This mosaic, found at Pompeii, was made in c.310 B.C., about thirteen years after his death.

**22.** The Pamir Plateau. Alexander once crossed these huge, bleak mountains to the wonderland of India.

23. The side of a trireme with oarsmen. Relief, c.450 B.C. Excessively long ships have a bad trim. To increase their size ancient sea-going vessels were therefore built higher instead of longer. The trireme was invented, a ship with three tiers of oars one above the other, which was the predominating type of craft until the 2nd century B.C. We still do not know exactly how the seating was arranged on these vessels.

24. Roman copper ingot bearing the image of an ox, the oldest form of Roman money, 4th century B.C. Payment was originally made in cattle. Linguistic formations also bring out the close connection between cattle and money in early Roman life: *pecus* means cattle, *pecunia* means money.

Pausanias himself keeps silent as to the source of his knowledge. But his somewhat earlier colleague, the Roman chronicler Pomponius Mela, who lived during the time of Cæsar, provides just the information we are after.

. . . Besides the natural philosophers and Homer, Cornelius Nepos, a more recent and credible historian, also asserts that the earth is surrounded by sea. He names Q. Metellus Celer as his authority for this. The latter reports the following: When he was proconsul in Gaul [62 B.C.] several Indians were presented to him as a gift by the king of the Suevans. On inquiring where these men had come from, he was told that they came from the Indian seas, having been carried by high winds across the intervening seas and finally cast up on the shores of Germany . . .

It is evident that these 'Indians' no more came from India than the copper-coloured natives whom Columbus found when he discovered America, and whom he too designated Indians. Whatever lay beyond the Ocean was called India. The mariners of India seem altogether to have contributed little to the discovery of the world, and there is no record of Indian ships ever having gone far outside the Indian Ocean. According to the geographical position Pomponius Mela's 'Indians' can only have come from America.

Besides manned and unmanned boats, many other things were naturally cast up on the shores of western Europe: pieces of wreckage, bamboo canes, 'sea-beans'—as we know, the seed of the *Entada gigas*, a creeper found on the Caribbean seaboard—foreign woods of high buoyancy, probably logs of the *cuipo* tree from South America, and similar objects. This flotsam and jetsam no doubt strengthened the existing hypothesis of a continent in the far west.

The view has recently been advanced, with the statements of Pomponius Mela and other classical authors in mind, that all these landings took place in northern latitudes and were made by Eskimoes. We cannot analyse this proposition here, but it is worthy of mention that one of Plutarch's (A.D. 46–120) reports does in fact relate to the far north. In his dialogue *On the Face in the Moon* Plato recounts that far west in the Ocean, in the latitude of Britain, lie some groups of islands beyond which, at the edge of the sea, stretches a great continent. These islands—and now follows the remark that renders this apparently fantastic report noteworthy—are distinguished by the fact that during a period of thirty days they have almost unbroken sunshine and light. During the night the sun ceases to be visible for about one hour, but it does not become quite dark—the western sky glows in a luminous twilight.

This *cannot* be an invention, but points unambiguously to an island to the west of Britain in the vicinity of the Arctic Circle. Such sober pieces of information as this are not products of the poetic imagination; the poet needs more exciting material to work on. There is not much point in trying to find out which island Plutarch might have meant. But there is no denying that his report gives one pause. According to the lie of the land, the great continent of which he speaks can really only be America.

At least we must admit that the reports cited here, which can be supplemented by a hundred corresponding quotations from the works of Strabo, Seneca, Ælianus and other classical geographers, are staggering. If we recall that long before the beginning of our era numerous antique ships ventured across the Indian Ocean, on a route that led some 1,250 miles over the open sea, i.e. about twenty-five days without sight of land, we must ask ourselves what serious difficulties would have impeded competent seamen if they had one day sailed westward with the north-east trade wind from west Africa, which they knew well, in order to reach India by this route. The Canaries and Azores had long been known by the time of the birth of Christ—even if this knowledge was later lost again—and if we take account of the fact that the north-east trade wind begins immediately west of Cape Verde and that it is sufficiently strong and constant to carry a ship a long way out, we must conclude that it is possible America was reached at an early period.

Up to the present, however, there is no unequivocal proof that this did actually happen. It is true that repeated efforts have been made, especially by Portuguese geographers, to produce unassailable evidence that the Atlantic was crossed long before Columbus. But probable as this is—we shall hear more about it in the next chapter—the arguments for it are as yet neither unimpeachable nor compelling. As regards navigation and shipbuilding technique, the possibility of conquering the Atlantic Ocean already existed in classical antiquity—there is no doubt of that. As long, however, as the proposition holds good: *Quod non est in actis, non est in mundo*—in plain English, what isn't written in black and white didn't happen at all—so long will voyages to America prior to Columbus, at least on the part of Mediterranean peoples, remain more or less hypothetical.

AN ancient legend was current in Temixtitan, Emperor Monte-zuma's magnificent city in the Valley of Mexico, an ancient legend that had been as unwilling to fall silent under the Toltecs, the erstwhile lords of the country, now poor fishermen and peasants, as under the mighty barons from Aztlan, who now ruled the land. A legend which the priesthood had not been able to exterminate, no matter how many twitching human hearts they offered on the altars of the god Huitzilopochtli during the centuries in which the Aztecs, who had emigrated from Aztlan, had been rulers of their new flourishing and fertile home. Now that had come to pass which the wise seers had prophesied and which was written in the sacred books for all to read: Far in the east the light-god Quetzalcoatl, born of a virgin, arose and set about recovering and making his own again the land of which the gods of the Aztecs had dispossessed him. And with him, the white god of light and of the clear, bright air, there approached a host of radiant celestial beings mounted upon four-footed dragon gods from whose nostrils the breath came forth like steam, who sped through the air like a hurricane, and whose manes and tails waved like the plumes of smoke that issued from the mouth of the ice-clad fire-mountain Popocatépetl. Thunder and lightning, said the scouts, the white gods bore in their hands; they themselves with their own eyes had seen many a brave man lay down his life before the thunder shot by the enraged white gods out of long tubes. There was no remedy against them, if their friendship could not be won.

A presentiment of approaching downfall ran through the land. The poets sang:

How sad! How heavy!
I know that our kingdom is sinking,
The stars are smoking,
The city of books, of flowers
Will soon be no more!

From everywhere menacing omens were reported. Evil comets appeared in the sky; temples burst into flames; the sacred lake of

Texcoco suddenly frothed up over its banks; low voices and agonized laments echoed down from the air.

The man to whom all these signs referred, Fernando Cortés, the leader of the 'White Gods', had at this time no inkling of the alarm evoked in Mexico by his existence. He was a minor Spanish nobleman, of a good old family, but as poor as a church mouse. He had just received—we are writing of November 1518—an order from the governor of Cuba to reconnoitre Yucatan and the coastal areas of Central America. Orders are orders, he had to obey, although he rather liked Cuba with all its hot-blooded señoritas. He sailed away disgruntled, and he was still disgruntled three months later when he dropped anchor in the estuary of the Tabasco and gave the necessary orders for landing operations the following morning.

During the night a dozen Indian arrows whistled over the fleet. Cortés was almost glad. There would be a battle. But there was only a massacre. When the Spaniards' ten brass cannons and four culverins began to speak, the Indians were frozen with mortal horror. In the evening the Cacique of Cintla sent a declaration of submission. As a sign of unconditional surrender, twenty lovely young Indian princesses came heavily decked with gold and accompanied by slaves wearing further gold ornaments.

Amongst these twenty young maidens is a light-skinned, imperious young woman, an Aztec princess exiled by Montezuma, a member of the imperial house. Very confidently, fully conscious at every second of her exalted origin, she goes up to Cortés. She looks the slim, elegant Spanish cavalier straight in the eyes. Then she hides her face in her hands and, a few paces from Cortés, falls to her knees. As though in the grip of profound religious emotion, as though face to face with a god incarnate, she bows down before the Spaniard.

Cortés is astonished, moved, impressed! Interpreters, forward!

Two *Indios*, who had picked up a few words of Spanish somewhere, drag themselves over the deck on their knees to Cortés. Night falls, torches are flickering in pitch-pans on the rail, stars are sparkling in the sky above the masts. In a ring behind the commander stand the officers, the crew line the forecastle shoulder to shoulder. Silent, nonplussed, gripped, they listen to the strange story which the princess relates and the interpreters hesitantly and clumsily translate.

Long, long ago, recounts the Aztec lady, many foreign ships appeared off the coast of Yucatan, the very country off whose shores the sons of the white gods are now anchored, and from these ships stepped tall, fair-haired, blue-eyed men. The gunwales of these ships glistened like the scales of a snake, and it looked as though giant, shimmering serpents were creeping slowly over the sea towards the shore. These unknown men wore strange clothes, and round their brows an ornament that manifestly represented the image of a coiled snake. Now the sacred serpent was one of the most ancient divinities worshipped by the Mayas of Yucatan. When those fair-skinned, serpent-crowned beings arrived in their scaly, gliding snake-ships, people believed these strangers to be sons of the sacred serpent, to be gods.

As the famous Doña Marina, the Aztec princess was for many years to be his truest comrade and the only trustworthy companion of his triumphant life.

None of Cortés's biographers relate how the first meeting between him and the only woman he really loved throughout his turbulent life actually took place. It may have differed in many details from the picture we have drawn here. But it seems certain that the great Spaniard first learnt from Doña Marina with what anxiety he was awaited by the Aztecs.

Doubtless, Doña Marina must have told him first of the Maya tradition described above, which has become famous as the 'Wotan' legend of the natives of Yucatan. For during the lifetime of the Aztec princess, all that lay but a few hundred years in the past. Round A.D. 1000 the Mayas had left their original home in the primeval forests of Guatemala and occupied territory on the Yucatan peninsula; hence any tales of ships appearing off the coast of the New Country must be a comparatively recent tradition. It manifestly arose at the same period as that in which the Vikings who had settled in Greenland were making their first attempts to establish colonies in America.

This 'Wotan' tradition has long been known. The most recent account of it is given by the American authoress, Anne Terry White, in her very interesting book *Lost Worlds*. Reading her description of it, we immediately recall the many old pictorial representations of the dragon-prowed ships of the Norsemen, whose gunwales were hung with the gleaming shields of the crew: ships from whose bows snakes' heads stared out over the sea and whose sides must have glistened like the scales of snakes. And from these long, narrow snake ships stepped men upon whose brows sparkled serpentine diadems, spiral ornamental fibulas perhaps, beloved of the Teutons, beautifully wound like coiled serpents—an emblem that was bound particularly to strike the Mayas. Anne Terry White relates further that the fair-haired, blue-eyed strangers of the 'Wotan' legend settled in Yucatan, that they lived amongst the Mayas and became their teachers and guides. Finally she recounts the strange radiations from this landing passed over to Mexico.

For one day, some time in the thirteenth or fourteenth century by our chronology, there appeared in Mexico an old man whom nobody knew. This unknown from the far east began forthwith to teach a new religion and a new code of ethics. He was clear-thinking and wise, kind-hearted and of a great gentleness. Deeds of blood and violence

*22. Viking ship from the Bayeux Tapestry. William the Conqueror setting out for the invasion of England in 1066. The illustration shows a dragon ship under full sail. In order to increase the freeboard the crew have attached their shields to the gunwale.*

he fervently abhorred, and he stopped his ears when men spoke of war. His skin was white and he had a long beard—Indians are almost beardless—and he was called Quetzalcoatl after the resplendent *quetzal* bird. To begin with, says the legend, the forefathers were for a long time obedient to him. Then they rose in revolt against him, so that he had to flee the country and return to his home far away in the east beyond the great sea. Before he disappeared, however, he prophesied that one day his white brothers would come to Mexico and conquer the country.

It stands to reason that this legend was very opportune to Cortés and that he did nothing to invalidate it. When he was told by one of Montezuma's envoys, after his landing on the Mexican seaboard, that the forefathers had worn such helmets as his Spanish morion in the days of Quetzalcoatl, and that one still hung in the temple of the War God, he may himself have half believed that he was only a successor of much earlier white discoverers. The Aztecs, at all events, were firmly convinced that the Spaniards were sons and brothers of the Light God from the east.

25.  The streets in old Roman towns were as narrow as this. The great corner balcony gives this house in Pompeii quite a modern look. But the stepping stone on the right of the picture, placed so that the wheels of vehicles would pass on either side of it, but allowing the pedestrian to cross the street dry-foot, shows what things must have been like on a rainy day.

26. The balsa raft *Kon-Tiki*, built and sailed by the well-known Norwegian ethnologist, Thor Heyerdahl.

27. *Kon-Tiki* in a heavy sea. Quite primitive craft may be capable of sailing on the high seas.

In this context we must not hide the fact that in the primordial Indian legends, which came into being long before the advent of the Aztecs, Quetzalcoatl is apparently *not* portrayed as a white god. The German Americanist, Walter Krickeberg, has drawn attention to this in his book *Legends of the Aztecs, Inca, Maya and Muisca* (see bibliography), where he declares:

It frequently happened that religious ardour or misunderstanding scented traces of Christian doctrine in ancient Indian stories, and added all sorts of arbitrary Christian trimmings to them . . . But we must take care not incredulously to reject whole legends as Spanish inventions because of a few Christian additions, e.g. if culture heroes like Quetzalcoatl, Bochica, or Virakocha are equipped with the outward characteristics of an Apostle . . . Here the chronicler doubtless began with features which were already present in the original tradition and drawn from the natural basis of the myth, merely adding to these certain Christian trimmings of his own invention. All other elements in the American legends which offer striking parallels to early Christian stories are merely to be counted amongst the great number of correspondences between the civilized peoples of the Old World and the New, which also exist in other spheres and whose explanation must be left to future research.

So far Walter Krickeberg, whom we have quoted at such length because he is not given to flights of fancy. Despite all his caution he emphatically stresses the 'striking' parallels between early Christian stories and ancient American legends, counting them amongst the 'great number of parallels' between the civilized peoples of the Old World and the New. Equally emphatically he warns against a too uncritical interpretation of Indian legends, whose chroniclers decked out the old myths with all sorts of Christian 'embellishments'.

Does this latter apply to the figure of Quetzalcoatl? In other words, did the Spaniards who, shortly after the conquest of Mexico, began to write down the myths and legends of this strange land, depict Quetzalcoatl after the image which they, as people of their age and nation, were bound to visualize as the appearance of the Redeemer? Did they portray the 'White Saviour' of Mexico as olive-skinned, dark-haired and dark-eyed, as the Spaniards five hundred years ago represented Christ and the Apostles, as they themselves looked then and still look today? Did these Spanish chroniclers portray Quetzalcoatl in the clothing which was traditionally supposed to have been customary during the lifetime of Christ—that is to say, in a kind of Greek *chlamys*, a long mantle of beautifully draped, heavy material, loosely girded round the loins and falling in voluminous folds down to the feet?

Nothing of the sort! Quetzalcoatl is depicted quite differently: he is not olive-skinned and dark-eyed, but fair and blue-eyed. Is that not odd? Nor does Quetzalcoatl wear a Greek *chlamys*. He is dressed in a garment worn all over Europe in the early Middle Ages, but which had long since vanished by the time of the Conquest, except amongst the Greenland Vikings, the descendants of that Leif the Happy who discovered America in *circa* A.D. 1000. And curiously enough, the weave of the fabric from which this garment was made is described as coarse, like sacking, precisely as the fabrics disinterred five hundred years later from the eternally frozen icy soil by Danish archæologists excavating Norse farm-buildings in Greenland.

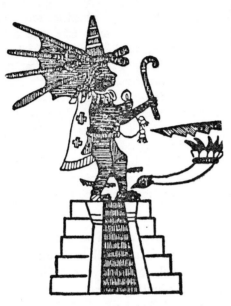

But let us listen to the prime source on Quetzalcoatl, the chronicle of the Spaniard Juan de Torquemada:

23. *Quetzalcoatl wearing a tiara and a cloak with crosses on it, holding a crozier and standing on a stepped pyramid. After an ancient Indian manuscript.*

A few years after the settlement of Tollan, certain tribes came from northern regions and landed in the area of Panuco. These were well-dressed people who wore long garments of black sacking, similar to those worn by the Turks etc. and resembling the *soutanes* of priests; these garments were open in front, without cowls, cut out round at the neck, and with short, wide sleeves that did not reach as far as the elbows. The natives still wear them today during their dances when they wish to represent those tribes. The latter pushed on indefatigably from Panuco without encountering any hostility, and when in due course they came to Tollan they were very friendlily received there, for they were very experienced and skilled and of great inventiveness and industry. They understood the working of gold and silver and were masters of every art, e.g. they were excellent lapidaries; they showed the greatest dexterity not only in such fine things as these, however, but also in other activities of a more utilitarian nature and in agriculture. In short, their admirable behaviour, industry and skill made them so well liked that wherever they went they were highly esteemed and shown great honour . . .

When the newcomers saw that they could not find a livelihood in Tollan, since the country was already densely populated, they sought to move on again and settled in Cholula, where they were also very friendlily received; the natives of the district, as is well-known, intermarried with them. For a long time they settled there and took root. The following story is told in this locality: When those tribes arrived in Tollan, they had with them a very distinguished person who was their leader and ruled over them. His name was Quetzalcoatl; the people of Cholula later revered him as a god. It is generally agreed that he was of pleasant exterior: white, fair-haired, bearded, finely built.

. . . It is asserted that Quetzalcoatl lived for twenty years in Cholula, and that at the end of this period he returned by the same route on which he had come. When he left he took with him four distinguished and virtuous youths from that city, but sent them back from Coatbacoalco (a province 150 leagues away, beside the sea), enjoining them to observe the good precepts which he had given them and to make the following announcement to the inhabitants of the city Cholula: Let them rest assured that at some future time white men with long beards like himself would come across the sea from the east. These men, his brothers, would become lords of the land of Mexico. Therefore the Indians always awaited the fulfilment of this prophecy, and when they saw the Christians arrive they called them gods, sons and brothers of Quetzalcoatl; although when they got to know and experience their works, they could by no means continue to regard them as divine.

Thus Torquemada. A curious report! For if the whole Quetzalcoatl myth, as is sometimes averred, was a Spanish invention, concocted to facilitate the conquest of Mexico and the victory of Christianity, how clumsy it all was, how small the propaganda value of this story to the cause of Spain! For if a militarily and culturally superior victor is to impose his gods on a subjugated people, he will naturally depict these gods as the quintessence of himself. But this is exactly what the Spaniards did not do—if they invented the story. On the contrary, Quetzalcoatl's appearance was so portrayed that the Aztecs could not fail to notice how little like the blond god the dark Spaniards were. The Aztecs were bound to conclude sooner or later that they could not be the sons of the Light God at all.

If the Spanish conquistadores did not portray the White Saviour of the Indians after their own image, however, then he cannot be a Spanish invention and the myth must be Indian in origin. In this case the question arises: how did the Aztecs know of the existence of fair-haired, blue-eyed men? How did they know articles of clothing which no one in Europe still wore at the beginning of the sixteenth century, but which were undoubtedly of European origin?

Carefully considered this leaves no other conclusion open than that the Light God Quetzalcoatl was a real person, that he was neither an invention of Spanish propaganda nor a legendary figment of Indian imagination, but that at some time in the early Middle Ages a white man from the Christian world came to Mexico, probably via Yucatan.


2


Ari was carried by the sea to the Land of the White Men, which some also call Greater Ireland. This lies in the west, near Vinland the Good. It is said to lie six days' journey west of Iceland. Ari could not leave this place, and he was baptized.

This is how the account stands in the *Landnámabók* or *Book of the Taking of the Land,* one of the most ancient of the Icelandic chronicles. If it gives the facts correctly, we must assume that Hvitramanna Land, this remarkable 'Land of the Palefaces', was an Irish settlement of long standing on the soil of North America appropriately known as 'Greater Ireland'.

Hvitramanna Land, Land of the White Men, Land of the Palefaces —it would never occur to a white man to give this name to the country in which he lived. At all events, when the Norsemen discovered America a little later they did not call it 'Paleface Land', but Vinland, Wine Land, after the wild vines that grew in such profusion in its southern regions. The expression Paleface Land can logically have been coined only by the coloured inhabitants of America, just as, many centuries later, the Indians of the great North American prairies called their white oppressors from across the seas to the east 'palefaces'.

A very ancient document is, in fact, extant which indicates very clearly that the term 'Paleface Land' really goes back to the brown-skinned aboriginal inhabitants of America. When the Icelandic merchant, Thorfin Karlsefni, attempted to plant a settlement in Massachusetts, the Vinland of the Vikings, in 1010, he and his companions one day met two Indian boys who told them that

. . . on the other side of their country there lay a land where people wore white clothes, shouted loudly, and bore before them rods with white cloths attached to them. This, people thought, must be Hvitramanna Land, the Land of the White Men, also called Greater Ireland.

There can be no denying that these reports are very striking. They are all the more astonishing because they undoubtedly arose independently of one another. In complete agreement, they both speak of a land far away in the western sea called Greater Ireland or Hvitramanna Land. It was known by this name to the natives as well. It is evident that some fact underlies these reports. There is the additional detail that Karlsefni's Indian informants related as a particular characteristic of the white men of Hvitramanna Land that they wore white clothes, bore before them long rods with cloths attached to them, and shouted or sang loudly. What does this describe if not a Christian procession with choral song, white robes and ecclesiastical banners? This would naturally be such a strange sight to the Indians as to impress itself upon them as a characteristic activity of the dwellers in White Man's Land. It is unthinkable that a European should have given such a naïve account of an ecclesiastical practice. It must stem from a native.

Admittedly, this inference is only circumstantial; but there is no getting away from the probability that for a time a colony of white men existed amidst the coloured population on the soil of the New World, perhaps south of the later Vinland of the Vikings. A good hundred years ago Alexander von Humboldt asserted pretty categorically that this 'Paleface Land' was situated in Florida. This cannot be proved, but it is supported by a continual crop of reports suggesting a very ancient, non-Indian colonization of Florida. Thus for example, in 1819, the American geographer J. Johnston reported that in the mideighteenth century a tradition was current in Florida and South Carolina to the effect that white settlers possessing weapons and implements of iron had once peopled this area. And it has been effectively argued by O. S. Reuter in his book *Germanic Astronomy* (see bibliography) that the Norsemen's voyages of reconnaissance along the coast of the New World took them as far as Florida.

If this was the case—and the 'Wotan' legends of the Mayas cited above render it very likely—then those Christian missionaries, whose story runs like a strand of European tradition through the mythology of America, did not have so very far to travel. From Florida to Cuba is a stone's throw. From Cuba to Yucatan and Mexico is no great distance either. Did northern Europeans really come to Central America? At present there is no proof of this, but equally it is not beyond the bounds of possibility. And when we learn from old Spanish sources that precisely in Yucatan the Mayas possessed a kind of Trinity dogma, and further, that the Aztecs believed Quetzalcoatl to have come to Mexico from Yucatan, we cannot help wondering.

The account of Ari the Viking's voyage to Hvitramanna Land, taken from the Icelandic *Landnámabók*, discloses that this European settlement must have existed long prior to A.D. 982, and that the Irish were certainly involved in the affair. This brings us to the innumerable Irish folk sagas, which also tell of a fruitful wonderland far to the west beyond the ocean. In the centre of all these traditions stands the legend of the voyage of St. Brandan, who was one day called upon by a divine voice to leave all his possessions and preach the word of God in a great, unknown land across the sea. Brandan obeyed this divine command, and after a long and difficult journey reached a land far to the west, where delicious wild vines grew 'so that all the branches were borne down to the ground by the weight of grapes'. Now we know from the reports of the Vikings, the first white men thereafter to set foot on American soil, that wild vines did indeed grow in great abundance on the new continent. Hence the name Vinland. Since the vine does not thrive anywhere north of Ireland, the glorious grape lands referred to must have lain in the New World and the report of them can hardly have arisen otherwise than through an eye-witness.

There really was such a person as St. Brandan; incontrovertible evidence indicates that he lived during the sixth century A.D. It is, however, doubtful whether he himself ever sailed the seas to any extent. Manifestly he was only, through some circumstance unknown to us, the crystallization point round which the numberless sea sagas current amongst the Irish condensed and precipitated. Thus the account of his alleged voyages, the *Navigatio Sancti Brandani,* is a collection of the most colourful fables, which probably contain a hard core of historical truth. Hence it is quite possible that the legend of St. Brandan represents a dim memory of the landfall on Hvitramanna Land of those whites whose identity cannot be exactly established, but to whose real existence everything points. The seafaring sagas of the Emerald Isle repeatedly refer to thick banks of mist, to bird and birds' egg islands in the western ocean; the obvious inference is that they relate to regions between the Labrador Current and the Gulf Stream, which might well have been reached by Irish seamen.

It must not be forgotten that numerous legends were also current amongst other Celtic tribes, such as the Bretons and the Welsh, to the effect that a great foreign country lay across the sea in the far west. This popular tradition was so strong that an expedition put to sea from Bristol as late as 1480 to seek for this remote western continent. It was inspired by information contained in two ancient MSS. from the Abbeys of Strata Florida (the Welsh Caron Uwch Clawdd) and Conway, relating to a great expedition launched by King Madoc of North Wales in the year 1170. Sailing round the south of Ireland, he and his many companions discovered vast tracts of land beyond the western sea. According to these ancient chronicles Madoc returned to Wales to enlist fresh colonists, having left a hundred and twenty settlers behind him. He then re-embarked with ten ships and several hundred passengers. This was the last that was heard of Madoc or those who accompanied him. So much for the MSS. The negative conclusion of their account does not, of course, necessarily imply that Madoc failed to reach his objective. As is proved by the Norsemen's voyages to America a hundred and fifty years later, it is by no means impossible that the ocean was crossed several times at about this period.

It is worth noting that these connections between the Old and New Worlds in North America seem to have left their mark in the blood of the latter's inhabitants. In many parts of the New World there are white Indians, whose European discoverers time and again declared: 'These are no Indians!' The natives of America are distinguished by a great variation in the colour of their skins. Alongside peoples with markedly red skins there are others with pale yellow or bronze skins, and the Dakota, Menomini and Zuñi look almost white, although their physiognomy is entirely Indian. Besides these 'almost white', but nonetheless Indian tribes there are peoples of completely European appearance, with white skins, fair hair, blue eyes, and altogether un-Indian features. The white Indians of Venezuela, who still exist, are mentioned in the chronicles of the Spanish conquerors, and the Boroanos Indians on the Rio Imperial in Chile were known to the conquistadores as 'white Indians'.

In North America too there is a whole series of white Indian tribes. In particular, the Tuscaroras of north-east America are thought to show signs of an age-old intermingling with European peoples. Alexander von Humboldt already drew attention to the 'whitish, often blue-eyed nation of the Tuscarora'. After him special attention was paid to the Mandan tribe who lived in the Mississippi basin, and some peculiar facts were observed. The Mandan were scattered over the whole area of the States of Dakota, Wisconsin and Minnesota. The districts of their settlements were not reached by the white farmers, who were thrusting ever farther westwards, until the middle of last century, shortly after the Mandan had been wiped out by a smallpox epidemic. But some two hundred and fifty years earlier the first obscure rumours of a tribe of whites living one thousand miles away in the western wilderness had come to the ears of the *courreurs du bois*, the intrepid French backwoodsmen who began to push out into the primeval forests from Montreal and Quebec round this time. Champlain, the first great French explorer, speaks of them in 1615. In 1630 another well-known backwoodsman, Jean Nicolet, packed a Chinese State robe in the bow of his birchbark canoe: he intended to don it when he came to the 'whites' in the west, who could only be Chinese and from whose territory there must be a passage to the certainly not far distant land of the Great Khan. Two years later, the Jesuit father, Lejeune, in Quebec, noted in his diary that an Algonquin Indian had told him that far, far away in the west there lived a great Indian nation whose towns, from his description, resembled those of Europe.

On the basis of these reports, but of course with the main purpose of reaching the Pacific, the French governor of Canada commissioned the fur trader and explorer, de la Verandrye, a born Canadian, to undertake an expedition to this remarkable people in 1738. Verandrye was the first white man to get to know the Mandan intimately, and his observations were calculated to arouse great interest. It transpired that the Mandan were so different from all other Indian tribes, in their customs and practices as well as in their physical constitution and appearance, that one could only suppose them to be of non-Indian origin. Contrary to most of the other Redskins, who had retreated before the white man and become nomads again, they had held fast to their settled way of life and to agriculture. They are said to have possessed not only numerous solidly built villages, but apparently also a few large, well-fortified towns. About a fifth of this strange people were white-skinned and blue-eyed. Fair hair was also not infrequent, and the physiognomy of all Mandan was entirely different from that of the usual Indian type.

All accounts of the Mandan Indians have been published in very out-of-the-way places. A few of them are, therefore, reproduced here. The first of these in order of importance are the communications of the American George Catlin, who wandered amongst the Indians, painting them and observing their customs and who made a close study of the Mandan at the beginning of the nineteenth century. The main points in his account (see bibliography) run as follows:

The Mandans are certainly a very interesting and pleasing people in their personal appearance and manners; differing in many respects, both in looks and customs, from all other tribes which I have seen. Being a small tribe, and unable to contend on the wide prairies with the Sioux and other roaming tribes, who are ten times more numerous, they have judiciously located themselves in a permanent village, which is strongly fortified and ensures their preservation. By this means they have advanced further in the arts of manufacture; have supplied their lodges more abundantly with the comforts, and even luxuries of life, than any Indian nation I know of. The consequence of this is, that this tribe have taken many steps ahead of other tribes in manners and refinements (if I may be allowed to apply the word refinement to Indian life); and are therefore familiarly (and correctly) denominated, by the Traders and others, who have been amongst them, 'the polite and friendly Mandans'.

There is certainly great justice in this remark; and so forcibly have I been struck with the peculiar ease and elegance of these people, together with the diversity of complexions, the various colours of their hair and eyes; the singularity of their language, and their peculiar and unaccountable customs, that I am fully convinced that they have sprung from some other origin than that of the other North American tribes, or that they are an amalgam of natives with some civilized race. Their *personal appearance* alone, independent of their modes and customs, pronounces them at once, as more or less, than savage.

A stranger in the Mandan village is first struck by the different shades of complexion, and various colours of hair which he sees crowd about him; and he is at once almost disposed to exclaim that 'these are not Indians'.

There are a great many of these people whose complexions appear as light as half breeds; and amongst the women particularly, there are many whose skins are almost white, with the most pleasing symmetry and proportion of features; with hazel, with grey, and with blue eyes—with mildness and sweetness of expression, and excessive modesty of demeanour, which render them exceedingly pleasing and beautiful.

In 1850, a few years after Catlin, D. Mitchell, the director of the United States Department for Indian Affairs, expressed himself similarly. He declared:

As far as I have been able to ascertain, the Mandans as a whole differ from all other North American Indians; and I have a close knowledge of most of the existing tribes. Apart from possessing their own language and customs, the Mandans are physically distinct. Very many of them have fair hair and blue or hazel eyes.

And the explorer de la Verandrye, mentioned above, states in the diary of his journey to the Mandan:

. . . This tribe is partly white and partly red skinned. The women are extremely beautiful, especially those who are white, some of whom have lovely fair hair. Both men and women are very industrious and work with a will. Their lodges are big and spacious; they are divided into several rooms by partitions of thick planks. Nothing is left lying about untidily; all objects are placed in large bags suspended from the posts . . . The men are tall, strong and courageous. They are very active, and of good appearance with pleasant features. Their women do not look in the least Indian . . .

This is all very remarkable information. But on top of it comes the fact that Mandan mythology explicitly tells that the first ancestor of this people was a white man who, in the mists of antiquity, came to the country in a canoe. Long before the first missionaries reached the Mandan they are alleged to have known of a gentle, kindly god who was born of a virgin and died a death of expiation; they told of a

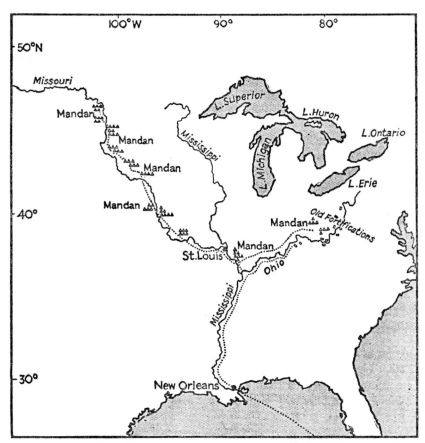

*XIV. The position of Mandan settlements and the alleged route followed by the Welsh settlers under Madoc. (After Catlin.)*

miracle having close affinities with the feeding of the five thousand; they related the story of the first mother of mankind and her fall, of the ark and of the dove with a green twig in its beak; they believed in a personal devil who sought to win over and subjugate to himself the world of men. Reports such as these could not fail to arouse attention, and the better acquainted the hearers were with Indian nations as a whole, the more convinced they became that the Mandan were the product of intermingling with Europeans. Catlin held this view and suggested specifically that the Mandan might be descended from the Welsh king, Madoc, of whom we spoke earlier.

The connection which Catlin suggests between the Mandan and King Madoc and his followers is, of course, pure surmise—though he is correct in his statements concerning the migrations of the Mandan. In the meantime, however, the problem has been complicated by the fact that it has become almost certain that the area occupied by the Mandan, 490 miles west of the Atlantic coast, was indeed settled by Europeans 130 years before Columbus. These settlers were neither Irish nor Welsh, however, but Scandinavian Vikings; and furthermore only a handful of men, whose biological force cannot have sufficed to Europeanize a whole Indian tribe. But the clear traces of European blood which the Mandan are said to have exhibited in 1750 cannot have been the outcome of a relatively fleeting contact with the white man; they must have sprung from some much more profound intermingling. What great adventure, what tragedy lies behind this strange and now vanished tribe? We do not know.

Many scholars regard the evidence for such early cultural relations between the Old World and the New as exceedingly tenuous. Their main argument against the existence of such contacts has always centred round the question: how did it happen that these alleged white immigrants brought with them their gods, but not knowledge of the wheel? For the wheel was unknown in pre-Columbian America. It must be conceded that wide tracts of American territory consisted of forest, mountains or swamps where the wheel and the cart would in any case have been useless. But there were also vast plains on which they could well have been used, and any hypothetical white immigrants would surely have utilized their knowledge and not kept it a closely guarded secret, as would appear to have been the case.

This objection sounds convincing, but it is not conclusive. The Islamic peoples also made no use of the wheel and the cart, despite their long and intimate contact with the West. Even today they prefer the riding-animal or the beast of burden to any wheeled vehicle. Furthermore, the assumption that the aboriginal inhabitants of the New World were unacquainted with the wheel is palpably false. The truth is that the Indians were so familiar with this principle that they even put children's toys on wheels. Recent excavations in Mexico, reported in the *National History Magazine*, New York, October 1950, prove this incontrovertibly. Yet neither the Toltecs, nor the Aztecs, nor the Chimus seem to have employed wheeled vehicles. For one thing, they lacked suitable draught animals. There were no horses in America prior to Columbus, and in the absence of suitable draught animals the sedan chair, which had long been in use, was a natural alternative. After the arrival of horses the absence of roads or a knowledge of road construction remained an obstacle to the use of carts by the Indians.

24. *The Inca and the Queen in a sedan chair decorated with crosses. Drawing from the picture chronicle of Huaman Poma de Ayala.*

It can, therefore, no longer be argued that the Indians were ignorant of the wheel and that this precludes the possibility of a pre-Columbian white immigration into the New World. The Indians knew the wheel, though they did not use it as we do. This may be incomprehensible to us, but there are many such inexplicable 'failures of expectation' in history. For example, the Egyptians and Phœnicians had mastered the art of making glass, and were producing glass *objets d'art*, thousands of years before the birth of Christ. Yet the Greeks, who had the closest commercial ties with both peoples, made absolutely no use of glass. It simply didn't interest them! To us glass seems such an immensely useful material that we cannot conceive why the Greeks should have failed to adopt it. If intercourse between Egyptians and Phœnicians on the one hand and Greeks on the other were not unimpeachably and richly documented, we should deduce from the latter's apparent ignorance of glass that no such contact existed. It is the same with the Romans. As we have said, their neighbours and forerunners the Etruscans were brilliant seamen. Yet although the Romans were so much intermarried with them that they adopted their gods and many things connected with everyday life, the inhabitants of the city on the Tiber were for a long time baffled by the sea and unable to make any use of the nautical knowledge of the Etruscans. This is another 'failure' which cannot be explained.

These things happen. Even where there is conclusive evidence of a pre-Columbian European settlement on American soil with solidly built houses and a great house of God—in other words, where there can be no doubt that carts were used for carrying timber, stones and other building materials—there is nothing to show that the Indians who watched, and perhaps helped, adopted the cart themselves. And yet these Indians, for three hundred years, gave their children European names, and later white discoverers were highly astonished to hear that some little Indian boy in the wilderness of the east American seaboard, apparently virgin territory where no white man's foot had ever trod before, was called 'Magnus'. But more of this presently.

3

Of gigantic stature, with mighty shoulders, helmet and breastplate freshly burnished and glistening, his arquebus over his shoulder and a huge double-handed sword in his sword-belt, Pedro de Candia stepped from the boat. A few cable lengths behind him Pizarro's caravels rode at anchor, broadside to the land, their port-holes open and gunners standing by with lighted matches in their hands. If things went wrong, Pedro de Candia had all the fire support a Spanish conquistador could wish for in 1527.

But things did not go wrong! On the contrary, Pedro de Candia, a Cretan by birth but a knight of his most Christian majesty the King of Spain, could only endorse the statements of his brother officer, Alonso de Molina, who had landed yesterday and was the first Spaniard to set foot on the soil of the holy Inca empire. Tumbez, the wealthy seaport of the wonderland Birú, stood open to the Spaniards, and its people grovelled in the dust as though before a god come down to earth. This was a little burdensome, Pedro found, and most inappropriate—for seen in his true light he was, after all, no more than a petty lieutenant in the freebooter armada of the highly dubious Señor Pizarro.

Candia walked between a lane of bowed figures. Foreheads were pressed to the dust on either side of his path. 'Virakocha, Virakocha', rose the whisper all around him.

Pedro de Candia had no idea what that meant. He felt awkward, irritated and ill at ease; and since he was still a very young man, he suddenly lifted his arquebus from his shoulder and fired a shot into the air.

The mortally terrified crowd bowed lower still. 'Illa Tiki, Illa Tiki!', 'The god of lightning', they whispered on all sides.

Pedro de Candia grew more and more embarrassed. He did not know that the brown-skinned natives actually took him for an incarnate god. He did not know that for weeks and months blood-red comets had been hurtling across the sky of the Inca country; that terrible quakes had thrown open the earth, laying bare its glowing entrails. He did not know that the augurs had predicted evil from their observation of the flight of birds; nor that the moon had been encircled by a treble ring—an infallible omen that the day of the last things was nigh.

'Virakocha, Illa Tiki!' rose the whisper, and every one of the fearful multitude was thinking how, the previous year, four thousand men and women, the closest servants of the Inca Huayna Capac, who had just gone home to the gods, had immolated themselves in the flames of his funeral pyre—because Virakocha stood wrathful and avenging at the frontiers of the country.

Virakocha! Today, after more than four hundred years, this form of address means simply 'lord' in Peru, Bolivia and Ecuador. In practice it is identical with 'white man'. Today the Whites are still the sons and people of Virakocha the Almighty.

Who and what is Virakocha?

There is a myth concerning a very, very ancient god, whom the Incas found when they first immigrated into Peru. Virakocha may mean something like 'holy man from the sea'. But not even this is known for sure. It is certain, however, that when the Incas discovered the giant city Tiahuanacu on Lake Titicaca, allegedly built by Virakocha and his followers, and even more when they came upon the grandiose divine city Pachacamac south of Lima, they invoked this strange god by the name Kon-Tiki, the Eternal, and that they called him Pachaya-chachi, Creator and Ruler of the World.

They relate that Virakocha was an unknown, aged bearded man, who bore a cross and set it up on an eminence. He preached, wept for the sins of the world, and then, as the Indian chronicler Pachacuti adds, he did something very strange: he splashed the head of one of the princes following him with water—to baptize him.

Cusco, the ancient capital of the Incas, was said to have been founded by Virakocha, and likewise the celebrated temple buildings on the Sun Island of Lake Titicaca. Here was once the main seat of the white saint. Here he was attacked and defeated by King Cari of the Coquim-botal. Here Virakocha's white men were slain and sacrificed to the gods, while the lives of the women and children were spared. From here the white god with a few of his closest followers escaped to the western ocean. There he preached a farewell sermon to his world and his creatures and spoke of things that would happen in time to come. False prophets would arise, but the people should not give ear to them. Then, when the time was come, he himself would send messengers to them, 'white, bearded men!' Then Kon-Tiki 'spread his cloak on the sea', stood upon it with his followers, and departed.

This is another very strange story. It might be regarded as a mere legend devoid of historical basis, if it were not well known that the first Spaniards to enter Peru in 1527 were greeted by the *Indios* with frightened awe as 'Virakochas'. This, as Siegfried Huber has pointed out in his book *In the Kingdom of the Incas* (see bibliography), would be 'utterly inexplicable in the absence of some pre-existent tradition, that is, unless white, bearded men had been known in olden times and their return in later ages expected'. It is therefore certain that the Virakocha myth is not an invention of either Indian or Spanish priests; this gives to the remarkable political testament of the last Inca to reign prior to the Spanish invasion, Huayna Capac the Great, the same importance as the celebrated act of abdication of Montezuma of Mexico reported by the Spanish chroniclers. Just like the Aztec in the latter document, so the Inca in the former lays his power in the hands of those unknown white men who had suddenly appeared off the coast of the vast South American theocracy. As he lay upon his deathbed, he called to him the chiefs of the Ayllus, the leading clans of his kingdom, and declared:

Many years ago it was revealed to me by our father, the Sun, that after the rule of twelve of his children, an alien people would come which had never been seen before in these regions and would conquer and subdue this kingdom and many others as well. I am inclined to suppose that this refers to the people recently sighted off our shores. They are said to be a powerful race, superior to us in everything. Now we know that with me the number of twelve Incas has been reached. Therefore I predict to you that a few years after I have gone to my ancestors, that strong people will appear and bring to fulfilment the prophecy of my father, the Sun; they will conquer our kingdom and rule over us. I command you to obey and serve them, for they are superior to us in everything, because their laws are better than ours, their weapons more powerful and invincible.

Peace be with you—I go now to my father, the Sun, who has called me . . .

When the Spaniards encountered the same prophecies of the advent of white, bearded men in South America that they had already met in Central America, they were naturally doubly dumbfounded. Then they also learnt that the Incas not only had auricular confession, which was received by priests bound to the strictest observance of the secret of the confessional, but that, just as in Europe, penances were imposed and final absolution given. The Spaniards were likewise struck by the symbols of the Trinity which they found before Peruvian altars: images of the 'Sun of the Lord', the 'Sun of the Son', and the 'Sun Brother', to which offerings were made and which invited comparison with the Christian Trinity. The Spaniards were also very much surprised to find that there were monastic orders practising bloody mortifications and regular strict fasts; that Peru had holy hermits who, just as in the Old World, lived in solitude and devoted their lives to meditation. They were most deeply impressed, however, by the large number of fair and white-skinned people they met amongst the Inca Ayllus, the Peruvian aristocracy. In particular, the *coyas*, the ladies of the great Inca families, seem in many cases to have looked exactly like European women. Pedro Pizarro, a cousin of the conqueror of Peru, writes of them with positive consternation in his *Story of the Discovery and Conquest of Peru*. These princesses were neat and clean, stately, and beautiful to behold, he reports. They considered themselves well-formed, and were so in fact. 'These people are corn-blond', continues Pizarro. 'Some of the ladies and gentlemen were actually whiter than Spaniards. I saw one woman with her child here of a whiteness such as is seldom seen. The Indians believe such people to be children of the *idolos*, the gods.'

The older generation of Americanists, who laid particular stress on the Mongolian features of the Indians, placed little credence in Pizarro's excellent report as regards this point. One feels inclined to agree with them. Indian squaws, by all other accounts, were not especially attractive beings. But either the nobility of the Spanish court at the time of Charles V and Philip II had ideals of beauty utterly different from our own—which, in view of the Spanish paintings of the period, is hardly conceivable—or Pedro Pizarro's delineation of the *coyas* is substantially correct. At all events, the haughty grandees of Castile, so proud of their noble birth, married the blond Inca princesses in large numbers, regarding them as their equals in birth and presenting them to their Spanish Majesties at court in Madrid. Two generations later, in 1603, a petition for tax relief signed by 567 representatives of old Inca families was presented to the crown of Spain. This speaks volumes—and in favour of Pedro Pizarro.

The Latin-speaking Spanish clerics who accompanied Pizarro to Peru made a number of interesting linguistic observations. The Indian word *capac* resembled in both sound and meaning the Latin *caput*, head or chief. Similarly, the Inca *suma*, best, was identical with the Latin *summus*. The Inca word for wave or flood was *uno*, the Latin *unda*. And if any of these clerics had ever read about the Goths, the quondam rulers of the Spanish Mark, he must have been struck by the fact that the Inca *marca* (boundary mark) corresponded to the Gothic German *Mark*, and that the thunderous '*Hailla*' with which the Inca warriors greeted their officers, had its counterpart in the Germanic '*Heil*'.

These external factors however, striking as they may be, excited the interest of the Western chaplains and bishops less than the supposed correspondences of a spiritual and religious kind. These latter have received particular attention from contemporary Scandinavian ethnologists and Americanists, amongst them the Norwegian Thor Heyerdahl, of whom we shall hear a great deal more shortly, and the Finnish Americanist, Rafael Karsten. The latter points out that, although the Incas, like all other Indians, were *per se* polytheists who worshipped a multiplicity of entirely anthropomorphic gods, they placed above this Olympus one super-god conceived, in quite un-Indian fashion, as a spiritual being: the creator god Virakocha, the knowledge and worship of whom the Incas had taken over from the unknown people of the Tiahuanacu culture. Virakocha stood high above the sun: 'The everlasting Lord, symbol of the world and its eternal first cause, master and ruler. He is the Sun of Suns. He is the Creator of the World . . .' says one of the most ancient Inca prayers. It is clear from this that Virakocha was not a sun-god, which invalidates the conjecture of certain Americanists that Virakocha's solar origin is the explanation of his beardedness, a notion which, in a beardless people, is most striking. The rays of the sun, think these scholars, were placed like a halo round the head of the sun-god and thus gave rise to the notion of a beard. This supposition is incompatible with the conception of the sun as a mere heavenly body and the bearded world-creator Virakocha as a sublime being far above it. Both Karsten and Heyerdahl are convinced that this is how the Incas saw them. The same view is held by Siegfried Huber, whom we mentioned earlier.

These legends of the appearance of a strange, white, long-bearded founder of religion, who one day came into the country from the east, are not confined to Mexico and Peru. They are to be found in many parts of Central and South America, and all of them agree in stating that, after a period of teaching and missionary activity, the central figure returned to his old home far away across the sea. As far as is known, there appear to have been six of these white founders of religions: in Mexico Quetzalcoatl, in Yucatan Zamno, in Peru Virakocha, in Brazil and Paraguay Zume, amongst the Tupi tribe the god Tupan, and in Colombia Bochica.

Next to Quetzalcoatl and Virakocha, Bochica is one of the most interesting of these white missionaries. He was the teacher of the Chibcha Indians of Colombia, and the astonishingly high cultural level of this people, upon which the Spanish conquistadores commented in wonderment, is perhaps attributable to him and his later emissaries. A long, long time ago, says the mythology of the Chibcha, men turned away from God. To punish them the Lord flooded the Valley of Bogotá with two mountain torrents, so that the majority of men perished. The survivors besought God for mercy on the mountain-tops. Then Bochica appeared on a rainbow and caused the flood to go back.

This legend might have come straight from the Book of Genesis. Since the first chroniclers to concern themselves with the history and mythology of the Indians were usually Spanish monks, there was a natural tendency for them to deck out ancient Indian legends in Christian garb. This did, in fact, often happen; frequently on the basis of some genuine misunderstanding, but in many cases quite consciously with the generous aim of fabricating a kind of 'Christian past' for the Indians as a means of protecting them from the often horrifyingly brutal excesses of Spanish adventurers. How necessary this was is shown by the fact that Pope Paul III, as early as 1537, punished enslavement of the Indians by excommunication: a quite unprecedented step, which greatly aided the missionaries in the New World in their work of conversion. So the grafting of Christian elements onto Indian legends was of frequent occurrence. It cannot, however, have taken place as regards the rainbow legend related above. For the rainbow was also an ancient mythological symbol of divine clemency in Peru and, as we shall hear later, in Polynesia—a very remarkable concordance with Western ideas.

When Bochica considered his mission fulfilled, he retired to an inaccessible region, where he lived as a hermit, fasting and praying for his people. Then he vanished. Later a priest came to the Chibcha from the far east, claiming that Bochica had sent him to lead his people back into the paths of righteousness. The Chibcha were instructed by this white-skinned, long-bearded, aged missionary in agriculture, astronomy, meteorology, and weaving. He also organized their State, built their towns, and gave them their rulers—a spiritual ruler and a temporal ruler subordinate to the spiritual. The text of the Bochica legend runs:

There descended into the savannah of Bacata a man coming from the east. Long was the hair of his head, and his beard hung down to his girdle. And he was full of years, and his feet were naked. He wore a cloak about his shoulders, and in his hand he bore a staff.

And the Chibcha fell to their knees before him and listened as he spoke. And they called the man Bochica, that is: Royal Mantle of Light.

And Bochica was good. He taught them to believe that their souls were immortal. And he taught them to believe that one day the good will be rewarded and the evil punished. He also taught them to believe in the resurrection of the body. And he enjoined them to give alms to the needy . . .

But in the princedom of Iraca they say of Bochica:

'There came a white man from the east. His hair was long and his beard fell to the club which he carried in his hand as a pilgrim's staff.

'On his head and on his arms he bore the sign of the cross. And he was full of years. And King Nompanem prayed to him. And he heard his teachings, and they seemed to him good.

'Then the prince commanded that the teachings of the Master should be followed throughout the land.

'And Nompanem asked the Master: "What punishment is meet for him that doth not obey thy teachings?"

'Said the Master: "Thou shalt not compel obedience to my teachings with the punishments of this world. Beyond, in the other world, there are punishments for the evil and rewards for those who obey the teachings of God." '

This is the legend of Bochica, which is recorded in very similar terms in a group of Spanish chronicles from the conquistadores period. No wonder the Spaniards were struck by it: it deviates so widely from the normal Indian notions of God as to raise doubts of whether it is really of pre-Columbian origin. But the Chibcha possessed an amazingly high level of culture in other spheres as well. Not only was their art of a very high standard, they also had a currency system based on gold and an absolutely modern calendar, according to which the year was divided into 365 days with twelve months beginning from the winter solstice on 22nd December. The latter information is particularly interesting because, as recent investigations have shown, the calendar

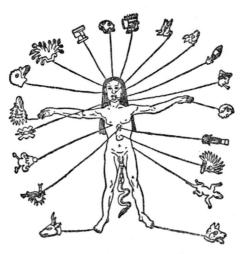

*25. Magical anatomy. Mexico, like medieval Europe, evolved a kind of 'blood-letting homunculus', in which the various organs of the human body were brought into magical relationship with the twenty heavenly signs of the calendar.*

of the Toltecs, the ancient Indian people who inhabited Mexico from the tenth to the twelfth centuries A.D. and were followed by the Aztecs in the thirteenth century, seems also to have undergone certain influences from the Old World. It is evident that problems relating to the calendar, with their intricate astronomical and mathematical substructure, cannot be solved in the course of isolated, brief contacts. If, therefore, European influences operated in this sphere, relations between the Old and the New Worlds must indeed have been very close.

Unfortunately, our knowledge of ancient American civilization is somewhat incomplete. We know that the Spanish conquistadores encountered numerous highly-developed cultures in America, and also that these were patently no more than faint echoes of much older and more brilliant periods. Again and again age-old ruins, of huge dimensions and still splendid in destruction, are found in the vast primeval forests of Central and South America. It may be assumed with some certainty that highly-evolved cultures flourished on the soil of the New

World from two to one thousand years B.C.; but that is about all we do know for sure.

Regrettably, no original literary records from those times have come down to us. Some of these ancient peoples, whose collapsed and crumbling Cyclopean edifices fill us with wonder, had mastered the art of

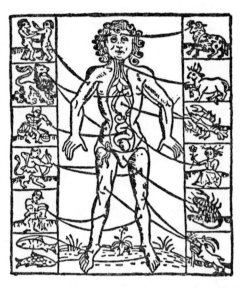

*26. 'Blood-letting homunculus' from medieval medicine in Europe.*

writing. But their written documents have, almost without exception, fallen victim to Time, either because they perished even before the arrival of the Spaniards in the merciless wars of annihilation waged by one people against another, or because they succumbed to the destructive effects of nature and the climate. The main damage, however, was undoubtedly perpetrated by the fanatical destructiveness of the white conquerors, whose priests imagined they were doing good in the sight of God by burning both the *Indios* themselves and their cultural works. The Bishop of Merida, in one tremendous *auto-da-fé* alone, destroyed two hundred and twenty-four Maya MSS., fifty-three altars, and five thousand statues. Hence out of the doubtless very extensive Maya literature only three works have survived, and these, up to the present, have been only very partially deciphered. Whether it will be possible to read these works of a vanished culture in their entirety remains to be seen.

What happened to the founders of these religions that so closely resemble Christianity? In one case alone is there a clue which seems so striking as to be worth following up: The Polynesians, 2500 miles to the west of Peru, worshipped as their primal ancestor and supreme god Kon-Tiki, The Eternal—and Kon-Tiki was the name bestowed by the Incas upon Virakocha, whom they adopted from their forerunners in Peru.

It has long been known that whole tribes, and not merely the intrepid crews of individual ships, have migrated across enormous expanses of ocean. The classical example of this is the curious island of Madagascar: although it is separated from the east coast of Africa only by the 250-mile-wide Mozambique Channel, it was not peopled from Africa nor by Negroes, but from Java and by Malayo-Polynesians.

The distance from Java to Madagascar is in the region of 4,000 miles, and the Indian Ocean can be quite especially unruly; the conjunction of the two, the prodigious stretch of open sea and the shattering storms common in these latitudes, caused scholars prolonged doubts as to whether the Arab sources from which our knowledge of the Malayo-Polynesian settlement of Madagascar is derived were reliable. But French investigations under the leadership of the Paris savant Gabriel Ferrand, and almost simultaneous German research going back to the Leipzig ethnologist Karl Weule, made it finally evident at the turn of the century that the old Arab geographers were right, and that the Malagasies did indeed immigrate to their island across the sea from Java. *How* that happened nobody can say. *When* it happened is almost equally uncertain, though the investigations of the German geographer, Eberhard Stechow, make it seem likely that the first waves of these trans-oceanic immigrants arrived in Madagascar before the beginning of the Christian era. It is in any case certain that the Malagasy Hova, who number more than three-quarters of a million, are Malayo-Polynesians. And it is also certain that the immigrants were able to traverse this vast expanse of sea only because their primitive craft were carried along by trade wind and current.

These facts might have been thought sufficient to inspire the study of other theoretically possible migrations carried out with the aid of the trade winds. Such studies have been made, but they never yielded more than cautious suggestions. Then the young Norwegian ethnologist, Thor Heyerdahl, cut the Gordian knot of scientific Ifs and Ands by an audacious expedition. In 1947, driven by the trade wind and the ocean currents, he crossed the Pacific in an ocean-going raft built after ancient American-Indian prototypes. He did not, of course, thereby solve every problem; but it is worth analysing the consequences of his voyage as reported in his interesting book *The Kon-Tiki Expedition— by raft across the South seas* (see bibliography).

It has been known for many decades that the Peruvian menhirs—

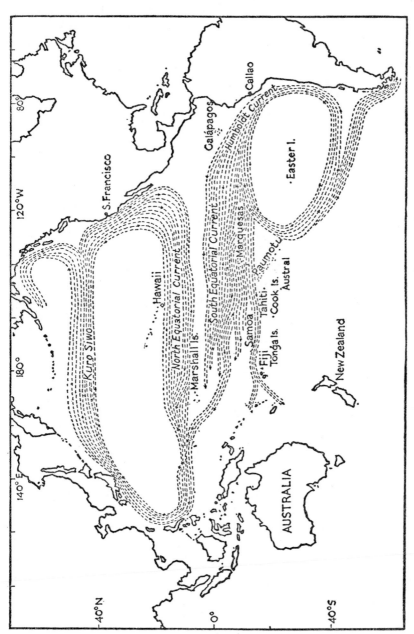

XV. *Currents in the Pacific Ocean.*

monoliths resembling those of Stone-Age Europe, but often carved by unknown sculptors into the form of a human face—had peculiar counterparts thousands of miles away on Easter Island. There too stood enormous giant heads, chiselled out of a single block, as high as a four-storey house, gazing out over the treeless island into the vast expanse of the eternal sea. Naturally, these colossal statues weighing several tons caught the eye of the first whites to reach the island, and the Dutch captain, Jacob Roggeween, who discovered the utterly lonely island on Easter Day, 1722, already mentions them. James Cook and his two German companions, the scholar Johann Reinhold Forster and his son Georg, wrote of them at length fifty years later. Since then, the guessing-game of Easter Island has gone on uninterruptedly. What was the meaning of the giant heads? Who erected them? When and how did men come to Easter Island?

Two thousand five hundred miles of sea stretched between the island and the mainland; it was about one thousand miles to the nearest Polynesian atoll. The little island lay in utter solitude amidst the vast sea. Was one to suppose that men of some western culture had been *cast away* there? This seemed altogether out of the question, for since time immemorial, wind and current had come day after day from the east. Was one to believe that the men who once peopled Easter Island sailed to this minute volcanic island consciously and to a preconceived plan? Wasn't that an even more outrageous idea?

Yet this assumption alone offered an explanation as to how it had been possible to hew these house-tall human faces from the rock of one of the volcanic craters of Easter Island and transport them several miles over undulating, deeply scored ground to their final positions. Since the smallest of these statues weighed considerably more than five tons, while the average weight was ten to twelve tons and the heaviest weighed more than fifty tons, the number of men required to shift them was such as could have reached Easter Island only by repeated, planned voyages. On no account could this feat be ascribed to a few castaways.

Or was Easter Island only the meagre remnant of a whole continent that had sunk down into the depths of the ocean? Did busy towns and thriving villages once stand here, did fertile acres and shady woods once stretch across the land? Was there an 'Atlantis' here that had sunk hundreds of fathoms deep onto the bed of the ocean? Many theosophists, supported by occult revelations, emphatically asserted this. They believed that the colossal idols of Easter Island were not created by men of our kind at all, but the gigantic inhabitants of the age-old continent 'Lemuria', which once filled the area of the Indian and Pacific Oceans and whose last residue was Easter Island. But paved roads were found leading down from the heights of the island to the harbours and landing-places on the seashore, harbours that are still serviceable today, indicating that their water-level has not changed. This spoke very clearly against the cataclysm theory. To accumulate further evidence, geologists were sent to Easter Island. They hammered and bored, investigating every nook and cranny. And it emerged with complete certainty that there could be no question of any large-scale seismic disaster. So Easter Island was *not* the relic of a submerged continent; its culture was *not* autochthonous; the island must have been peopled somehow and from somewhere.

27. *Menhir circles on the Sillustani Peninsula near Umayo in Peru. The layout reminds us of Stonehenge.*

This left the scholars of all civilized countries with the same insoluble puzzles as before. Then in 1864 several wooden tablets, a hand's breadth wide and mostly a span in length, the so-called *kohau rongo-rongo* or 'news-woods', thickly decorated with figures and 'hieroglyphs', were found at the feet of the colossal carved steles of Easter Island. It was at least surmised that the signs on these tablets were some kind of picture-writing. None of the present natives of the island could give any satisfactory information concerning these pieces of talking wood; the observations of the earliest white discoverers suggest that these 'writing' tablets were employed in some religious cult. Subsequently, the *kohau rongo-rongo* were destroyed by the Christianized Easter Islanders as works of the devil; only nineteen of the tablets survived this holocaust, which did not give scholars much to work on.

In the early twenties, it looked for a time as though a clue to the mystery of the Easter Island tablets had been found. When the English archæologist, John Marshall, began to excavate the ruins of the two five-thousand-year-old, once thriving great industrial centres on the Indus, the cities of Mohenjo-daro and Harappā in the south-west Punjab in 1922, he discovered in the subterranean parts of these cities inscriptions whose 'written' characters seemed to correspond to those of the mysterious Easter Island tablets. In 1938 the American ethnolo-

28. *An Easter Island 'writing-tablet'.*

gist, Alfred Métraux, was able to demonstrate, after a fresh and thorough investigation of Easter Island and its phenomena, that Marshall's conjectures were erroneous. Fortunately, it must be added, since this saves us from the truly neck-breaking contortions that would have been necessary to find even the most threadbare explanation for such an early and distant cultural contact. To his own great astonishment, Alfred Métraux ascertained that the famous 'writing' tablets of Easter Island were less than two hundred years old and carved out of driftwood dating from the eighteenth century. Hence there could be no question of any connection between the scripts of the ancient Indus and of Easter Island.

Nonetheless, the fact remains that the tables of comparison between the Mohenjo-daro and Easter Island scripts drawn up by scholars show a number of similarities. This is undeniable. And, on the other hand, investigations carried out by prehistorians in both south Asia and Oceania seem to show that, as the Viennese prehistorian, Robert Heine-Geldern, puts it, 'the genesis of Polynesian culture, or at any rate of one of its most important components in the Formosa-Philippines-North Celebes area, is to be explained by the mingling of the

Austronesian socketed celt culture with the Austro-Asian palstave celt culture'. In plain English, it appears that, at some time in the mists of antiquity, certain Polynesian islands received their first wave of settlers from the west.

29. *Comparative table of the script signs of the Mohenjo-daro culture with those of Easter Island. Left: Mohenjo-daro. Right: Easter Island.*

This view is also held by zoologists. Whereas neither the chicken nor the pig existed in pre-Columbian America, at least not as domestic animals, both these ancient companions of man were to be found in Polynesia. This is unequivocally attested by the first white discoverers.

They also report that the Polynesians had dogs, and science quickly established that the house dogs of the South Sea Islanders were closely related to Australian and Indonesian breeds. It was the same with the chicken and the pig. The primary forms of the Polynesian varieties likewise came from the Austronesian zone.

Since it has now been demonstrated that India and China knew the domestic chicken some three and a half millennia ago, the hypothesis that certain Polynesian islands were peopled from the west at a very early period may well be correct. The totally different climatic and meteorological conditions that no doubt obtained in the Pacific during and for a long time after the Ice Age, including the considerable narrowing of the trade-wind belt between the enormously enlarged ice-capes at the north and south poles, may have led to quite different states of wind and current, and so made it possible to launch out to the east, even with quite primitive craft. Under no circumstances, however, does this apply to proto-historical and historical times, and a glance at a map of the Pacific will convince anyone of the pristine solitude that lies upon these waters. How could prehistoric peoples have traversed these vast stretches of ocean in their unsteady dugouts and primitive rafts, against wind and currents? And if the theory is propounded that these unknown early men reached not only Easter Island, but also South America, one is bound to ask why Stone-Age Europeans did not also sail in hordes to America, across the much narrower reach of sea that separates the Old World from the New.

The puzzle does not stop here, however. When the first Europeans visited Easter Island at the beginning of the eighteenth century, they encountered people who were almost white. Several of the men had long beards—a form of hair distribution otherwise as unknown in the South Seas as amongst American Indians—and related that many of their forebears had been white-skinned, whilst others had been brown. They repeated a tradition carefully handed down by word of mouth from one generation to the next—as William E. Thompson, purser of the American battleship *Mohican,* who spent some time on the island in 1886, states in his official report—that their white ancestors had once come to the island in great vessels 'from a mountainous land in the east which was parched by the sun, sailing always towards the setting sun'. A similar story met the ears of the first Europeans to reach Polynesia. There too, particularly amongst the chiefs and nobles, they found many white-skinned natives with red to blond hair, blue-grey eyes, and finely curved, aquiline noses. Here too there were ancient legends to the effect that the original home of the Polynesians had lain far to the east, and that the sun-god Tiki had brought his people thence to Polynesia in bygone ages on great rafts. Alongside these almost white and entirely European-looking natives, there were others with brown skins, raven hair, and the flat noses usual in the South Seas. And in Polynesia too, the names of all the chiefs had been preserved by word of mouth right back to the time when the islands were first peopled.

This information was either greeted with complete incredulity, or —which was perhaps worse—it was falsified to conform with the 'noble savage' theories of Rousseau. When Cook and the Forsters got back to Europe everyone was under the influence of Rousseau's philosophy of nature. Thus the reports of half-white, half-brown, friendly and engaging natives arrived at an opportune moment; and when the beautiful dream of man's innocence was distorted into the ridiculous pastoral idylls of the court, science threw the facts overboard with the caricature. So it was a hundred years before anyone delved into the matter.

The trail was blazed by Peter H. Buck, director of the Bernice H. Bishop Museum in Hawaii, a distinguished ethnologist and anthro-

pologist, who, in the early twenties, carried out an extensive anthropo-
metric survey amongst the Polynesians. Buck, who is himself a
Polynesian on his mother's side, established by thousands of individual
examinations that the inhabitants of the Polynesian islands are undoubtedly Europoid. His findings are summed up in the sentence:

As a result of the studies made on the living in all parts of Polynesia it
is evident that the master mariners of the Pacific must be Europoid, for they
are not characterized by the woolly hair, black skins and thin lower legs of
the Negroids nor by the flat face, short stature and drooping inner eyefold
of the Mongoloids. (*Vikings of the Sunrise,* p. 16; see bibliography.)

This is entirely in accord with the impression gained by Captain
Cook during his second voyage in the South Seas in 1773: 'We met
hundreds of true European faces and many genuine Roman noses
among them.' And Georg Forster states of the inhabitants of the
Marquesas Islands: 'Many of them could have been set alongside the
masterpieces of classical art, without losing anything by the comparison.' Of O Aheatua, king of Tahiti-iti, he even writes: 'He was
lighter in colour than all his subjects and had long, sleek, light-brown
hair, shading off into reddish-brown at the ends.'

Sceptics may be of the opinion that Cook and his scientific companions exaggerated somewhat in their enthusiasm over their discovery.
But the Polynesians themselves were patently struck by their resemblance to the miraculous strangers. At all events, Georg Forster relates
with the greatest amusement that the Polynesian Porea, who had come
aboard in Tahiti, after a time asked to be allowed to dress like a
European during landings on other Polynesian islands.

He went on land with us dressed in a linen jacket and seaman's trousers.
He carried Captain Cook's powderhorn and ammunition pouch and desired
to be taken for one of us. To this end he never spoke his mother tongue, but
muttered all sorts of unintelligible sounds, which really duped the local
population. To favour the deception still more, he wished no longer to be
called by his Tahitian name, Porea, but to have an English one . . .

This is extraordinarily significant. For it reveals that Porea knew
himself to resemble his European friends so closely that in European
clothes only his Polynesian name and his inability to speak English
would betray him. And his compatriots, as Georg Forster confirms,
did in fact take him for a white.

This is undoubtedly valid proof. Accordingly, there is little room
for doubt that at some time or other a great host of white men poured
into the Pacific island zone. Whence can these whites have come?

There is, of course, no doubt that at one time India was inhabited by light-skinned Indo-Europeans. Certainly too, isolated Indo-European tribes advanced much farther into Asia. But it is equally certain that the Pacific Ocean barred their progress, at least during historical epochs, when nautical conditions on this largest ocean on earth were exactly the same as they are today. On the other hand, however, it cannot be doubted that this white immigration into the South Seas is of comparatively recent date. Both on Easter Island and in Polynesia, the natives state that the advent of their forefathers to the Pacific islands took place fifty to sixty generations back—in other words, if we take this literally, twelve centuries ago. This may be inexact or exaggerated. But that the Polynesian migration cannot have taken place prior to the Middle Ages is compellingly attested by the fact that all Polynesians, from latitude 20° N. to latitude 40° S., speak a common tongue. Cook and the Forsters have already related with great surprise that their Tahiti-born companion, Porea, was equally well understood everywhere throughout the islands. And Peter H. Buck, who speaks a southern Polynesian dialect, confirms that in our own day one and the same language is spoken across thousands of miles from Hawaii to Tahiti. Likewise, the same genealogy is everywhere taught by the native chroniclers. Buck declares in this connection:

> The names of the ancestors (who colonized Polynesia) are everywhere the same, even in groups of islands as far apart as New Zealand, the Cook Islands, the Society Islands, the Tuamotu group of islands, the Austral and Marquesas Islands, the Gambier Islands and Hawaii. This proves that all Polynesian peoples had common ancestors in historical times.

This proves irrefutably that the Polynesian immigration *must* have occurred during historical times; it further argues strongly for the belief that the immigrants came not from the west, from Indo-Malaya, where there were no longer any Stone-Age peoples in the Middle Ages, but from the east, from America, whose cultures were essentially of a Stone-Age character up to the time of the Spanish invasion.

This may appear a very bold assumption. But if the evidence cited above is accepted in its entirety, this conclusion is almost inescapable. Furthermore, both the technical-material and the spiritual-religious culture of the Polynesians exhibit extensive correspondences with South American culture. Attention has repeatedly been drawn to this aspect of the matter, most recently by the Scandinavian ethnologist, Erland Nordenskiöld, who, in 1931, listed the points of identity which emerge on comparison of the material culture of Peru with that of

Polynesia. Not only are weapons the same—the blowpipe and strange, swordlike wooden clubs; not only are personal adornments and toilet articles identical, e.g. wide bracelets of metal, tortoiseshell or seashells, as well as a sort of combined brush and comb, which exists only in Peru and Polynesia; not only do we find in both places the double canoe, the characteristic triangular sail and the fish hook—all of which might have been acquired through fleeting contacts; but much more complex knowledge was also trans-mitted from Peru to Poly-nesia. This included the artificial irrigation of ter-raced fields rising up the mountainside; the difficult art of blowing the conch-shell horn; the extremely queer custom of skull tre-panning, which is as wide-spread in western South America as in Polynesia; the use of wooden chairs; the wearing of dance masks in religious rites; and most especially the invention of the celebrated knot 'writing', which was employed both by the Incas and by the Polynesians.

30. *Inca scribe with* quipu *and abacus. Drawing from the picture chronicle of Huaman Poma de Ayala.*

The unprejudiced reader will probably feel that these few examples from Norden-skiöld's long list of identities are already sufficient to dispose of the argument that they are mere coincidences. In particular, the fact that an attempt was made in both Peru and Polynesia—but nowhere else in the world—to evolve a kind of 'writing' by arranging knots of various sizes and various types in a significant order as aids to memory, cannot be explained by coinci-dence. There can be little doubt that the similarity in procedure pre-supposes intensive contacts between the two cultures.

This view receives strong support from the following argument: when the first Europeans landed in Polynesia, they noted to their surprise that one of the cultivated plants which they had brought with

them for the islanders had long been known on the Polynesian islands
—the potato! It grew there in the sweet variety, was unknown to the
west of the islands and was confined to the zone occupied by the Polynesian people. On the other hand, it occurred farther east, on both Easter
Island and in South America, where this *Ipomœa batatas* had been
cultivated in certain regions since the earliest times. Since the potato is
highly susceptible to sea water, which rots it immediately, it could not
have drifted to the oceanic islands, but must have been brought by
men. The American ethnologist, R. B. Dixon, who made a special
study of this question in the early thirties, states, 'This plant could have
been brought from America to Polynesia only by the hand of man',
and Peter H. Buck expressly confirms that the sweet potato was planted
in Hawaii not later than *circa* A.D. 1250, and in New Zealand not more
than a hundred years after. He points out further that in the Quechua
dialect of north Peru the sweet potato is called *kumar,* while in Polynesia its name is *kumara.* This observation is important in that it
localizes the point of departure for relations between South America
and Polynesia. The designation *kumar* is unknown in south Peru.
Thus the connections between Peru and Polynesia, at least as far as the
sweet potato is concerned, must have had their juncture in north Peru.

A variety of linguistic correspondences point to north Peru having
been the starting point for the mysterious links between South America
and Oceania. Here are some of them:

| On Easter Island | In North Peru | |
| --- | --- | --- |
| unu | unu | water |
| hapay | apay | to carry |
| kiri | kiri | skin |
| toki | toki | axe |
| ariki | awki | chief |
| tuu | tunu | post, stake |
| karu | koroa | distant |
| poko-poko | ponko | shaft, deep hole |
| rarako | raku | light colour, snow |
| kimi | kimi | bottle gourd |

This identity between important words is naturally no chance—
especially not in the case of the last on the list, *kimi* for the bottle
gourd, *Lagenaria vulgaris.* Like the sweet potato, the bottle gourd—
and all other varieties of gourd—originated in America. The bottle
gourd in particular is a plant of the primeval American forest. Both in
Polynesia and Peru not only the fruit, but also the shell of this plant
have been used since time immemorial. Dried over the fire the shells

make excellent water-containers. Both the Polynesian sailors and fisher-men and the coastal Indians of Peru put them to this use centuries before any contact with the conquistadores and discoverers from the Old World. No type of gourd, however, can resist salt water, even for a short time. Thus the bottle gourd, the turban gourd, or any of the other gourds distributed throughout Polynesia can have reached the South Seas only in vessels navigated by man. The fact that the *Lagenaria vulgaris* is called *kimi* on both sides of the Pacific is a further pointer to the American origin of the plant. To end this list of correspondences we have the *Sapindus saponaria,* a medicinal plant originating from tropical America that has an astringent effect and can also be used as soap. This plant also grows in Polynesia and, remarkably enough, it bears the same name amongst the Easter Islanders as in America: in both places it is called *para-para.*

The situation is just the same in the spiritual and religious sphere. While the Peruvian Virakocha myth states that the white religion-founder one day spread his mantle on the western sea, seated himself upon it, and vanished in the ocean, an ancient legend on the Tonga Islands in south-west Polynesia tells of the magical departure of early Polynesians to a land far away in the east across the ocean. When the waters of the great Flood, sent upon the earth at the dawn of time by Tangaloa, the supreme god, had subsided, he appointed two of his sons with their families to occupy land in Polynesia. But one of them, an envious, lazy man, murdered his industrious and inventive brother. Then Tangaloa was wroth. He removed the family of the murdered man to the east, say the Tongans, to a distant land across the sea; he bestowed upon all its people white skins, amazing skill, immense wealth, and the ability to build large ships. Then Tangaloa announced: 'The wind shall blow from your country to Tonga. But the others shall remain in Tonga, have dark skins and no riches. Your white brothers shall bring them to you and trade with you.'

This was written in 1818 by the Englishman, F. Merian, who was one of the first systematically to explore Polynesia and to make equally systematic notes of what he found. He was sure that this was a very ancient legend. And when the German explorer, Georg Gerland, who made a study of Flood legends, examined the Tonga myths a century later, he too expressed the opinion: 'Here the subsequent advent of the Whites was pragmatically linked to a certain very old myth relating to the Gods' Land of Pu-Lotu and its light-skinned, divine inhabitants, who often came to Tonga.'

Virakocha vanishing westward into the sea, Tangaloa's grand-

children translated eastward across the vast ocean into another land,
both of them white-skinned and distinguished from their dark brothers
by greater skill and immense wealth—thus the two shores of the
Pacific, through their children, reached out their hands to one another
in ancient times! Hence Kon-Tiki, the Peruvian god, is also worshipped
in Polynesia—significantly, above all in east and central Polynesia.

*31. Metal beaker from Peru.
The figure bears on its head
a crown or circlet exactly
like that found on the idols
of St. Agostino in Colombia
or on Easter Island.*

Hence Tane, one of Virakocha's followers, as Thor Heyerdahl reports, also
crops up in north-east Polynesia: as a
secondary god to Kon-Tiki, as the god
of craftsmen and manual skill—as the
god and tribal ancestor of the whites, as
Peter H. Buck remarks in parenthesis
long before Heyerdahl and quite independently of him!

In the context of our account as a
whole, we cannot help being struck by
this. The fact that gods like Tiki and
Tane are known equally on both shores
of the Pacific suggests very close links
between them. For the transference of
gods is as difficult as that of weapons and
ornaments is easy. It requires firm bridges,
prolonged and undisturbed relations between people and people; and as a rule
some kinship of race or blood is a necessary pre-condition. Close connections
between Peru and Polynesia are also clearly indicated in the sphere of
art; particularly by statues of the Easter Island type, which occur in
Colombia and Peru and in Polynesia. On Easter Island itself these
statues have an altogether European look: they are narrow-faced, with
prominent, sharply profiled noses, thin lips curled as though in contempt, and jutting chins with pointed beards. Anyone who has seen
them, or even illustrations of them, will agree that they cannot possibly
have been carved after Mongoloid or Negroid models. Unless we
suppose the Easter Island statues to have sprung solely from the un-
fettered creative imagination of their sculptors, who gave their works
the appearance of a white man quite by chance, we can only conclude
that these statues are in the nature of portraits, or at least that they
represent the traditional conception of the forefathers as reverently
handed down through the generations. This is Heyerdahl's deduction.

He reports further that, according to genealogical tradition on Easter Island, white men came to the lonely isle in the Pacific with great vessels from the east between A.D. 400 and 500, while the brown population stems from the Polynesian islands. Peter H. Buck, who must be considered the leading authority on all questions affecting Polynesia, clearly knows nothing of this. He reports the results of his anthropological investigation, which convinced him that the Polynesians were Europeans; he states that the craftsman's god, Tane, is regarded as the ancestor of the whites; he relates that in the past there were two kings on the Mangareva Islands, the Akariki-tea, the white king, and the Akariki-pangu, the dark king. But he mani-festly ascribes little importance to these traditions, doubtless because, at the time he wrote his book, he could find no adequate explanation as to whence his white Polynesians could have come. Hence Buck asserts that the stone-carvers who produced the giant heads on Easter Island could only have originated from the Marquesas Islands or Raivavae, where similar huge statues occur; whereas only smaller stone figures have been erected on the Society Islands, Hawaii and New Zealand. He makes no mention of Peru or any connection between Easter Island and South America.

*32. An Easter Island* ariki *in a canoe with a feather head-dress tied in triangular bundles. Script sign from an Easter Island tablet.*

*33. Chieftain with head-dress in triangular bundles. Another script sign from Easter Island.*

Now, most of the Easter Island figures have round the body a curious girdle, carved in relief from the volcanic tufa, which is also to be seen on the giant Peruvian heads by Lake Titicaca. This, as Heyerdahl points out, represents the rainbow girdle, the mythic symbol of Kon-Tiki. On the Mangareva group in Polynesia, ancient legends have been handed down according to which the sun-god stretched out his rainbow girdle before him and crossed by it to Mangareva, as though over a South American suspension bridge. Yet no girdle reliefs are known from Mangareva. This seems to suggest that artistic contacts between Peru and Easter Island were closer than between Easter Island and the Marquesas.

This is corroborated by a series of minor pieces of evidence, which, although they have all been well known for years, have rarely been assessed in the context of the

34. *Feather mosaic from the sheet-silver ornament of Pachacamac. The head-dress of triangular bundles is also known in Peru.*

problem as a whole. Bishop Jaussen, who was for many years the Easter Islanders' spiritual guide and also made a study of them, included in his dictionary of the Easter Island language the two signs reproduced in figs. 32 and 33. They show a canoe bearing men whose hair or feather head-dress is tied into triangular bundles. Such triangular bundling of hair or feather plaits is known from only two other regions of the world: the Amazon, where the ethnologist, I. Fr. Ph. von Martius, saw it among the Yuris, a savage Indian tribe, at the beginning of last century—and Peru, as fig. 34 from Pachacamac demonstrates. On the front of this sheet-silver ornament two demons with long plaits tied in triangular bundles are portrayed in feather mosaic.

The famous 'Trujillo jug' from Peru, a glorious piece of old Indian craftsmanship which is represented in every major work on art history, bears the figure depicted in fig. 35, which portrays a stylized bird framed by two upright rods. It is possible that this represents the *inti* bird, the winged companion that fluttered round Virakocha and, like Odin's raven, knew everything, both past and future. This symbol is strikingly reminiscent of cultic bird images from Melanesia, particularly those from the Negroes of the Solomon Islands off New Guinea. Symbols similar to those found in Peru also figure on the Easter Island writing tablets. And we know from Captain Cook and the Forsters

35. *Mythological bird framed by two rods. Symbol from the temple jug of Trujillo, Peru.*

that sculptures of a bird, occasionally paired with images of a fish, frequently occurred on the *marai,* the pyramidal burial places of Polynesian chiefs and heroes. It would be very strange if these correspondences were the outcome of mere chance!

One more item must be listed here that more or less completes the picture: this is a decoration on the back of a figure on the so-called Puma Box in the Berlin Ethnological Museum. This decoration, which is scalloped and might be interpreted as feathers, fur or scales, is also known from two mutually independent Easter Island tablets: the tablet in the Leningrad Hermitage, and that in the Braine-le-Comte Museum in Belgium. No symbol of this kind is known from any other part of the world. It occurs only in Peru and on Easter Island, which is remarkable to say the least.

It is very typical that attention was drawn to this strange identity not by a strictly orthodox scientist, but by the woman painter, K. von Möller, who reported it about a dozen years ago in the *Zeitschrift für Ethnologie* (the *Journal of Ethnology*). That is to say, by an outsider who can with impunity indicate such visual resemblances and draw from them the conclusions that common sense inevitably *must* draw: viz., that contacts and connections existed here, of which we know very little, but which cannot be dismissed as figments of the imagination merely because of the absence of written records.

*36. Mythological birds framed by two rods. Script signs from Easter Island.*

What are we to make of all these things? Are they all coincidences? Or have the scientists, who have been accumulating evidence bit by bit for nearly two centuries, perhaps been on the wrong track altogether? Have they perhaps all been working under the compulsion of a preconceived opinion, and observing only those facts that fit their theories? In concrete terms, was the Pacific really crossed from east to west, from America to the Polynesian islands—or was it, on the contrary, the Polynesians, first-rate seamen as they were, who sailed to America?

One may assume as highly probable that ocean-going outrigger boats now and again reached the west coast of America. These landings must have taken place not in Peru, however, but considerably farther south, at the point where the cold westerly current of the Pacific touches its eastern shore. This lies in the area of latitude 40° S., between Valdivia and Valparaiso, far south of Peru. But—here there was no sweet potato called *kumar*, no bottle gourd and no *Sapindus saponaria*, no knot writing, no gods named Tiki or Tane, no giant statues, and no legends of white founders of religions from a far land to the east. All this is confined to Peru, and to north Peru in particular, suggesting that American-Oceanic communications proceeded from America, not from Polynesia. Wind and ocean currents were bound to carry vessels which put to sea from Peru, and were caught up by the Humboldt Current, to Oceania.

Furthermore, in spite of the masterly nautical skill of their captains, the Polynesian outriggers were technically primitive craft. The outrigger construction compelled all sailing to be done in such a manner that the outrigger always remained to windward, i.e. so that when the main boat was tilted over by the sail pressure the outrigger was raised out of the water and not submerged beneath it. This is self-evident to anyone acquainted with sailing ships. Nonetheless, it was not easy to obtain confirmation of it from men who had themselves been in the South Seas in their youth—mainly because, under the influence of Europeans, outrigger sailing has become a lost art, even in the South Seas. All that could be learnt was that not one of these ancient mariners, washed by the waters of all the seven seas, could remember ever having seen a Polynesian boat tacking into the wind under full sail. Adalbert von Chamisso still had an opportunity, during his world tour in 1815–18, about forty years after Captain Cook and the two Forsters, to watch Polynesian outriggers, such as are now in our museums, under sail. He describes such craft as follows:

A swinging platform is fastened amidships, projecting over the water on both sides: a shorter distance to leeward, a greater distance to windward, where this light wooden structure curves down at the end and is attached to an outrigger float parallel with the hull of the ship. On this platform, to windward of the hull, is the mast, attached by several ropes and leaning forrard, carrying a simple triangular sail, one corner of which is attached to the prow. Steering is done at the stern with a hand rudder. The crew stand or lie on the platform, closer to the float during a strong wind and during a weak one closer to the main body of the craft . . .

This shows clearly that the Polynesians used the outrigger as a kind of balancing pole. As long as the rigging held, such boats could ride the strongest wind and no doubt attain fantastic speeds. It is also quite unquestionable that the sailors who manned these craft were capable of holding their course from Tahiti to Hawaii or vice versa at right angles to the prevailing wind. What could not be done with these vessels was to tack in our sense of the word for long distances. And this is precisely what would have had to be done, for endless periods and across infinite distances, in order to sail from Polynesia to South America. Isolated vessels no doubt managed it from time to time. But it is quite out of the question that whole fleets, with women, children, provisions and cattle on board, ever ventured across the vast wastes of water separating Polynesia from America under the conditions of wind and current prevailing in historical times.

Just how did these forgotten South American emigrants get to Polynesia? Chamisso asserted: 'No American people was ever a maritime people', and this assertion has been repeated again and again since his time and rarely disputed. Of course, the Indians, as far as we know, generally had rather primitive canoes or reed rafts—river craft, which could also be used on the sea immediately offshore. Besides these, however, they possessed, at least in South America, large seagoing sailing rafts, constructed of huge balsa logs and given a certain capacity for holding to a course by numerous centre-boards fixed between the logs. The Spanish captain, Bartolomeo Ruiz, who was attached to one of Pizarro's preparatory expeditions, vividly reports the great shock he received when, in 1525, he espied a large vessel under full sail far off the coast of Ecuador. He was forced to suppose, he relates, that the immense swelling sails belonged to a Spanish ship, and that some other caballero in search of El Dorado had got there before him. He breathed a sigh of relief when he observed that it was no Spanish caravel which rose up before him, but 'merely' an Indian high-seas raft, a vessel with a displacement of about thirty tons and a crew of some twenty men.

This incident, which Prescott retails at length in his famous history of the conquest of Peru by Pizarro, has been read and re-read a hundred thousand times and as often overlooked. The millennia in which our early European forefathers took the tremendous step from sailing raft to boat are so immensely distant, that our experienced navigators cannot imagine how such an unwieldy thing can have been navigated. Apart from anything else, they thought the crew of such a craft would be swept overboard by the first large breaker. It therefore seemed utterly impossible that these ungainly rafts could have been steered across the thousands of miles of the Pacific with any prospect of reaching the other side.

Proof that even landlubbers could manage it was furnished by a small group of Norwegians, who allowed themselves to be driven by the Humboldt Current and the trade winds from Callao, the port of Lima, to Polynesia in a hundred days on a sailing raft built after old Indian prototypes—the celebrated 'Kon-Tiki Expedition', to which we have already referred. These six Norwegians, authentic descendants of those Norsemen about whom we have had so much to say here, but with no experience of the sea, afforded by their expedition absolutely irrefutable proof that incredible distances can be traversed with the most primitive craft. After the successful completion of this experiment, there can be no further doubt that Polynesia *may* really have been peopled from the east. At least it must be admitted that Heyerdahl's theories have gained immense weight by the fact that he and his five comrades staked their lives on them. To be fair, it is now up to the proponents of the theory that America was reached by vessels from Oceania prior to Columbus to put out to sea eastward from Polynesia in an Oceanic high-seas canoe. As far as I am aware, no such project has been so much as discussed.

All the same, Heyerdahl's magnificent drift voyage still does not prove that Polynesia actually *was* peopled from the east across the Pacific. For Heyerdahl and his comrades at least knew that land awaited them at the end of their journey. They were acquainted with the globe. They had ocean charts on board. They were in constant touch with the civilized world by radio. The alleged white immigrants of the middle of the first century A.D. did not have these modern technical aids at their disposal. They had neither radio nor ocean charts. Apparently they just sailed into the blue, man, wife and child.

Can we assume this? Can we believe that the first settlers put to sea without the slightest inkling of where their voyage might end? That they entrusted themselves to the enormous South Seas on their simple rafts, without knowing for sure that, with some luck, wind and current would carry them to land? Such things just do not happen. When we observe, in a future chapter, how cautiously the Icelandic Norsemen felt their way to Greenland, how carefully and thoroughly they investigated the new land and its living conditions, we shall realize how such colonizations were carried out. It is quite unthinkable that those Polynesian seafarers crossed the sea blindly, gambling with Fate.

Heyerdahl does not suppose that the white exiles from Peru utilized ocean-going ships of the type used in Europe during these centuries—though this theory is by no means preposterous, if one accepts the idea of a white population of Peru prior to Columbus at all. His conjecture is that they employed the balsa rafts of ancient Indian tradition. He can support this belief by the fact that rafts of a similar type were still in use on the east Polynesian islands of the Mangareva group after their discovery by Europeans. Buck also went into this problem, expressing the view that rafts were used in the Mangareva exclusively for the transport of goods between nearby islands, whereas longer trips were made in double or outrigger canoes. Rafts were still employed, he claimed, only because they were quicker to make and required less wood and fewer highly specialized craftsmen than sea-going canoes. This argument might also have been valid for our white refugees on the coast of Peru, since they probably had little time in hand following Chief Cari's attack, and since they had laboriously to transport the wood for the rafts from the mountain forests of the Andes to the coast.

Heyerdahl makes no more than an allusion to this important pre-liminary question which his expedition had to consider. He surmised that Kon-Tiki embarked on the rafts after Cari's onslaught, solely to escape his enemies, and was then swept westward against his own intention by the Humboldt Current. Apparently, however, rumours concerning the presence of land in the western ocean were current in early times. Tradition has it that the Inca Tupac Yupanqui, monarch of Peru and Ecuador, put to sea with a large fleet of rafts in search of these islands shortly before the arrival of the Spaniards. It appears that he found the Galapagos Islands. Anyway, he succeeded in returning home nearly nine months later. One is therefore disposed to assume that Virakocha knew, or at least hoped, that he would come to land in the west.

Heyerdahl reports in his book that his raft traversed 60 to 80 nautical miles in twenty-four hours—a speed of 3 knots. It is quite unthinkable that primitive craft could have sailed eastward *against* such strong currents. Hence Heyerdahl dismisses the idea that South America can have been peopled from the west via the seaway as impossible.

4

The only thing which appears certain at the outset is that Basques and Celts, at a pretty early period, sailed into the north-west Atlantic and thereby into the immediate vicinity of America. Among the Basques, many vivid oral traditions are extant of the discovery, several centuries ago, of 'Stockfish Land', i.e. the Newfoundland seaboard, which is exceptionally rich in fish; no written documents are available, since the archives of the Basque cities were destroyed to the last scrap of paper. Eugen Geleich has proved with almost complete certainty that Gascon fishermen were at home in American waters long before Columbus. It is therefore not particularly surprising that numerous reports should be current of the discovery of Gallo-Celtic words in American Indian languages; indeed, some claim that it is possible to converse tolerably successfully with certain Indian tribes by using modern Irish or Welsh. Paul Gaffarel quotes several such reports in his pamphlet *The Irish in America before Columbus* (see bibliography). They related to districts in Kentucky, Virginia and Carolina, that is to say, to those regions which we have already named as the main seats of the Tuscarora and other 'white' Indians. In fact, it has been expressly stated that the aboriginal Welsh inhabitants of Carolina have preserved a vivid recollection of the voyages of their tribal hero, Madoc. Particular reference is made to the Tuscarora Indians in this connection. An English geographer named Owen relates in his *Collection of Breton Antiquities* (London, 1877) the adventures of one Jonas Morgan, who was taken prisoner by the Tuscarora in Virginia in 1685. As he could speak Welsh he was not scalped, but treated in a very friendly manner. He remained with them for four months, and was able to converse with them without much trouble in Welsh.

It is as well to maintain a critical attitude towards these and similar reports, especially as Phœnician and Egyptian roots have also been 'discovered' in Indian languages. Condamine asserted in 1746 that he had noted Hebrew words in the language of the Incas. The Englishman Donelly 'found' ancient Armenian stems in Mexican place names, while his countryman Hyde Clark 'disclosed' linguistic concords between African and Mexican tongues. In the face of such flights of fancy (the American, Augustus Le Plongeon, went so far as to declare in his book *Sacred Mysteries among the Mayas and the Quichuas 11,500 Years ago* in 1886: 'The Maya language is one third purest Greek'!) it is desirable to bear continually in mind the words with which Alexander von Humboldt castigated these follies: 'The structure of American languages appears extraordinarily bizarre to those peoples who speak modern European languages. Hence one is easily deceived by chance resemblances.'

Nonetheless, the so-called 'inscription of Parahyba' in Brazil in 1874 aroused immense interest throughout the scientific world, which had long grossly over-estimated the nautical capacities of the Phœnicians. For nearly twenty years it was considered genuine and regarded as proof that Phœnicians had been cast away on the coast of South America.

A still longer life was enjoyed by an alleged ancient Phœnician rock inscription discovered in 1899 not far from Rio de Janeiro, ostensibly by Professor Ladislaus Netto, the distinguished director of the Brazilian National Museum, and reported at length in a scientific geographical periodical of North Africa shortly afterwards. This inscription ran as follows:

We are here, sons of the land of Canaan in Syria. We are pursued by misfortune. It is terrible to be stranded as we are. We certainly have not much longer to live. Despair has seized us—and what despair! We shall soon see the ninth, yea the tenth year of our sojourn here draw to a close . . . Unbearable heat reigns here. The little water that there is to drink is quite bad . . . What an accursed land this is! Fevers consume us and it is like a glowing oven here. We have no other consolation than Baal . . .

*37. The alleged 'Phœnician' inscription discovered near Rio de Janeiro.*

This obscurely published inscription seems to have remained unknown to European orientalists for a long time, so that the German geographer, Richard Hennig, was still able to report it in 1940. He too queried it profoundly, but it was recognized that nothing is more difficult than the investigation of such ancient and, on the whole, still little understood languages. The conflict which raged round the first finds of Persian cuneiform script last century is typical. Studies of this

Rio de Janeiro inscription allegedly made by philologists led to the conjecture that its authors were Carthaginians who had fled overseas after the fall of their city in the year 146 B.C., or had been carried overseas by high winds while in flight. This cannot be dismissed as entirely impossible, since it is certain that there were Carthaginians on the Azores some three hundred years prior to this date.

The riddle seems to have been solved recently. Study of the facsimile of the alleged Phœnician inscription, reproduced in fig. 37, by a German orientalist revealed it to be a forgery. The Brazilian Ministry of Education, whose opinion the author of this book obtained, also declares it such. This presumably puts an end to the mystery and reduces it, like many other South American 'enigmas', to an error or a fake—immensely difficult though it is in the present state of our knowledge of Phœnician to forge a text that makes sense.

*38. A genuine Phœnician inscription from the ninth century B.C.*

Despite the doubts of scholars regarding alleged Phœnician inscriptions in South America, a further rock engraving, ostensibly in Phœnician cuneiform script, was discovered not far from Rio de Janeiro. Three thousand feet up on a vertical wall of rock in the little holiday resort of Pedra da Gavea are a series of scratches looking like an inscription and visible from a great distance. This 'inscription' had for a long time been attributed to some unknown prehistoric American people, until closer examination apparently revealed that it was Phœnician. It is said to contain the following words: 'Tyre, Phœnicia, Badezir, Firstborn of Jethbaal . . .'

If this interpretation is correct, the Pedra da Gavea inscription is some two thousand years old. Badezir ruled Phœnicia from 855 to 850 B.C., and his father, Ittobaal or Jethbaal, from 887 to 856 B.C.

The scholar who made this discovery was a most unusual man. His name was Bernardo da Silva Ramos, he came from Manaos in the Brazilian interior, and was originally a *cauchero*, a rubber tapper, in the vast primeval forests of Brazil. More diligent, cleverer, and presumably also luckier than his fellows, he soon attained independence and a fortune. From rubber-tapper he became a rubber industrialist—and he chose for his relaxation a hobby rare in the jungles of the Amazon:

he became a coin-collector. In order to devote himself entirely to his passion, he finally sold his business and retired altogether from the rubber industry.

This was before the fall in rubber at the beginning of this century. Bernardo da Silva Ramos kept his fortune; he went to Europe and published, in Rome, a three-volume work on his collection of coins. Then he undertook a study tour of Egypt, Syria and Greece lasting for several years; after this, when he was over fifty, he returned once more to Amazonia.

Only now did his real life's work begin. It had long been known that from time to time blocks of stone were found in the primeval forest on the Amazon that seemed to bear some kind of inscription. But no one had hitherto paid any heed to them. Now Silva Ramos went in search of them, and it appeared to his eye, trained in Egypt and Asia Minor, that the blocks bore Phœnician characters. He knew no Phœnician, however. So he copied down the remarkable signs he thought he saw, returned to Manaos on foot through jungle and swamp, and placed his drawings before the learned Rabbi of the age-old Jewish community in Manaos. And behold, the Jewish scholar was able to decipher the intricate scratches! These inscriptions stemmed from an early Semitic language, which could only be Phœnician.

The expectation of life of anyone who had worked as a *cauchero* in the inferno of the Amazon jungle was short in those days. Any man who passed the age of fifty must be favoured by the gods. But anyone who still had the energy at that age to hunt the jungle year after year for a few old stones must be possessed. This remarkable man sought, photographed and drew stone engravings in the Amazon jungles till his death of a fever in 1931 at the age of seventy-three—consumed by the prodigious hardships of these two decades, but full of fierce, stubborn energy to his last breath. He left behind him a thick, two-volume work listing two thousand eight hundred ancient historical inscriptions, most of which—in his opinion—are Greek and Phœnician.

His hometown, Manaos, elected him President of the local Geographico-Historical Institute and still honours his memory. One part of the rest of the scientific world laughs at him, as it once laughed at Don Marcellino de Sautuola for his Spanish cave paintings, as it laughed at the merchant Heinrich Schliemann, when he thought he had dug up Troy. In Rio de Janeiro they do not laugh. There they are horrified: 'We see here an author who wasted his talent in depicting the simplest things erroneously and thereby propounding absurd and illogical theories . . .'

Naturally, the author of this book made inquiries concerning the Gavea inscription in Rio de Janeiro. As was to be expected, official archæology in Brazil adopted a completely negative attitude towards this 'inscription' as well. The Ministry of Education and Health stated emphatically that examination by geologists had proved it to be nothing more than the effect of weather erosion which happened to look like an inscription. The official opinion of the appropriate Brazilian authority concludes with the words: 'Brazilian archæology denies altogether the existence of Phœnician inscriptions in any part of the country whatsoever.' This is so final that it leaves nothing more to be said, unless the advance of research at some time brings to light fresh facts.

Whether that will ever happen no one can say. But the bold exploit of one man, the French physician and oceanographer Dr. Louis Alain Bombard, who crossed the Atlantic on a fragile rubber and canvas raft, does show the problem in a fundamentally new light. Of course, nothing was farther from the intention of Dr. Bombard, who put out from Casablanca in North Africa at the end of August 1952, and landed safely in Bridgetown on the island of Barbados in the Antilles on Christmas Eve the same year, after a drift voyage of sixty-five days, than to prove that the Punic armada of which we spoke above reached America with the north-east trade wind on its flight from the Romans. He was concerned to complete investigations begun by the Norwegian ethnologist, Thor Heyerdahl, on his famous Kon-Tiki expedition and also carried out by other experimenters. He was concerned with the question of whether a shipwrecked man of normal constitution was capable of living for weeks on nothing but plankton and fish, and whether it was possible to satisfy the human body's need for fluids by salt water and the liquid squeezed from raw fish.

The successful conclusion of his undertaking answered these questions once and for all. In the context of our narrative it demonstrated furthermore that it must undoubtedly have been possible, even in early times, to cross the Atlantic. This lends fresh weight to all hypotheses of ocean-crossing prior to Columbus, beginning with the news received by Odysseus from the enchantress Circe, of Persephone's Land of the Dead beyond the Ocean, and ending with the works of Bernardo da Silva Ramos, the butt of scientific laughter.

For the present we must leave it at that. I did not wish to omit these matters from our account, since it must be borne in mind that what we are dealing with are not a few isolated reports from which early links with the New World might be inferred, but a closely woven web made up of a vast variety of individual threads. It is the very multiplicity of these reports, which are entirely independent of one another, and relate to the most disparate spheres of human life and activity, which makes it probable that true and factual events underlie them.

By and large, this is the standpoint adopted by scholars, who, with a few exceptions, are convinced of the extreme probability that early links existed between Europe and America.

Moreover, it is not only geographers who hold this opinion. Many historians too have given expression to it, particularly in relation to the Irish. Thus, for example, the German Julius Pokorny, one of the leading experts on the early history of Ireland, has explicitly stated that the discovery of America by Irish mariners is entirely possible. Another well-known investigator, the Scot W. F. Skeene, expresses the same view. Concerning the stories of the Brandan cycle he declares: 'They rest upon a basis of historical fact.' A similar opinion is held by the Irish historian, E. O'Curry, who assesses the sea legends of his people in the following terms: 'These very ancient accounts are naturally inexact and laden with many poetic and romantic elements. Nevertheless, there can be no doubt that they rest upon facts. It is extremely probable that they would be of immense value if only we knew them in their original form.'

Similar quotations could be made from the works of innumerable other scholars. It is therefore clear that we must not dismiss all apparently fanciful traditions as mere legends. This gives a certain significance to the saga of Hvitramanna Land. Of course, this problem is not yet solved, and it does not look as though a solution is in immediate prospect. The discovery of America by white men even before the Scandinavians is eminently probable, but it cannot be definitively proved. Hvitramanna Land is therefore one more of those geographical and historical puzzles which render ancient geography such a fascinating subject.

## PART SEVEN

# THE RUNE STONE OF KENSINGTON AND THE MYSTERY OF THE GREENLAND VIKINGS

WITH a shower of sparks the pickaxe sprang back out of the ground. The man wiped the sweat angrily from his brow. Damned hot this August 1898! Now there was some stone or other in the way; this was going to be the devil of a job. But he'd got to get rid of the tree whose roots he was uncovering. A pity—it was a fine tree. Slender and straight as a mast, and a good sixty or seventy years old. There was nothing for it, however, even though aspens didn't cast nearly as much shadow as other trees. This was just where he wanted to put the vegetable garden, and it had to have sun.

Once more the pickaxe. Again sparks flew. That was quite a chunk down there! He took up the spade and prodded the soil to see how big the stone really was. As the sun climbed higher in the sky, the man dug and heaved, until he had it out. Encrusted with sand, a rectangular, surprisingly regular stone 31 inches long, 16 inches wide and 6 inches thick lay on the edge of the hole he had dug. It must have been down there a long time. The roots of the tree, which had clasped it at both ends, had been quite flattened on one side by the pressure of the stone. It must already have been in the ground when the aspen seed first settled in the soil.

In the scorching heat of this August afternoon, it wasn't long before the sand covering the block dried. As the sand fell off it revealed what looked like writing, writing chiselled in the stone—good God, those were runes!

The man was deeply moved. For he had seen runes as a child, long, long ago, before he crossed the wide ocean and bought this farm here in Minnesota. That was at home in Helsingeland, Sweden, where he was born and went to school. His teacher had once shown him a rune stone in the museum, and told him of the ancients who cut runes in beech staves, and who had set up stones with runic inscriptions in Scandinavia, in the great land of Russia, in Denmark, and farther south, in Germany, as a sign of their presence.

A feeling of nostalgia overcame the man. Runes! He must show his youngster, who knew nothing of the old homeland across the water. And even more the neighbours. There were many Swedes living in the locality. They were all certain to have seen runes in the old days at home, as children. How *they* would stare! There was plenty of writing too. "Let's have a look: one, two, three, four . . . nine lines; and there were another three long lines running down the edge.

Olof Ohman called his son. He sent the farmhand to the neighbours. How did these runes get here, right in the middle of the U.S.A., 940 miles from the Atlantic, here in Solem near Kensington in Minnesota, immediately west of the Great Lakes?

## 2

The lawyer and notary, R. J. Rasmusson, had been living for some years in Douglas County, Minnesota. He acted as legal adviser and Notary Public to the many Scandinavian settlers in the neighbourhood. He was an upright and prosperous man.

One day in the year 1909, three men called on him, and R. J. Rasmusson registed the strangest affidavit of his life. The three men were Olof Ohman, farmer, living in Section Fourteen of the Township of Solem, Minnesota, aged fifty-four, married, of blameless character, and domiciled in American since 1881. One of his companions was obviously also a farmer. His name was Nils Flaten, he was a neighbour of Olof Ohman and came, like him, from Sweden. Both men wished to swear an affidavit to be registered by the notary. The third man was a great deal younger. His name was Hjalmar R. Holand; he looked as though he were from the city and was unquestionably no farmer. He really had nothing to do with the affair, and had simply accompanied Ohman and Flaten.

R. J. Rasmusson sent the other two into the waiting-room, while he listened to Ohman's story. At the end of it the notary drafted a summary of this long and remarkable tale, which was read and sworn by Ohman. This is the affidavit registered by R. J. Rasmusson:

I, Olof Ohman, of the town of Solem, Douglas County, State of Minnesota, being duly sworn, make the following statement:

I am fifty-four years of age, and was born in Helsingeland, Sweden, from where I emigrated to America in the year 1881, and settled upon my farm in Section Fourteen, Township of Solem, in 1891. In the month of August, 1898, while accompanied by my son, Edward, I was engaged in grubbing upon a timbered elevation, surrounded by marshes, in the southeast corner of my land, about 500 feet west of my neighbour's, Nils Flaten's house, and in full view thereof. Upon removing an asp, measuring about 10 inches in diameter at its base, I discovered a flat stone inscribed with characters, to me unintelligible. The stone lay just beneath the surface of the ground in a slightly slanting position, with one corner almost protruding. The two largest roots of the tree clasped the stone in such a manner that the stone must have been there at least as long as the tree. One of the roots penetrated directly downward and was flat on the side next to the stone. The other root extended almost horizontally across the stone and made at its edge a right angled turn downward. At this turn the root was flattened on the side toward the stone. This root was about three inches in diameter. Upon washing off the surface dirt, the inscription presented a weathered appearance, which to me appeared just as old as the untouched parts of the stone. I immediately called my neighbour's, Nils Flaten's attention to the discovery, and he came over the same afternoon and inspected the stone and the stump under which it was found.

I kept the stone in my possession for a few days; and then left it in the Bank of Kensington, where it remained for inspection for several months. During this interval, it was sent to Chicago for inspection and soon returned in the same state in which it was sent. Since then I kept it at my farm until August, 1907, when I presented the stone to H. R. Holand. The stone, as I remember, was about 30 inches long, 16 inches wide, and 7 inches thick, and I recognized the illustration on page 16 of H. R. Holand's History of the Norwegian Settlements of America, as being a photographic reproduction of the stone's inscription.

(*Signed*)  Olof  Ohman.

Witness:

R. J. Rasmusson
George H. Mehres

After signing this affidavit, Ohman was sent into the waiting-room and Nils Flaten, his neighbour, was asked in. He made his statement, which tallied with Ohman's; Rasmusson swore Nils Flaten, got him to sign his affidavit, and then registered this second document.

One dubious point is immediately evident in this exceedingly curious story, and of course R. J. Rasmusson straight away inquired into it.

The greywacke block with the runic inscription was found in 1898. Why was it that Olof Ohman had not developed the wish to record the fact and circumstances of his find in sworn and certified form until 1909, eleven years later? And another question: could Ohman still remember all the details of the stone's position in the roots of the tree clearly after so many years? For if the stone had really lain between the roots of the tree in the manner described by Ohman, this would prove it to be exceedingly old. Round 1830, when Ohman's aspen took root and began to grow, the whole area of Douglas County, Solem and Kensington was nothing but untouched and unexplored wilderness. There were no white men there at all, let alone white men who carved runes on chunks of stone.

Was Ohman's deposition true? Edward Ohman, the farmer's son, had said the same as he, and so had his neighbour, Nils Flaten. But who was this third man with them, who looked as though he were from the city? What had this young man to do with the whole thing?

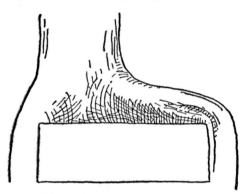

39. *The position of the rune stone of Kensington between the roots of the aspen. (After Hjalmar R. Holand.)*

R. J. Rasmusson called all three together in his office. Now the following facts emerged:

Both Ohman and his neighbours had immediately been of the opinion, when the stone was found, that the characters of the inscription could only be runic, such as they had seen in Sweden long ago. None of them could read runes, however. So they made a copy of the signs cut in the stone—a fragment of this copy has been preserved by the Minnesota Historical Association—and sent it to O. J. Breda, Professor of Scandinavian Languages at the University of Minnesota. The latter made a translation of the words which he was able to decipher, which read as follow:

— Swedes and — Norwegians on a discovery-journey from Vinland west — we had camp — — — one day's journey north from this stone. We — — fished one day. When we came home found — men red with blood and dead. A. V. M. save from — have — men by the ocean to look after our ships — day's journey from this island. Year —

To this partial translation, Breda added in an interview that he did not believe in the authenticity of the inscription. Firstly, it was very rare for Swedes and Norwegians to band together for expeditions of exploration or plunder; and secondly, the language of the inscription was not Old Norse, but a mixture of Swedish, Norwegian and English, which was, of course, impossible in the early Middle Ages.

In 1900 Breda was an authority in Minnesota. Since his attitude to the Kensington Stone seemed unmistakably negative, the latter was almost universally regarded as a fake carried out by one of the many Swedish immigrants in the district. The Scandinavist at the North-Western University of Evanston, Professor George O. Curme, reached the same conclusion, stigmatizing the rune stone of Kensington 'a clumsy fraud'. For the time being, this closed the discussion of Olof Ohman's find, which had originally aroused a great deal of interest.

The finder himself had been pretty clearly shown up as a liar and a trickster; extremely angry, Ohman used the 'lying rune stone' as a doorstep to his granary, where it was useful as a block for straightening bent nails and hammering leather.

This was approximately what Notary Rasmusson learnt from his two clients. First of all, it was obvious that Ohman and Flaten had suffered so much annoyance over the whole thing that they could remember it all perfectly clearly eleven years after the finding of the stone. There could be no doubt that all the circumstances had deeply impressed themselves on their minds. It emerged further that no advantage of

8 göter ok 22 normmen på
oppagelsefard fro
winlanp of west wi
hape läger wep 2 skjar en
pags ride norr fro penv sten
wi war ok fiske en pagh äptir
wi kom hem fan 10 man ro po
af leop og pep AVM
fräelse af illy
har 10 mans we hawet at se
äftir wore skip 14 pagh rise
främ peno öh ahr 1362

40. *The inscription on the Kensington Runestone. (After Holand.)*

any kind had accrued to either Ohman or Flaten from the affair. On the contrary, they had been made to look ridiculous and called forgers—a particularly unpleasant name for an immigrant to have to bear. Hence it was psychologically quite understandable that Ohman should have made a doorstep out of the stone, so that he could, quite literally, trample it underfoot every day. What had happened to make Ohman rake up the old story again? So much water had flowed under the bridge since then that he was no longer in need of 'rehabilitation'. Had he not cause to fear losing his reputation completely, if the whole business started off all over again? Or wasn't he a forger at all? Had he perhaps been right?

This was where Hjalmar R. Holand, the young man who had accompanied Ohman and Flaten, came in. He stated that, according to the figures contained in the U.S. Department of Agriculture's bulletin dealing with the growth of aspens in the West, the Swedish farmer's aspen must really have been sixty to seventy years old. So the Kensington Stone must have been buried since the 1820's at the latest, i.e. since a time when there was no white settlement yet west of the Great Lakes. The first white settler made his home here in 1858; the first Scandinavian not until 1867.

In 1907, nine years after the original find, Hjalmar R. Holand, an American of Swedish extraction, happened to be in this neighbourhood. He heard of Ohman's find, and the fantastic possibility that the runic inscription might after all be genuine, in spite of the verdict passed on it, gave him no peace. He looked at the stone, which bore the longest of all known cut runic texts, deciphered it, and, being convinced of the authenticity of the stone and its inscription, requested Ohman to confirm the circumstances of its discovery under oath before a notary public. This was the text of the runic inscription:

> [We are] 8 Goths [Swedes] and 22 Norwegians on
> [an] exploration-journey from
> Vinland over the West [i.e. through the western regions] We had camp
> by 2 skerries [i.e. a lake wherein are two skerries] one day's-journey
> north from this stone
> We were [out] and fished one day After
> we came home [we] found 10 [of our] men red
> with blood and dead Ave Maria
> save us from evil

In addition to these nine lines on the face of the stone, the following three lines were cut in the 6-inch-wide edge:

> [We] have 10 of our party by the sea to look
> after our ships [or ship] 14 day's-journey
> from this island Year 1362

This translation, published by Hjalmar R. Holand in January 1908, re-started discussion of the Kensington Stone amongst scholars and scientists. It had therefore become necessary to have a properly documented record of the circumstances of its discovery.

## 3

Early summer, 1948. There had been rather a lot of rain in the Middle West that year. Then the temperature suddenly rose. The corn grew at a tremendous pace; the wheat flowered in no time, and immediately afterwards the grain was there; the harvest began, and the work which was normally spread over a period of weeks had to be accomplished in a few short days. Hence, apart from a few scholars, no one in the whole of Minnesota and Wisconsin noticed that the Kensington Stone, the national relic of these States so to speak, was on its way to Washington. For some time previously it had rested at Alexandria, Minn. The United States Government had decided to transfer the famous stone, as the most outstanding historical monument yet found on the soil of North America, to the Smithsonian Institution of the National Museum in Washington.

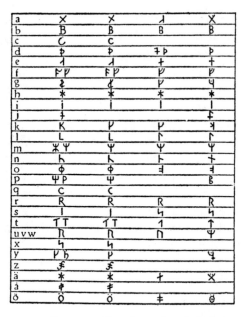

41. *Four medieval runic alphabets (after Holand). First and second columns: alphabets from Dalecarlia. Third column: alphabet from Skone, circa 1250. Right: alphabet of the Kensington Stone.*

Prior to this, European runologists and archæologists were invited to America to give their opinion on the genuineness of the stone, which had already been scrutinized by American scholars. Opinions varied. Whereas the runologists, with a few exceptions, took the view that the inscription must be a forgery, the majority of the archæologists followed the geographers and historians in declaring it authentic.

For its part, the National Museum in Washington had decided to publicly display the Kensington Stone. A crucial factor in this decision was the examination of the rune stone's weathering, which would naturally have to tally with the age of the inscription as given by the date 1362. Chemical and microscopic tests were carried out by the North-Western University of Chicago, whose geological specialists had already declared in 1899: 'The external appearance of the stone . . . is such that the inscription may well be six hundred years old.' Ten years later, the Wisconsin State geologist, Professor Hotchkiss, examined the stone. His report ran: 'I have carefully examined the various phases of weathering on the Kensington Stone, and with all respect for the opinions of philologists, I am persuaded that the inscription cannot have been made in recent years . . .' And Professor Winchell, the Minnesota State geologist, whose test lasted more than a year, declared officially that its runic engraving was about five hundred years old. Since it is practically impossible to produce weathering effects that would stand up to expert scrutiny 'artificially' on minerals, the National Museum in Washington considered itself justified in deciding the Stone deserved to be exhibited. It published in August 1951 a comprehensive study of the historical and philological problems raised by the Kensington Stone and an equally puzzling runic stone found near Upernivik in north-west Greenland, *Two Runic Stones* by William Thalbitzer, in which the authenticity of the Kensington Stone is strongly supported after exhaustive consideration of the evidence and of the objections raised by other scholars.

So much for the declaration of William Thalbitzer, which is logically incontestable and leaves little room for doubt, despite objections by certain runologists.

To this must be added the fact that four respectable citizens of Solem, all neighbours of Olof Ohman, stated on oath that they saw the stone shortly after its disinterment and, amongst other things, had clearly observed the flattening of the roots of the aspen clasping it produced by the pressure of the block.

They stuck to this important statement, like Ohman himself, although subjected for years to cross-examination by newspapermen and scholars. If they had compounded together to make a false statement, some crack must have appeared in the façade of misrepresentation during the fifty years that have elapsed since the recovery of the stone. Moreover, none of these simple farmers, who were intellectually no match for the journalists and professors who questioned them, have derived the slightest advantage from the whole affair, which has caused them nothing but vexation. Hence there is no answer to the all-important question, *cui bono?*, who stands to gain?, which is so vital in judging any question of forgery.

We must therefore assume that Olof Ohman's stone really lay for about seventy years at the root of his tree. If this is correct, however, the stone is undoubtedly genuine. For then the forgery, if there had been one, would have to have been perpetrated in the 1820's. The perpetrator would have had to be an expert in ancient Scandinavian languages and in runology and to have known, 130 years ago, that the whole of the area west of the Great Lakes would one day come to be of interest to Scandinavists. This is absurd, of course. Indeed, the presence of a genius at forgery, equally versed in runology, chemistry, linguistics and history, in the wilderness west of the Great Lakes around 1820 would represent a far greater miracle than the existence of a runic inscription from the fourteenth century.

We have discussed this problem at such length because the rune stone of Kensington has acquired a certain celebrity through the frequent references to it in the Press of the world during recent years, so that the reader may be interested to know the true facts about this strange find. The Kensington Stone has, of course, long been known in circles concerned with ancient American history. After repeated allusions to it in the American Press, Hjalmar R. Holand himself recounted in his extremely interesting book, *The Kensington Stone. A study in pre-Columbian American history* (1932), the results of twenty-five years of work on the problems involved. This first book was followed by two others (H. R. Holand: *Westward from Vinland*, 1942, and H. R. Holand: *America 1355–1364. A new chapter in pre-Columbian history*, 1946), in which his grandiose thesis that America was temporarily settled by Greenland Vikings during the Middle Ages is buttressed and expanded by a series of fresh investigations.

This may sound altogether fanciful when heard for the first time, out of its context and in ignorance of the centuries of preliminary work undertaken by the Norsemen prior to risking the magnificent leap across the Atlantic. But the story of this feat is no flight of fancy, nor is it mere hypothesis. It is established fact. And it is also a fact that these glorious voyages of exploration by the Greenland Vikings did not remain unknown to the Europe of their day. Not only did the seafarers and navigators hear of them—including in all probability, later on, Columbus—but the Vatican was no less well-informed, and with it no doubt also the great financial and mercantile houses of Europe during the high Middle Ages.

4

We must, however, begin by speaking of the preparations, the preliminary expeditions by which the Norsemen felt their way step by step towards their great goal beyond the western ocean. This gradual, groping advance was not systematic, but more or less fortuitous.

Naturally, men began to sail the seas of northern Europe and to use them, like those of the south, for commercial exchanges at a very early period. But just as people are still under the impression that the great voyages of discovery began round the middle of the fifteenth century, so the idea is still rife that there were no seagoing craft, no ships capable of crossing the ocean, until the latter part of the Middle Ages. We immediately see a mental picture of the high-decked caravels in which the various great discoverers, Columbus, Vasco da Gama, Magellan and the rest, made their voyages. Going back farther, we conjure up images of the Græco-Roman galleys; little or nothing is said of the achievements of the north European shipwrights, and few people can call to mind their beautifully streamlined ships, which crossed all the seas from the North Sea to the Persian Gulf long before the Portuguese and the Spaniards.

As stated in Part One, the Neolithic Age, a period about five thousand years back, must already have known a lively and extensive sea traffic. Naturally, there is no documentary evidence of this, nor have any of these early craft been preserved. On the other hand, a paddle from the seventh millennium, the oldest wooden implement in the world, was found years ago in the Duvensee marshes in Schleswig-Holstein. Furthermore, there exist some rough rock drawings, the so-called *hällristningar*, of which the most celebrated are those at Bohuslän on the Kattegatt, which furnish irrefutable proof that these remote and ancient times were already acquainted with seagoing craft. Above all, however, thousands of finds have been made which clearly show that the men of the Stone Age made long voyages by sea. Remains of sea-fish, such as cod and herring, have been found in the Neolithic kitchen middens, the famous *kökkenmöddingar* of Denmark. This means that the Neolithic Period possessed seagoing craft. It is evident, of course, that apart from military campaigns, the risks of sea transport were worthwhile only for luxury articles and particularly valuable raw materials. The chief of such goods and materials were flint and the tools and weapons manufactured from it. The trade routes started from the various flint-mining areas of France, Belgium and southern Britain. They ran straight across the North Sea to the south of Sweden; along the coast between the Calais region and the estuaries of the Schelde and the Elbe; from Warnemünde to Gjedser; from Swinemünde via Bornholm to the southern tip of Sweden; from Truso to Gothland. At an early stage they made the Baltic provinces an emporium of Swedish trade. Thus, for example, whole stores of this costly raw material have been found in Bornholm and Gothland, where flint does not occur naturally. Flint axes and other implements have been unearthed all over northern Sweden, which are assumed to have been brought from Scania and Denmark, and certainly came by sea.

Towards the end of the Stone Age, round about the third millennium B.C., maritime travel seems to have reached a high level. It was at this period that the first great immigration of Swedish peasants into Finland

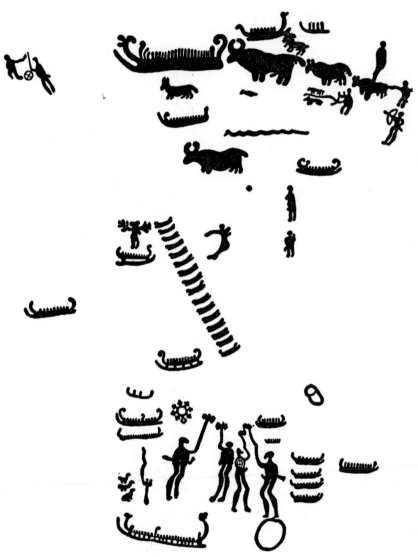

*42. Drawings scratched on rocks near Tanum, Sweden. Ships, rams, dogs, and men fighting are the subjects most often portrayed in Nordic rock drawings.*

and the Baltic provinces took place. The immigrants went straight across the Baltic, and the crossing of this 160-mile stretch of sea presupposes the existence of large, seagoing craft capable of bearing heavy loads. The emigrants' lines of communication with their homeland had also to be safeguarded: there must have been regular traffic between their old and their new home that was more or less independent of the weather. Anyone who has personally experienced the malignity of the Baltic with its short, heavy breakers will be able to assess the demands made by regular sea traffic upon the still fragile and imperfect craft of

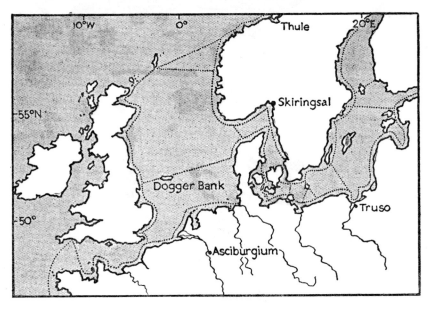

*XVI. Stone Age sea routes.*

the Stone Age. At a speed of two to three knots, the highest these boats of sewn skins can have attained, they must have been at sea for hours without sight of land, even if the crossing was made via the island of Gottland, as it presumably was. And that not beneath the mild skies of the Mediterranean or the sub-tropics, but in the squalls, the billowing mist and the cold of northern waters!

At about the same period a brisk traffic was plied in the North Sea, which apparently did not shrink from a crossing of approximately 440 miles from Sweden to the coast of Britain. This seems to be attested by the finding of tombs in western Sweden and Britain whose arrangement differs from anything discovered in Germany, Denmark, or Norway. These tombs suggest close links between eastern Britain and western Sweden. There is no proof, of course, that the vessels which established the link did not hug the coast all the way round, merely crossing the Straits of Dover. But the finding of flint tools on Heligoland, where flint does not occur naturally, together with the obvious risk of attack by marauders on the long coastal routes, suggests that bold skippers preferred to take their precious cargo by the shortest

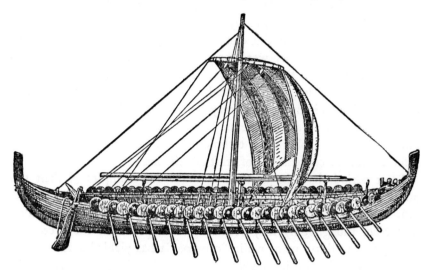

*43. Viking ship, sixth to eighth century A.D. Ships of this kind— very fast, seaworthy, but of such shallow draught that they could also be used on fairly small rivers—were for a long time the favourite Viking craft. They were built in proper shipbuilding yards with slips and runways by highly paid specialists of great skill. The mast was regularly attached in such a manner that, as in a modern racing yacht, it could be lowered in a few movements. Shrouds and back-stays were made of walrus skin, the sail of firmly sewn strips of frieze. The sail could be hauled close or squared by means of blocks-and-pulleys corresponding to our long-tackle.*

route—straight across the open sea. Moreover, it must be borne in mind that in all probability the level of northern European seas has risen considerably—at the rate of about sixteen feet every thousand years. If this is correct—and recent investigations leave little doubt of it—the present Dogger Bank area, which is now some fifty feet under water, would still have been an island around 2000 B.C. This would have rendered the North Sea crossing a good deal easier, especially as, with the lower sea level, the coastline would also have been considerably to seaward of its present position. Taking all these factors into account, there are good grounds for supposing that there was sea traffic in both the Baltic and the North Sea around 2000 B.C., including voyages on the high seas.

Unfortunately, no seagoing vessels from this period have been preserved. All we have is a series of rather rough rock-drawings dating from the beginning of the Bronze Age, showing vessels without sails and propelled by oars or long paddles. These must have been coastal craft. If the North Sea was really crossed in those days it can only have been by sailing vessels; the distance is surely too great for rowing vessels, especially if they were carrying a heavy cargo. The largest of the craft depicted in these rock-drawings have twenty oarsmen, which would make the length, calculated on the space required for each oarsman, about eighty feet. It may be surmised, however, that these drawings represent an exaggerated glorification of reality—it is not likely that the shipbuilding technique of that time can have been sufficient for the construction of craft of this size.

Later periods have bequeathed us numerous examples of their seagoing craft, above all the turbulent era of the third and fourth centuries A.D. A series of dugouts has been unearthed in Lower Saxony, some of which, though only fifty feet long, had provision for a crew of twenty-five to thirty men; while Scandinavia has yielded a few vessels which leave a lasting impression of the shipbuilding capacities of the northern Europeans. One of them, the famous Gokstad ship, which was discovered in 1880 and dates from the sixth century A.D., may be accepted as typical of the Viking galleys of the period, apart from its dimensions, which are rather below the average. She has an over-all length of nearly eighty feet and a beam of about sixteen feet. Her draught is about three feet and her freeboard amidships gives her gunwale a height of two feet above the waterline. She is clinker-built of oak and equally adapted to rowing or sailing. Her structure would have enabled her to weather the worst storms on the high seas and closely resembles that of the modern lifeboat. She was certainly capable of remaining at sea for weeks on end without contact with the shore.

This hypothesis deduced from the construction of the Gokstad galley received interesting practical corroboration a dozen years after its discovery, when an exact replica of the Gokstad ship, the *Viking*, sailed from Norway to America in 1893 on the occasion of the World Fair at Chicago. It was an outstanding feat to sail from Europe to America in a ship of a pattern that was almost two thousand years old. Hence this voyage contributed greatly to the fame of the Viking longships; but it remained difficult to accept the fact that intrepid seafarers

28. On the mountains live the gods. To the right Popocatepetl, on the left Ixtaccihuatl, as seen from Mexico. Cortes once passed between these two mountains into the Valley of Tenochtitlan.

29.  Like serpents the ships crept over the sea. . . . This is how the 'Wotan' legends of the Mayas of Yucatan speak of the attack by a seafaring race of fair, blue-eyed white men in times long past.

30.  Ruins of the temple pyramid of Chichen Itzá in Yucatan. Did the Vikings once mount the steps of this famous Maya sanctuary? Were they the victims of fanatical priests or were they their 'White Gods'?

with vessels like this might very well have preceded Columbus by half a millennium in the discovery which brought him celebrity and suffering.

Longships like the Gokstad galley cannot, of course, be regarded as the real ocean-going vessels of the Scandinavians. They were exceptionally fast, being capable of doing more than ten knots, i.e. almost as much as a modern tramp-steamer. But high speed is only important for warships; and this was the main use to which the long Norse boats, called 'dragon ships' because of their beautifully curved and often artistically carved fore and aft posts, were put. They proved their worth amongst the skerries and fjords of the northern seas, as well as in the Mediterranean and the Black Sea and along the great rivers of Europe. In the ocean-swell, however, their skippers must have wished their vessels were broader in the beam, with a higher free-board, and above all shorter. Many long, slender dragon ships must have broken across on the crests of the rolling waves, like the Swedish replica which broke up and went down with all hands in the Bay of Heligoland in the summer of 1950.

44. *This is a* knorr, *the Vikings' ocean craft, a forerunner of the Hanseatic* kogge. *Representation on the oldest seal of Danzig, 1299.*

Consequently, the Vikings tended more and more to employ on longer ocean voyages, i.e. on the routes to Britain, Iceland and Greenland, a type of craft known as the *knorr,* a broad, high-decked, tubby sailing ship, which stood up to heavy seas much better than the dragon ships and could also carry much more sail. Whereas the longships weighed some fifty tons, the *knorrs* were between sixty and one hundred tons; and since their speed was little less than that of the Norse warships, thanks to their greater area of sail, they gradually replaced the longships. At later periods, dragon ships seem only to have been used for rapid swoops in calm waters and as reconnaissance craft; one can imagine that the Scandinavians who sailed to America in heavy *knorrs* left these vessels at anchor while they reconnoitred the coasts and rivers on hastily constructed longships.

Unfortunately, it is not yet finally clear what aids to navigation the Vikings possessed. It is certain, however, that they were much more extensive than was for long supposed. By A.D. 1000 they were able to estimate latitude, and round this time they also learnt to determine the north magnetically. Their great voyages of discovery could not otherwise be explained. Of the Norse voyages to America tradition specifically states that they reached the precise point at which they were aiming. The major problem was the calculation of latitude. For it must quickly have struck the Norwegian navigator that the shadow of his mast was very much shorter off the shores of France and Spain than at home, and that in these southern latitudes the Pole Star was lower than above the fjords of his homeland. At the same time, he must have noticed that the day, which in the north lasted up to twenty-four hours, drew to a close much more rapidly in the south. Naturally, therefore, he paid more attention to the estimation of the latitude in which he was sailing than of the longitude.

As long as the sun shone, the problem of estimating latitude was easily solved. It naturally became difficult when the sky was overcast for weeks on end, rendering it impossible to measure the altitude of the sun or the length of shadows. Even today, navigation is difficult under these conditions in the absence of radio direction-finding equipment. In such cases the Vikings had recourse to the *leidarsteinn*, or lodestone.

The *leidarsteinn*—described in detail in the mid-thirteenth century by the Picard, Peter of Marincourt, who saw the stone being used by Italian navigators in Naples—is always regarded as an important forerunner of the compass in magnetic direction-finding. It is frequently referred to in Norse sagas, and much earlier than any mention of it in the south. It was the north, where it was much more urgently needed because of the frequency of dull weather, rather than the south which invented the compass—at any rate in Europe.

In the north, as in the south, the measurement of longitude remained an intractable problem for the navigator. For a long time it was generally done by a dead reckoning, i.e. the navigator calculated his longitude by the direction of his course and the distance he had travelled. The simplest part of this was undoubtedly the estimation of his speed, which, prior to the invention of the log, had to be done by eye. Impossible as it seems to the landsman to assess the speed of a ship without fixed points of reference, the sailor can acquire great accuracy in it. The skippers and helmsmen of sailing ships brought it to a fine art, so that as a rule they had no need of the log. The Scandinavians, who spent all their lives at sea, must have become very expert at it.

The measurement of time must have been a far more difficult matter, and it is interesting that the Vikings, like the seafaring peoples of the south, adopted water clocks to provide them with an unvarying measure of time. These water clocks, which were probably already gimbal-mounted, so that they were not disturbed by the motion of the ship, ran out in three, twelve, or twenty-four hours. The latter type was called *ættmal*; this word came to mean not only a measure of time, but also of distance. It corresponded to the sailing distance covered under normal circumstances in twenty-four hours. These methods were certainly far from exact; but they must have stood the Vikings in good stead, as the manner in which they sailed straight to their goal across great distances shows.

We have already had occasion to speak of the nautical knowledge of the ancient south. The results achieved there were also very striking. They do not astonish us quite so much, however, because climatic conditions in the south were in every way notably superior to those of the north. Dull weather with an overcast sky was an exception; the sun was regularly visible during the day. The nights were clear, so that even if an observation was impossible during the day, bearings could be taken from the stars. This was rarely possible to the Scandinavians in their home waters. As a rule, the sun set for a few hours only, and it was a very difficult task to take reliable bearings from the stars during the bright twilight of the northern night.

Despite all this, we should no longer be surprised that bold seafarers, with the nautical knowledge and the vessels that the Vikings possessed, should have been able to traverse the seas of half the world and make them their own. The seas of the north were naturally the first to attract them, and there is incontestable historical evidence that the Scandinavians first reached Iceland in A.D. 863.

## 5

To begin with, the voyage to Iceland was extremely perilous. Although it did not take so very long to reach, Iceland was one of the more distant objectives at that time, and the voyage from Norway was generally undertaken in the summer months only. The voyagers wintered on the island and usually returned home the following summer. The Vikings made the first part of the trip on courses with which they had long been familiar—via the British Isles, the Orkneys, the Shetlands and the Faeroes—and then made their way to the south-east coast of Iceland with the aid of the westerly arm of the North Atlantic Drift, the northern offshoot of the Gulf Stream. Mariners from the British Isles and the string of islands leading up towards it had already explored Iceland prior to the arrival of the Vikings.

It has even been asserted recently by American numismatists that Iceland must have been discovered five hundred years before the advent of the Vikings. This assertion is based on the finding of some Roman coins from the period of the Emperor Diocletian. Since, however, there is no means of knowing how long these coins had been lying in the ground, so that they might have been brought to the island by the Vikings themselves, this assertion is not very credible. But it does seem that the Irish, who, like the inhabitants of the Shetlands, had been under Scandinavian domination since the sixth century, sailed to Iceland in *circa* A.D. 795—long before its official discovery by the Northmen. These were not colonizing expeditions, but more likely small bands of monks in flight from the world and seeking, like St. Brandan, a hermitage on some solitary isle.

In addition to ancient Irish sources, the Scandinavians themselves attest that there were Irishmen living on Iceland before them. This is recorded in the *Landnámabók*, the great written document of their settlement of Iceland. Although this book was not written until A.D. 1200, it has proved reliable over so many points that great importance must be attached to its testimony regarding the discovery of Iceland by the Irish. The *Landnámabók* account runs:

At that time Iceland was covered with trees between the shore and the mountains. There lived here then Christian men called by the Northmen *papar*. These men later went away, because they did not wish to live with heathens. They left behind bells, crosiers and Irish books from which it could be seen that the people were from Ireland.

This is pretty convincing evidence that Iceland was first visited by the Irish. No traces of any earlier settlement have been found on this remote island, so the view that the aboriginal inhabitants of Iceland were Celts can hardly be incorrect. The island was too far from any other habitable country to be peopled before sea travel had reached a relatively high level of development. The Norwegians themselves did not sail to Iceland by the direct sea route until some time after its first settlement.

Men had to be hardy to brave the rigours of these northern seas. They had to be quite especially hardy and resolute to transplant their whole clan to Iceland, land of ice and fire. We know for certain that the decision to carry out this migration was not made lightly, but only after thorough investigation of the new country. Despite the poverty of the soil and the harshness of the climate, living conditions which the Northmen found in Iceland were no worse than in their Norwegian and Swedish homelands, particularly in the ninth century, when the deterioration of the climate, which probably took place later, had not yet begun. Although the lonely isle lay climatically on the borderline

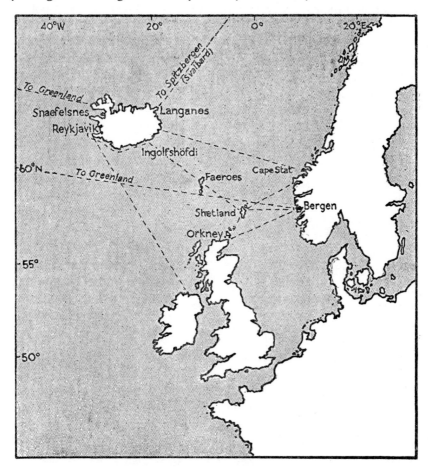

*XVII. Viking routes to Iceland.*

between the temperate and the Polar zone, it certainly did not belong to the latter. This was due to the effect of the North Atlantic Drift, which kept sufficient warm water circulating round the island to raise its temperature above that of the Polar zone proper. This exceptional condition was (and is) confined to the seaboard, however; the highlands of the interior of Iceland were and are cold and infertile. It may, in any case, be assumed that the first impression made by Iceland upon the Vikings was not an unfriendly one.

In the coastal areas, particularly in the south and south-west, they found everywhere magnificent meadows, many of them lusher than those in Scandinavia; round the sheltered fjords gardens could be planted which flourished as well as in Norway. The rivers and the rocky waters round the coast were seething with fish. Only corn could not be satisfactorily grown in sufficient quantity for the needs of the settlement. The summer was too short for this, although the light nights secured less interruption in the growth of plants than had been the case at home. There was also a complete absence of metal ores, which the Norsemen needed as urgently in peace as in war. The lack of these two vital natural products could, however, be overcome by imports from Norway.

Consequently, settlement in Iceland did not mean any reduction in the accustomed standard of living. What was required of the Iceland colonists was adaptation to slightly different natural conditions, rather than the adoption of an entirely new way of life. Dairy farming had to take precedence over agriculture; but since the Norwegian farmer had already engaged extensively in cattle-breeding, this did not present the settler with any fundamentally new problem.

These economic considerations, great as was their influence on the choice of a new settlement, were not the driving force behind the Norwegian emigration. This latter was of quite a different character and strong enough to send Norsemen to Greenland, where conditions were in sharp contrast to those in Norway, once the habitable areas of Iceland had all been colonized. Although shortage of land in Norway —owing to the type of economy practised by its inhabitants, which called for a great deal of space—was doubtless one reason for the raiding and colonizing expeditions of the Northmen, it was certainly not the primary incentive to the settlement of Iceland. The motive for this was not economic, but political: flight from the ruthless hand of Harald Fairhair, king of one of the Norwegian provinces, who, at the end of the ninth century, extended his sway over the whole of Norway.

This flight, which involved every class of society, brought men from all parts of Norway, from Halogaland in the north to Vik and the Upplönd in the south. According to the *Landnámabók*, the districts round the Hardangerfjord and the Sognefjord made a particularly large contribution to the emigration.

Soon a positive flood of Northmen was pouring into Iceland. By about A.D. 1000, there were some twenty to thirty thousand people living on the lonely island, and excavations in Norway have disclosed that in the districts of Agder and Rogaland whole communities were abandoned; not only younger sons emigrated, but whole families with bag and baggage, so that land which had once been tilled became wilderness once more. To prevent the depopulation of Norway, an 'emigration tax' was instituted: everyone wishing to go to Iceland had to pay the king ten *öre*, and later on as much as half a gold crown. Of course, many left the land in secret. In only four instances does the *Landnámabók* state that emigration took place with Harald Fairhair's foreknowledge. Many people emigrated for personal reasons. The *Landnámabók* frequently relates that Iceland-farers had to leave their homeland because they were guilty of murder or manslaughter, or because of old clan feuds, which made it impossible for the children of the second or third generation to stay in Norway. This brief survey shows how manifold were the causes of emigration from Norway. If political reasons preponderated, there were all sorts of other motives as well, and the internal cohesion of the colonists of Iceland must not, therefore, be overrated.

In addition to the Norwegians, who formed the main contingent of colonists, members of many other nations also took part. One of the first men to explore Iceland, Gardar, was a Swede. It is recorded further that Ingolf's brother had several Irish slaves on board. The *Landáma-bók* contains information on this point too. It carefully records the names of the most important foreigners who participated in the colonization of Iceland. In addition to Ireland, Scotland, Denmark and the Hebrides, Sweden and Gothland were particularly strongly represented. There were also Lapps and Finns, the latter mostly as slaves and domestic servants among the immigrants. They and the many Celts introduced an alien element into the otherwise homogeneous blood of the Iceland-farers, which may have contributed to the Icelanders' gradually becoming independent of their Norwegian mother country. None the less, the Icelanders, as well as the Norse Greenlanders, remained closely linked to the mother country in their ways and customs. We shall have more to say of this later. It is worth bearing in mind from the outset, however, that all these people, scattered over the whole world, whether in Iceland, Greenland or Vinland-America, were and remained Europeans. This point will arise when we discuss the decline of the Greenland Norsemen.

Iceland was the first step taken by the Scandinavians in the direction of their ultimate destination—America. This step was taken quite unconsciously, of course, and appeared to contemporaries no more than the discovery of one more new country in the unbroken chain of foreign shores. Looking back from the present, the coming of the Norsemen to Iceland seems to have been determined by something more than mere chance. For Greenland now lay on their doorstep; sooner or later it was *bound* to be discovered by the Vikings. But the

*XVIII. Iceland with the dwelling places of Eric the Red in Dranga-land, Haukadal and Öxney.*

door that opened on Greenland opened on a trap: Greenland had neither wood nor metal, it could not support the Norsemen and they had to leave.

Where were they to go? Their route led from Greenland straight across the Arctic Ocean to America, with its inexhaustible supplies of both timber and metal. The way was clear to the Greenland Vikings as soon as they found Markland, the vast forest area of Nova Scotia, New Brunswick and Maine. And it looks as though, with Vinland as their starting-point, they penetrated to the metalliferous regions round the Great Lakes. But many of them realized too late that their settlement of Greenland had led them into a blind alley; the link with Europe grew more and more tenuous and finally broke, leaving them helplessly imprisoned in Greenland's ice. No longer able to leave— because, being without timber, they were without ships of their own— they perished, man, woman and child.

6

The summer of 1721 was hot and dry. Day after day the sun blazed down upon the parched soil; meadows and fields dried up; the fountains in the parks of the gentry no longer played; the peasants prayed for rain.

To Hans Egede from Trondenaes in the Lofotens, on his way to Greenland at just this time, this searing chastisement of the world was a sign from God. The seals, the Greenland Eskimoes' main source of food, had moved far north; the little slit-eyed trolls were hungry, and the man whose stomach is empty is usually ready to open his ears to the word of God. And to bring the word of God to the Eskimoes was Hans Egede's mission in life.

The ice too had retreated much farther north than usual this summer. True, it thundered down incessantly from the lofty cliffs. Whole icebergs broke away from the sharp edges of the cliffs and tumbled down with a hellish roaring, grating and rumbling into the foaming sea, sending the water high into the air. But the endless icefields, which the English skippers, Davis and Baffin, had reported a hundred years earlier, had vanished. Thus it came about that Hans Egede anchored well up to the north, at the mouth of a fjord that cut deep into the land, in Godthaab, the harbour of 'Good Hope', at almost 65° N.

He had no idea that white men had lived in this region four hundred years earlier. Perhaps some unknown ancestor of his own family had here cast overboard the sacred pillar of the high seat, in order to take land at the point where it drifted ashore, guided by the gods. Great farms had stood here once, a two-storeyed granary had been erected, a dignified church built. But the missionary found nothing!

That their forebears had once discovered and colonized Greenland was well known in Norway and Denmark; but people had been led astray by the clever scholars. It is written in the sagas, said these learned gentlemen, that the main Norse colony was called *Eystribyggd*, 'Eastern Settlement', and the second and smaller one *Vestribyggd*, 'Western Settlement'. Consequently, they deduced, the powerful Eystribyggd must have lain on the east coast of Greenland, the poorer Vestribyggd, which moreover perished as early as 1342, on the west coast. This was a misconception: in point of fact both settlements were situated on the west of the country, but the Eastern Settlement lay at the extreme inner end of the fjord, while Vestribyggd was to the west of it, closer to the open sea.

Hans Egede too had believed the men of learning. And he had silently hoped, in spite of all the intervening centuries, to find some trace of his old Norwegian compatriots where he believed Eystribyggd to have been. He gave no thought to Vestribyggd, where he actually landed. That had been too small, and had ceased to exist too long ago, to have left any visible signs. So he paid no heed to the ruins which still stand there, monuments to a poignant tragedy of hunger and abandonment. He did not notice that here and there he was stepping over graves.

He found nothing. 'As regards the old Greenland Eystribyggd, I believe without a doubt that it is still alive and filled with the offspring of a pure Norwegian people, who, with God's help, will in due course be discovered,' he wrote home. In the summer of 1723, he re-embarked and sailed, in constant danger of his life, along the calving glaciers of inland ice. He sailed along almost the whole of the Eystribyggd coast; it was all within reach of his hand: the ruins of the old monasteries, the huge walls of the see of the Bishop of Greenland at Gardar near the modern Julianehaab, the vast cemeteries in whose icy graves the dead were waiting patiently for one of their own people to come, the blossoming gardens of the Vikings still bright with many European plants foreign to the soil of Greenland. Within reach of his hand! But Hans Egede passed it by. It was not his destiny to be an excavator, an archæologist; he was to become the apostle to the Eskimoes. And when he died many, many years later on the Danish island of Falster, his soul was accompanied by the praises of countless Christian Eskimoes in far-away Greenland, whom he had freed from the fear of their demons.

Just two hundred years after Hans Egede's voyage to Greenland, in the hot summer of 1921, another expedition landed there with the specific aim of searching for its ancient Norse inhabitants. Again

Europe was parched by a blazing sun, and again in Greenland the ice had retreated far to the north. The frozen soil of the seaboard had become soft and willingly yielded its hidden contents.

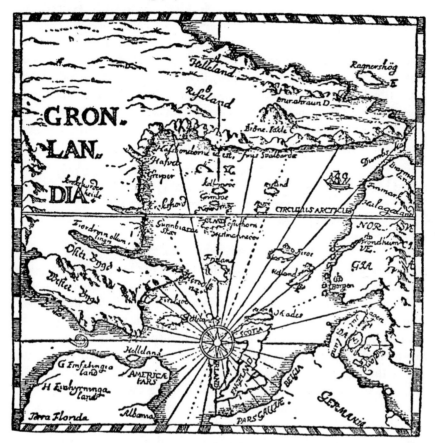

45. *'Öster-Bygd' and 'Wester-Bygd', the two Norse settlements on Greenland, on the map of Jon Gudmundsson circa 1600. Northern Asia with Finmark and Bjarmaland is separated from Greenland only by a narrow channel. The Eastern Settlement lies on Greenland's east coast, the Western on the Atlantic side of the island. Between Greenland and America there is likewise only a narrow channel.*

As early as 1586, the English navigator and explorer, John Davis, had come across a grave marked by a cross in Greenland. And ever since whalers had begun to anchor off the west coast of Greenland, reports of the finding of graves and skeletons had been accumulating in Copenhagen. These finds, which were all made on the west coast of Greenland, corroborated the scholars' new theory that Eystribyggd and Vestribyggd had both lain on the western littoral of this icy land. This theory won more and more credence, and immediately after the First World War Denmark sent a scientific commission to Greenland headed by the archæologist Paul Nörlund. And what Hans Egede missed, this expedition found: their own Norwegian forefathers.

They had been dead for four centuries. Their farms were destroyed, their churches in ruins, their fields and gardens smothered by weeds and horsehair oats. But down below, in the graves, in the depths of the eternally frozen soil, time had stood still. There lay the Vikings, as they had once been put to rest. They found Bishop Jon Smyrill, nicknamed the Sparrowhawk, with his bishop's ring and crosier, the latter beautifully carved from a walrus tusk by the pastor's wife, Margret.

*46. Gudveig's rune rod from the Herjulfsnes cemetery.*

There lay the maiden Ingibjourg, who died more than eight hundred years ago and whose loving parents had placed her in a fine grave framed in sandstone and bearing a runic inscription. There slumbered Ozuur Asbjarnarson, who died one winter's day on a little island in the fjord, and was laid to rest in unhallowed ground. But when the grave was filled in, a stake was stood on his chest. And when spring came round and the ice melted, the stake was pulled out and a priest poured consecrated water through the hole onto his chest. Now he too rested in hallowed ground. In the grave of the goodwife Gudveig there lay nothing but a rune rod. On this rod can be read the words: 'This woman, who was called Gudveig, was lowered into the Greenland sea.' Gudveig died at sea and was buried there, in the manner of sailors, sewn up in a sailcloth with a stone from the ballast tied to her feet. But the sea is not hallowed, it is the abode of the devil. So the rune rod was buried in hallowed ground as her proxy. There were children's graves: the little ones lay peacefully with folded hands, a cross between their stiff fingers and, in the corner of the grave, their toys.

All this can be read in Paul Nörlund's scholarly, but harrowing, book, *Viking Settlements in Greenland,* published in 1937. Harrowing not so much because it treats of those who died and left others to weep for them, but rather because all these dead were severely crippled, dwarf-like in stature, frightfully undernourished, bent and twisted with rickets, and probably riddled with tuberculosis. Harrowing because hardly any of these poor creatures, stigmatized by generations of malnutrition, lived to be much more than twenty. Harrowing because all of them, including the children, were dressed in the latest fashions current in Europe at the time—not made from silk and velvet, like their

*XIX. Greenland with Eystribyggd and Vestribyggd. Vestribyggd, the Western Settlement, lay some way north of the Eastern Settlement. The distance between the two was about 200 miles, or, in the words of an old chronicle, 'six days' rowing with six men in a six-oar boat'. Since the seaway ran past dangerous glaciers, whose sharp-cornered calf-ice often blocked the channel completely, contact between the two colonies cannot have been particularly close.*

distant relatives in Scandinavia, but of the coarse woollen frieze manufactured in Greenland itself. Yet this coarse cloth was made up into elegant surcoats and caps like those worn during the high Middle Ages in Europe, into knee-length *cothards* such as were the height of fashion in fourteenth-century France, into the hoods with a queue familiar to us from the descriptions of Dante and Petrarch, into the tall Burgundian caps painted by Memling and others as the headgear of the great gentlemen of their time and worn by Charles the Bold (1433–77) and Louis XI of France (1423–83).

This can only mean that these poorest of the poor, lost and forgotten in the solitude of unending ice, maintained contact with Europe till late in the fifteenth century, that foreign ships came to their shores, that merchants and mariners landed there and, finally, that to the very last these crippled Greenland dwarfs retained their determination to dress fashionably.

At the birth of Eric the Red, the son of Thorvald Asvaldsson from Jaederen near Stavanger in Norway, no one foresaw that he would one day go to his rest many thousands of miles to the west in the everlastingly frozen soil of Greenland, and not amongst the meadows and ploughlands of his Norwegian farm. It was certain from his youth, however, that he would find no peace until his death. For his grandfather had been involved in many violent quarrels, and his father likewise. Even after he had reached years of discretion, the latter's life continued to be stormy, and in 960 he went too far: he killed a man and was forced to flee his ancestral home and emigrate with his family to Iceland.

At this time, his son Eric was about ten, old enough to realize that the farm in Drangaland, one of the harshest and most inhospitable districts in northern Iceland, was in no way comparable to the homestead in Jaederen. But there was no choice. All the land of Iceland had been parcelled out seventy years ago. Late arrivals like Thorvald, a fugitive from justice to boot, had to be content with what they could get. Thorvald accepted the situation. But not his son. He knew that his father's clan had been one of the most respected and powerful in Jaederen. Here in Iceland they were of no account at all.

Like so many happenings in the early days of Iceland, Thorvald Asvaldsson's arrival is related at length in the *Landnámabók*. He and his son Eric settled in Hornstrand on Dranger. The father died, Eric the Red took over the farm, married, and thereby became related to one of the most respected Iceland families. This enabled him to acquire a new farm in Haukadal, farther to the south. But now he got into difficulties. Like his father and grandfather before him, Eric got involved in quarrels, and when it happened twice in succession that the wild Norwegian's adversaries were left dead on the field, the Thing at Thornes early in 982 punished him and his people with three years' banishment from Iceland. The *Landnámabók* concludes its account with the words:

Eric fitted out a ship in Eric's Bay . . . He said he wished to seek for the land which Gunnbjörn, the son of Ulf Krake, espied when he was drifting on the sea west of Iceland, and which has since then been called Gunnbjörn-skerry. He assured his friends that he would return to them when he had found the land. They parted in all friendship. Eric promised them his aid, if he could give any and if they should have need of it.

Thus the *Landnámabók,* whose detailed and precise report can be relied upon. Early in 982, probably in May or June, Eric the Red put out from Iceland on a westerly course to seek an unknown land in the ocean, which had been fleetingly glimpsed in 900, i.e. over eighty years previously. The truth about this land west of Iceland is uncertain. When it was first sighted by Gunnbjörn, one of the earliest settlers, it aroused great interest in Iceland, so that the oldest inhabitants could still remember its discovery. Manifestly Gunnbjörn Ulfson, like other navigators, had embarked on the circumnavigation of Iceland, but he must have set a course that took him farther west. It is recorded that he could see the Snaefells glacier on Iceland, when another glacier emerged from the sea to the west at the same time. This statement was originally construed to mean that the 'skerries' discovered by Gunnbjörn were perhaps the small islands off Cape Farewell, the southern tip of Greenland. This is not certain, however, and Gunnbjörn's course remains doubtful. It must not be forgotten that atmospheric reflections are a common phenomenon in summer at these latitudes, and also that the ice-gleam, i.e. the reflection of the rays of the sun scattered by the vast surfaces of Greenland's snow and ice, is visible much farther than the glaciers themselves. Furthermore, it must be borne in mind that in the area round Iceland, which is characterized by violent volcanic and seismic action, the sudden appearance, and equally sudden disappearance, of islands and rocks is entirely possible.

However that may be, the Gunnbjörn skerries were the not very palpable incentive to the discovery of Greenland. For, as the result of sailing far out to the west, Eric the Red came into the area of the northern arm of the North Atlantic Drift, which at this point curves round to the west and, with a favourable wind, was bound to carry him to Greenland. As luck would have it, he landed not on the east coast of Greenland, which is barred by pack-ice and bleakly inhospitable, but on the south-west coast beyond Cape Farewell, i.e. in the climatically most favourable area of the country. For even at this latitude, the influence of the Gulf Stream, of which the North Atlantic Drift is an offshoot, produces an unusually high temperature. The mean annual temperature here is almost 9° F. above what would be expected from its latitude and in comparison with the temperatures of the North American continent. Of course, the temperature in Greenland drops steeply as one moves inland. The influence of the Gulf Stream is

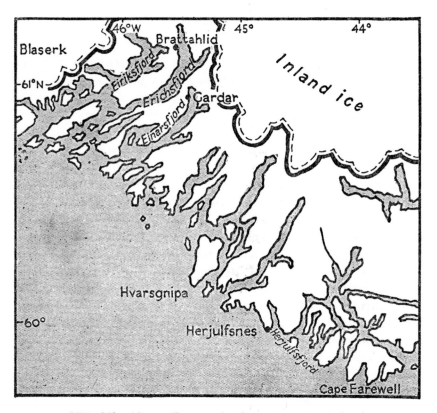

*XX. The Norse Eastern Settlement on Greenland.*

considerably reduced, and the cooling effect of the immense ice-cap, which covers Greenland and penetrates deep into the magma masses of the earth's interior, defies all attempts at colonization.

True, Eric the Red knew nothing of the course of the isotherms, and the warming effect of the Gulf Stream was also unknown to him. But as the prudent elder of his clan and the responsible leader of his followers, he used the three summers of his banishment to make a thorough inspection of Greenland; and when he returned to Iceland at the end of his period of outlawry he knew very well that the south-west of Greenland was habitable and where he himself proposed to settle. This was the deep Eric's Fjord, now called Tunugdliarfik, which was sheltered from the icy gales by high mountains and climatically the most favourable spot in the whole of Greenland. The new settlement of the fugitive Northman was sited with great care and forethought.

Eric the Red did not stay long in Iceland after his return from exile. He set sail for Greenland the very next summer, this time to settle there permanently. This enterprise too is faithfully recorded in the *Landnámabók*. It is also described in detail in the *Heimskringla*, or *Lives of the Norse Kings,* an historical work written in Iceland at the turn of the twelfth to the thirteenth century.

These two witnesses give a pretty exact picture of the way in which the settlement of Greenland proceeded. Eric the Red's original expedition, in which his family with several small children and five or six servants took part, was undoubtedly lavishly equipped and provided with all the essentials of life for a longish period. But this voyage was nothing against the real taking-of-the-land. Twenty-five ships put out to sea, and since they must certainly all have been *knorrs* they must have carried some seven hundred souls together with a large cargo of livestock and household goods. It may therefore be inferred with some certainty that Eric the Red's plan for the colonization of Greenland must have caused a great stir in Iceland. No doubt conditions on the island were not altogether satisfactory, in consequence of its over-population; but these difficulties were probably less decisive than the great respect in which Eric was held and his glowing descriptions of the economic and climatic conditions in the new country. Eric the Red doubtless laid it on pretty thick; not for nothing does it say in the *Landnámabók* that he called his country the Green Land, 'because he believed that more people would go thither if the country had a beautiful name'. Anyway, the difference between the Greenland East Settlement and Iceland was not so great that an Icelander need shrink from emigrating there.

Only one thing was missing, and that was timber. Whereas Iceland was fairly heavily wooded in parts at the time of the taking-of-the-land, there was nothing on Greenland but a few miserable birches. Driftwood was washed ashore from Siberia by the North Polar Current, but this was no use for building ships. Eric the Red had undoubtedly observed this shortage; but he was primarily a farmer and cattle-breeder, not a seaman. Perhaps he relied upon being able to obtain the necessary timber without difficulty from Iceland or Norway. At all events, he had no idea that the shortage of timber would one day become a fatal difficulty and that, despite all his forethought, his decision to settle in Greenland had led into a blind alley.

As the statements of the *Landnámabók* reveal, all settlements without exception were located on fjords. This constitutes a fundamental difference between the colonization of Greenland by the Northmen, and its later occupation by the Eskimoes. The Eskimo remained attached to the sea and the seaboard. He was exclusively a hunter and fisherman, and therefore lived on the outermost ring of islands and skerries round the coast. Only in summer did he occasionally enter the fjords to hunt reindeer. The Northman, on the other hand, was primarily a stockbreeder and farmer. He was dependent upon fields and pastures and therefore kept to the hinterland round the fjords, which was climatically particularly favourable. The innermost creeks of the fjords were sheltered from the wind by high walls of rock, consequently their temperatures were several degrees higher than that of the land round about. It is even alleged that occasionally apples ripened here. At all events, the Greenland cleric, Ivar Bardsen, reported round the middle of the fourteenth century that there were 'fruit,' shaped like certain apples, with the most excellent aroma'; and from the eighteenth century, Hans Egede relates that, in particularly sheltered spots, it is possible to grow turnips and cabbages. Nowadays the Greenlanders, with appropriate methods, are able to cultivate radishes, carrots, rhubarb and potatoes. Hence the northmen were undoubtedly able, at the beginning, to breed horses and pigs—although this would no longer be possible today, for reasons which will be explained later. Immediately inland from the fjords, however, begins the region of perpetually frozen soil and inland ice.

The Greenland Vikings lived on dairy produce and meat. Even today the Eskimoes on Greenland are chiefly concerned, after fishing, with livestock farming; but they confine themselves almost exclusively to sheep and goats, whereas the old Norsemen for the most part kept cows. This would be altogether out of the question today. On the farm of Eric the Red, for example, the ruins of four cowsheds containing a total of forty individual stalls were found. The head of cattle on the bishop's estate at nearby Gardar was even greater. Its two great cowsheds, the longest buildings in the whole Greenland, had accommodation for about a hundred beasts. But even the average farm in the East Settlement must have possessed fifteen to twenty head, a quite considerable number. All these byres are situated in an area which is today utterly bleak. Either the pastures of the Norsemen have deteriorated into barren tundras, or the fjords have been rendered totally impassable by calf ice from the inland glaciers. This leads to the inference that in the early Middle Ages the climate was more temperate and the flora richer than at present.

In regions as climatically precarious as the sub-Polar areas of south-west Greenland, however, even the slightest alteration in the climate was fraught with the direst consequences. Even before the change, cattle-breeding and dairy-farming could only be carried on in the sheltered fjords, whose high summer temperatures made it possible to cultivate extensive pasturage. Even here the warm season was extremely short. The water started to freeze by the end of August, and in the course of October the fjords became icebound. There were hard months ahead for anyone whose winter provender was not in the barns by then, especially as the vegetable components of his diet—consisting principally of berries, angelica, and certain edible grasses and seaweeds —were inadequate at best. Hence the difficulties of getting in the harvest during the few weeks of fine weather in the summer were tremendous. Bearing in mind the length of the winter that had to be provided for, it is hardly conceivable that individual farms could have coped with the task on their own. The quantity of fodder consumed by the animals was enormous.

The major portion of the hay harvested went to the cows. During most of the winter, the sheep, goats and horses had to take second place. According to old Icelandic figures, about 25 pounds were reckoned per head of cattle per day. Since the winter, during which the cows were kept in the cowshed, lasted around 220 days in Greenland, each cow consumed approximately 5,500 pounds of hay. An average East Settlement farm possessed something like twenty cows. It therefore required more than 450 tons of hay for fodder. From the viewpoint of the labour involved alone this was an impossibility, especially as most of this hay had to be transported across the fjords in boats.

The difficulty of providing for the beasts during the winter led to their fodder being supplemented with fish or fish offal—which is still done in Norway—or else to their being only very meagrely fed, as was the case in more southerly countries as well during the Middle Ages. When they were put out to graze again at the beginning of spring, the animals were generally so weak that they had to be carried. Milk production dropped to a very low level during the winter. Consequently, the milk obtained during the summer was preserved, i.e. soured and salted, so as to produce *skyr*, a kind of condensed milk, which could be kept for a considerable time in tubs. Large quantities of butter and cheese were also prepared and stored for the winter. Since there was no lack of meat—principally seal meat—the real shortage was confined to vegetables and cereals. As long as the link with Iceland and Norway

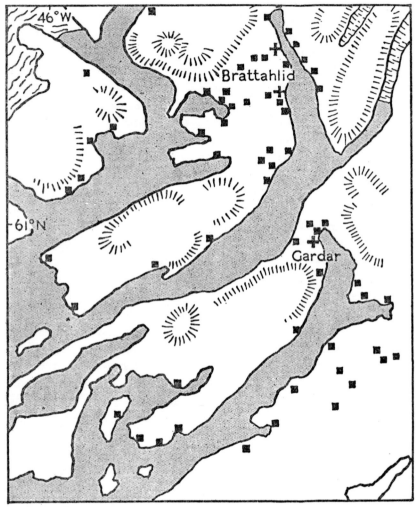

*XXI. Brattahlid on Eric's Fjord and Gardar on Einar's Fjord, the two main centres of the Norse Eastern Settlement in Greenland.*

held this was no cause for concern, since the necessary supplement of carbohydrates could be imported. Later on the situation changed, as we shall hear.

To begin with, the Scandinavian settlement of Greenland was pretty dense. On the inland reaches of the fjords, every little vale was filled with farms; wherever there were a few acres of grass and pasture, a

Viking peasant settled. It is estimated that in the whole of Greenland there were 280 farms, of which about 180 belonged to the East Settlement, Eystribyggd. This would put the population at around 3,000. If we recall that the present population of the same tracts of land, amounting to between 4,000 and 5,000, is largely dependent upon food from Europe and America, we can see what a prodigious feat of colonization the Norsemen achieved in populating this barren soil so thickly. It also shows the great adaptability of the Nordic peoples to the conditions of the Arctic and sub-Polar zone—an adaptability which they were to demonstrate a little later in sub-tropical regions of the south, like Sicily.

The Northmen encountered a further difficulty in the lack of iron. True, there are large iron deposits in Greenland on Disco Bay north of Vestribyggd, just where the Vikings had their main hunting ground. But they were first discovered by the Swedish explorer, Nordenskiöld, and not exploited until 1870. So the Greenland Vikings were dependent upon surface iron. There were large deposits of this too; but the production of iron even from this surface ore was greatly impeded by lack of fuel. As in Iceland, the underwood was quickly destroyed by reckless felling and damage by cattle—the young cattle had a predilection for chewing off the fresh shoots—so that they were dependent on driftwood and imports from Europe and America. This same lack of timber prevented the construction of ships. When the link with Europe broke in later centuries, the Northmen were marooned on Greenland. To begin with, they had recourse to timber from America, especially from 'Markland' (the name means 'forest land'), which the Greenland Vikings discovered round A.D. 1000. Ships plied regularly between Greenland and Markland up to the mid-fourteenth century. This is shown by the following entry in the *Icelandic Annals* of the Bishop of Skalholt in Iceland for the year 1347.

There came a ship from Greenland, even smaller than the little Iceland-farers. It sailed into the outer Straumfjord and had no anchor. It bore seventeen men who had sailed to Markland, but had been driven here by high winds.

Later, such long voyages seem to have become less frequent or even ceased altogether; perhaps because the Northmen, undernourished through the breakdown of their dairy-farming, lacked the strength; perhaps because, owing to the acute shortage of iron, they had no nails with which to fix together the planks of larger, seagoing ships. This casts a grim light on the situation of the later generations of Greenland

Vikings. Without iron, without timber, without adequate nutrition, the maintenance of their mode of life and their culture was impossible. In a country which offered plenty of living space to the Eskimo, the Northman was bound finally to succumb, once his supply lines were cut.

# 7

At the beginning there was no hint of what was in store. Intercourse between Greenland and Norway was brisk and the Greenlanders receive all the imports they needed. At the outset, navigators were unwilling to make the run straight from Norway to Greenland, preferring to sail first to Iceland. But after a time the majority of them seem to have taken the direct route, which, as we know, ran either from Bergen, the neighbouring Herö, or the Stadt Promontory, past the Shetlands and Faeroes and south of Iceland to Cape Farewell, the Viking Hvarf. According to the old chronicles, the first to sail the direct route was Leif, son of Eric the Red. Neither of his two voyages was uneventful, we are told, but on both occasions he made port safely.

By no means all skippers were as fortunate. Many ships sank without a trace. Others were lost in the pack-ice which is carried down from the north by the Polar Current and driven by the North Atlantic Drift against the east coast of Greenland; the most luckless escaped from their stranded vessels across the fringe of ice and reached the uninhabited, stony shore. The most luckless—for now they were confronted by a slow and agonizing death. Only once did the attempt to escape from this inferno of howling winds, biting cold and utter desolation by marching westward across the inland ice, nearly succeed. The Icelander, Einar Thorgeirsson, crossed the inland ice with two companions to within a day's march of the first farms. There he and his men collapsed from exhaustion. Their bodies were later laid to rest in the cemetery of Herjulfsnes.

But despite all the shipwrecks on the Greenland run, there were always men ready to tempt Fate. The profits to be made on these runs were exceptionally high. Timber, iron goods, corn and salt were all things the Greenlanders urgently needed and for which they paid high prices. Payment was by barter, of course. Besides butter, cheese and wool, the Greenlanders could offer their frieze cloths, which for a long time were much sought after in Europe, as well as white and blue fox-furs, Polar-bear skins, walrus and narwhal tusks, and walrus skins.

The last three articles in particular were in great demand with the European merchant mariners. As long as the Saracen pirates in the Mediterranean rendered genuine elephant ivory hard to come by, walrus tusks were considered a perfect substitute. They were as highly prized a commodity as amber had once been to the northern Teutonic

*47. Cologne in 1490. In the foreground a* knorr *for the traffic with Iceland. Woodcut by Wilhelm Pleydenwurff for Hartmann Schedel's* World Chronicle, *1492. The drawing for this woodcut is attributed to Albrecht Dürer.*

tribes in the Baltic, and were worth even the long and hazardous voyage to Greenland, which was looked upon as the end of the world. Narwhal tusks also enjoyed high esteem; they were given out to be the horn of the mysterious unicorn and credited with great medicinal properties.

These narwhal tusks were more or less a monopoly of the Greenland Scandinavians, and were for a long time instrumental in keeping intercourse with Europe alive. But the Norwegians began to hunt walruses in the waters to the east round Novaya Zemlya, and it was naturally cheaper for merchants from central Europe to purchase their walrus tusks in Norway than to sail all the way to Greenland. To this was added the fact that communications through the Mediterranean gradually became safer, so that elephant ivory became easier to obtain. Most important of all, however, was the waning of the vogue for ivory. The Greenlanders then pinned their faith to the narwhal tusk, which remained a saleable commodity not as an ivory substitute, but because of its supposed magic properties. Walrus-skin hawsers were also much coveted articles. The traditional mart for these was Cologne, and from here anchor cables and sail ropes of Greenland walrus skin went all over Europe.

Walruses were not particularly easy to catch, however. Some were to be found on the east coast of Greenland, which was therefore occasionally visited by Norse hunting parties, though these probably never went beyond Angmagssalik. In the main, however, they were hunted in *Nordrsetur*, the hunting grounds in the Disco Bay area on latitude 70° N. The records speak of whole fleets of hunting boats sailing to Disco Bay each summer, and no doubt the hunting of creatures so well able to defend themselves as the narwhal and the walrus provided the sort of excitement dear to the hearts of the intrepid Northmen. When the boats returned to the home farms at the end of summer, they were eagerly awaited. A good bag meant that during the coming year corn, metal goods and other precious articles could be purchased from European traders.

So whole cargoes of walrus and narwhal tusks left Greenland for the south. To begin with, these goods were transported almost exclusively in Norwegian freighters. Later, Hanseatic *Koggen*, a type of ship better suited to long ocean voyages, entered the Greenland trade. The fact that the Hansa city of Cologne was the main centre for the trade in walrus skins strongly suggests that at an early stage commerce with Greenland was largely in the hands of Hanseatic seamen and shipowners. The numerous pieces of brown stoneware of Rhenish origin that have been found in Greenland lend support to this view.

In any case, it is certain that by 1300 Greenland's trade with Norway was rapidly decreasing. The reason for this was the obsolescence of the Norwegian merchant navy, which still employed numbers of low-gunwaled rowing vessels. Every one of the high-gunwaled Hanseatic *Koggen* carried sail; they required smaller crews, took bigger cargoes, and were much more seaworthy. Considerable capital would have been needed to modernize the Norwegian merchant navy; but those who could have furnished the capital, the great ecclesiastical and temporal landowners, began at just this period to withdraw from the field of overseas trade with all its agitations and risks. The universal prosperity during the high Middle Ages guaranteed them an adequate profit on the sale of their corn and other agricultural products.

There were other important obstacles too. Scandinavia was twice ravaged by the 'Black Death', the plague. Between 1349 and 1351, during the first attack of the frightful pestilence on Norway, thousands upon thousands died; in 1392 the horror broke loose again, threatening the country with depopulation. A year later, in 1393, Bergen, the principal port for the Greenland run, was attacked by pirates and so devastated that it took a long time to recover. Obviously, compared with these afflictions, concern about maintaining contact with the far-away Greenlanders must have faded very much into the background.

But the final and decisive blow to intercourse with the Greenlanders was probably dealt by political difficulties. By letter patent from King Eric VI of Norway, the right to trade with Greenland was reserved exclusively to Norwegian merchants, especially those from Bergen. All others were prohibited from making the trip. This was aimed particularly at the Hanseatic League; but in practice the restriction affected Norwegian traders as well. For the Norwegian State, beginning in 1294, had used the distribution of letters patent gradually to create a monopoly in the Greenland run for itself. Ever since 1261 when the Greenlanders attached themselves to Norway, a State merchantman, the *Knarre* (the same word as *knorr,* the type of Scandinavian ship which superseded the Viking longships), seems to have plied between Bergen and Greenland; and it may be assumed that the offer of a regular State shipping service from Norway must have been a powerful enticement to the Greenlanders to relinquish their independence. There are repeated references in later documents, particularly from the first half of the fourteenth century, to this Greenland *Knarre*.

In 1369, one of the King's Greenland ships foundered not far off-shore on its return to Bergen. The whole crew was saved; but the ship, with its no doubt very valuable cargo, was lost. It appears that this mishap spelt the end of official Norwegian traffic with Greenland. At all events, nothing is heard of any new *Knarre*. This did not, however, result in the lifting of the ban on trade and traffic with Greenland by private individuals. On the contrary, it was intensified. Finally, the Crown made any unauthorized voyage to Greenland a capital offence, and when some sailors were driven on to its shore by gales in 1389 they escaped execution by a hair's breadth. The Act of Union between Sweden, Norway and Denmark, drawn up at Kalmar in 1397 and conferring the three crowns on Queen Margaret of Denmark, brought official sailing to Greenland to a complete stop. To those in Copenhagen, the Greenland colony seemed even more remote than it had to the Norwegians. Obviously, the revival of trade with Greenland meant nothing to Queen Margaret.

As has been said, the breach was very largely filled by the Hanseatic League. In sailing to Greenland they were transgressing not only Norwegian law, but also their own regulations as repeatedly laid down by the Hanseatic Diet. In 1416 a ban was issued on voyages to the Shetlands, Orkneys and Faeroes, and the Hanseatic Diet of 1434 expressly extended this ban to Iceland. But the Hanseatic towns, especially Hamburg and Bremen, nevertheless traded widely in the northern seas, particularly with Iceland. It may be assumed that no small proportion of the goods brought by the Hansas went on from there to Greenland. To what extent the latter was itself within the range of activities of the Hanseatic shipowners and merchants is an open question.

Records from the sixteenth century speak of two Hamburg ships being 'driven aground' on Greenland in rather rapid succession while on their way to Iceland. According to the records, the crews of these two vessels, which re-entered the port of Hamburg on 1st July 1537 and 9th August 1539 respectively, did not go ashore on Greenland. This is rather dubious, however. For a few years later, in 1541, a *Kraffel*, the largest type of Hanseatic ship at that time, was dispatched by the city of Hamburg to explore Greenland. This would certainly not have been done without reasonable expectation of success, and it may be assumed that the aim of the expedition was to bring the transit traffic from Iceland to Greenland into the hands of the Hamburg shippers. The voyage cannot have been undertaken solely for purposes of exploration, because a ship of the largest type would not have been chosen for this. It is stated to have failed and been abandoned because it did not succeed in 'coming upon men'. The section of the account of the greatest interest to us runs:

> In spring a *Kraffel* was sent to Greenland for the first time to investigate the land. The skipper's name was Gert Mestemaker. He found the land, but could not come upon any men there. Therefore he at once returned home.

What really happened on this 1541 expedition, and whether Gert Mestemaker landed on the uninhabited east coast of Greenland, remains obscure. It is fairly certain, however, that this voyage into the Arctic Ocean was the last of its kind for years to come. With its failure, the last thin thread binding the Greenland of the Norsemen to the Old World was broken.

8

Certain connections with Europe had held firm for a surprisingly long time. One of these was the link with the Church at Rome. The Catholic Church played the same important role in the extreme north as in the rest of medieval Europe. The rigid organization of the Church offered the existing powers in Greenland, as elsewhere, an effective medium through which to operate. Above the mutual rivalries of the old fjord farmers rose a central power whose grip ran through the priests and Christian missionaries to the humblest commoner. True, tradition has it that Eric the Red rejected Christianity; but he does not appear to have accepted the old faith wholeheartedly either. When the pillar of his high seat was washed ashore on Greenland at what seemed to him an unfavourable spot, he had no hesitation in correcting this error on the part of Destiny and building his house at Brattahlid, in the position of his own choice. When Christianity was introduced into Greenland around 1000 by his son Leif, he did not embrace it himself, but at the same time he took no steps to combat it. As the powerful leader of the Greenland colonists, he could easily have prevented the spread of Christianity if he had wished.

But the way to Greenland was long, and living conditions, even for the dignitaries of the Church, were rather hard. Hence the bishops were usually in no hurry to come to Gardar, and if an ecclesiastical conference called them to some other part of the world, years not infrequently passed before they returned to their bishopric. During the fourteenth century, the northernmost diocese of the Church of Rome was deserted for almost twenty years: Greenland was without a bishop from 1349 to 1368.

During this period the very pious King Magnus Erikson of Norway, who regarded the propagation of Christianity as his life's work, sprang into the breach. It is perhaps thanks to him that the Greenland Vikings, at least in Eystribyggd, survived the difficult times in the middle of the fourteenth century. His aid came too late for Vestribyggd, however: this settlement seems to have perished in 1342—in consequence, it has long been surmised, of an attack by the *Skrælings*, the Eskimoes. The first news of this to reach the Norwegian court was probably a report from the priest Ivar Bardsen of Gardar, received in 1348. Bardsen had come to Greenland in 1341. A year later he was ordered by the head of the East Settlement to go to Vestribyggd and see if all was well there. He reported on this expedition as follows:

From Eystribyggd to Vestribyggd is a twelve days' sail. There is nothing but desolation. In Vestribyggd is a large church, which stands at Stesnes. For a time it was the principal church and the bishop's seat. The Skrælings have now plundered the whole of Vestribyggd, so that there are only goats, sheep, cattle and horses there now, all of them wild, but no men, neither Christian nor heathen. All this was reported by the Greenlander, Ivar Bardsen, who was for many years steward of the bishop's seat at Gardar. He saw it all himself and was one of those sent to Vestribyggd by the law-speaker to drive away the Skrælings. When they arrived in Vestribyggd they found no man there, neither Christian nor heathen. But they found a few cattle and sheep grazing wild. They ate some of the cattle and took as many with them as the ship would hold. Then they sailed homeward.

This sober report, together with others like it, was manifestly what prompted the great relief expedition organized by King Magnus Erikson a few years later. This undertaking, with which we shall be concerned more closely presently, was under the command of Powell Knutsson, a member of the royal bodyguard and a greatly respected and powerful man; it put to sea in 1355. Magnus Erikson's edict order-ing this expedition is extant. Since it is important to our narrative it is given herewith:

King Magni letter of command given to Powell Knutsson at Anarm [probably Onarheim] to sail to Greenland.

Magnus, by the Grace of God, King of Norway, Sweden, and Skone, sends to all men who see or hear this letter good health and happiness in God.

We desire to make known to you that you are to take all the men who shall go in the *knorr* whether they be named or not named, from my body-guard or other men's attendants or of other men whom you may induce to go with you, and that Powell Knutsson, who is to be commandant on the *knorr,* shall have full authority to name the men whom he thinks are best, both as officers and men. We ask that you accept this our command with a right good will for the cause, as we do it for the honour of God and for the sake of our soul and our predecessors, who have introduced Christianity in Greenland and maintained it to this day, and we will not let it perish in our days. Let it be known that whoever breaks this our command shall feel our displeasure and pay us in full for the offence.

Executed in Bergen on the Monday after St. Simon and St. Jude's Day [i.e. October 28th] in the 35th year of our rule [i.e., 1354] Herr Örmer Östinsson, our Lord High Constable, set the seal. (See William Thalbitzer: *Two Runic Stones,* Smithsonian Institution, 1951, p. 49.)

It is not known what success attended this expedition in Greenland. Undoubtedly, however, it was a grandiose and determined act of State, calculated to bring assistance to the hard-pressed Greenlanders in the East Settlement—at least by removing from friend and foe the impression that the Norwegian dominion had been forgotten in the mother country.

9

Even in the course of the Greenland colony's very last decades, however, it was not only pious Catholic kings who concerned themselves about their protégés—even if only in fits and starts; finally Rome itself sought to give aid. There exists a papal brief written by Pope Alexander VI in 1492, bewailing the decline of Christian ecclesiastical life in Greenland in poignant terms and appointing the Benedictine monk Matthias, who had apparently travelled from Scandinavia to Rome expressly for the purpose, Bishop of Greenland.

Alexander VI would certainly not have written this brief if he had not been reliably informed of the existence of a Christian community in Greenland, and if he had not believed that it would be possible to get help to it. What became of this bishop appointed in 1492 is unknown. It cannot be assumed that he really went to Greenland; at all events, there is no record of his having done so. Probably, like so many of his predecessors and his last successor, he could find no ship to take him there. For Matthias also had a successor, in the person of Vincentius Pedersen Kampe, the confessor of Christian II of Denmark. Vincentius, at Christian's suggestion, was nominated Bishop of Greenland by Pope Leo X in 1520; Christian gave an explicit assurance that he would furnish a ship to take the new bishop to his diocese. But this last attempt to establish contact with the Norse Greenlanders was not put into execution either. Accidents to persons taking a leading part in the enterprise, and political difficulties, prevented Christian II of Denmark from carrying out his purpose. The last Bishop of Gardar never reached his bishopric.

At about the same time, then, as the cessation of all worldly contact of the Greenland Northmen with Europe, the spiritual links, which had lasted altogether nearly five hundred years and had been of great practical significance to the Greenlanders, also broke.

The religious outlook engendered by these links played its part in determining the Norsemen's attitude to the Skrælings, the Eskimoes. Eskimoes seem already to have been living in Greenland when Eric the Red first settled there. At all events, Ari Frode says so in the *Icelanders Book*, which he wrote in the first quarter of the twelfth century. But at that time the Norsemen do not seem actually to have seen the Eskimoes. It appears that their first actual meeting took place towards the end of the twelfth century. At this period, ancient chronicles relate, the Greenland Norsemen's hunting expeditions to the far north of their settlements came upon little people whom they called Skrælings. 'They have no iron', these chronicles state, 'and they use walrus tusks as throwing weapons and sharp edged stones as knives.'

In the fourteenth century, there was a succession of alarming reports about the Skræling advance in northern Greenland. We have already heard tell of Ivar Bardsen's fruitless voyage to Vestribyggd in 1342 and his call for aid to King Magnus Erikson of Norway. But there are innumerable other records which speak of increasingly frequent clashes between Northmen and Eskimoes, who razed many Viking homesteads to the ground.

Excavations in Greenland have not so far furnished any confirmation of these accounts; though investigations at Vestribyggd revealed traces of devastation on one of the biggest farms, which might well imply the hasty flight of its owners. Fairly large-scale fights between the two peoples, including perhaps attacks on lonely farmsteads, may have taken place here and there. By and large, however, the Danish excavations corroborate the surprising picture which confronted Ivar Bardsen in Vestribyggd in 1342: the whole place empty and obviously plundered, and in the meadows masterless livestock—goats, sheep, cattle and horses—grazing wild. But nothing to suggest any hard fighting. Nowhere does Ivar Bardsen say that churches and farms went up in flames and now lay in ruins. His report states that the Skrælings had looted the settlement, which now lay in lonely desolation. This account, supported by the excavations is very striking. What really happened at Vestribyggd? we wonder. Why did the Vikings abandon their settlement? Where did they go?

Even today there is no unequivocal and convincing answer to these questions. But there are a number of feasible hypotheses. The worsening of climatic conditions in the North Atlantic zone during the Middle Ages was apparently accompanied, as investigations at Vestribyggd have shown, by a change in the vegetation brought about by a sudden drought. This catastrophe, which must have had a completely devastating effect on the Northmen's livestock industry, is thought to have coincided with the end of the Viking period. We know that cattle-breeding was the basis of the Greenland Northmen's economic existence. Once it became impossible to keep animals, they were faced with the alternative of either adopting the Skræling way of life and living, like them, on fish and blubber—or emigrating.

The Vestribyggd Vikings appear to have chosen the latter solution. In the *Icelandic Annals* of the Bishop of Skalholt, Gisle Oddson, we find the following entry for the year 1342:

> 1342. The inhabitants of Greenland fell voluntarily from the true faith and the religion of the Christians, and having abandoned all good manners and true virtues, they turned to the peoples of America. Some are of opinion that Greenland is quite close to the western regions of the world. This was the reason why the Christians began to refrain from the Greenlandic naviga-tion . . . (See Thalbitzer: *Two Runic Stones*, p. 51.)

It must be made clear that, in the form extant, this astonishing record dates only from the seventeenth century. When the archives of the main church of Skalholt in Iceland were burnt in 1630, Bishop Oddson re-wrote from memory what he regarded as the most important docu-ments. The entry quoted was amongst these, which naturally reduces its value as evidence. None the less, it does not sound improbable. America—the fruitful Vinland and the well-timbered Markland—was, after all, only a few days' sail from Greenland, and, as we have already heard, there is explicit testimony to a voyage to Markland by the Greenlanders as late as 1347. Although this concerned sea-farers from the East Settlement, there is no reason why the people of Vestribyggd should not have been just as well able to make their way to Markland five years earlier—especially as the report in question stresses that the Markland ship was smaller than the smallest Iceland-farer.

It may also be inferred from Ivar Bardsen's account that the emi-grants had not gone so far afield that they could not return to their Greenland home to fetch their beasts. He states expressly that there were cattle, horses, goats and sheep in Vestribyggd. None of these animals could have survived the Arctic winter without cover in that icy waste. Bardsen must, therefore, have arrived in the West Settlement almost immediately after the departure of its inhabitants, who had not yet had time to return for the remainder of their livestock.

Once they had decided on this, however, they had no alternative but to cross the Davis Straits and seek territory on the other side. The conjecture that they did this—and it is no more than a conjecture—receives remarkable support from the numerous reports of the existence of white, tall, fair-haired and blue-eyed 'Eskimoes' in this area.

The first of these reports comes from an English fishing captain, who, round the middle of the seventeenth century, found below 72° N., alongside small, dark-skinned and short-legged Eskimoes, a large number of tall, well-built and rather fair-skinned natives, whose appearance clearly suggested a mixture of some Eskimo with a great deal of Scandinavian blood.

John Franklin was the next to reach the area inhabited by European-looking Eskimoes. He met one of these 'blond' Eskimoes in 1824 and describes him as follows:

The oval face bore a prominent nose and differed little from European faces, apart from the small eyes and low forehead. His skin was fresh and ruddy, and his beard the longest I have ever seen amongst American natives.

Thirteen years later, in 1837, two American Arctic explorers, Dease and Simpson, encountered Eskimoes in the same district. 'One of them', they reported, 'looked distinguished, and might almost have been a Scandinavian.'

The literature on the Arctic is full of similar reports. They were collected by the American scholar, A. W. Greely, and published at the beginning of this century. On the basis of these reports, Greely undertook an intensive investigation of the problem of the white men of the Arctic. This disclosed the existence of many Eskimo legends to the effect that long ago a tall race of foreigners had migrated into the country, who were called by its aboriginal inhabitants, in Labrador as well as on Baffin Island, *Tunnits*. Soon after, this remarkable people was found in the flesh by the Icelandic Arctic explorer, Stefansson, on the isolated Victoria Island off the north coast of the Canadian mainland. Stefansson landed on Victoria Island, which was considered totally uninhabited and even uninhabitable, in 1908 with the express aim of searching for the white Eskimoes. In the middle of May 1910, he succeeded in finding them on Cape Bexley to the north-east of the island. They were feared by the other Eskimoes as brutal and malevolent, but they proved pleasant and peaceable folk, who welcomed the *kablunat*, the white man, hospitably because he looked almost the same as themselves. The resemblance struck Stefansson's Eskimo companions. They exclaimed: 'These aren't Eskimoes, they only dress and behave like Eskimoes!' The encounter with these strange people is vividly described by Stefansson himself:

When I saw the people in front of me, I felt myself to be on the eve of a scientific discovery. Familiar since childhood with Nordic literature, I remembered the Scandinavian adventurers who in groups of a hundred, and sometimes even of a thousand, vanished from time to time into the mists of the Arctic Ocean. Either I had tracked down evidence of those historical

31.  Ruins of the temple fortress of Ollantaitambo near Cuzco. The gigantic blocks of porphyry, weighing up to 40 tons apiece, were quarried from the mountains visible in the background, lowered 5,000 feet into the valley, transported over the Urubamba, and then carried up to the summit of the old temple mountain of Ollantaitambo.

32.  This child's toy of burnt clay, recently unearthed in Mexico, seems to prove that the Indians were acquainted with the principle of the wheel.

34. The monastery of San Domingo in Cuzco stands on the old foundations of the sun temple Coricancha. No explanation has yet been found as to how the Incas were able to cut the semi-circular andesite blocks of the

33. These two 26-foot towers rise above the ruins of Sillustani on the Umayo Peninsula. They are built of huge, accurately hewn blocks and are presumably mausoleums. What ancient people erected these towers is

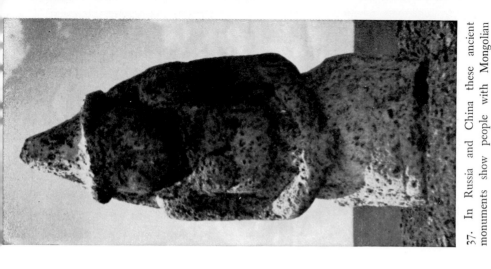

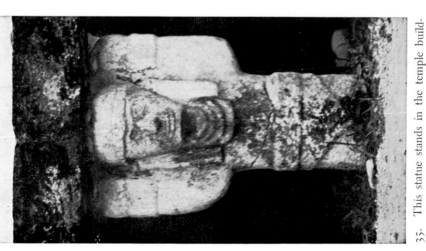

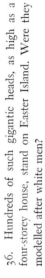

35. This statue stands in the temple buildings of Chichen Itzá in Yucatan. Is it the image of the 'White Gods'?

36. Hundreds of such gigantic heads, as high as a four-storey house, stand on Easter Island. Were they modelled after white men?

37. In Russia and China these ancient monuments show people with Mongolian features. They are the images of their creators.

38. This is Drangaland on Iceland, the barren, rocky area in which Eric the Red originally settled.

39. The glaciers are calving. The spray flies up into the air, in a moment a terrible tidal wave will break loose. Such mortal dangers as these lurked everywhere along the route from the eastern to the western Viking settlements.

events, or I had posed a new question: Why did these Ekimoes look like Europeans if they were not of European descent? . . . A few of them have fair hairs in their moustaches, less often in their beards. Some of the moustaches are dark brown. I have never seen this colour in the west (Mackenzie, Alaska). Here (on Victoria Island) there are men with thick beards, 3 inches long, which are light brown towards the edge and darker by the chin. Their faces and proportions recall those of sun-tanned Scandinavians . . .

These aren't Eskimoes—that was also what Stefansson thought. He spent several years among the Tunnits and wrote a long book about them on his return to civilization. Whereas Eskimoes, being descended from Mongolian tribes, are short of stature, yellow-skinned, black-haired and dark-eyed, the Tunnits were tall, fair-skinned people, often with grey eyes and light brown or reddish hair. 'There are three men here whose beards are almost as fair as my own', noted Stefansson on 16th May 1910, the day of his first meeting with the white inhabitants of the Arctic.

On the very same day he struck to the core of the whole problem. The offspring of unions between Eskimoes and Europeans generally look like Eskimoes. The Tunnits were undoubtedly a mixed race—yet their appearance was European. When Stefansson measured the skulls of his new friends the figures led to the same conclusion: the proportions were not those of Eskimoes, but of Europeans. This means that a strong group of Europeans interbred with a numerically much weaker group of Eskimoes. Therefore this racial evidence of contact between white and Mongolian Eskimoes cannot be derived from the sporadic visits of whalers, whose crews are far too few. Besides which, it is almost certain that there were only two occasions on which whalers or trappers penetrated anything like so far north prior to Stefansson.

Hence, says Stefansson, the mystery of these strange 'Eskimoes' remains unsolved; to the unprejudiced observer the most likely solution would seem to lie with the Greenland Norsemen. Not only were the latter sufficiently numerous to transmit hereditary characteristics through many generations, but also the distance between Victoria Island and the Viking settlements on Greenland was relatively so small that it could have been traversed in about one year. 'If the Victoria Eskimoes really have European blood in their veins,' concludes Stefansson, 'then the Scandinavian settlers of Greenland offer the only historically possible explanation of its source.'

The assumption that the Greenland Norsemen of Vestribyggd were the forebears of the present-day 'white Eskimoes' remains, however, no more than a conjecture.

When the last Northmen vanished from Greenland—which need not have had anything to do with any attack by Skrælings—is somewhat uncertain. According to the testimony of the Icelandic Bishop Oegmund of Skalholt, who was blown into Greenland waters while on his way from Norway to Iceland, he and his men could still see people in Herjulfsnes as they sailed past, in 1534. Evening had fallen, but they sailed so close to the shore that they could clearly distinguish people, sheepfolds, sheep and lambs.

The last European to see a Greenland Viking, though only as a corpse, was probably the Icelandic skipper Jon, who sailed the Hamburg-Iceland run and was given the surname "Greenlander'. This Jon Greenlander made a trip in 1540 of which he left the following account:

He was carried by the wind to Greenland on a German merchantman in 1540. This ship sailed into a fjord dotted with many islands, some of which had been occupied by Eskimoes. They were afraid to land there, and sailed on to a small, uninhabited island lying by itself. There they found boat-houses and stone walls, such as there are on Iceland. There too they saw a dead man, lying face down. On his head he wore a hood, well sewn, and for the rest he had clothes of sealskin and frieze. Beside him lay a curved dagger with a sheath, bent and worn very thin by frequent sharpening. This knife they took with them as a memento.

Since the Hamburg skipper, Gert Mestemaker, as we heard, found no one on Greenland in 1541, a year later, the dead man seen by Jon Greenlander was presumably the last of the Norsemen, whom there was nobody left alive to bury.

In his ill-starred sortie to new shores—which, according to the geographical conceptions of the ancients, must have lain in the immediate vicinity of *Ginnungagap* (yawning gap), the terrible cosmic whirlpool—Eric the Red was obeying more than his own tragic destiny. He was unwittingly impelled by the world's new governing principle, which, after the end of the Græco-Roman Empire, shifted the centre of gravity of future development to the west and north. By his migration to Greenland, Eric set the stage for those who soon afterwards landed on the far western country across the sea, which had so long been the object of Europe's unspoken hopes.

## PART EIGHT

# WINELAND

*Bjarni Herjulfsson, the first man to cross the Atlantic · Leif Ericson sails to Vinland · The wild vine, wild corn, and the salmon · Was Vinland in Massachusetts? · Professor E. F. Gray and 'Leifbudir' · Mr. Dodd and the Beardmore grave · What does* leitadi *mean? · May a bishop desert? · The Vatican knew about Vinland · The Native Copper District on Lake Superior · The Mandan Indians again · Is Magnus an Indian name? · Vikings and the Pining-Pothorst expedition · Burgundian caps in Greenland · John Cabot discovers Markland · The fairy-tale island of Brazil · Did Columbus go to Iceland? · Columbus and the Vinland tradition.*

WHEN Bjarni, the son of Herjulf and his wife Thorgard, returned from Norway to his father's homestead at Eyrar in Iceland in the summer of 985, he found the place deserted. He learnt from the neighbours that his parents had joined forces with Eric the Red and crossed the sea to Greenland. Although still in his early twenties, Bjarni was a widely-travelled and experienced navigator. It did not take him long to make up his mind that he would follow his father to Greenland and winter with him there, as he had previously done in Iceland. In the course of this voyage he became the first European of whom there is definite evidence that he found America.

Let us have a look at Bjarni's account of his voyage to America. He put out from Eyrar in western Iceland and sailed for three days on a westerly course until the land disappeared below the horizon behind him. In good weather—and naturally he waited for good weather before setting out—the high mountains of Iceland remain visible to a distance of about 100 miles. Therefore on the fourth day of the voyage, when the mist came, Bjarni lay 100 miles west of Iceland in the Denmark Strait, only about 80 miles off Greenland. Now, under a grey sky, a northerly wind sprang up, sending the ship off on a southerly course, or rather, since the effect of the East Greenland Drift must be taken into account as well, on a south-westerly course. This went on for several days, as the account states. When the sun finally shone again, and they were able to take their bearings once more, Bjarni had no idea where they were. He was not acquainted with the Greenland Current, since he had never been in Greenland. Hence he did not suspect that they had been carried south-west, and decided to steer westward. Greenland lay west of Iceland, so his decision was logical. He and his men held to this course for a day, when they suddenly saw land that was somewhat hilly and moreover wooded.

What country can this have been? Unquestionably America, that is certain. But what part of its east coast? It can hardly have been Newfoundland, because the Newfoundland littoral rises to a height of

2,600 feet. These are no small hills, but very considerable eminences, especially when viewed from the sea. North Labrador is likewise ruled out. At Port Manvers and Nain the mountains reach a height of 6,600

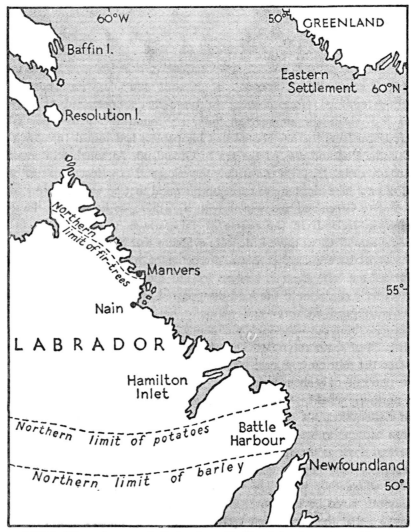

XXII. *The shores of Labrador, Baffin Island and south-west Greenland.*

feet, besides which the northern limit of trees runs along the fifty-seventh parallel, so that its woods are thin and sparse. But in south Labrador, in the Hamilton Inlet region, there is a generally flat landscape broken only by a few hills, which accords with Bjarni's description. Here, too, there are great tracts of forest with magnificent trees, and since the land the Northmen sighted must have been some part of America, there is a great deal of evidence to suggest that their first landfall was here in south Labrador.

After sighting the unknown shore, we are told, they left it on their port side and sailed on. After two days, they sighted land anew. Here too was forest, and Bjarni's men would have liked to take advantage of a calm to anchor and fetch fresh water and firewood from the shore. Their captain vigorously opposed the idea, paying no heed to the grumbles of his crew.

Bjarni's will prevailed against that of his men, and he put out to sea with a south-westerly wind, again in a generally northerly direction, but also a few points west. After a short time they sighted high mountains and glaciers—a country which obviously resembled Greenland, but which did not seem to Bjarni sufficiently inviting. According to the information he had received about Greenland, which certainly spoke of pleasant fjords and lush pastures in keeping with its name, he was convinced that this third country could not be Greenland either. He had sighted the southern part of Baffin Island, where, in addition to high mountains, there are also large glaciers, which is not the case on Labrador.

That this third country cannot, in any case, have been Greenland is clear from the latter part of the account. It says there that the Vikings put out into the open sea with a stiff south-westerly wind, and, riding the storm with sails reefed, reached Greenland in the neighbourhood of Herjulfsnes in four days. Such a course, roughly east-south-east, would clearly have been impossible if the Northmen had really been already in Greenland. The third country they sighted can only have been the southern part of Baffin Island.

Thus the first man of whom we possess certain evidence that he discovered America was Bjarni Herjulfsson, with his voyage in 985. Apparently he never repeated this expedition—surprisingly, it must be added. For since he made his permanent abode in Herjulfsnes, the modern Ikigeit, in south-west Greenland, he might have been expected to make occasional sorties to Markland—as the forest country sighted by Bjarnia was later called—to replenish his stocks of timber. Probably he did, in fact, do so; perhaps the only reason we have heard nothing of it is because the Bjarni tradition has been outshone by the more brilliant accounts of his successor, Leif Ericson, the eldest son of Eric the Red, and Thorfin Karlsefni, an Icelandic merchant. Undoubtedly, too, his voyage only acquired its importance through the expeditions of Leif and Thorfin.

The saga relates that after the death of his father, Bjarni paid a visit to Norway, where he received lively reproaches at the court of Eric the Jarl for not having explored the land he sighted. With these reproaches in his heart he returned to Greenland, and here he manifestly spoke freely of his anger and the new country in the west. This, so we are told, spurred the Greenlanders to seek the unknown western lands. Apparently then, it was only the disapproval of his contemporaries which brought home to Bjarni the fact that the new shores beyond the ocean might be of some importance, so that he now spoke more about them and his voyage thither. On the other hand, it may have been a question of the Greenlanders gradually coming to realize the importance to them of a forested country within reach. It is in any case surprising that it did not occur to the enterprising Greenland Vikings, accustomed as they were to long sea voyages, to migrate to the unknown lands discovered by Bjarni until A.D. 1000, fifteen years after the storm had carried him to their shores.

## 2

The clan of Eric the Red, uncrowned king of Greenland, were naturally amongst the most ardent supporters of the plan to emigrate, when it was finally broached; and Eric's oldest son, Leif, was himself at the head of a large-scale expedition to the western lands. The *Heimskringla* relates of this expedition:

Now is to be told that Biarne Herjulfson came over from Greenland on a visit to Eric the Jarl and the jarl greeted him well. Biarne told him of his voyage, when he saw afore-mentioned lands; and it was thought he had not been very anxious to know about things when he was unable to tell anything about these lands, and for this he was blamed. Biarne became the jarl's bodyguardsman, and the next summer he sailed for Greenland; and there they spoke much about finding new lands. Leif, son of Eric the Red of Brattalid, came to Biarne Herjulfson and bought the ship from him, and obtained a crew so that they were thirty-five men altogether. Leif asked his father Eric to be chief of the voyage. He excused himself, saying he was too old, and not so able to stand wet and cold weather as in former days. Leif replied that he among all their kinsmen would have the most luck on such a voyage. Eric finally gave way, and rode from home with Leif when they were ready for sea; but when they were a short distance from the ship the horse on which Eric was riding stumbled so that Eric fell to the ground and his foot was hurt. Then said Eric, 'It is not fated that I shall discover more lands than Greenland, on which we live: and we ought not to proceed all together on this voyage.' Eric now went home again to Brattalid; but Leif, with his crew, in all thirty-five men, made their vessel ready for sea. On this voyage there was a man from a southern country and his name was Tyrker. The ship was made ready, and they proceeded to sea, and found first the land which Biarne and his men had found last. They sailed to it, dropped anchor, put out a boat, and went on land; but saw no grass. There were big snow-fells inland, but from the shore to the snow-fells the land was all stone, and they thought the land was of no use. Leif said, 'Now we won't have it said of us, as it was of Biarne, that we did not go ashore. I will now give the land a name and call it Helluland [a naked land of rocks].' Afterwards they went on board, sailed away and found another land and sailed near it and dropped anchor. They put out a boat, and landed. This land was flat and covered with wood; and wherever they walked the strand consisted of white sand, with a low beach. Leif said, 'This land shall have a name according to its appearance, and we shall call it Markland [a forest land].' They hurried afterwards to the ship and sailed away. It was blowing a gale from north-east, and they sailed for two days before they saw land. When they came near it, they saw it was an island which was situated on the north side of the land. There they landed in good weather, and found that there was some dew on the grass. It happened that they touched the dew with their fingers and put it to their mouths, and they thought they had never tasted anything so sweet before. Afterwards they went on board, and sailed into a sound situated between this island and a ness which projected northwards and they proceeded west past the ness. The water was very shallow at ebb tide, and their ship lay dry, so it was a long way from the ship to the sea. But they were so keen to get on land that they would not wait for flood tide, but leaped ashore and came to a small river which flowed from a lake. But when their ship was afloat, they went to their boat and rowed to the ship. They towed her up the river, and then into the lake. There they anchored and bore their belongings out of the ship and built some booths. They decided to settle there for the winter, and soon commenced building a big house. They had no shortage of salmon, either in the river or in the lake; and the salmon was larger than they had ever seen. The land was thought to be so fertile, that they needed not to store cattle fodder for the winter. There was no frost in the winter and the grass did not wither much. Day and night were more equally divided than in Greenland or Iceland. The sun was there in the position of eyktarstad and dagmalastad during the shortest winter days. When they were ready with their house-building, Leif said to his followers: 'I will now divide the men into two parts, in order to explore the country; and half of you shall stay at home and the other half shall get to know the land, but nobody shall go farther away than that they can come back the same day, and you must not walk far apart from each other.' This they did for some time. Leif changed about, sometimes he went with them, and other times he stayed at home. Leif was a big and strong man, and of manly looks; besides a wise and careful man in all things.

One evening it happened that a man of the party was missing; and it was the South-country man, Tyrker. Leif was very concerned about it; because Tyrker had lived with his father and fostered Leif in his childhood. Leif gave his men the blame, and arranged to go with twelve men and search for him; but they had come only a short way from the house when Tyrker came to meet them. He was joyfully greeted. Leif soon saw that his foster-father was merry. Tyrker had sharp eyes, and was little in size and ugly with a small face, but was very skilled in all kinds of sports. Leif said to him, 'Why art thou so late, my foster-father? and why didst thou leave thy comrades?' At first he spoke in Turkish,[1] rolled his eyes and frowned, but they could not understand what he said. After a while he said in Norse, 'I did not go much farther than the others; but I have something new to tell, for I found vines and grapes.' 'Can that be true, my foster-father?' said Leif. 'Yes, it is true,' answered he, 'for I come from a country where there are plenty of vines and grapes.' They slept all night and the next morning Leif said to his men, 'We have now two things to look after each day, first to gather grapes and cut vines, and next to fell wood in the forest as cargo for our vessel.' And this they did. It is told that their tender was fully loaded with grapes. Then a cargo of wood was cut for the ship. They found wheat fields which were self-sown and a tree which is called massur. Of everything they took some quantities, and the trees were so large that they could use them for building houses. When spring came they made themselves ready and left the country. Leif gave the land a name after its products, and called it Vinland (Wineland). (*Heimskringla,* Monsen and Smith's translation, pp. 190–3.)

Thus the story of Leif Ericson's voyage to Vinland as told in the *Heimskringla.* The tone of this account reveals that its aim is something quite different to Bjarni's log-book. The specifically nautical aspect recedes largely into the background. Interest centres not so much upon landmarks, wind-directions and sailing-courses, as upon marvellous occurrences in the Utopian paradise on the new shores. True, nautical matters are also mentioned, e.g. where the nature of the inhospitable Helluland or the thickly-forested Markland is discussed and where an attempt is made to indicate latitude by stating the altitude of the sun on the shortest day of the year. But this account is more than a simple ship's log and includes much sensational information about the new country, a great deal of which must have sounded like a fairy-tale to the Greenlanders. In fact, however, even details like the sweet dew are no fairy-tales. In many regions of North America a so-called honey-

---

[1] Other versions of the same story refer to Tyrker as a German.

dew is still to be found; it is the sweet-tasting, dew-like excreta of certain plant-lice and flies. The report of the finding of vines is also correct. In north-eastern America there are no less than thirty different varieties of wild vine, growing to within a short distance of the Gulf of St. Lawrence. Nansen contested this, and consequently dismissed the whole narrative as a Viking wish-dream. This is undoubtedly mistaken. Even today one of the subsidiary bays of the Gulf of St. Lawrence is still called *Baie du Vin*, Wine Bay, from the time of its colonization by the French; likewise an island in the Nantucket Sound bears the name Martha's Vineyard. When the Italian, Verrazano, came to this district in 1524 he reported:

The vines twine themselves round the trees exactly as may be seen in the south of France. If they were cultivated and tended, it would be possible to produce the finest wine from their grapes. For they are sweet and scarcely inferior to our own.

Similar reports have continued right up to our own day. Accordingly, there can be no doubt that the Northmen's statements about Vinland are correct on this point, and in view of the truly sensational significance to them of the occurrence of the vine, it is not surprising that they named the new country after it.

A subsequent voyage to Vinland was made by the Icelandic merchant, Thorfin Karlsefni, a lengthy account of whose attempts at colonization is given in the *Saga of Eric the Red*, which is consequently often known as the *Karlsefni Saga*. He was forced to abandon his settlement as the result of attacks by the Skrælings. The Karlsefni Saga contains much geographical information of importance in siting Vinland.

Naturally, the Northmen did not know that they had discovered a new continent. Some five hundred years later, the Icelander, Sigurd Stefansson, drew a map of Helluland, Markland, and the Vinland promontory, in which all these areas are represented as connected by land with Greenland, and the latter in turn with Bjarmaland, or Siberia. But they did know that something great had been achieved, something worthy to stand alongside the heroic saga deeds from the time of the taking-of-the-land in Iceland, something, indeed, which perhaps surpassed the latter—and of this achievement they were justly proud.

3

It remains uncertain at which particular point on the coast Leif halted. Massachusetts is the place most frequently named in the very extensive scientific discussion of this problem. None the less, it is still a moot point; hence there are always those who would transplant Leif Ericson's Vinland to Virginia, Florida, New England or Newfoundland. Yet none of the objections to Massachusetts are very convincing.

48. *Map of the Vinland voyages by Sigurd Stefansson, 1570. Sigurd Stefansson was Rector of the College at Skalholt in southern Iceland. The original was lost. Bishop Thord Thorlaksson of Skalholt found a copy of Sigurd Stefansson's map, which he worked on. It can be seen that according to the ideas of the period Norway, Bjarmaland, Greenland and Vinland formed a single complex land mass.*

Of great importance in establishing the site of Vinland is the sagas' statement that the winter frost was so light there that the grass scarcely withered and the cattle were able to remain in the open throughout the cold season. This, as American scientists have pointed out, is possible on the Massachusetts seaboard, but out of the question immediately north of it. Quebec already has a mean January temperature of 23 degrees of frost, and Montreal, farther inland, is colder still.

Climatic conditions south of Massachusetts would, of course, have been even more favourable, so that the statement about the mild winter would be much more generally applicable there. This has led to Vinland being sought in Virginia, North Carolina, or even Florida. Such a belief is, however, contradicted by the reported occurrence of immense numbers of large salmon, a fish well known to the Scandinavians from Greenland and Norway. The salmon is a cold-water fish, and is met on the eastern seaboard of America only as far south as 41° N. Assuming climatic conditions at the time of the Vinland voyages to have been approximately the same as today, the mention of salmon sets a definite southern limit to the situation of Vinland. A northern limit is set by the reference to wild vines, which do not grow farther north than 47°. These facts point to a region between Boston and New York.

Against this has been set the indications contained in the *Heimskringla's* remark that, at the time of the winter solstice, the sun reached *eykarstad* and *dagmalastad*. This statement has always engaged the attention of experts and has been the subject of many varying interpretations, none of which has yet gained universal acceptance. The present tendency seems to be to place Vinland farther south than previously, on the basis of this statement. The German scholar, Otto Sigfrid Reuter, deduces from it that Vinland lay between 27° and 31° N. —i.e. in Florida—while the Norwegian, Mjelde, places it in the Chesapeake Bay area below 37° N. The uncertainty arises from the fact that the concepts *eykt* and *dagmal*, which describe certain positions of sunrise and sunset, could be established by the Norsemen only approximately. An inaccuracy of as little as 14 minutes in the observation of the altitude of the sun results in an error of 3° in the latitude calculated from it, i.e., more than 100 miles. Hence it would be a mistake to attach overmuch weight to this statement. All that is meant by it is: 'We were so far south that on the shortest day of the year we still had many hours of light'—a remark which must have been of the greatest interest to the Northmen living on Greenland, because they spent the whole winter in dusk or darkness.

It appears that our present knowledge does not enable us to do more than state the limits between which Vinland must have lain. Nevertheless, much patient research has been devoted to determining the position of Leifbudir, the real Vinland colony of the Vikings. As an indication of how exhaustive research on this point has been, we will briefly outline the hypothesis advanced by one of the most outstanding experts on the subject, the American geographer E. F. Gray, according to whom the Viking settlement must be sought in the vicinity of the Barnstable Peninsula, south of Boston.

This hypothesis is based on the saga accounts of the voyages of both Leif and Karlsefni, together with a personal examination of the possible sites. According to Gray the course of Karlsefni's expedition, after reaching the Barnstable Peninsula, was as follows: after the first landing in the Chatham Harbour area, where the Northmen found sweet dew on the grass, they entered the Nantucket Sound and crossed this in the direction of the narrow channel between the island called Martha's Vineyard and the southernmost promontory of the Barnstable Peninsula. The ness mentioned in the sagas as jutting out northwards into the sea is identified as the projecting northern tip of Martha's Vineyard. Martha's Vineyard itself is synonymous with Karlsefni's Stream-island (Straumsey), and the Nantucket Sound, together with the channel between Martha's Vineyard and the mainland, corresponds to the Stream-firth (Straumfjord). These designations are entirely apposite, since a strong current flows along the coast in an easterly direction at this point.

Here on Straumsey, according to the sagas, eider birds nested in such numbers that it was hardly possible to pick a way between their eggs. This, Gray assures us, is still true of Martha's Vineyard today— though appreciably earlier in the year. Since Leif and Karlsefni launched their enterprises in the early summer, they would have reached Barnstable at the beginning of high summer, when the eider ducks would have finished breeding. Gray explains this discrepancy by the fact that Martha's Vineyard is occasionally swept by storm-tides, which destroy the nests and eggs; when this happens, the birds—eider ducks, sea swallows and gulls—breed afresh, so that large numbers of eggs are still to be seen from the middle of July to the beginning of August. These dates agree with those for the first ripening of wild grapes. If, therefore, we accept Gray's assumption, and also the saga statements about the finding of birds' eggs and grapes, we have an approximate date for Karlsefni's arrival in Vinland—late July or early August.

After overcoming the currents in the Nantucket Sound, the Northmen, we are told in the sagas, sailed west past the northern tip of

Martha's Vineyard. At ebb-tide the channel was very shallow here, so that they finally ran aground. This too applies to existing conditions

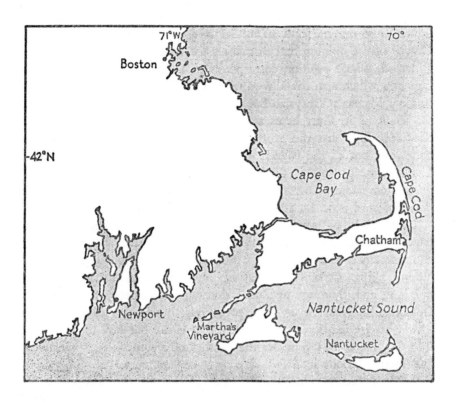

*XXIII. The position of Vinland (after E. Gray). The islands of Nantucket and Martha's Vineyard were formerly joined to No Man's Land (Leifsbudir), so that Nantucket Sound (Straumfjord) really was a fjord. Cape Cod is identified with Kjalarnes, the long sandy shore of Barnstable with Furdurstrandr (Wonderstrands), the Nantucket Sound with Straumfjord, Martha's Vineyard with Straumsey and a point on the northern shore of the Barnstable Peninsula with Krossanes. Gray points out that all early expeditions to America landed here; e.g. Verrazano 1524, Allefonsce 1542, Gosnold 1602, Champlain 1604, Smith, 1614, Hunt 1614, Bermer 1619, the Mayflower 1620. Wild vines still grow here, the white sandy beach on the east coast of Barnstable is still striking and the strong northward-flowing current reduces sailing speed so much that the time it takes to pass them still causes 'wonder'. Gray points out further that the powerful currents in the Straumfjord prevented the explorer Gosnold from sailing through it in 1602.*

on the northern littoral of the island. Navigation is rendered exceedingly difficult by a number of very shallow sand-banks.

After their ship was stranded, Leif and his men did not wait for the rising tide to float it, but waded ashore. They found a small river flowing into the sea from an inland lake, and towed their ship up it. Gray is of the opinion that this refers to Lake Menemsha on Martha's Vineyard, whose position corresponds to the indications given in the saga and which also contains salmon. Leifbudir, where Leif wintered, was not Martha's Vineyard, but the little island of No Man's Land to the south of it. Gray bases this supposition on the statement in the *Karlsefni Saga* that the Northmen on Straumsey had a hard winter and 'went out to the island'. He takes 'the island' to be No Man's Land, whose position in the path of the warm Gulf Stream gives it a winter temperature corresponding to that implied by the saga, which does not hold good for the area round Lake Menemsha.

There is a lot to be said for Gray's theory. It is strengthened by newspaper reports in summer 1952 that digging on the Barnstable Peninsula had unearthed rotting timber which appeared to be the remains of Viking ships. Other investigators, however, hold totally different opinions, and, thorough as Gray's researches have been, it can be seen from this brief review on what precarious foundations all attempts to give a precise location to Vinland rest. It is not our task to go deeper into the matter and consider the conflict of assumptions, conjectures, and interpretations in detail. We must content ourselves with noting that Massachusetts corresponds most closely to the indications of Vinland's position given in the sagas, and that there can be absolutely no doubt about the east coast of America having been reached by the Northmen, and in particular by Leif Ericson and Thorfin Karlsefni.

There is equally little doubt as to when this happened. It was during the early years of our millennium. To be more exact: Leif probably launched his expedition in the early summer of 1000 and returned to Greenland in spring 1001. Bjarni Herjulfsson was certainly the first historically attested Northman to sight America. But the discoverer of the New World was Leif Ericson. It is therefore just that a magnificent monument should have been erected in Boston to him, and not to Bjarni. His was one of the most brilliant exploits of Nordic discovery. Not only did his expedition cover a distance of about 5,000 miles— from Baffin Island to Massachusetts alone is almost 2,200 miles—but the demands made upon the leader's intelligence and nautical skill during the voyage were exceptionally great. The fact that he was equal to these demands and that, although the journey took him more than a

year, he was able systematically to explore Vinland and, despite all
hazards, return to Greenland with his company safe and sound, places
him in the front rank of all discoverers. He is worthy to stand alongside
men like Columbus and Magellan.

From the time of Leif's and Thorfin Karlsefni's contemporaries right
up to the present, the information that the Vikings had come up against

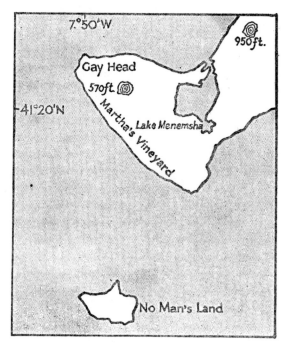

XXIV. *Lake Menemsha and No Man's Land near Barnstable.*
(*After E. Gray.*)

'Skrælings' and had decided to abandon the colonization of America
on their account, has aroused particular interest. At first it was thought
that 'hide-canoes' referred to by the American Vikings could only
have been Eskimo kayaks. Recently, however, scientists have come
round to the view that these Skrælings were Indians rather than
Eskimoes. For in addition to the well-known light birch-bark canoes,
the Indians also possessed hide-boats, and whereas the Eskimoes used
either the one-man kayak, or the women's boat holding nine—the
*umiak*—the Indians in the north of America generally employed a
medium-sized craft corresponding to the descriptions in the sagas.

Moreover, the Eskimoes have always lived much farther north than the regions in which we must seek Vinland. Their settlements were confined almost exclusively to unwooded coasts. Where there were forests, they were usually exterminated by Indians. Evidence that these Skrælings were really Indians is also afforded by a reference in the Saga to a 'dark-coloured ball', which they hurled at their Viking foes by means of a long stick. This probably magic weapon may correspond to the so-called 'demon's head' of the Algonquin Indians south-west of the Gulf of St. Lawrence. This is reported by European settlers from the time of their first clashes with the Redskins. It was a stone wrapped in a painted skin and thrown by the Indians into the midst of their enemies during the battle with the aid of a long throwing-stick; it was intended to be taken for dangerous magic and to strike terror into their adversaries. By this time, white men had lost their fear of demonic weapons. But this was not so with the Northmen. They were convinced from the outset that the brown trolls confronting them could work magic, as they likewise supposed of the Finns and Lapps. So it is easy to understand that the Skrælings' 'dark-coloured balls' filled them with dread. To be frightened of magic, and if possible to flee from it, was no disgrace to the Vikings. Where superhuman forces intervened, all courage was useless. There was nothing left but flight!

The sagas' references to wild grapes and corn have been taken by many writers, in particular Nansen, as an indication that the whole Vinland story is nothing more than a Norse version of the universal legend of a wonderland of plenty, exemplified by the classical Fortunate Isles. This point is discussed at length by G. M. Gathorne-Hardy in his book *The Norse Discoverers of America* (Oxford: Clarendon Press, 1921, pp. 154–62). After bringing to bear an overwhelming weight of evidence, he concludes: 'That wild grapes, at all events, were discovered, I regard as indisputable.' Although 'identification of the wild corn will always be an insoluble problem', there are a number of plants to which the term might have been applied by the Northmen. As Gathorne-Hardy writes: 'The older commentators on these sagas used to consider that maize was indicated, but this is not, properly speaking, a wild plant, and moreover bears singularly little resemblance to any European cereal. The later school mostly identifies the corn of the sagas with wild rice, but this is open to the objection that it is an aquatic plant.' He himself regards something in the nature of lyme-grass (*Arundo arenaria*) as being the most likely explanation. Such minor doubts and uncertainties, however, do nothing to invalidate the Norse discovery of America as a firmly established historical fact.

4

There was a colony of Vikings in America in the eleventh century. It is even possible that this colony stood for about 200 years, and that one section of those who emigrated from Vestribyggd around 1342 went in search of this outpost in the far west. But that is a long story.

This story begins at its last phase on 24th May 1930, in the vicinity

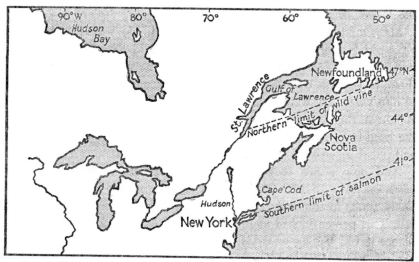

*XXV. Where was Vinland? Since the southern limit of the salmon lies on 41° and the northern limit of the wild vine on 47°, Vinland must be sought between these two extremes.*

of Beardmore, a small town near Lake Nipigon in Ontario. Its heroes are firstly Mr. James Edward Dodd, a freight conductor of the Canadian National Railway, in his spare time a mining prospector, and secondly an unknown Norse warrior, dead for nearly a thousand years and buried with full arms and armour, whose grave Mr. Dodds chanced to unearth. A third part in the story will be played by Eirik Gnupson, the first Viking Bishop of Greenland, who vanished in Vinland on an official visit a few years after arriving in his diocese.

This strange grave was found in a very prosaic manner. On the morning of 24th May 1930, Mr. Dodd discovered on his claim a vein of quartz, which looked to him promising and which he wished to follow to its end. After a few cuts with the spade, however, he came on an obstacle. Deeply embedded in the earth was the stump of a birch tree, so hard that neither axe nor crowbar could make any impression on it.

This was a case for dynamite! Expertly Mr. Dodd packed the charge, lit the fuse, and threw himself flat on the ground; the stump flew in the air with a deafening roar. The rock was laid bare to a depth of 3 feet 6 inches: at the bottom there was schist, and embedded in it a rusty iron object—an old sword, as Mr. Dodd observed on closer inspection—together with an equally rusty old axe, a kind of hand-grip, also terribly rusty, and finally a broken bowl-shaped object, rusted right through, which immediately fell to pieces and had to be got out of the hole with a shovel.

Mr. Dodd was not impressed by his find. He wasn't looking for rusty old bits of iron, but what on earth could they be? Some prospector long before him must have thrown the stuff away and left it there; or perhaps they were old Indian implements. It made little odds to him what they were. But all the same, when he went home to Port Arthur in the evening he took the iron objects with him; he even took the trouble to scrape together a few fragments of the crumbled bowl and put them in with the rest.

And now events took much the same course as they had thirty years earlier with Mr. Olof Ohman of Solem near Kensington. Mr. Dodd spoke to someone about his find, which he would have liked to sell. This person looked at the objects and was struck by their resemblance to old Viking weapons. Before Mr. Dodd knew what was happening, he found himself suspected of staging a fraud. Beardmore is 1,030 miles from the coast. No one had ever before heard of such finds in the district, and there were Scandinavians living all around. It was understandable that the newspapers should suspect Mr. Dodd of trying to gain notoriety.

The flurry in the newspaper caught the attention of Dr. Curelly, director of the Institute of Archæology in Toronto. He was an expert in such matters and it immediately struck him that Samuel Champlain, one of Canada's great pioneers, had reported in 1610 an ancient Indian tradition to the effect that in olden days there had been 'white wooden-boat-men' on Hudson Bay. It wasn't far from Hudson Bay to Lake Nipigon. Could the strange find be genuine? Viking weapons, a Viking grave?

Dr. Curelly travelled to Beardmore. He saw at once that these were Norse weapons, almost a thousand years old, from the early part of the eleventh century. There was a sword, a battle-axe, the hand-grip of a shield, and the remains of a shallow convex shield-boss. This was subsequently confirmed by the directors of European museums. And Dr. Curelly also knew at once that these four homogeneous objects could not have fallen by chance into the hands of Indians and then been lost. For Indians immediately divide their spoils; even a thousand years ago, they would most certainly have shared out things as precious as these keen-edged weapons. So if they had been in the possession of Indians they would never have been found all together now.

Then a Northman must have been buried here. Buried by whom? Again, certainly not by Indians. If this Viking had been a prisoner of war, his weapons would have been taken from him after he was slain. Nor would Indians have taken the trouble to bury the dead, and now quite worthless, white captive so deep in the earth. This man must have been buried by his own people, and by so many of them, so well armed, that they did not consider it necessary to relieve their dead comrade of his weapons: not a lost, half-starved band of despairing men, concluded Dr. Curelly, but an organized troop, perhaps an expedition, who laid one of their number to rest carefully and at a considerable depth.

In themselves, finds of early Scandinavian weapons and implements in North America were no great rarity—though each one of them was a tremendous piece of luck. The eighty thousand Goths who once settled in Italy left in their graves for the archæologists no more than some thirty fibulas, those large and artistically exquisite precursors of the modern safety-pin used in olden times to fasten the ample folds of garments. Thus finds from the Scandinavian epoch in the vast expanse of America were on a par with a very small needle in a very large haystack.

None the less there has been a whole series of such finds. Long before the possibility of a Viking colony on American soil had been seriously considered, ancient Norse weapons and utensils, such as spoons, arrowheads, silver-work, etc., were taken from pre-Columbian graves in the region of Middlesborough and Four Corners in Massachusetts; and as early as 1892, when he published his great book on America, the German Americanist, Rudolf Cronau, expressed the opinion that lasting cultural influences must have been exercised on eastern America by the Greenland Norsemen.

Then Hjalmar R. Holand, whom we have already met as the expert investigator of the Kensington Stone, appeared on the scene. With admirable persistence, he followed up every report of Scandinavian finds. Starting from Nova Scotia, where an old battle-axe, probably dating from the eleventh century, was found in 1880, he followed the trail of the nine finds of ancient Scandinavian weapons made up to then, through Michigan and Minnesota. By the most careful investigation of each find and the circumstances under which it was made he enabled a few rays of light to penetrate the obscurity surrounding the Viking epoch of America.

But the Beardmore find, which permitted such interesting and logically convincing deductions of early and successful colonial ventures by the Northmen in America, was quite isolated and unique of its kind.

5

Scholars began to examine the old Scandinavian sources afresh. In the process they came upon a brief entry in the *Icelandic Annals* for 1121, which read: *eirik bykop leitadi Vinlandz* (Bishop Eric went to seek Vinland). This statement, repeated somewhat more fully in a later entry, had actually been known since the latter half of last century. But since at this time the Vinland expeditions of the Greenland Vikings were held to have been unsuccessful ventures that were soon discontinued, the word *leitadi* was interpreted as meaning that Bishop Eric went in search of Vinland, and as a further proof that it had not really been found before.

In the meantime we have learnt that there can have been no question of 'seeking' Vinland at that period. Every child in Greenland knew where 'Vinland the Good' lay; and as G. M. Gathorne-Hardy points out in *The Norse Discoverers of America*, many instances have been found in which the verb *leita* is used meaning simply 'to visit'. In other words, this sentence states that Bishop Eric visited Vinland in 1121.

We are then confronted by the question of Bishop Eric's purpose in going to Vinland. As the Danish historian, Gustav Storm, has established, Eric arrived in Greenland in 1112 as the first bishop of the most northerly diocese in the world. He was a member of the highly respected family of Icelandic chieftains, the Gnupsons, and doubtless he was a tough and rugged Viking of the type needed in the farthest north. But his exalted origin did not release him from the duty of obedience to the Church, indeed he was even more bound by it than a priest of lower estate. And however much he may have been impelled by the Viking blood of his forefathers, it is altogether unthinkable that he, a bishop, would have put out 'in search of' Vinland. He sailed thither to *visit* it, because it was part of his diocese, because it had souls to be saved, because the Vikings' American colony had a very special right to be strengthened by the flesh and blood of Christ in its savage, heathen surroundings. It is even possible, as G. M. Gathorne-Hardy suggests, that Eric had formed the 'bold resolve to make an end of the one obstacle to settlement by converting the Skrælings to Christianity'. Anyhow, we can be sure that the shepherd abandoned his flock only because he felt that his presence was more urgently needed across the ocean to the west than in Greenland itself.

It must be admitted that up to the present no entirely cogent evidence has emerged in support of this hypothesis. Lukas Jelič, a well-known Catholic scholar, announced at the International Catholic Congress at Brussels in 1895 that his investigations had disclosed that Eric Gnupson was consecrated by Pope Pascal II (1098–1118) in 1112, Bishop of Greenland *regionumque finitimarum* (and the neighbouring regions): in other words, he was to be the pastor of Vinland as well. Only when Eric Gnupson made up his mind to remain in Vinland did the Greenland Norsemen, at a Thing held in 1121, request that they should be sent a new bishop. Up to now, however, no documentary evidence has been forthcoming to support this thesis, either in the archives of the Vatican or elsewhere. If such documents still exist at all, time may eventually bring them to light. They must certainly have existed once.

It is certain that the Curia at Rome had thorough and first-hand information about Greenland and Vinland, because there are absolutely reliable records of frequent visits to the capital of Christendom by Icelanders and Greenlanders. Just as, a few centuries later, the Vatican knew all about the Christian Abyssinians, the St. Thomas's Christians in India, the Great Khan in Caracorum, and the strange land of China, far away in the infinitely remote East, so at this period it was doubtless very well informed concerning the new lands in the west. But the old books are silent, and perhaps for this reason the stones will continue to raise their voices, as they have already begun to do in our own day. Up to now, all North American finds have been made by chance. There are grounds for expecting that systematic search by archæologists will bring to light all sorts of fresh discoveries in years to come.

What can the Viking explorers of 1362 have been seeking besides the Great Lakes? True, we know already that the Vikings frequently ventured into much more impassable country than Minnesota or anywhere else in North America—namely the icy wastes of the Arctic—without any visible reason other than sheer love of adventure. We shall hear later of the thousands of miles they advanced southward; we shall learn that they perhaps penetrated farther east than Novaya Zemlya. But most of these undertakings were of only short duration. Quite unlike them, the expeditions to America seem to have been carried on

over a period of centuries. The weapons found at Beardmore date from
the eleventh century, the Kensington Stone and all the other finds in
Michigan, Wisconsin and Minnesota from the fourteenth. The fact that
all these finds have been made in the same area cannot be attributed
to mere coincidence. It is much more likely that the Vikings had some
specific reason for advancing all this way inland.

We have no definite information on this point, but prehistory may
provide us with a clue. It has been established that the Indians knew
of the extensive copper deposits in the Native Copper District on Lake
Superior long before the advent of the white man. Indian tribes used
to trek to this mining area from quite far afield. It was the source of the
indispensable raw material for weapons and implements which travelled
as far as the Atlantic in the east, the Mississippi in the west, and the
Gulf of Mexico in the south. Ornamental plaques, beads and other
personal adornments, as well as axes, lance heads, knives and awls,
unearthed in a variety of places, bear witness to the importance of the
Lake Superior copper-mines. And they were real mines that the Redskins operated. Many traces of them are still visible: shafts more than
seventeen feet deep, wooden pitprops, built into the earth, massive
ladders, huge lumps of copper, stone hammers and mallets of copper,
large wooden bowls and buckets for bailing water out of the pits, and
so forth.

We must conclude from this that the Great Lakes region was once
one of the centres of North American Indian culture. The Northmen
probably heard of it. Possibly they believed the red metal described to
them by the Indians to be gold, possibly they were simply attracted
by the existence of rich metal deposits. For to a white colony entirely
dependent upon its own resources, even copper was of the greatest
value. By skilful cold-working this naturally soft metal could be
sufficiently hardened for arrow and spear heads, daggers and short
swords to be made from it. The Norse colonists in Vinland, suffering
as they did from an acute metal shortage which could not be relieved
from Greenland, were certainly glad of what metal they could get.

6

At the beginning of this section it was suggested that Fate had laid
a trap for the Vikings when she enticed them to Greenland. They
perished, leaving only a few wretched traces of their erstwhile existence,
of their proud voyages of conquest and discovery. For a long time this

was the universal opinion. But just as, according to the teaching of theoretical physics, both matter and energy are indestructible—undergoing perpetual modification one into the other and back into themselves, changing their manifest form, but never ceasing to be—so it seems that the paths of mankind, looked at as a whole, never run meaninglessly astray. Anyhow, the frequently expressed view that the Vikings' voyages to America were fundamentally pointless is wrong. For a straight line leads from these Norse pioneers to certain voyages made half a millennium later. Columbus's voyages of discovery, be it said at once, do not lie directly on this line, even though it is probable that the Genoese knew of the Westland voyages of the Greenland Vikings. But what Columbus sought was not lands in the western ocean, but India and China and the western route to them. All the same, the news that unknown lands had been found in the west of the ocean must have strengthened his expectations of success.

The straight line that connects the Northmen with their later successors runs first to the old seafaring districts of Flanders, the Netherlands and Friesland. Walrus tusks and walrus skin were much sought-after commodities there, and we have already heard of Greenland's monopoly in walrus tusks which lasted until the high Middle Ages. Greenland also had many connections with southern Europe, however, particularly with Rome through the organization of the Church. As late as 1327 Greenland was still paying its Peter's pence, or Rome scot, and its Crusade tithe. In this year the papal nuncio, Bernard of Ortolis, issued a receipt for about one ton of walrus tusks—a very considerable contribution for the little Greenland colony! Other direct references to the Arctic diocese by high dignitaries of the Church are by no means rare. The Popes themselves remembered it, even at times when officially Greenland was almost forgotten.

Even in southern Europe, however, knowledge of Greenland was not confined to the Church. There can scarcely have been direct commercial relations between Greenland and the south—although the presence of glass windows in the church at Hvalsey points very forcibly to contact with Venice, the only place in Europe at that period which produced glass on any scale. In the south it was the great secular lords who, for a very special reason, concerned themselves with Greenland. One of the favourite sports of the medieval kings and princes was hawking. The white Greenland falcons were universally considered the best hunters, and since they were comparatively rare and difficult to obtain, huge sums were paid for them. This kept knowledge of Greenland very much alive, and it is significant that the Emperor

Frederick II was able to assume in his book *De arte venandi cum avibus* (*On the art of falconry*), written in 1250, that his readers knew of Greenland and its position not far from Iceland. Since Frederick II lived mainly in Norse Sicily, he was acquainted with Viking tradition. But at the fifteenth century other textbooks on hawking still expressly stated that Greenland falcons were the most suitable for this sport of kings. From this it may be inferred that knowledge of the far-away land in the north was much more widespread than might have been supposed.

During the fourteenth century the collection and recording of Vinland sagas reached its peak in Iceland. Hence the news of unknown countries long ago discovered in the western ocean began to seep through to Europe in a more general form than previously. Not only was the information more widely disseminated, but now it was differently received, inasmuch as the numerous expeditions of the Portuguese had created a widespread readiness for voyages of exploration. For it was in Portugal that the trend towards a re-direction of attention began. Interests in commercial, Christian, geographical and political matters were combined in a remarkable fashion in her ruling house. King Alfonso IV (1325–57) seems to have initiated long voyages to the west, probably the Canaries, as early as the first quarter of the fourteenth century. This tradition was taken up and continued by Prince Henry the Navigator (1394–1460) with the aim of finding a seaway to India round the southern tip of Africa. Expedition after expedition sailed from Lisbon, each of them got a little farther, but the Dark Continent extended much farther south than Henry had supposed, and towards the end of his life he realized that it would be a long time before the seaway to India was discovered—if it existed at all.

Round about the same time as this realization came to him, Henry received from his uncle, King Eric of Denmark, a gift which interested him immensely. This was a copy of the great map of northern Europe drawn in 1427 by Claudius Clavus, one of the most celebrated Scandinavian geographers of the period. This map seems to have set Henry the Navigator wondering whether he would not do better to seek a north-western seaway to India. Perhaps this route was much shorter than the south-eastern one, on which he had already expended so much blood and wealth in seeking. Thanks to Marco Polo's accounts people were pretty well informed about India and China, and it was obvious to the perspicacious that these countries could be reached by the western, and not only by the eastern route. Apparently Henry the

Navigator proposed to King Eric of Denmark that an expedition should be dispatched to the north-west. But Eric died soon after, leaving the proposal to be adopted by his successor, Christian I. In 1473 a big Luso-Norwegian enterprise was launched from Iceland, which went north along the old Viking routes. It is not impossible that this expedition reached America eighteen years before Columbus along the course followed by Bjarni Herjulfsson.

The somewhat inaccessible accounts of this voyage have been known for quite a long time. The key to them was provided in 1909 by the finding of a letter from the Burgomaster of Kiel, Karsten Grip, to King Christian III of Denmark, which is dated 1551, i.e. eighty years after the expedition, and reads:

> May Your Royal Highness be informed by these presents that Your Majesty's land of Greenland extends on both sides toward the New World and toward the islands which were found by the Spaniards and Portuguese, so that it is possible to come thither by land from Greenland. This year I saw a map which has appeared relating to Your Majesty's land of Iceland, with a description of all the wonders to be seen there. This map was made in Paris in France. It is also said that Iceland is twice as large as Sicily, which lies beyond Italy. It is further stated therein that the two admirals of Your father, His Royal Majesty Christian I, Pining and Pothorst, on the instructions of His Royal Majesty the King of Portugal, etc., were sent with several ships on a voyage to the new islands and the continents in the north. It is noted therein that they constructed and erected a great seamark on the rock of Wydthszerck [Hvitserk] off Greenland opposite the Sniefeldsickel [Snaefellsjökull] on Iceland, on account of the Greenland pirates, who attack in large numbers with many keelless ships . . .

This document shows the goals pursued by the expedition of 1473. It went in search of the 'new islands' and the continents in the north, and it may be assumed that it was aiming for north-east America. In any case, Burgomaster Karsten Grip is aware that Greenland is not far from the islands and lands in the west, and that these form part of the New World beyond the ocean discovered by the Spaniards.

It has been conjectured that, besides Pining and Pothorst, two German captains in Danish service, a third leading personality took part in this voyage of reconnaissance—the Portuguese João Corte Real. There is no record of his having taken part in any other expedition, yet he was rewarded by the King of Portugal with the post of Governor of the Island of Terceira in the Azores for having discovered 'Stockfish Land', which must certainly be taken to refer to the shores of Newfoundland and Labrador with their wealth of fish. He must, therefore, have been a member of the undertaking led by Pining and Pothorst, and Scandinavian experts have recently lent strong support to the view that Corte Real participated in the Pining-Pothorst expedition as liaison officer to the Portuguese crown. This seems plausible, in the first place because the stimulus to the whole enterprise came from Portugal, and in the second because in 1500 Corte Real's sons, as though following a family tradition, made a particular effort to explore these northern regions of America.

In a very remarkable way, this João Vaz Corte Real and his sons Gaspar and Miquel, who disappeared in Newfoundland in 1502, constituted a link between the old Viking America pioneers and Columbus, the real discoverer of America. Las Casas, Columbus's biographer, records that the great discoverer knew Gaspar and Miquel Corte Real. This can only mean that he also learnt of their father's voyage to Stockfish Land, and of Pining and Pothorst, the heroes of this venture. Thus he knew that there was land in the west, and that there had been repeated voyages to this land. For it would have been very strange if Corte Real and Columbus had not heard of the Vinland tradition of the Vikings.

Thus Germans, Danes and Portuguese may have set foot on the American continent some twenty-five years before Columbus, who reached the mainland, as opposed to the islands surrounding it, on 1st August 1498. The English, under the leadership of the Venetian Giovanni Caboto (John Cabot), also got to America before Columbus. This enterprise too, the inspiration for which was partly derived from the voyages of exploration to the legendary islands of Brazil related in medieval romances, was also largely stimulated by the Viking tradition.

The oldest account of this remarkable voyage is contained in a chronicle attributed to the English priest William of Worcester, who lived in the fifteenth century. There it says:

15.7.1480. *John Jay Junior,* 80 tons, set sail from the port of Bristol for the island of Brazylle west of Ireland . . . On the 18th September news reached Bristol that the ship had sailed round on the water for about nine weeks. But they had not found the island and had returned because of heavy storms . . .

The island of Brazil, stated here to have been the *Jon Jay Junior's* objective, was one of those fairy-tale islands dreamed up by mankind since time immemorial. In the early Middle Ages, the beautiful tale of the wonderful island far out in the western ocean made its way via Rome and Gaul to Ireland. There this ancient legend was overlaid by the natural phenomenon of the Fata Morgana, which, although it is chiefly known from the desert regions of the southern and eastern hemispheres, is also of frequent occurrence off the west coast of Ireland. Whereas in the former areas smiling oases and inviting lakes present themselves to the thirsty pilgrim, in the latter place it is green and fertile islands that rise up ghostlike over the rim of the horizon, only to evade the fisherman who sails towards them as magically as the oases vanish from the caravan leader in the desert. Only by casting a piece of iron on these islands or by shooting an arrow on to them can they be rendered 'solid', say the Irish folk tales. But beneath this Irish disguise the antique legend remains clearly visible. Brazil is more fruitful than any other country in the world. Golden apples grow there, and a dyestuff with which the white wool of sheep can be dyed purple. This, as we can see, comes straight from Phœnician and Greek antiquity. At that period fertility, golden apples and purple dye may have been sufficient to constitute felicity. But the Irish were not content with this and peopled the islands with multitudes of sailor-loving damsels. After this they felt justified in dubbing the lonely island in the ocean 'Brazil the Fortunate'.

It is understandable that both the multitude of damsels and the costly purple stuffs of this legend should have deeply impressed contemporaries and inspired in them the desire to discover this happy isle in the west. The mapmakers of the early Middle Ages did their best to meet this desire. From west of Ireland to south of the Canaries, they enlivened the otherwise empty surface of the ocean with Brandan's, Canary, and Brazil Islands. The Pizigano map of 1367, perhaps in order to increase its international sale, showed three separate Brazil Islands: one west of Ireland, another to the south-west of it, and a third in the area of the Canary Islands. So strong was the ancient legend's power of illusion that the name Brazil was still used by Findlay in 1851, in his map of the ocean currents, to designate an imaginary rock in the Atlantic.

Now it is hardly to be supposed that the level-headed merchant princes of the powerful port of Bristol were disposed in 1480 to spend their money on reaching an island with sailor-loving beauties. Nor are they likely to have been attracted by sheep, golden apples or dyestuffs producing a deep red. The secret of Phœnician purple had lost most of its fascination, since other ways of achieving a lustrous, warm red had been found in the meantime. The owners of the *Jon Jay Junior* and other vessels that put to sea from Bristol round this time were probably concerned, like their Portuguese and Spanish colleagues, to reach

India and Cathay (China). There, as had been learned from the accounts of Marco Polo and other travellers, unimaginable riches beckoned. It looks very much as though the evocative name Brazil was used simply to attract crews. One could hardly expect any seaman to risk his life for the remote and somewhat nebulous 'Lands of the Great Khan'. The fortunate island of Brazil was a much greater draw. This was the reason, we may fairly surmise, why Brazil, and not the 'Lands of the Great Khan', was named as the destination.

Seven such voyages were launched from Bristol from 1480 onwards —all without result. Then, at the end of 1495 or the beginning of 1496, Giovanni Caboto (John Cabot), a Venetian mariner who had been living for some time in Bristol, and his three sons, took charge of these enterprises. This introduced a new phase in the history of these expeditions. Of course, he did not discover the island of Brazil either, and the shores of North America, which Cabot reached before Columbus in 1497, proved bare, harsh and infertile. In any case, the new country had nothing in common with India or Cathay. This epoch of Brazil-America voyaging is reported in a number of mutually independent sources from amongst which we will quote a private letter from the Venetian ambassador in London, Pasqualigo, to whom Cabot may have unfolded his plans at some length.

Pasqualigo wrote to his family in 1497:

Our Venetian, who sailed from Bristol some while ago in a small vessel, is now back and relates that he reached the continent under the sovereignty of the Great Khan 700 Italian miles away. He sailed along 300 miles of the coast of this land and saw no man. Nevertheless, he gave the king of that place several traps for catching wild beasts and a needle for making nets. Moreover, he found trees bearing notches. From this he concluded that the territory is not uninhabited. For reasons of prudence he re-embarked. He was away for three months. This is reliable. He lives in Bristol with his wife and sons . . . He bears the title of Grand Admiral and is treated with great honour. He dresses in silk, and the English run after him like fools. He, however, wants nothing to do with them . . . The discoverer of this territory hoisted the English flag there, but also the flag of St. Mark, since he is a Venetian. So our banner has been planted in a far-off land . . .

Great value must be attached to this report; it clearly reveals that Cabot, like the Luso-Danish expedition led by Pining and Pothorst, sought to get to the lands of the Great Khan, i.e. eastern Asia, and further, that he actually reached the coast of America. What part of the New World he discovered is, unfortunately, not stated. As a rule, the territory discovered by Cabot is placed in south Labrador, New-

49. *Map of the world from Hartman Schedel's World Chronicle. This map reproduces the geographical ideas generally prevalent at the end of the fifteenth century. Asia and Africa are joined at the southern edge, the Indian Ocean is an inland sea. West of North Africa lie the 'Isles of the Blessed'. Scandinavia is an island, and the Arctic Ocean reaches as far as Prussia and Saxony. The large island in the Indian Ocean is not Australia, but Ceylon.*

foundland or Nova Scotia, that is to say, in what the Vikings called Markland. Since it is dependably recorded that Cabot made his voyage on the Bristol ship *Matthew*, which normally plied between that city and Iceland, it is very probable that he received the stimulus to his undertaking from the many Icelanders who cast anchor at Bristol, the main port for Anglo-Icelandic trade. Possibly his crew of eighteen included some Icelanders as pilots. Anyhow, he reached America via Iceland along the old sailing routes of the Vikings.

No proof is needed that the importance of the Viking voyages to Vinland and Markland was heavily underlined by the Pining-Pothorst, Corte Real and Cabot expeditions. Looked at from this angle, the discovery of America in the fifteenth century appears as the re-discovery of old, long-travelled and tested routes; it was no chance phenomenon, but a more or less direct link with the old tradition. Hence the view that the Vikings' voyages to America were devoid of practical value is fallacious and, in this categorical form, untenable.

This tradition, and its revival by the great voyages to the south-west in the latter half of the fifteenth century, was not without importance to Columbus as well. As we know, he was acquainted with Corte Real's sons and may be assumed to have questioned them closely on their father's discoveries. It is possible, however, that his knowledge of these matters was much more direct. In his biography of Columbus, Las Casas reproduces a short note which is probably taken from one of Columbus's letters to his son and runs as follows:

In February 1477 I sailed about 100 miles beyond Thule, the northern part of which lies on 73°, not on 63°, as is asserted by many. And Thule does not lie on the meridian which constitutes the beginning of the west, but much farther westward. To this island, which is as large as Britain, the English sail with their goods, especially from Bristol. When I was there, the sea was not covered with ice. At some points here the difference between high and low tides amounts to 26 *braccia*.

This very definite statement does not sound unplausible, particularly as Columbus made a whole series of voyages before setting out in 1492 to discover America. Consequently, this passage in Las Casas's book has long been considered genuine. The Norwegian school of geographers in particular has clung to it right up to the present, and only recently Samuel Eliot Morison, in his book on Columbus, ex-pressed the opinion that the Genoese really did go to Iceland. All the same, there is no getting away from the fact that Las Casas's quotation contains a great many inconsistencies. At no point on Iceland does the difference between tides reach 26 *braccia* (a *braccio* measured 22 inches);

41. The crozier carved from walrus tusk by Margret, the pastor's wife, for the Bishop of Greenland, Jon Smyrill.

40. Short-sleeved male garment of very coarse frieze from the graveyards of the Greenland Vikings.

42. Ruins of the church at Hvalsey (Qaqortog) near Julianehaab. This imposing two-storey building, erected in 1100, was the most famous of all the Greenland Vikings' churches. It even had glass windows.

43. Aerial photograph of Brattahlid. In the foreground cattle sheds and fodder barns, on the right the ruins of the church with the cemetery, in the background, facing the water, the homestead of Eric the Red.

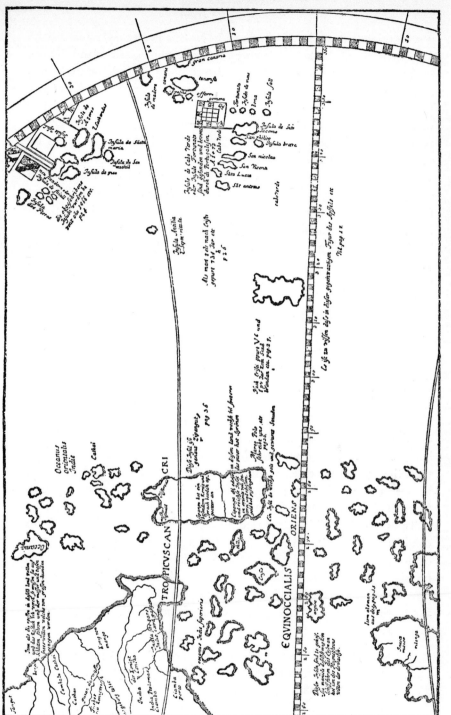

50. The Atlantic islands. Section from Martin Behaim's globe, 1493.

nor is Iceland situated on latitude 73° N.; it is nearer 65°, and this 8°
displacement of the long-known and frequently visited island is very
strange, despite the inexactitude in determining latitude at that time.
Finally it is striking that the Genoese claims to have been in Iceland in
February. This is extremely unusual, since navigation in these waters
generally ceased during the winter. All these points, while they do not
prove that Columbus was never in Iceland, do cast certain doubts on
the authenticity of the document Las Casas quotes.

The question of whether or not Columbus went to Iceland is relatively unimportant, however, because his aims were quite different
from those of the Greenland Vikings, whose Vinland tradition therefore meant little to him. The things which so impressed them—the
broad forests, the grapes, the fields of wild corn, wonders indeed to
dwellers amidst the icy wastes of Greenland—were no enticement to a
traveller from sunny Italy. When Columbus set out to find the lands
of the Great Khan, his inner eye was focused on the visions conjured
up by Marco Polo's descriptions of what he had seen in Cathay and
heard of India and Chipangu (Japan): fertile lands swarming with
people beneath an eternally blue sky, with great cities, incalculable
hoards of gold, silver and the most magnificent gems, with huge bales
of costly silk and mountains of all the various spices so highly prized
and so expensive in Europe. *These* countries were Columbus's goal.
Even if he did go to Iceland and, as would have been likely, there heard
of Vinland, he would have made no direct use of the information;
because the territory discovered by the Vikings lay much farther north
than the regions of eastern Asia which he was seeking, and moreover
because the descriptions of these lands did not in any way tally with
Marco Polo's accounts of Cathay.

Tales of the Viking tradition must, however, have increased his
confidence. They proved the existence of a large country in the western
ocean and so removed the fear of sailing about in a shoreless sea, with
no sight of land and no opportunity of obtaining fresh water and
provisions. On the other hand, Cathay was believed to extend very
far to the north. Martin Behaim noted of these regions on his globe
in 1492:

Item when the Russians travel into that same land, for the sake of costly
furs, they have to travel on sledges drawn by large dogs, because of the
water and the deep snow.

If, therefore, Columbus gathered from the Viking tradition that
there were glaciers in Helluland, and in Markland many beasts of the

chase, he may well have believed, with Cabot, that these regions were Tartary or northern Cathay, and that India must lie to the south of them. This confers a fresh and impressive significance on the ancient tradition. To be familiar with this tradition Columbus had no need of a trip to Iceland, or of acquaintance with the Corte Reals. It was enough for him to have been in England during the 1470's, as we know, from an entry in his log-book for 21st December 1492, that he was. We have seen how close sea traffic between England and Iceland was at this period. Hence nothing is more likely than that Columbus, who was always on the lookout for information about the western lands, should have heard of the Greenland Vikings and their voyages to Vinland during this stay in England.

This does not detract from Columbus's achievement. But it shows that achievement to have been, not an absolutely independent flash of genius, but an organic link in a living chain that leads from the Greenland Vikings via Columbus to our own day. The Norse sea-farers who sailed to America nearly a thousand years ago were the precursors and forebears of those who went later. The criticism that their voyages were, in the long run, ineffectual is shown to be without foundation; they provide one more confirmation of the old proverb: he goes farthest who knows not where he is going.

## PART NINE

# FROM JOTUNHEIMAR AND SVALBARD TO BAGDAD AND CANTON

*'Tickets to Zaitun sold out,' says Head Steward Suleiman · Chinese junks with suites, bathrooms and lavatories · Law student Ibn Batuta becomes a globetrotter · Ibn Batuta sees the Indian rope trick · How much does a concubine cost? · Ibn Batuta's women, the coconut and hashish · On satin, the 'perfume nut' and silk · Chinese paper money · What is the* Konnungsskuggsja *and who wrote it? · How did Dante know about the Southern Cross? · Idrisi's map of the world and the* Rogerian Treatise · *Polar bear skins in Egypt · Arab accounts of skiing in Norway · Ibrahim Ibn Jaqub is astonished in Mainz · Did the Scandinavians use Arab currency? · A Moorish 'Baedeker' for the journey from Magdeburg to Prague · Was Nestor of Kiev telling the truth? · Miklagard and the Varangian Vikings in Bagdad · Captain Othere in Archangel · As far as the Urals and to Siberia · The Arabs'* Bahr Varenk · *The Hönen rune stone · Do virgins become pregnant through drinking water? · Jotunheimar is the land of the kobolds and 'Svalbard' means 'Cold Shores'.*

THE distinguished diplomat came to an indignant stop on the gang-plank of the China boat. His bearers and servants stood as though turned to stone behind him. A sudden silence seemed to have descended on the harbour. The sound of the wavelets slapping against the jetty falls echoed clearly, the wind rustled in the ship's gigantic matting sails, and at the end of the gang-board the women giggled and whispered.

For naturally an exalted dignitary like His Excellency Abu Abdullah Mohammed, ambassador of the Sultan Mohammed of Delhi in India, on an important mission to the Emperor of China, was traveling with his harem—legal wives, concubines and slave girls.

His Excellency stopped short when the supercargo of the China boat hurried to him in great agitation, mopping the perspiration from his brow. The supercargo salaamed reverently and poured out a flood of words, from which the Sultan's ambassador gathered with annoyance that all First Class suites on this ship were already taken.

Abu Abdullah Mohammed, Ibn Abdullah, Ibn Ibrahim, known for about seven hundred years, under the name Ibn Batuta, as one of the most inveterate globe-trotters of all time, left his own account of what happened in *circa* 1330 on the China boat in the port of Calicut, in the memoirs which he wrote at the request of the Sultan of Morocco.

'The Chinese merchants have taken the cabins for the journey here and back,' declared the Arab supercargo, Suleiman of Safad near Acre in Palestine. 'But my brother-in-law has a cabin which I can give you. Unfortunately it has no lavatory. Perhaps Your Excellency may be able to exchange it with one of the Chinese merchants on the way.'

So Ibn Batuta started the journey in a little cabin without lavatory or bathroom, but no doubt he was able, with the aid of the time-honoured Oriental institution backsheesh, to obtain the accommodation he wanted. For, as he wrote later:

I need a cabin to myself because of the slave girls, for it is my custom always to take them with me . . . A cabin is divided into rooms and has its own lavatory and washroom. The door of the cabin can be locked by its occupant, who is accompanied by his slave girls and wives. It often happens that a man remains in his cabin unknown to any of his fellow-passengers until they meet on landing at some port.

First Class suites, bathrooms, lavatories, return bookings?—yes, the huge junks which plied between China and India had all these things early in the fourteenth century. The matter of fact tone in which Ibn Batuta speaks of them suggests that in his day they were nothing new, but had already come to be taken for granted.

We have plenty of information about sailing conditions at this period and even earlier, through the numerous extant accounts. One of these was left by the Chinese Buddhist Fa-hien, who sailed from Java across the China Sea to Canton in a comfortably appointed trading ship carrying two hundred passengers in addition to its cargo, in A.D. 414—nearly a thousand years before Ibn Batuta. We have plenty of descriptions of the first great seafaring operations of Indian ship-owners, who sent their vessels across the Bay of Bengal to Malaya and Indonesia carrying strings of horses, which went on from there to China. Finally there are the old Roman sailing manuals from the first century A.D.

These ancient Oriental transoceanic sailing vessels cannot have had bath-cabins and private lavatories. But compelling hygienic necessity, not regard for the comfort of a handful of rich merchants, must have led to their installation at quite an early stage. For on board one of these enormous craft there was some twelve hundred people, as many as in the average medieval town, and the vessel was often months at sea. The crew itself, including oarsmen and sailors, numbered six hundred—a prodigious figure, but the huge sails of bamboo rods plaited like mats were immensely heavy and required many hands to cope with them. Oars were still needed on occasion, and each of these gigantic beams thirty feet or more in length was wielded by a dozen or so slaves. Then there were four hundred 'marines', mostly Abyssinians, because they were the fiercest fighters, armed with crossbows from which they shot burning arrows dipped in naphtha. They too were a bitter necessity. Pirates lurked everywhere, and anyone not in a position either to defend himself or to pay an exorbitant ransom was flung mercilessly into the sea. In addition to the ship's company of one thousand, there were two hundred to three hundred passengers. Such numbers made the provision of lavatories and bathrooms absolutely necessary. Since these craft were primarily cargo vessels, and therefore packed to the rail with goods of all sorts, their proportions were enormous; they had a displacement of 2,000 to 3,000 tons and would have made Columbus's caravels look like toys.

This may sound rather a tall story. But we have Ibn Batuta's first-hand account of these giant ships:

The large Chinese ships have up to twelve sails, which are made of bamboo rods plaited like mats. They are never lowered, but kept turned into the direction from which the wind is blowing. When the ship is at anchor the sails are left floating in the wind. A ship's company consists of a thousand men, six hundred of whom are sailors and four hundred men-at-arms, including archers, men with shields, and arbalists, who thrown naphtha . . . These vessels are built only in the towns of Zaytun and Sin-Kalan [Canton] . . . At the sides of the ship are the oars, which are as big as ship's masts and each wielded by ten to fifteen men. Rowing is done by two groups standing facing one another. Two enormous ropes, as strong as wooden staves, are attached to the oars. The two groups pull on these ropes alternately, first this way and then that. The vessel has four decks and contains rooms, cabins, and saloons for merchants . . .

Twenty years before Ibn Batuta took up the pen, another had written similarly—the Dominican Jordanus of Sévérac, Bishop of Columbum (the Latinized form of Kaulam, now Quilon, on the coast of Travancore in south-west India). In 1330 he published, for the benefit of members of his order in distant Europe, a handwritten booklet entitled *Mirabilia descripta*, the description of wonders, wherein he tells—with a white man's arrogance, and incidentally in execrable dog Latin—of Chinese junks:

*Navigia quae navigant in Cathay sunt permaxima.* The vessels with which they navigate to Cathay are very big, and have upon the ship's hull more than one hundred cabins, and with a fair wind they carry ten sails. They are very bulky, being made of three thicknesses of plank . . . They are in truth of very strong construction. Yet they do not venture far out to sea; the Indian Ocean is rarely if ever rough, and when a sea is running which they consider might be dangerous, our seamen would say it was fine weather. Without exaggeration, one of our sailors would be worth a hundred or more of these men at sea . . .

Here truth and falsehood mingle. No doubt European mariners were ahead of their coloured comrades in many respects. They had certainly advanced farther in the field of navigation. But when Jordanus writes that the Cathay junks were mere coastal vessels this is an unjustified and erroneous belittlement. The Bishop of Quilon is a great deal more just in writing about the Indian sailors, though what he was really describing were mostly ships of Arab construction and carrying an Arab crew, but belonging to Indian shipowners. For it was a long time before the Indian went to sea himself—like all the obviously inland Indo-European peoples, he did not take to it naturally. Anyhow, Bishop Jordanus finds the ships of 'these Indians' wonderful: '*sunt mirabilia*,' he says,

for although they are very large, they are not bound with iron. Instead they are sewn with a needle and with thread manufactured from a certain plant. The ships never have a deck, but are always open and ship so much water that the sailors always or almost always have to stand in a pool to bail out the water.

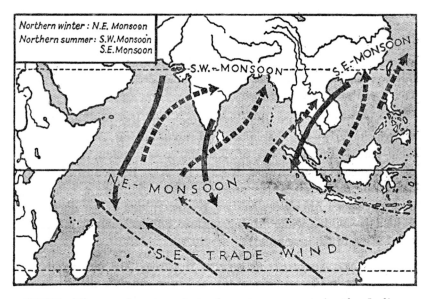

*XXVI. The north-east and south-west monsoons in the Indian Ocean.*

This too may sound like a story from the *Thousand and One Nights* told by Sinbad the Sailor. But Bishop Jordanus was a worthy man who had no truck with fairy-tales. What he relates here is the absolute truth. For these 'sewn' ships still exist. They are the '*mausim*-farers', the monsoon vessels, which today, as three thousand years ago, traverse the 2,800 miles between the Malabar coast in India and Zanzibar in East Africa, tack across the 1,300 miles between Calicut and Socotra, or ply between Ceylon and Sumatra at a speed of four to five knots.

There are no bolts, no nails in the hulls of these 'sewn ships'. Spars, keel, planks, storm-boards—everything is sewn or tied together, stopped with pitch and knotted with the tough and water-resistant coir yarn, a thread painstakingly woven from the fibre of the coconut husk. *Ntepe* these craft are called today; they are open or half-decked vessels of about forty tons, with a low bow rising abruptly to a high stern, forward-leaning masts and huge, gracefully swinging triangular lateen sails.

2

So much for the *ntepe* and Bishop Jordanus of Columbum, and back to Ibn Batuta. Despite his interesting descriptions of Chinese ships, he was no mariner, but merely a traveller with a gift for recounting his experiences, rather like the Greek, Herodotus, many years before him. He began as a law student, but never took his exams. Not through laziness—he was quite a diligent student. But it is the duty of every Moslem, particularly a studious Moslem of good family, to make at least one pilgrimage to Mecca in the course of his life. So on Thursday, 2nd Rajab 725 (14th June 1325), at the age of twenty-two, Batuta left Tangier, his birthplace, on a pilgrimage to the Holy House (Mahomet's birthplace at Mecca) and the Tomb of the Prophet at Medina.

He had no presentiment that he would not return for twenty-nine years when, 'moved by an irresistible desire to visit those glorious sanctuaries', he resolved to leave home and friends behind him. His parents were still alive, and the parting was grievous to both him and them.

A few months later Ibn Batuta was in Mecca. He had walked seven times round the Kaaba as prescribed, he had kissed the *hadshar el aswad*, the black, silver-framed meteorite set in the Kaaba—now it was time to go home. But the wanderlust had taken possession of him. When a caravan left for south-east Africa he joined it, and he roamed to and fro about the world for half a lifetime: to Egypt, Syria and Persia, across Asia Minor and the Black Sea to the Crimea, up the Volga to Bulghar, a great commercial city at the junction of the Kama, and thence past the Caspian and Aral Seas along an ancient caravan road through Afghanistan to India. After several years' stay in Delhi he travelled to China, and five years after leaving Delhi, twenty-two years after his departure from Tangier, he returned to India and across Persia and Egypt to Mecca. In January 1354, he arrived in Fez, capital of Morocco and the seat of its Sultan, where he 'settled down under the wing of the Sultan's bounty' to dictate his memoirs, which were completed on 9th December 1355.

This travel-narrative is a thick tome, long-winded in places, but containing much that is intensely interesting. The fact that Batuta was no wealthy pleasure-seeker, but a man who earned his livelihood as he travelled—as a merchant, a travelling-companion, a cadi (magistrate), and a diplomat—gives his accounts a palpable vitality and freshness. The young man who, in these pages, marches over steppes and deserts, across swamps, through endless forests, and over the frozen passes of skyscraping mountains to busy cities has his eyes open and a receptive mind. He tells stories and listens while others tell them, with all the Arab's uninhibited delight in talk, in tales and legends. But he remained watchful, this ex-law student, he listened critically, sceptically, incredulously. Consequently when at last he was back home again he did not write a collection of fantastic tales after the manner of Sinbad the Sailor, but a book of travel memoirs which, examined closely, is a veritable mine of information on the geography and culture of the Oriental world of his day.

When he arrived in India, this vast country had been under Mohammedan rule for a full century. Ibn Batuta felt almost as though he were at home. Wherever he went he met his countrymen. The factor of the ship that took him to China as ambassador of the Sultan was an Arab from Palestine. In China he met the celebrated Arab jurist, Kiwam ed-Din es-Sebti, who came from Ceuta near Tangier. When Ibn Batuta crossed the Sahara to Timbuctoo, twenty-five years later, he met there the brother of the man whose acquaintance he had made in China. 'What a distance separates the two brothers!' he noted in his diary.

What a distance indeed! The whole world seemed to have become Arabian, from Spain deep into China and to the South Seas, from Timbuctoo in the Sahara and from the mouth of the Zambezi right into Russia. But it was only a thin stratum of wealthy noblemen, enterprising skippers and venturesome merchants who went out into the world, borne by the winds, the ocean currents and the winding rivers. The mass of the Arab people had never left the plains and deserts of their homeland. When Ibn Batuta later recounted his experiences, he met the same incredulity as Marco Polo, whose tales of China earned him the nickname Messer Milione, Master Million, in mockery of his supposed exaggerations.

Batuta's memoirs, too, far exceeded the powers of comprehension of his own era; it was half a millennium before he was properly understood and assessed at his true value. He recounts so many remarkable adventures and so many observations which were bound to strike the

Western World as fabulous, that their worth was not recognized until subsequent writers confirmed them.

There is, for example, a description—probably the very first—of the famous Indian rope trick of the fakirs, the secret of which is still hidden. Of this Ibn Batuta speaks as follows (in the translation of the English Orientalist, H. A. R. Gibb):

That same night a certain juggler, one of the Qán's slaves, was there. The amír said to him, 'Show us some of your feats.' So he took a wooden ball with holes in which there were long leather thongs, and threw it into the air. It rose right out of our sight, for we were sitting in the middle of the palace court, during the season of intense heat. When nothing but a short piece of the cord remained in his hand, he ordered one of his apprentices to go up the rope, which he did until he too disappeared from our sight. The juggler called him three times without receiving any reply, so he took a knife in his hand, as if he were enraged, and climbed up the rope until he disappeared as well. The next thing was that he threw the boy's hand to the ground, and then threw down his foot, followed by his other hand, then his other foot, then his trunk, and finally his head. After that he came down himself puffing and blowing, with his clothes all smeared with blood, and kissed the ground in front of the amír, saying something to him in Chinese. The amír gave him some order, and thereupon he took the boy's limbs, placed them each touching the other, and gave him a kick, and up he rose as sound as ever. I was amazed and took palpitation of the heart, just as had happened to me when I saw something similar at the court of the king of India, so they administered some potion to me which removed my distress. The qádí Afkhar ad-Dín was sitting beside me, and he said to me: By God, there was no climbing or coming down or cutting up of limbs at all; the whole thing is just hocus-pocus. (*Selections from the Travels of Ibn Battúta*, Routledge, 1929, pp. 296 f.)

The possibility of this trick, even as an illusion, has been repeatedly denied; the English Orientalist E. Denison Ross declared it to be no more than a legend. 'No one has ever been found who saw the trick with his own eyes. The whole thing is a tradition. Once the story had come into being, it aroused such an echo in the people that it never quite disappeared again. It became a rumour passed on from mouth to mouth by Indian villagers. There is no question of hypnosis being the explanation!' Queen Victoria is known to have offered £2,000 for the secret of this trick. The sum was later increased to £10,000; but it still lies in the vaults of the Bank of England, no one having come forward to claim it. None the less, the Indian rope trick has been seen and confirmed by men alive today. Whatever the truth behind the events which Batuta describes, he certainly saw them himself, since nothing of the kind had ever been recorded before in his day.

Ibn Batuta also devoted his attention to more ordinary matters, however. One such was the *Berid*, the Indian State Post, by which the Arab traveller was much impressed. In India, he relates, there is an express post, the *Ulak*, which is as swift as the falcon and can traverse the immense distance from the northern mountains to the southern sea in a few days, by means of a highly organized system of relays; besides this there is the ordinary *Berid*, and also a State service used exclusively by the Sultan and operated by relay runners. In itself this was nothing new. But the Middle Ages had long since forgotten that Cyrus and Darius, Artaxerxes and the Sassanids, employed relays of messengers. It had forgotten that the Egyptians had a postal system with set times of delivery, proper post offices and official postmen, that there had long been an efficient telegraphic system with a code of light signals. It had no idea of the speed at which the *carruca dormitoria—wagons lits* so softly upholstered that the statesmen's secretaries and the generals' adjutants had no difficulty in taking down shorthand notes in them— had sped along the streets of Rome during the last century before Christ; it did not recall that this system had been inherited by Byzantium, so that the Indians and Mongols with their State Post were merely heirs and successors of earlier times. Ibn Batuta did not know this anyhow. Patently too, with the typical ingenuousness of Western travellers lost in the labyrinth of Oriental despotism, he had no inkling that the *Berid* was simultaneously a secret intelligence and security service. The *Sahib-el-berid*, the Postmaster, of which there was one in each Indian provincial capital, was a political officer directly subordinate to the Caliph whose sole task consisted in supervising the machinery of the State. Even the governors, the official representatives of the central power, were spied upon by the *Sahib-el-berid* and lived in perpetual fear of what the Postmaster might report to Delhi about them. Apparently Ibn Batuta knew nothing of these undercurrents. Political matters did not interest him, or perhaps he thought it wise to withhold this information from his benefactor, the Sultan of Morocco. At all events, he says nothing about it. On the other hand, being the son of a merchant and a member of an old mercantile people, he goes into great detail on the subject of Indian prices:

In the whole world there is no country with cheaper prices. I saw, as in Bengal, a milch cow sold for 3 silver dinars [about 6s]. . . . Young doves were sold at the rate of 15 for 1 dirhem [about 9d.]. I watched a fat ram bought for 2 dirhems; a pound of sugar for 4 dirhems; a pound of syrup for

8 dirhems; a pound of cooking butter for 4 and a pound of sesamum oil for 2 dirhems. I saw fine cotton of the best quality sold at the rate of 2 dinars for a length of 30 ells; while a charming young slave girl could be had as a concubine for a single gold dinar, which is as much as 2½ Magrevinian dinars [£3] . . .

He also considered pepper an important substance. This was one of the condiments which for centuries the Arabs had bought from the Far Eastern trading caravans, earning huge profits by re-selling it to the merchants of Europe, where it was the object of enormous interest though little or nothing was known about it. Another important commodity was cinnamon wood, the celebrated sappan or brazil wood, whose reddish-yellow pith was used by dyers and, in Europe, was worth its weight in gold. There was also the coconut, the first batches of which had just been landed in Europe and to which every conceivable medicinal property had been ascribed, including one which rendered it particularly valuable in Arab eyes: it was considered to be an aphrodisiac!

'The majority of the trees on the Maldive Islands,' writes Ibn Batuta, 'are coco-palms. These, together with sea-fish, provide the staple diet of the inhabitants. The coco-palm is a wonderful tree. Each tree bears twelve bunches of coconuts a year, one every month. Some bunches are small, some large; some dry and some still green, without any interruption. Milk, oil and honey are made from these coconuts. From the honey they make sweetmeats, which are eaten with the dried coconuts. From these foods and from the fish which they eat the islanders gain incomparable erotic potency. Their performances in this respect are extraordinary. I myself had four legal wives in this country, apart from concubines. I was ready for all of them all day long and also spent the whole night with the one whose turn it was; I lived in this manner for a year and a half.'

This passage may strike the European reader as one of those tall stories with which every traveller spices the record of his adventures. To the Arab world, however, this account was of special significance. There the rite of circumcision is traditionally practised on both men *and* women, with the result that both sexes suffer a dulling of the sexual appetite amounting in the women to frigidity. Consequently aphrodisiacs are particularly highly prized and, in a sense, sociologically necessary. Amongst the broad masses of the Oriental Arabic world, the custom of male and female circumcision has continued up to the present. Hence sexual stimulants are as important there today as in the time of Ibn Batuta; this results in the universal smoking of hashish, a drug which, in certain doses, has a stimulating effect. As long as the barbaric custom of circumcision continues it will remain indispensable. The moderate use of good-quality hashish is said to be no more deleterious than alcohol. When accompanied by malnutrition, however, the toxin has a devastating effect, and in advanced stages of chronic intoxication other narcotics are generally used as well. These are the reasons why it is manifestly impossible to suppress the drug traffic in the Middle East.

After five years in India, Ibn Batuta moved on to China. This happened as follows: the Chinese Emperor sent the Sultan of Delhi an embassy with gifts—a hundred male and female slaves, five hundred garments of *Zaituniah* satin from the city of Zayton (this word, through the *Zettani* of medieval Italian or *Aceytuni* of medieval Spanish, is the origin of our *Satin*), and a hundred garments of Hansa (Hangchow) silk. An embassy naturally had to be sent to the Emperor of China in return, and Ibn Batuta was appointed one of its leaders.

The journey took rather a long time. But time was of even less importance in the Far East then than it is now. So Ibn Batuta had plenty of leisure for observation on the way. Since the route took him via the Sunda Islands, at that period the centre of the clove industry, Ibn Batuta used the occasion to make inquiries about this plant. The European *giaour*, or infidels, sprinkled dried clove blossoms in to their wine and small beer by the handful; the Arabs couldn't get enough of it to satisfy their demand. Some more knowledge about the plant might be very useful.

The clove trees live for a very long time and are of great girth. They are more numerous in the territory of the infidels than in the region of the Muslims, and because they are so numerous there is no private property in them. What we call 'cloves' are a part of the blossom, which falls from the tree and looks like orange blossom. The fruit of the clove tree is the nutmeg, called in our country *jauz-el-tib,* 'perfume nut'. The blossom of this tree is the nutmeg blossom. I have seen all this with my own eyes.

Many months later and after various perilous adventures, Ibn Batuta disembarked in China. To his great astonishment, he met a large number of compatriots here as well. At the outset, the Arabs were anything but seafarers and explorers. They were a nomadic trading people with as great an aversion to the sea as the first Phœnicians a few thousand years before them. Like the Phœnicians, it took the Arabs a long time to grow sufficiently accustomed to the sea to venture out on its waves. The first Arab fleet was built by Caliph Muraviya in about A.D. 650, and used by him in an attempt to conquer Byzantium.

Greek fire, a blazing projectile made up of naphtha, burnt chalk and saltpetre, invented under Constantine the Great around A.D. 330, brought all Muraviya's attacks to naught; but the idea of an Arab fleet was now established, and a little later considerable areas of the Mediterranean were controlled by Arab warships.

Round about 650 the ancient Suez Canal between the Nile and the Red Sea, in Egypt, was dredged, and shortly afterwards Arab ships appeared in the Persian Gulf, on the east coast of Africa, and in India. By the end of the seventh century Arab colonies fringed the west coast of India right down to the southern tip, and soon became the points of departure for Arab trade with the Far East. The principal commercial centre of China appears to have been Khanfu (Canton). A large Perso-Arab colony had existed there since 750; a few years later this colony had grown so strong that it was able one day to attack and plunder the Chinese city. A good hundred years later the foreigners were repaid for this injury to Chinese national pride. On the occasion of the revolution unleashed by the officer of the guard, Wang-chow, and directed particularly against foreigners, a frightful massacre took place in Canton which cost the lives of thousands of foreigners of all creeds and nationalities.

Thereafter Canton lost its pre-eminence in trade with the Arab and Persian world. Its place was taken by Arab colonies on the Yangtse Kiang; Hang-chow, Marco Polo's Quinsay, and the northern city of Ming-chow (Ming-po) already played an important role. We have precise information on this from the Arab geographer Ibn Kordadbeh (*circa* 880) and the Arab merchant Ibn Wahab (*circa* 870), who was himself in China and went as far as the Imperial Court at Nanking. From these two we know that the main commodity imported into China by the Arabs, apart from Indian gems and pearls, was spices from the Moluccas; Indian cotton was also of some importance. There is no evidence that the Arabs imported opium. After about A.D. 870 a new commodity, much prized in China, was carried in the Arab dhows: Negro slaves from east Africa. Even at this early date the value of 'black ivory' was such as to justify long and dangerous voyages.

For the India–China run was an exceedingly hazardous trip. It appears from Chinese sources that the compass was used by foreign navigators on this run from the middle of the eleventh century—the Chinese, who were acquainted with the magnetic stone, employed it for purposes of religious ritual only; none the less the Indian Ocean remained unpredictable, and many a ship must have gone down with all hands.

Ibn Batuta, after surviving many perils, arrived safely in the Middle Kingdom. He possessed neither Marco Polo's intellectual calibre nor his status as a minister of the Chinese Emperor. But he saw enough of the remote and alien land to keep him in a perpetual state of astonishment. A hundred giant junks, all of them as big as the one on which he travelled, lie in the harbour of Zayton, where he landed. The number of smaller craft is beyond counting. It is the largest port in the world. The milling crowd is made up of men of all races. Everyone is dressed in silk. Therefore silk must be cheap, deduces the Arab. Why is it so cheap? 'Because the worms which produce it cleave to certain fruits, eat those fruits, and do not require much looking after.' Ibn Batuta does not see the prodigious amount of work involved in manufacturing silk. He does not notice that the enormously expanding population makes labour a cheap commodity in China, and that this is the only reason why the product of that labour, silk, costs so little that it 'even serves to clothe the poor and wretched of the country'. Only a thoroughgoing capitalist could pass this judgment and then continue: 'If there were no merchants, silk would be of no value at all. A single cotton garment is sold in China for the price of many silk garments.'

He is equally dumbfounded by the 'marvel' of paper money, a marvel which can be explained only by the absolute, overwhelming power of the Emperor. For there was no question of any cover for the pieces of paper as big as the palm of the hand and bearing the Emperor's signature; a few decades later, when the rulers of India and Persia endeavoured to resuscitate their countries' failing finances they achieved nothing but utter chaos. Power is sufficient coverage for an internal bill of exchange only so long as enough internationally valid currency is available for foreign trade; in other words, as long as the internal paper money is simply a certificate of claim to reward for labour. Thoughts like these never entered Ibn Batuta's head, however: he sees, he marvels, he relates.

3

It is time to take leave of Ibn Batuta, the ex-law student, the explorer and travel journalist, the sometime cadi, diplomat and merchant. The flux of our narrative sweeps us unexpectedly northwards again to Scandinavia. There an unknown man sits at the court of the king of Norway, a few decades before the emergence of Ibn Batuta, and broods over the world and its enigmas. Unknown because, although history has brought us his book, the work of a man of genius, his name is lost to us. We do not know who or what he was. That he was a man of standing, however, is evident from the fact that his book was written on orders from the king as a textbook for that ruler's growing son. His instructions must have called for a cosmography, a description of the world, containing all the knowledge of the age. Nothing was more important to a ruler than to be able to visualize correctly the earth with its lands and seas, its currents and winds, its hot and cold zones. A king, of all people, must never forget that there are other men living over the high mountains. To make this clear to the king of Norway's spirited son was the educator's primary task.

This was how the *Konnungsskuggsja*, the *King's Mirror*, the textbook for princes which we have already mentioned and which summarizes, in the shape of a dialogue between father and son, the geographical and scientific knowledge of the period, came to be written in Norway around 1250. We find in this book the following passage:

Now you must understand that the earth is spherical in shape and not equally close to the sun at all points. And there where the curved orbit of the sun brings it closest to the earth it is hottest, and the countries that lie directly opposite its unbroken rays are partially uninhabitable. But those which lie in such a position that the sun strikes them with slanting rays, those countries can be lived in . . .

I have mentioned that a hot zone encircles the earth from east to west like a ring. If I was right in saying this, then I consider it certain that the earth is just as cold at its southern as at its northern end. Further I believe that all countries which are near that hot zone, whether to the south or north, are warm; but those which lie farther away on either side are cold. If you notice, my son, that all people say the countries get warmer the farther south one travels, this comes, I believe, from the fact that you have never found anyone who has travelled so far to the south as to have reached countries as far south of the hot path as those of which I have spoken are to the north of it. And if you have spoken of the winds that come from southern regions being warmer than others, it is, of course, natural for the wind to grow warm when it comes to us, even if it starts out from the frozen southern end of the world, because it blows through the curved ring of the burning path, and so reaches the north warm, even if it blows cold from the south. If men live as close to the cold zones on the southerly side as the Greenlanders do to the northerly, I regard it as certain that the north wind comes to them as warm as the south wind does to us, for they must look northward to the meridian and to the whole motion of the sun, as we have to look southwards, since we live north of the sun . . . And when the sun moves to the extreme southern edge of its diagonal path, those people have summer and abundance of sunlight who live at the southern extremity of the earth; but we have winter and lack of sun. When it turns to the extreme northern edge, however, *we* have abundance of sunshine and *they* winter cold; and so it goes on all the time, rising for the north when it descends for the south, and when it descends for the north, it begins to rise for the southern side . . .

Considering that the doctrine of the spherical shape of the earth— taught by Pythagoras (580–500 B.C.) and after him by Aristotle (384– 324 B.C.), but then completely forgotten again—was still far from being universally recognized in the fifteenth century, this short exposition is very remarkable. Not only does it assert that the earth is a sphere, it also proceeds to the various implications arising out of this conception, e.g. that the earth has a hot zone running round it like a belt, that the North and South Poles must be equally cold, and finally that winter and summer must alternate as between the northern and southern hemispheres. So sure of his business is the unknown author of the *King's Mirror*, one of the greatest geographers of the Middle Ages, that he effectively disposes of the objection that all mariners who have sailed far south have reported that it becomes hotter there, never that it grows colder. This means a lot, and one feels the inclination to attribute his clearsightedness on this point to a brilliant piece of intuitive insight. But such flashes of intuition are rare in the science of geography, which is built up on diligent research and experience. This must apply here. What the *King's Mirror* teaches is not the outcome of logical deduction, but knowledge gained on actual voyages to far places.

Now there is no record of the Northmen ever having found their way as far south as the cold zones of the Antarctic. They didn't even get as far as the equator. How then can they have known that the temperate and cold regions of the north had their counterparts in the southern hemisphere?

This is puzzling, but there are many such puzzles. To name one of them, Dante (1265–1321) wrote the following lines in the First Canto of his *Purgatory*:

> Io mi volsi a man destra, e puosi mente
> All'altro polo, e vidi quattro stelle
> Non viste mai fuor ch'alla prima gente.
> Goder pareva il ciel di lor fiammelle:
> Oh settentrional vedovo sito,
> Poi che privato sei di mirar quelle!

> To the right hand I turned, and fixed my mind
> On the other pole attentive, where I saw
> Four stars ne'er seen before save by the ken
> Of our first parents. Heaven of their rays
> Seemed joyous. O thou northern site! bereft
> Indeed, and widowed, since of these deprived.

(Translated H. F. Cary, Oxford University Press, 1921, p. 121)

This passage (lines 22–7) was already interpreted by Alexander von Humboldt as a description of the Southern Cross, and as such closely examined. Since, however, this constellation, characteristic of southern latitudes, is not visible at all north of 30° N., Dante's familiarity with it is rather mysterious. It was not known in Europe until the mid-fifteenth century, after the great voyages of discovery had begun! His knowledge of this striking group of four stars—which, as Dante indicates, was once visible in the northern hemisphere as well, until it sank beneath the horizon before the beginning of our era in consequence of the procession of the equinoxes—reveals that Dante had been able to draw upon very ancient sources for his astronomical information. He was also aware that the Great Bear, or Charles's Wain, the constellation of the north, sinks lower and lower the farther south one goes and the higher the Southern Cross rises. For the passage from the First Canto of the *Purgatory*, quoted above, continues:

> Com'io da loro sguardo fui partito,
> Un poco me volgendo all'altro polo,
> Là onde il Carro già era sparito
> Vidi presso di me un veglio solo . . .

> As from this view I had desisted, straight
> Turning a little towards the other pole,
> There from whence now the wain had disappeared,
> I saw an old man standing by my side . . .

(Translated H. F. Cary, Oxford University Press, 1921, pp. 121 f.)

Elsewhere in the *Purgatory* Dante relates that he went over to the southern hemisphere and there saw the sun in the north. To the ordinary man of his time and place this was an altogether bizarre idea, and we must infer that the great Florentine did not acquire knowledge of this sort by theoretical reasoning alone. It is too exact for that. He must somehow have learnt that the constellation of the Great Bear in the northern hemisphere was paralleled by an equally striking constellation in the southern hemisphere, the Southern Cross. But the conviction that the earth was a sphere did not start to win universal acceptance in Europe until a hundred years later. How, then, did Dante acquire his knowledge?

We must suppose that it came to him from the court of the Norse king Roger of Sicily (1130–54), at whose palace all the geographical knowledge of the northern Vikings and the Arab seafarers and explorers converged.

Palermo, Roger's seat of government, was one of the few points of intersection between the spheres of power of the northern and southern sea rovers. The two peoples had long been acquainted with one another. They had been measured against each other in numberless sea battles and skirmishes. Arab women and girls had found their way north as captives; Viking galley slaves rowed Moorish warships, and there were Viking bodyguards in the retinues of Moorish noblemen. The two peoples resembled one another in many respects; they were bound together by a strange relationship of mingled love and hate.

In the early ninth century the Norsemen entered the Mediterranean through the Norfa Sound (the Straits of Gibraltar), and by 1059 they had firmly established themselves in Sicily and the whole of lower Italy. These areas had long been settled by the Greeks. In the early Middle Ages a thin layer of Arab warriors and landowners had superimposed itself upon the Græco-Italic colonial peoples; they were followed, for a hundred and fifty years, by the Norsemen.

The latter were Christians, but most of the time they were engaged in violent quarrels with Rome. In any case, the long arm of the Church did not reach as far as the lecture-halls and studies of Sicily; consequently a scientist was free to speak his mind—even if he were an Arab. Indeed, the fair-haired northern barbarians were full of respect for Arab wisdom, and so it happened that an Arab philosopher, physician and geographer, Ibn Idrisi, entered into collaboration with Roger II. The joint efforts of these two such different men produced three pieces of work embodying the accumulated knowledge of their two peoples: a celestial sphere, a disk representing the known world of the day—both in silver—and a geographical treatise, the famous *Al Rojari* or *Rogerian Treatise*.

Both Roger and Idrisi had a strictly scientific approach. They were in search of knowledge, of truth—a modern trait which presaged the emergence of a new human type—and they disregarded everything in the flood of reports, tales and legends which reached them which they themselves did not consider thoroughly credible. They were undoubtedly acquainted with the Scandinavian saga traditions concern-

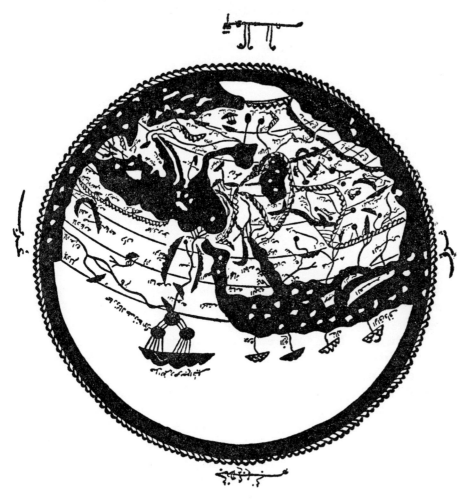

*51. Idrisi's terrestrial disk. Like the original, this fifteenth-century copy of the famous terrestrial disk is orientated towards the north. In the extreme north lies Scandinavia, drawn as an island, so that there is a narrow channel between the Baltic and the Arctic Ocean. The British Isles are unrecognizably distorted. Northern Germany contains a number of lakes: with a little good will we can see in these the Oder Haff, the Frisches Haff and perhaps the Zuider Zee. Spain is a great æstuarium, the boot-shaped outline of Italy is suggested, the Black and Caspian Seas are indicated, so are the Urals, the Red Sea and the Persian Gulf are there, Ceylon is drawn in the quadrilateral shape typical of early maps—but Africa extends immensely far to the east, and the Nile puts out a western arm right across the Black Continent to the Atlantic Ocean.*

ing Greenland and Vinland. But these countries are not represented on the globe nor alluded to in the treatise. For nothing definite was yet known about these regions, and the welter of reports of them current in the Norse world were still passed on only by word of mouth and so vague and embellished that the two sober-minded men at the mapping table in the Court of Palermo dismissed the whole thing as a sailor's yarn. Hence Ireland and the Canaries represent the western extremity of the known world.

It is just the same in the Far East. Japan is mentioned, under the name 'Sila Islands', but nothing is said of Polynesia and the Pacific island world. Yet the existence of these clouds of islands was as well known to the eastern Arabs as Greenland and Vinland were to the Viking seafarers. They had even been described in writing—by Ali Masudi, an Arab geographer and author of travel books born in Bagdad at the beginning of the tenth century. But what he wrote of Polynesia in his *Murudsh al-Dhabab,* (*Meadows of Gold,*) was presumably not precise enough for Roger and Idrisi. It sounded to them too fabulous, too vague; so they ignored it and ended the eastern world with Java, Sumatra and the Philippines.

To the north their vision extended as far as Archangel and the fur-hunting region on the Pechora. The districts round Lakes Ladoga and Onega are named, as well as those on the Rivers Neva and Dvina, and the Rivers Volga, Don, Dniester and Dnieper. In Asia they knew, amongst other things, Lake Baikal and the Rivers Onon, Amur, Ili and Yenisei. They also had a fairly clear picture of Tibet and the gigantic mountains of inner Asia. Naturally enough, central Europe is clearly depicted with the Danube, the Rhine and the Elbe, its great cities, its seas and coasts. But in west Africa they felt sure of nothing beyond southern Morocco, so they omitted everything they had heard about it. And whereas on the east African coast Arab dhows had long sailed to the Zambezi and Sofala, Roger and Idrisi clung to the old Ptolemaic notion that south Africa swept round to the east in a wide arc and finally joined up with Asia, reducing the Indian Ocean to the status of an inland sea.

Much light and many shadows mingle here. But the two go together, and the shadows are indispensable if we wish to see things in three dimensions. That a great deal of knowledge of what lay outside the area illuminated by Roger and Idrisi existed, cannot be doubted. Both Dante and that unknown magus of the north who wrote the *King's Mirror* knew much that was disregarded or not known at all in Palermo. For the link between the Arabs and the Norsemen, although up to the

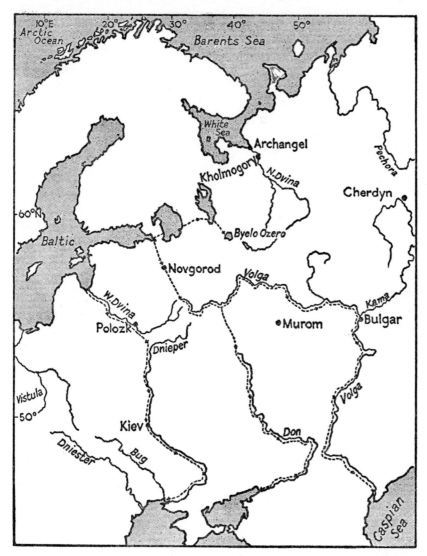

XXVII. *Prehistoric and proto-historic trade routes in Russia. In addition to the Vistula–Dniester route to Olbia and the Baltic road along the W. Dvina and the Dnieper, the N. Dvina–Volga and the Percha–Kama–Volga routes were much used. Amber from the Samland coast (N. Prussia) and furs from western Siberia, which were carried as far as India, were the principal commodities transported along these roads. The precise position of Gelonos is unknown; it probably stood on the site of the later Bulghar. Holmgard was, of course, founded during the Middle Ages. This colony, which was greatly influenced by Norway, was probably established on the site of a prehistoric village of hunters and fishers.*

time of the crusades it was confined to the upper strata of venturesome merchants and audacious fighting-men, was manifestly a good deal closer than was for a long time supposed.

This link seems to have been forged by fashion, in particular the vogue for furs, which lasted right through the Middle Ages. Oddly enough, in view of their climate, the Arabs shared this predilection for wearing furs. Anyhow, a brisk trade soon developed between the far north, the home of valuable furs, and sub-tropical or even tropical countries like Persia, Egypt, Arabia and India. This trade was mainly in the hands of Arab merchants, and furs fetched such prices that great profits were made. As a result of this trade, there were Polar bear skins in Egypt and ermine capes in India. For the sake of the profits, Oriental merchants took upon themselves great discomforts and dangers. To begin with, they travelled only as far as Bulghar, the capital of a Turkish people living at the junction of the Volga and the Kama round A.D. 700. Later on, they went considerably farther north, reaching both Siberia and the White Sea, where Cholmogory, not far from Archangel, the Viking Holmgard, was one of the centres of the European fur trade.

These districts, which cannot all be precisely located, are spoken of by Ibn Fudhlan, a Greek resident in Baghdad who had been converted to Islam and held a position of trust in the court of the Caliph Muktedir (908–32). This Ibn Fudhlan, a clever man obviously greatly interested in geography, was sent as an envoy to the court of King Almus of Bulghar in 920, and has left a comprehensive account in which his own experiences are skilfully blended with information gleaned from others. Of the lands of 'Gog and Magog', the Northmen, he relates so much which is characteristic that the Arabs must have been able to form an accurate picture of the, to them, very strange conditions obtaining amongst the Vikings. The section of his account which is of the greatest interest to us runs:

At a distance of twenty days' journey from the land of Bulghar lies a district called Isu, and beyond Isu is a people called the Yura . . . The inhabitants of Bulghar make journeys into their country and bring back articles of clothing, salt and other goods in which they trade. To transport these things they have made vehicles in the nature of small carts, which are drawn by dogs, since there is much snow and ice there and another animal would not be able to move in this country. The men bind the bones of cattle on the soles of their feet, each one takes two pointed sticks in his hands, thrusts them into the snow behind him and so slides along on the surface of the snow . . .

The King of the Bulghars has told me that at a distance of three months' journey beyond his country there is a people called Vishu, amongst whom the night is less than an hour long. In a sea of this region lives a fish from whose tusk they make knives and sword-hilts. If a ship sails on this sea in the direction of the Pole Star, it comes to a region where in summer there is no night at all and where in winter, on the contrary, the sun does not become visible overhead and revolves in the circle of the firmament like a mill. And then follows a region where the whole year numbers only one day and one night . . .

Of the Vikings themselves Ibn Fudhlan has the following to say:

I never saw people more perfectly developed; they were tall as palm-trees, and ruddy of countenance with red hair. They wear neither coat nor caftan, but the men have only a coarse cloak, which they hand over their shoulders so that one hand is left free. Every man carries an axe, a knife or a sword with him; they are never seen without these weapons. Their swords are broad and decorated with wavy ornamentation and Frankish work. On one side of the sword from the point to the hilt are depicted trees, figures and the like. The women wear a breastplate of iron, silver, copper or gold according to the wealth of their husbands. On the breastplate is a ring and

*52. Skiing in the sixteenth century. Woodcut after Olaus Magnus:* History of the Northern Peoples.

to this, likewise on the breast, is attached a knife. Round their necks they wear gold and silver necklaces. For if a man possesses 10,000 dirhems he has a necklace made for his wife. If he has 20,000 she receives two, and the woman always receives a fresh necklace every time the man becomes richer by 10,000 dirhems. For this reason a woman of the Rus often has a multitude of necklaces round her neck. The finest jewellery of this people is glass beads of the kind which are also to be found on their ships. They value them very highly and pay a dirhem for them and thread them on strings for their wives . . .

The main features of this short extract from Ibn Fudhlan's comprehensive travel-narrative are doubtless authentic and the product of excellent powers of observation combined with the ability to distinguish between truth and fiction in what he was told. How strange it must have been for dwellers in the tropics to hear of people sliding over the snow on cattle-bones—the forerunners of our skiers—and being drawn by dog teams. Even to the Norsemen, skiing seems to have been something of a novelty. This may be inferred from the way in which it is described in the *King's Mirror*. The author is at great pains to make his meaning clear and seems to anticipate incredulity, or at least ignorance, on the part of his readers:

But it will appear a still greater wonder to learn that there are people who can so tame pieces of wood or boards that someone who is no swifter than others when he is only wearing shoes or is barefoot, as soon as he ties under his feet boards eight or nine ells long surpasses the birds in their flight or the greyhound, which is the swiftest runner, or the reindeer, which is twice as fast as the stag . . . Now this will be difficult to believe and will appear marvellous in all countries where people do not know by what art and skill it is possible to bring mere boards to such a speed that up in the mountains there is no earthbound creature which can hope to escape by speed of running from a man, as soon as he has the boards on his feet. But as soon as he takes the boards from his feet he is no swifter than others. But where people are not used to it, it will be almost impossible to find a nimble man who does not seem to lose all his swiftness as soon as pieces of wood, such as I have described, are tied under his feet. We, however, understand this matter well and every winter, as soon as snow lies on the ground, have the opportunity of watching plenty of people who know this art.

How much more incredible must such accounts have seemed to people who did not know what snow really was and whose conception of rapid travel was limited to riding the horse or dromedary. That Ibn Fudhlan risked his reputation at the Bagdad court by putting out such apparently mendacious statements suggests that the same facts had already been reported by the diplomats of his master, Caliph Muktedir. In general, the transmission of information during the first millennium A.D. was probably a great deal more efficient than we tend to suppose. Trade relations too were very nearly as close as they are today. Thus an Arabian account of the German imperial city of Mainz dating from 973, the work of a Moorish physician and merchant named Ibrahim Ibn Jaqub, is extant which clearly reflects the author's astonishment at this city's links with the Far East. Ibrahim Ibn Jaqub relates:

Magandsha [Mainz] is a very big city of which part is inhabited and the rest agricultural land. It lies in the country of the Franks on a river called the Rin and is rich in wheat, barley, spelt [German wheat], vineyards and fruit. There one can see dirhems from the Samarkand Mint of the years 301 and 302 according to the Hejira [A.D. 913–14] with the name of the Master of the Mint and the date of coinage. I take them to be coins of the Samanide Nasr

53. *Map of central Europe from Hartmann Schedel's World Chronicle of 1492. In view of the astonishing knowledge of central Germany which the Arabs already possessed in the tenth century, it is strange that geographical knowledge should have been so restricted at the end of the fifteenth century as this illustration indicates.*

Ibn Ahmed [912–42]. It is also strange that there are spices there which occur only in the farthest Orient, whereas the city lies in the farthest Occident, e.g. pepper, ginger, cloves, spikenard, costmary and galingale. They are imported from India, whence they come in large quantities . . .

Reports of this kind, indicating the great importance of Arabian coins to east and central Europe round the turn of the first millennium, are to be found elsewhere—so frequently that the discovery of Arabian coins even in Iceland (not collector's pieces, but coins brought by the first *landnama* generation) comes as no great surprise. For many hundreds of thousands of such coins, originating from the Near East and obviously currency in these remote regions of the north, have been unearthed from the soil of Scandinavia, Russia and Germany bearing dates from the three centuries A.D. 700 to 1000. Three thousand Arabian coins of this period have been found in Gothland alone, and hundreds of further finds of varying sizes have been reported. Even in Sweden, which no Arab merchant ever visited, about a hundred and seventy sites of finds were known up to 1857.

54. *Byzantine and Cufic coins found in Russia.*

Large quantities of Hither Asian coins were, of course, plundered by the Norsemen on their marauding campaigns, which took them as far as the Caspian Sea and Bagdad. But even when this is taken into full account, the migration of such enormous sums of money remains altogether inexplicable. For the trade carried on by the Arabs was naturally executed more by barter than by monetary payment. It must therefore be supposed that Hither Asian coins were accepted as internal currency in Russia, Scandinavia and Germany. This surmise is to some extent borne out by the fact that the system of weights used by the Swedish Vikings was based on the Persian system. The basic unit was a drachma (our dram, $\frac{1}{16}$ oz. avoirdupois), the Swedish pound weighing 96 drachmas.

This question, like so many problems arising on the borderline between history and geography, remains even now an absolute enigma. On the one hand we know from the itineraries of medieval rulers how difficult travel was and how insecure their communications. On the other hand trade seems to have been more fluid than at any time except the period immediately preceding 1914. How well informed the Arabs were about central Germany in the tenth century is disclosed by the following itinerary for the stretch from Magdeburg to Prague, also taken from Ibn Jaqub:

The road from Magdifung [Magdeburg] to the land of the Buislav [Boleslav II of Bohemia, 964–98], and from there to the fortress of Kalbe [on the Saale] is 10 miles, and from there to Nub Grad [Naumburg] 2 miles. This is a fortified town built of stones and mortar; it lies on the River Salava [Saale], into which flows the River Bode. From Nub Grad to the salt mines of the Jews [Dürrenberg], which also lies on the Salava, 30 miles. From there to Burdshin [Wurzen]—this stronghold lies on the River Muldava [Mulde] —and then on to the beginning of the forest is 25 miles. The latter extends from beginning to end over 40 miles and is situated in pathless mountains [Erzgebirge]. There stands a wooden bridge [probably in the region of Brüx] over the swamp after 2 miles. From the end of the forest one comes into the city of Braga [Prague].

From the fact that Ibn Jaqub felt it necessary to give such a detailed account of his travels in central Europe, which led him from Mainz and Magdeburg to Prague and Cracow, to Poland and Mecklenburg, to Schleswig and *Itraht* (Utrecht), *Vaterburuna* (Paderborn) and *Ebulda* (Fulda)—all in the time of the great German king Huto (Otto the Great)—we may infer that he was not the only one to journey through these regions. Perhaps itinerant Arab merchants were no infrequent sight on the highways of Europe a thousand years ago.

### 4

Just as the Arabs seem at times to have roamed the whole of Europe, so the Vikings too were to be found in all parts of the Western World. They kept close to the seas and rivers, however; from eastern America to the Urals and from Spitzbergen to Bagdad, their activities were mainly confined to the seaboard and the river lands. To the south-east, of course, the Norse migration had to follow the courses of the rivers. The Dnieper, the Don and the Volga carried the Viking penetration deep into the heart of Europe.

This took place round the middle of the ninth century. At this time the Swedish Vikings, the Varangians or Værings, invaded Russia. According to saga tradition, certain Slav peoples called in the Varangians to restore order and found a State in their countries. This is recorded by Monk Nestor of Kiev, the father of early Russian historical writing, in the chronicle which he wrote at the beginning of the twelfth century. He relates there:

In the year 6357 [Anno Mundi, A.D. 859] the Varangians crossed the sea and demanded tribute from the Chudans, the Slavs, the Merans, the Vesses and the Kriviches. In the year 6370 [862] the latter drove the Varangians back over the sea, gave them no tribute, and began to govern themselves. And there was no law amongst them, family rose up against family, and dissension and disunity were rife. And they began to make war upon one another. Then they said to each other: 'Let us seek a prince who will rule over us and who can decide what is the law!' And they went over the sea to the Varangians, to the Rus, for so these are called, as others are called Svians, others Nurmans, others Anglanes, and yet others Goths. And the Chudans, the Kriviches and the Vesses said to the Rus: 'Our country is large and fertile, but no order prevails, therefore come and govern us and rule over us.' And three Rus were chosen with their clans, and these took all the Rus with them and came across the sea. And the eldest, Rurik, ruled in Novgorod. And the second, Sineus, on Lake Byelo Ozero; and the third, Truvor, in Izborsk. And the land, especially that round Novgorod, was called after these Rus. These are the people of Novgorod of Varangian descent, formerly the people of Novgorod were Slavs. But after two years Sineus and his brother Truvor died. Rurik then became sole master and distributed cities among his followers, to the one Polotosk, to another Rostov, and to yet another Byelo Ozero. And the Varangians entered these cities; before them there were Slavs in Novgorod, Kriviches in Polotosk, Merans in Rostov, Vesses in Byelo Ozero, and Muromans in Murom. But all these made Rurik their ruler.

The chronicle of Nestor of Kiev, doubtless for good reasons, has recently been contested. It is not our task to weigh up the pros and cons of this dispute. It must probably be accepted, however, that Rurik's *Gardarrike* (Kingdom of Fortresses), whose main purpose was no doubt to safeguard the Varangian trading centres and provide a springboard for further inroads, was the nucleus of the Russian State. To establish such a State it was necessary to dominate the areas round the sources of the Dnieper and the Volga, which provided a route for water traffic through the forest regions of Russia. And it was from here that the Varangians began to extend their influence over Russia. Rurik's first base, Aldaigyuborg on Lake Ladoga, opened the way to

44.   Skraeling canoes. The Vikings in America believed that some kind of mill was in motion on the sea. They had never seen boats driven by paddles.

45.   Svalbard. Amid heavy clouds, with forbidding mountains and surrounded by ice, Svalbard, the 'Cold Shores' of the Vikings, the modern Spitzbergen, rises up out of the sea.

46. Viking weapons in North America. The axe comes from the Beardmore grave, the fire-steel in the centre and the halberd on the right were found b Lake Norway, not far from Kensington.

47. Viking sword from the Beardmore grave. The sword is in the typical Viking style of the first quarter of the 11th century.

48. The Kensington Runestone.

the Volga across Lake Onega and Lake Byelo Ozero; his second seat of government, Novgorod, founded *circa* 860, at the point where the Volkov flows into Lake Ilmen, afforded access to both the Volga and the Dnieper.

The philological explanation of the name Rus—which was previously traced back to the Slav *rusyi*, blond, but is now generally regarded as coming from the Finnish name Ruotsi, meaning men from the land of 'Roslagen' on the northern shore of the Baltic—lends support to the theory that the Varangian settlement of Russia started from the area on the Gulf of Finland. The names of the Varangian leaders given by Nestor of Kiev are undoubtedly of Norse origin. Rurik is the Scandinavian Hrorik, Sineus corresponds to Signjut and Truvor to the Nordic Thorvard. Although leadership of the Viking expedition to Russia seems to have been in the hands of the Swedish Varangians, there can be no doubt that Norwegians, Danes and Finns also took part in it. The term 'Varangians' was applied by the Slavs indiscriminately to all these groups.

At the same time as Rurik went to Novgorod, which had been an important trading centre since the dawn of history, two other Varangians not of Rurik's clan, Haskuld and Dyri, also set out for the land of the Slavs. A few centuries earlier Rome had been the goal in the sunny south that beckoned to the Vikings; now it was Byzantium, which the Varangians called *Miklagard* (Great Garth) or *Tzargard*. But Haskuld and Dyri were no more successful in conquering Byzantium than any other Viking after them. On their journey down the Dnieper, a route which had been explored by the Northmen as far as the Black Sea long before Rurik, they came first to Kiev. This city, the capital of the Polanians, pleased them so much that they decided to stay. Their rule over the Polanians, whom they quickly overthrew, lasted for twenty years. Then they were attacked by Helgi, the son and successor of Rurik, who defeated and slew them in 882. Henceforth Kiev was the capital of the Russo-Varangian kingdom. It is recorded that as late as the eleventh century, the majority of the inhabitants of the Viking seat of government were still Scandinavians.

Despite this settlement, the lure of Byzantium remained. In 907 Helgi reached the Golden Horn, allegedly with two thousand ships. An enormous ransom freed the city from the danger of falling into the hands of the Varangians. In 941 another Northman, Ingvar, Helgi's son, knocked at the gates of Miklagard. This time 'Greek fire', which took a terrible toll of the Northmen, saved the threatened metropolis. But a few years later, Ingvar, whom the Slavs called Igor, was back

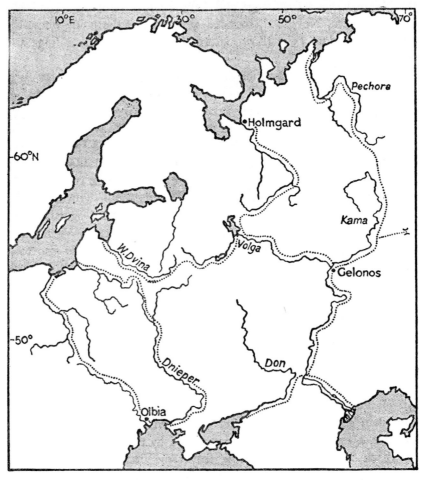

*XXVIII. The Viking lines of advance into Russia.*

again weapon in hand. Again Byzantium paid ransom. And again this availed her for one generation. Since then, Russia has made repeated attempts to bring Constantinople under her sway.

The Vikings were not well advised when, in order to be nearer Byzantium, they shifted their capital from Novgorod to Kiev. By so doing, they lengthened their lines of communication with their old homeland so much that their link with it was fatally loosened. The influence of the Slav environment became so overwhelming that the Varangians were soon completely submerged in the population of the subject country. The Icelanders continued to call Russia 'Greater Sweden', and the envoys of the Byzantine emperor Theophilus to the

German emperor Louis the Pious, who arrived at Ingelheim in the Palatinate in 839, declared that the Rus were of Swedish extraction. Even at the beginning of the fourteenth century Novgorod was still a Scandinavian city. But a little later this last Varangian outpost too was swamped by the Slav flood. Only in the *bylini*, the heroic ballads of Russian popular poetry, which have remained alive amongst the people of northern Russia right up to our own day, have traces of Varangian influence been preserved. These ballads are all that remain to remind us of those early Viking days in Russia. All else has long since sunk into oblivion.

As we have heard, the Varangians never succeeded in conquering Constantinople. They infiltrated into the city in large numbers as merchants and soldiers, however. In a military respect especially they soon gained considerable influence. For the Byzantine emperors, who could not always place full reliance on the loyalty of their compatriots, took to composing their bodyguard entirely of Varangians. The majority of the latter came from Russia, but no doubt there was a sprinkling from Scandinavia. The first Northman named as being in the service of the Emperor was actually an Icelander who arrived in the Golden City before 950, through a very strange concatenation of circumstances. Ultimately the Varangian Guard of the Byzantine autocrats formed a State within the State, with its own laws and its own jurisdiction. Naturally its leader was always a Varangian; one of them, Harald the Hard (Harald Haardraade), who later became king of Norway, we shall meet again. By the thirteenth century the number of Vikings who came to Byzantium had considerably diminished. The ranks of the Varangian Guard were then largely filled by Englishmen. It continued to exist until 1453, when Constantinople was taken by the Turks.

Apart from the Dnieper and the Don, the main channel for the Varangian advance to the south was the Volga. Oddly enough, there is no mention whatsoever in Norse literature of the great enterprises which carried the Vikings to Persia and Bagdad. This is all the more surprising because Bagdad had long been the terminus for many convoys from the Far East, which went from the Malabar coast, Hormuz and the Persian Gulf of Basra. After the Caliph transferred his capital to Bagdad in 760 the city began to overshadow the old Egyptian metropolis, Cairo. One would expect, therefore, to find some reference in Scandinavian sources to Bagdad, the junction with shipping routes from the Orient. It is not mentioned at all. There are plenty of allusions to Byzantium and the feats of arms performed in the struggle

with the Greeks; but for the much more extensive campaigns that took
the Vikings into the land of the Caliphs we are entirely dependent upon
Arab sources.

Viking traders seem to have got to Bagdad quite early on. At all
events the Arab geographer, Ibn Kordadbeh, speaks in his great book
on the roads of the Caliph's kingdom (845) of the Viking merchants
who had come to Bagdad. These Viking traders, however, were only
the advance guard of the Northmen, who invaded northern Persia in
crushing strength during the decade from 870 to 880. But the heaviest
onslaughts did not take place until the tenth century, from 909 to 912,
and in 943–4. Of the campaigns of 909–12 we have a full account in
the chronicle of Abul Hazan Masudi, the *Murudsh al Dhabab*. The
main points in his account run as follows:

As soon as the Viking ships had reached the fortress at the entrance to
the æstuarium [Sea of Azov] they sent emissaries to the king of the Khazars
to ask his permission to pass through his country, to sail on the river [Don]
and into the Sea of the Khazars [Caspian Sea] . . . They promised him half
of the booty they would obtain. He gave his permission. Thereupon they
sailed into the æstuarium and into the River Don and then into the Khazar
River [Volga] past the city of Itil [an ancient historical city near Astrakhan]
and out through the mouth of this river into the Sea of the Khazars.

The Rus remained several months in this sea. It was impossible for the
inhabitants of the coast to drive them away . . . When the Vikings had taken
sufficient booty and prisoners, they sailed back to the River of the Khazars
and sent emissaries with gold and booty to the king, in accordance with the
conditions they had accepted. The king of the Khazars had no ships on this
sea, for the Khazars are no sailors. If they were they would constitute a very
grave danger to the Mohammedans . . .

There can be little doubt that the long voyages which took the
Vikings thousands of miles from their northern home were made for
military and mercantile, rather than for geographical reasons. Plunder
or profit was their main motive. But curiosity may have been an added
incentive. The desire to find out what lands lie beyond the haze of
distance is typical of the Scandinavian character. This desire drove the
Vikings to every point of the compass: from 75° N.—the inhospitable
shores of the Smith Sound in Greenland—to around 34° N., the
latitude of Bagdad, and from 75° W., the approximate longitude of
Cape Cod on the east coast of America, to 70° E., the longitude of
Novaya Zemlya and the northern Urals.

Voyages of exploration and trade to these remote north-easterly
regions probably started before those in other directions, since here

the Northmen had only to sail along the Scandinavian coast to find themselves in a foreign country. And this foreign country proved to be very rich in furs, walrus tusks and many other commercially valuable goods. It is certain that the first Northmen entered the coastal lands of the Arctic Ocean by the eighth century at the latest. The first documentary evidence of such voyages, however, dates from the ninth century. The voyage we are about to discuss was made in about 870. At the time, it was nothing exceptional. At least Scandinavian sagas indicate that in the ninth century voyages to Bjarmaland were fairly common. The importance of this particular voyage lies in the fact that it is recorded in detail.

It was made by the Norseman Othere, a big farmer from Halogaland in northern Norway, who, despite his wealth—it is recorded that he owned six hundred reindeer—was in the habit of supplementing his income by walrus-hunting and trading expeditions by sea. This Othere, of whom we otherwise know little, seems to have been a noted seafarer in his day. Anyhow, King Alfred the Great of England called him to his court to aid his plans for an English fleet by acting as instructor to English navigators and seamen. The account of Othere's voyage to the White Sea, in the form in which it has come down to us, was written by Alfred the Great himself and runs:

Then Othere told King Alfred that of all Northmen he dwelt farthest to the north. He sailed along the coast towards the north. The land here stretches a long way northward, but it is absolutely desolate apart from a few places inhabited by Finns, who hunt in winter and fish in summer. As he related, he desired to learn how far the land extended and what lay north of the waste land. He therefore sailed due north along the coast. For three days he had the sea on his left hand, the desolate land to his right. Then he came as far north as the whale fishers usually go. But he sailed farther on to the north, as far as can be reached in another three days. Then the land receded to the east—or the sea runs into the land—he could not say which. There, however, he had to wait for wind from the west or west-north-west. Then he sailed close to the shore east by south as far as he could go in four days. There he had to wait until a north wind came, because the land went to the south. Then he sailed close to the land southwards for five days. Here a great river came out of the land. They sailed into the estuary of the river, not wanting to sail farther for fear of enemies. For beyond the river the land was thickly populated and cultivated. This was so for the first time since he had left his own farmstead. For during the whole voyage the land had been inhabited only by fishers, hunters and bird-catchers, and all these were Finns. But to the left he had never seen anything but the open sea.

There lay the land of the Bjarmers, a well-cultivated land, but he was not permitted to set foot on it. The country where the Terfinns dwelt, on the other hand, was desolate and uncultivated; there only hunters, fishermen and men who went bird-catching lived. The Bjarmers told Othere much about their own country and about neighbouring countries. But he did not know how much of it was true. It seemed to him that Finns and Bjarmers spoke roughly the same language. He had sailed hither because he wished to explore the land, and also on account of the whales and walruses. For the latter have very good ivory in their tusks.

*55. The Maelstrom. An old woodcut by Olaus Magnus.*

Othere's report is very precise and probably reliable, though the statements of sailing-days are rather doubtful as they stand. Exactly where he went and, in particular, which river on the White Sea coast he sailed up, is not stated explicitly in the account as recorded by King Alfred. The river was probably the Dvina, whose estuary had been a trading point of great importance since the dawn of history. Here Cholmogory, and later Archangel, sprang up, not by chance or at the command of some absolute monarch, but as the result of practical commercial necessity. This is the only place where there could have been tilled fields at that period. For the Murman coast must have been as desolate then as it is now.

The northern and eastern parts of the Baltic also entered the seafarer's ken round about this time. Not much was known about these areas as yet, and even Othere could tell King Alfred but little. All the more interesting, therefore, must the English king have found his acquaintance with the skipper Wulfstan, who had sailed the Baltic as far as the Frisches Haff. Who Wulfstan was, whether a Saxon or a Norseman like Othere, is unknown. Nor can it be ascertained when he made his Baltic voyage. Probably it was round about the time when Othere visited the White Sea, i.e. between 870 and 880.

The Vikings' true field of action, however, was the north-west. This was the direction to which they were principally drawn. Here lay Eric the Red's Greenland, here Vinland the Good. Harald Haardraade, the famous commander of the Varangian Guard of the Eastern Roman (Byzantine) Emperor, who was mainly responsible for the exploration of southern Europe, was finally also drawn to the north. In his day, Vinland was a clearly defined geographical concept throughout Scandinavia; it would have been astonishing if Harald had disregarded its call. The voyage thither cannot have appeared particularly difficult. It took a bare week to reach Iceland, and four days from there to the coast of Greenland. Another four days were needed to sail along the coast to the settlements of the Greenland Vikings, and then Vinland was only a stone's throw: the whole voyage couldn't take many weeks. So Harald set sail for Vinland, probably in 1065, the only reasonably peaceful year in the life of this reckless soldier of fortune.

There is a strong element of conjecture in statements concerning Harald Haardraade's expedition, since the only records are a brief note by Adam of Bremen and an inscription on a rune stone at Hönen in Ringerike, Norway. However, Gustav Neckel, who has made a close study of the subject, considers it reasonable to surmise that 'King Harald's bold and extended voyage was an endeavour to incorporate Vinland, which was so much discussed just then, into his kingdom. The project would have been worthy of its author.' Whether or not this conclusion is correct, Harald Haardraade is certainly to be included in the company of intrepid explorers of the Arctic who, throughout history, have obeyed the lure of the north. How many this company numbers in all will remain for ever unknown; those of whom a record exists are only a fraction of the total.

Typical of the incompleteness of our knowledge concerning Viking voyages to the north, their own specific domain, is the following strange note of an expedition from Greenland into the Arctic Ocean occurring in the *Monumenta Historica Norwegiæ*, a collection of medieval sources on the history of Norway, which runs:

Some sea-captains wished to return from Iceland to Norway. But they were borne northward by contrary whirlwinds, and finally landed in a region lying between the Bjarmers and the Greenlanders. They asserted that they

Von mancherlay gestaltnus der menschen schreibt Plinius: Augustinus vnd ysidorus die hernachge melte ding. Jn dem land india sind menschẽ myt hunds köpffen vnd reden pellede. nerñ sich mit fogelgefeng vñ klaiden sich mit thierhewtten. Jtem ettlich haben allain ein aug an der stirñ ob der nasen vnnd essen allain thier fleisch. Jtem in dem land libia werden ettlich on hawbt geporn vnd haben mund vnd augen. Ettlich sind bederlay geslechts. die recht prust ist in manlich vnd die lingk weibisch vnd vermischen sich vndereinand vñ gepern. Jtem gegen dem paradis bey dem fluss Ganges sind ettlich menschen die essen nichts. dann sie haben so klainen mund das sie das getranck mit einẽ halm einflössen vnd leben vom gesmack der öpffel vnd plumen. vnd sterben pald von bösem gesmack. Daselbst sind auch lewt an nasen eins ebnen angesichts. Ettlich haben vnden so gross lebsfizen das sie das gantz angesicht damit bedeckẽ Jtem ettlich an zungen. die deütten einander ir maynũg mit wincken als die closterlewt. Jtem in dem land Sicilia haben ettlich so grosse orñ das sie den gantzen leib da mit bedecken. Jtem in dem land ethiopia wandern ettlich nidergebogen als das vih. vnd ettlich lebẽ vierhundert iar. Jtem ettlich haben hörner. lang nasen vnd gaißfüß das findest du in sand Anthonius gantzer legẽd. Jtẽ in ethiopia gein dem nidergang sind lewt mit einem prayten füß. vñ so schnell das sie die wilden thier erfolgen. Jtem in dem land Sathia haben sie menschẽ gestalt vñ pferds füess. Jtem alda sind auch lewt fünff elnpogen langk vnd werden nicht kranck bis zum tod. Jtem in dẽ geschichtẽ des grossen Alexanders liset man das in india menschen seyen mit sechs henden. Jtem ettlich nacket vñ rawh in den flüssen wonend. ettlich die an henden vnd füssen sechs finger haben. ettlich in dem wassern wonẽde halb menschen vnd halbs pferds gestalt habende. Jtẽ weiber mit perten bis auff die prust auff dẽ hawbt eben vnd an har. Jtem in ethiopia gegen dem nidergang haben ettlich vier awgẽ. So sind in Eripia schön lewt mit kranchßhelsen vnnd snebeln. Doch ist als Augustinus schreibt nit zuglawben das ettliche menschẽ an dem ort der erden gegen vns da die sunn auff geet. so sie wider ñ geet die versen gegent vnsern füssen kerẽ. Doch ist ein grosser streyt in der schrifft wider den wone des gemaynen volcks. das geringßumb allenthalben menschẽ auff der erden seyen. vnd die füß gegen einander kerende dar auff steen. vnnd doch alle menschen ir schayttel gem hi mel kerẽ. in verwunderũg warũmb doch wir oder die die ir fersen gegen vnns wennden nit fallen. Aber das kömbt auß der natur. dann gleicherweis als der stul des fedrs nynndert ist denn in den federn. der wasser nynndert denn in den wassern. vnnd des gayts nynndert denn in dem gayst. also auch der stul der erden nynndert anderß wo denn in irselbs.

56. *The peoples in the lands of the Great Khan. Woodcut from* Schedel's World Chronicle *of 1493. These pictures show the ideas generally current in sixteenth-century Europe about India and the other lands of the Great Khan. The text reads:*

'Pliny, Augustinus and Isidoris write the following things concerning the various shapes of men. In the land of India there are men with dog's heads who talk by barking. They feed by catching birds and wear the skins of animals. Others again have only one eye in the forehead over the nose and eat only the flesh of animals. In Libya many are born without heads and have a mouth and eyes. Many are of both sexes. The right breast is male and they mingle with one another and bear children. Close to Paradise on the River Ganges live men who eat nothing. For they have such small mouths that they absorb liquid nourishment through a straw, they live on the juice of flowers and apples, and almost die from a bad smell. Likewise there are people without noses and with otherwise flat faces. Many have such large underlips that they can cover their whole faces with them. Many have no tongues; they converse with each other by signs, like people in monasteries. In the land of Sicilia many have such large ears that they can cover their whole bodies with them. In the land of Ethiopia many people walk bent down like cattle, and many live four hundred years. Many have horns, long noses and goat's feet, this you will find in the whole legend of St. Anthony. In Ethiopia towards the west there are people with a single broad foot and so swift that they can run as fast as wild beasts. In the land of Scythia they have human forms and horses's feet. There too are men five ells long who never become ill until their deaths. In the history of the great Alexander we read that in India live men with six hands. Many dwell naked and rough in the rivers, many, who have six fingers on their hands and feet, many who dwell in the waters, have half the form of men, half that of horses. Item, also women with beards down to the breast, but no hair on the head. In Ethiopia towards the west many have four eyes. Thus in Eripia there live beautiful people with the necks and bills of cranes. But men cannot believe that, as Augustinus writes, the people who live in the place opposite to us where the sun rises, and those who live where it sets, have their feet towards ours. But there is great argumentation in literature against the madness of the common man in wondering why either we, or those whose feet are turned towards ours [i.e. live in the antipodes] do not fall off the earth. For right round the earth live people with their feet turned towards each other and their heads towards the sky. It would be contrary to nature for them to fall off. For just as the seat of fire is nowhere else than in fires, that of water nowhere else than in the waters, and that of the spirit nowhere else than in the spirit, so too is the seat of the earth nowhere else than in itself'—meaning presumably that the things of the earth cannot fall away from, but only towards, the earth to which they belong.

had seen here extraordinarily tall men, and found the country where virgins become pregnant through drinking water. The Greenlanders are separated from them by icy frozen skerries.

It is obvious at a glance that some honest skipper has launched out into a far-fetched sailor's yarn under the influence of a plentiful supply of mead. On the other hand, the story of the virgins who become pregnant by drinking water was part of the permanent 'repertoire' of all Arctic explorers during the Middle Ages. Thus the captain who has the honour to be mentioned in the famous *Monumenta* was only repeating what his comrades from other ships had related before him, and what the landlubbers certainly expected to hear.

This story of the remarkable virgins also came to the ears of Adam of Bremen. He moves their domain to the Gulf of Bothnia and adds in his account:

And when they give birth, the children of the male sex are dogheads, those of the female sex the most beautiful women. The latter live only with their own sex and disdain intercourse with men, whom, if any come, they resolutely repulse. Dogheads are creatures who have their heads on their breasts . . .

Now Amazon myths are of widespread occurrence amongst many peoples of the earth. They have been interpreted as recollections of an earlier, predominantly matriarchal social order. Legends of dog-headed men are not rare either. They have been explained by reference to the great 'collective unconscious' of modern depth psychology and its dim memories of the time, hundreds of thousands of years ago, when the forefathers of *homo sapiens* really did possess doglike muzzles, or else as the outcome of encounters with aboriginal peoples of strongly prognathous physiognomy.

The explanation for the legend of the country of women referred to by the *Monumenta* and Adam of Bremen is relatively simple, however. Philologists have pointed out that the Finno-Ugric name for Finland, *Kainulaiset*, was corrupted by the Swedes into 'Quaenland', and since *quaen*, *cwino* or *queen* meant 'woman' from Iceland to the Alemannic Provinces, it was natural that Quaenland should be translated 'Womanland' and that every Arctic-farer worth his salt had to tell of this land of women.

The learned editors of the *Monumenta Historica Norwegiæ* did not, of course, include this note in order to discuss the virgins impregnated by water, but because of a report which occurs a little later in the *Saga of Samson the Beautiful* (1350). It is stated therein that north-east of Russia lies the country of Jotunheimar, the land of trolls and kobolds. 'And from here in the direction of the wastes of Greenland stretches the land called Svalbard.' In addition to this, there is an entry in the *Icelandic Annals* for the year 1194 which says: 'Svalbard found.'

At first sight this series of reports is mystifying. Svalbard means 'Cold Shore' and must represent the northernmost area reached by the Vikings. There is, however, no clear indication of what country was called 'Cold Shore' by the Northmen, to whom cold was no novelty. Consequently the above accounts have been taken as referring variously to north-east Greenland, Jan Mayen Island, Spitzbergen, northern Siberia and Franz Josef Land. Of these Jan Mayen Island, to which the word shore is inapplicable, and also northern Siberia and Franz Josef Land can be eliminated at once; for it has been clear since Nansen's expedition to the Arctic and his reports on drift and ice conditions, that the two latter could not have been reached by any chance run before the wind.

This only leaves Spitzbergen—an assumption emphatically supported by Nansen. He has pointed out that a ship sailing north from Greenland along the edge of the east Greenland ice must automatically come to Spitzbergen. This interpretation gains probability from the fact that even today Spitzbergen is rich in valuable fur-bearing animals. Since it was no more difficult to sail to Spitzbergen than anywhere else in the Arctic Ocean during the summer months—the *Landnámabók* later gave the sailing distance as four days—it was natural for the Norsemen to visit it. Hence there is good reason to suppose that the name Svalbard referred to the modern Spitzbergen.

If this assumption is correct then the land of Jotunheimar must be Novaya Zemlya. We have already heard that the Scandinavians reached the area of the Pechora. Once having got this far it was a short step to the islands of Novaya Zemlya, which lay across their path to the east.

Svalbard seems to have been the Vikings' last Arctic discovery. Their main interest was no doubt directed towards south-west Greenland on the one hand, and the rich lands round the White Sea and the Pechora on the other, rather than to the icy wastes of the north and north-east. This is very understandable. The man whose everyday life is hard seldom has time or inclination to journey out into the world for the mere pleasure of discovery. He needs some goal that will make his journey worth while. This goal offered itself on the path that led past Greenland. It lay far beyond that frozen country, but it was not outside the reach of a brave man. As we know, it was called Wineland, and it beckoned with vines that grew wild, with fields of self-sown corn, and with timber.

What ways have been travelled, what seas sailed! How wide open lay the world, how many new shores rose up from the salt waves of the sea! Was there still a country which the white man had not traversed by the end of the Middle Ages? One feels inclined to doubt it. For the next section will show that even Asia, buried in the sands of its vast deserts, was crossed by a multitude of paths and trodden by the feet of many men, long before the Portuguese set out to discover India.

## PART TEN

# THE CRUSADES, PRESTER JOHN AND THE GREAT KHAN

*The inscribed stone of Singanfu · Father Trigault is no forger · Is Mary the Mother of God? · The history of the silk road · Professor Lactantius on the amorality of geography · Bias in early travel-narratives · Who were the 'Three Wise Men from the East'? · St. Thomas's Christians · Why Napoleon did not build the Suez Canal · Emperor Justinian practises economic espionage, but the Persians beat him to it · Medieval 'Baedeker' for the journey to the Holy Land · Who is Prester John? · Prester John's open letter, forgery or fantasy? · The story of the* sidicus · *An embassy from the Great Khan · Papal legates in Caracorum · Transylvanian experts in the Altai Mountains ·* 'Visum fuit mihi, quod evasissem de manibus dæmonum' · *Two monks desert · 'If you can work magic, I'll become a Christian,' says the Emperor of China · Marco Polo freezes on the 'Roof of the World' · Chinese paper money · The magic island of Chipangu · John of Monte Corvino becomes Archbishop of China · Report from the land where pepper grows · Hanns Schiltberger among the heathen · Franciscans in Astrakhan.*

GAIN we start with the inscription on an ancient stone. This time the stone is found not in America, but in China and the inscription is not cut in runes, but in ancient Chinese characters. Nor is the site of the find virgin wilderness, but the honourable city of Singanfu, capital of the province of Shen-Si, for a long time the junction of great trade routes to the east and south of the Middle Kingdom and since time immemorial the terminus of the silk road leading to the barbaric countries of the West.

Just outside the huge, forty-foot-high city walls a dozen coolies were at work one day in the early spring of A.D. 1625, excavating the cellars for a new house. It had taken the coolies a long time to grasp why a house which was going to stand above ground should be started underneath it. Not many houses in the province of Shen-Si had cellars. But that was how the foreign devils from the West, protected by the Emperor's grace, wanted it. They must live underground like rats!

The coolies were putting their back into the work. There'd be cash in the evening, beautiful gleaming money. They would polish it till it shone, thread a cord through the square hole in the centre and hang it round their necks; they would buy tea that had come all the way from far-off Sze-Chwan; they would at last be able to drink the smoke of forgetfulness once more in the House of Dreams.

Then deep in the earth one of the spades struck a stone, an enormous block 8 feet 3 inches high, 3 feet 4 inches wide and 10 inches thick. Although the coolies could neither read nor write themselves, they knew the difference between writing and chance scratches: they realized at once that they had found something important. One of them immediately ran over to the house in which the imperial governor had lodged the white foreign devils. Fortunately Father Trigault, who had spent half a lifetime in Asia, was in the mission. He came at once, and observed to his astonishment that the stone, which was covered in ancient Chinese and Syriac characters, told of a Christian Bishop Adam, who had once lived here in Singanfu and who, at the time when the inscription was cut, was 'Priest and Master of the Law in Tsinistan'. An emperor named Tai-tsung was also mentioned on the stone. And, wonder of wonders, it related that Christianity had come to China long, long ago, that its teachings had been examined 'in the private chambers of the Emperor', and that when Tai-tsung had recognized its justice and truth he ordered it to be preached and propagated in his country.

*57. Inscribed tablet of Singanfu with Nestorian cross. Erected A.D. 781 as a memorial to the spread of the 'illustrious Tach'in religion' (Christianity) in the Middle Kingdom.*

It was easily established that this Emperor Tai-tsung had really existed. He reigned from A.D. 626 to 649, and was the second emperor of the Tang Dynasty and an outstanding personality. To begin with, however, this was all Father Trigault was able to learn. Nothing was known of the presence of Christian missionaries in China at such an early date. The Roman Catholic Church had only just received permission to send a few missionaries to China. All around them these brave men, mostly Jesuits, found nothing but the darkest paganism. There was not the slightest trace of an earlier Christian influence. And then this stone asserted that there had been Christians in the country at the time of Tai-tsung? Christianity was preached? There was a bishop? Christian churches had stood in every town, and here in Singanfu a splendid cathedral was erected in 638 by order of the Emperor?

Father Trigault was also a Jesuit. Unfortunately, it might be added. For in the West, which was at that time shaken by the fevers of the Reformation, the Counter-Reformation and the scepticism of the Freethinkers, the prestige of the Society of Jesus did not stand high. Consequently Father Trigault was not believed. He was regarded as a cunning forger, for whom the end justified the means, and it was about two hundred and fifty years before this verdict was reversed. Not until the middle of the last century was it definitively proved that Christianity really did attain widespread currency in China during the seventh and eighth centuries.

It was, of course, not Roman Catholic, but Nestorian Christianity. This takes us back another two hundred years into the nascent fifth century A.D.; to Nestorius, Patriarch of Constantinople, a very clever, very pious man, who meditated very deeply on the nature of Christ. He believed that the divine and the human had preserved in the person of the Saviour their own characteristic qualities: Christ was *homoiousios*, similar to God, but not *homousios*, identical with God. He was a man, and, in essential aspects of his existence, remained so; hence Mary his mother could not be called the Mother of God, but only the Mother of Christ.

To modern man, unconcerned with theological subtleties, this may appear rather unimportant. At the time, 1,500 years ago, such problems were of immense significance. If Christ, who was nailed to the cross as the bearer of the sins of the world, died beneath the burden of these sins, and then re-ascended into heaven, was indeed the Son of God, then the prospect of salvation was a great deal brighter for suffering humanity. Neither Thor nor Zeus, neither Jupiter nor Ammon, neither Jahveh, the god of the Jews, nor Borvon, the supreme god of the Celts, had ever given birth to a religion of salvation. There was only punishment and vengeance: an eye for an eye and a tooth for a tooth, unto the third and fourth generations. But in the whole of the West, with its many young and, in the truest sense of the word, believing peoples, spiritual life cried out for grace and redemption. Here Christ was *bound* to be understood as God Himself and as nothing else, here it seemed obvious that Mary was the Mother of God.

In Asia the situation was quite different. There the great conception of mankind's redemption by the grace of God was nothing new. On the contrary, so many doctrines of salvation had been showered down upon the inhabitants of the Near East that they had grown sceptical and indifferent towards them and more disposed to accept a religion which stressed the human aspect of the redeeming god. When Nestorius was condemned by the general council summoned by the Emperor Theodosius II at Ephesius in A.D. 431, Nestorianism spread like wildfire in Asia, and in a few centuries it had overrun this vast continent from end to end, winning a myriad followers. The whole of Asia Minor, Persia and India were under the influence of Nestorianism, and at this early period China too was within a hair's breadth of adopting Nestorian Christianity.

We must briefly sketch the events leading up to this memorable instant in history. The true age of the caravan roads linking Europe with China is uncertain. They may be of great antiquity. But Europe really became aware of their existence at the beginning of the second century B.C., when the Middle Kingdom succeeded in breaking through the ring of warlike nomads which barred its path to the west. Apparently the first contact with the West was actually made on Chinese initiative. Under the Han Emperor Wu-ti (186–140 B.C.) the Middle Kingdom experienced a period of the greatest prosperity and progress. The high pressure of industrial production which seems to have arisen during this epoch, and the strong national feeling which animated the ruling classes in this huge country, explain why a sudden acceleration took place in the development of commercial relations with the West, which had been tentatively growing since 100 B.C. Up to twelve caravans yearly, with a hundred men and a corresponding number of pack animals apiece, left China for the West at this period, according to the German authority on the silk roads, Albert Herrmann.

Beyond the Pamir Passes, the goods were mostly taken over from the Chinese caravan leaders and transported farther by the tribes of Iran. The main centre of this commerce was clearly the long-famous Bactria in eastern Iran. This part of the living bridge that spanned the tremendous distance between the two great empires, the Eastern in China and the Western in Rome, was constituted by the Parthians. Syria formed the last pillar and was the area in which this 6,250-miles-long trade bridge ended. Its enormous economic importance to Rome at the end of the republican and the beginning of the imperial period has already been mentioned earlier on in this book.

Around the time when Rome overcame the might of Egypt and so gained possession of the sea communications with India and China, i.e. shortly before the birth of Christ, the caravan traffic on the silk road was abruptly halted for two generations. The Hiung-nu, forerunners of the Huns, made themselves masters of the Tarim region and severed the inter-continental trade connection. This was a more painful loss to the Parthians and Bactrians than for Rome, which was able to circumvent the Tarim basin blockade by a southerly detour at sea. As might be expected, therefore, it was the western peoples this time, the Bactrians and the Persians, who thrust eastwards at the turn from the first to the second century A.D. They found the Tarim basin blockade raised, for meanwhile China had recovered and driven back

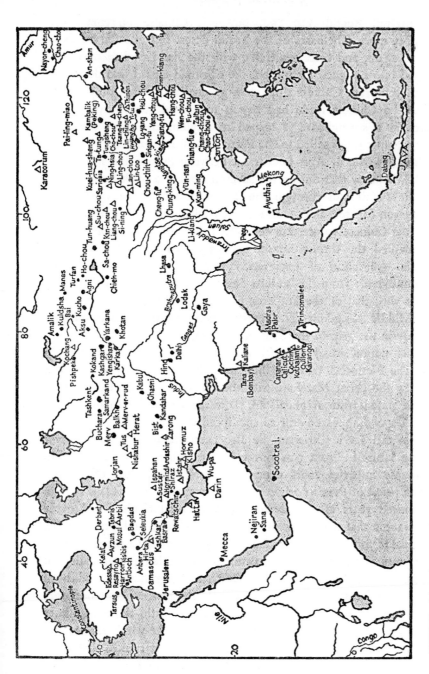

XXIX. Sketch map showing the distribution of Nestorians in Asia during the Middle Ages (after P. Y. Saeki and J. Thauren). During the Middle Ages there were Christian communities from Constantinople to Peking. Numerous bishops (△) ruled over the faithful, and Christian finds (●) have been made even in Mecca, Caracorum, Lhasa and Delhi.

the Hiung-nu. Round A.D. 130, however, Chinese supremacy collapsed once more. The oases of the Tarim desert fell into the hands of
the Huns again, and since sea traffic with the Far East had meantime
developed into a regular institution, the silk road lapsed into desuetude
for many centuries. Chinese ships, too, gradually appeared on the seas.
By A.D. 400 Chinese trade had begun to extend southwards. Using
Mallacca as a springboard it leaped to Ceylon, and after the sixth
century gigantic junks sailed to the Persian Gulf and back.

In the early Middle Ages land traffic between Europe and inner Asia
revived. We know that during the seventh century a brisk trade moved
across the Pamir and through the Tarim desert. There was a very
simple reason for this. In 618 an energetic adventurer made his appearance in the Chinese palace. He compelled the ruling emperor to abdi-
cate, mounted the throne himself and founded the Tang Dynasty.
With his assumption of government, Chinese power spread to its
maximum extent: from the Yellow Sea almost to the Volga there was
only one will, that of the Emperor of China, only one authority, that
of the Middle Kingdom. The Tarim basin and the Persian Empire
was firmly in the grip of the Sons of Heaven.

At this period many Nestorian missionaries made their way to
China. The Nestorian tablet of Singanfu, inscribed in *circa* 780, was
written by the priest Mar-Its-Busid, the son of a Christian cleric who
had immigrated from Afghanistan. Towards 640 a Syrian missionary
named Olopoen appeared and so convinced the Empress that it would
be fair to call her a Christian; he also exercised great influence over
Tai-tsung himself. From 711 onwards, Byzantine embassies came to
the Chinese imperial court every ten years; the arrival of a high
Christian priest of Persian origin in 750 is recorded, and as late as 840,
two hundred years after Tai-tsung's death, Nestorianism had made
such advances that a quarter of a million Chinese, and precisely the
ruling class of ministers and officers of the Court, were Christians.

Five years later, the whole structure of Christian power collapsed
like a house of cards. In 845 Christianity, and significantly Buddhism
as well, were forbidden by imperial edict; all Christian churches were
razed to the ground, the leaders were done to death, those who bore
the taint crawled away and hid, the rest ignored the whole matter and
forgot. And so complete were destruction and forgetfulness that eight
hundred years later Father Trigault was suspected of having faked the
stone of Singanfu. Once more it looks as though a blind path had led
men deep into an alien world and then petered out in total futility.
And yet some dim memory of the Christian communities of the Orient

remained alive in those unconscious or semi-conscious levels of the human mind that give birth to myths and legends. The mysteriously menacing radiance which later played round the figure of 'Prester John', and enveloped the bloody apparitions of the Mongolian Great Khans, rose up from these subterranean depths.

Nevertheless, although hundreds or even thousands of people may have made the long journey from Hither Asia to China during those years, their numbers remained limited to refugees, missionaries, envoys of emperors and kings, a handful of merchants, sea-captains and caravan leaders.

2

The œcumenical consciousness which characterized the ancient world, the immediately experienced fact of belonging to a universal sphere of culture, was lost during the turmoil of the Migration of the Peoples and with the passing of the Roman Empire. The world-wide knowledge of the classical period was also forgotten; it had to be regained with infinite labour. Moreover, thirst for knowledge and delight in the acquisition of new information were altogether alien to the Middle Ages, and there can be no doubt that Christianity, which was originally confined to the lower strata of society, for a long time showed itself hostile to culture. As a rule, the benison of faith was bestowed upon those who were weary and bowed down in mind as well as body. What need had they of knowledge, of new facts? The life of the mind no longer derived its laws from the mind itself, but from dogma. Geographical ignorance in particular was deemed positively meritorious and pleasing to God, as Lactantius, the tutor of Constantine the Great's son, expressed it in *circa* A.D. 300. Hence for a long time only the barbarian peoples on the fringe of civilization had engaged in exploration and discovery, ranging far afield in the saddles of their horses or on board ship. In the north, Viking ships sped from Iceland to Greenland, crossed the Davis Straits, and landed in America. In the south, Arab caravans penetrated deep into the African interior, in the east they crossed the central Asiatic deserts in endless treks.

In central Europe, meanwhile, the forces of the individual, liberated by the breakdown of the old universalist world, turned first of all inward, towards the kingdom of God. Round about 925, a revivalist movement was born in Cluny and Lorraine which had prodigious consequences. The impulses behind it soon turned outwards. The miserable heathen peoples all over the world were to have their share in salvation: exploration and discovery became a religious task.

It was no coincidence that the idea of the crusades was propounded by a supporter of Cluny and on the soil of southern France, in a world which, despite all its ecclesiastical zeal, had retained the best elements of chivalry. But precisely because of the rather narrow circle within which it originated, Pope Urban II, who issued his famous call to the crusades after the conclusion of the Council of Clermont-Ferrand in 1095, must have been much surprised by the widespread acclamation accorded to his idea and the way in which this spiritual and chivalrous adventure developed into a mass movement full of Apocalyptic fantasies.

The often very bloody military expeditions to the Orient during these centuries brought great gains to geographical knowledge. True, they never went outside areas long known to the Greeks and Romans; even the vague rumours that reached the crusaders through the mouths of Arab and Indian traders were of a world with which antiquity, at the beginning of the recently terminated first millennium, had been quite well acquainted. But it was the fact that thousands and thousands of people, not just a few isolated individuals, came into personal contact with the Orient, and that this contact with the wonders of the East was renewed again and again over many decades, indeed centuries, which gave the crusades their inestimable influence on the history of geography.

How deep was the impression made on Europe by this close contact with an alien culture is shown by the number of Arab words that crept into the Western languages during the epoch of the crusades. The first expressions to be adopted were mostly nautical. The words admiral, arsenal, cable and corvette are all of Arabic origin. The process was repeated in the field of arms and armour—many weapons, e.g. the crossbow, were not known in Europe at all before the crusades —after which it invaded the sphere of everyday life: lute, alcove, sofa, mattress, cotton, carafe and amber all come from the Arabic. Finally Oriental foodstuffs and particularly spices began to pour into Europe in vast quantities, bringing their Arabic names with them. Very soon spices became an inalienable element in European diet.

The most important commodities exported to Europe were naturally those produced in Syria and Palestine themselves. Pre-eminent amongst these were fruits like raisins, dates, figs, lemons, oranges, apricots, almonds, carobs, and especially cane sugar. Of the medicaments and aromatics native to Asia Minor, balsam and the resins of the rubber, myrrh and terebinth trees were especially prized. From inner Asia and Arabia came ambergris, aloe and frankincense—for the most part via Bagdad and Damascus. Rice and maize were also brought by the caravans, and most particularly of course, pepper, cloves, cardamom and nutmeg.

The chief industrial products were textiles like cotton, made from the home-grown plant, silken fabrics such as satin, muslin or damask, manufactured from either imported or local raw material, glass, especially mirrors, which replaced the European substitutes made of polished metal sheets, and paper. Carpets also captured the interest of the West round about this time, and soon they were being used in Europe just as the crusaders had seen them used by Arabs. Amongst the latter, they were spread on the floors of tents and hung on tent walls. Exactly the same was done in the castles of Europe. Here too there were carpets everywhere, and in view of the cold stone floors and walls of their usually extremely bleak dwellings, the nobility must have felt very thankful for this Oriental innovation.

The lion's share in all these refinements of good living naturally went to the merchant—especially the merchants of northern Italy in Genoa, Pisa and Venice, though German merchants in Augsburg and Nuremberg did not do too badly either. Italian shipowners, who began by monopolizing the passage to the Holy Land, also netted a very considerable proportion of the bounty which the crusades showered down on the West. The simple pilgrim paid £3 for the voyage to Syria and back, no mean sum at that period. The knight's esquire had to pay about £3 10s. for a place on deck, while a place in the cabin cost his master, the knight, £6. As a rule there were one thousand to fifteen hundred passengers on a crusaders' ship. Thus the shipowner had made a turnover of £3,000 to £5,000 before the ship left port. Of course, his risk was big. Efforts were made to reduce it by sailing in convoy as a protection against pirates, and as a rule the ships hugged the coast throughout the voyage. So the passage— which was begun either early in spring, enabling the travellers to be in Jerusalem for Easter, or at the end of June, reaching Palestine at the end of August or beginning of September—took two months. But there was more chance of getting the ship home safe and sound than if they had sailed straight across the sea and risked having the first gale blow the convoy apart and driving the isolated vessels right into the arms of the pirates.

All the Italian ports without exception laid the foundations for their subsequent wealth during these decades. They were already active in the Levantine and Oriental trade. But the business that was to be done now surpassed anything they had ever seen before. For not only the transport of passengers, but also the delivery of arms, munitions and supplies was in their hands. Their monopoly in communications with the Orient guaranteed them a soft cushion to fall back on, should the crusader trade ever dwindle. And in a short time the West was so dependent for its standard of living upon imports from the East that any reduction in their volume was unthinkable.

This situation has been analysed in order to demonstrate what a profound break in the continuity of European history the crusades represented. Without a shadow of doubt, the development that led via the Renaissance and Humanism to the Modern Era began here. Not only did a new outward mode of life, contrary to the old patriarchal customs, arise; new aspects of man's spiritual and mental being were also brought into play. For the collision with other forms of culture, society and civilization afforded an unparalleled opportunity of realizing one's own potentialities by comparison. This refers primarily, of course, to comparison with the forms of Oriental existence; secondarily, however, the Frenchman, the Englishman, the German and the Italian each gained a clearer picture of his national individuality by comparison with the rest. The concept of the 'ego', which the Cluniac reform had brought to light in the spiritual sphere, here took on secular shape.

This had important repercussions on the general attitude to travel and discovery. Up to now the impulse behind exploration had been, so to speak, anonymous: a divine mission, such as sent St. Brandan to America before any other white man; religious oppression which made life in the home country impossible, as happened to the Jews or the Nestorian Christians; or the group instinct of self-preservation, in response to which the Vikings made their way to Vinland in search of timber and other essential raw materials. Now, however, more personal motives seem to be at work. Certainly, 'anonymous' impulses were still operative in men like Marco Polo. But one has the impression that individual and personal components were much more active in him than in his forerunners. He is undoubtedly already to be numbered amongst the men of the Renaissance, who sought adventure for adventure's sake, because it represented self-affirmation and self-enhancement.

## 3

We know that Marco Polo was far from being the first to journey far to the East after the start of the crusades. His travels were certainly very extensive. Of greater significance than their extensiveness, however, was the fact that they were considered important and interesting by his age. This was something entirely new. True, various bold journeys had been commemorated by the medieval chroniclers long before the Venetian. But the records were rarely more than a brief, dry note. The focus of the chroniclers' interest was elsewhere. The fact that someone went on an expedition, that in the course of this expedition he underwent many strange experiences which he subsequently reported, was not in itself important. The value and importance of an expedition lay in a command from the Emperor or a call from the Vatican, in the aim of bringing back some religious relic or the like, i.e. in its incentive rather than in the events which accompanied it.

Thus we learn from the *Topographia christiana*, written in *circa* 530 by Cosmas Indicopleustes (India-farer), an Egyptian merchant who later became a monk and lived in a monastery on Sinai, many ridiculous theories as to the shape of the earth—which, according to him, is a rectangle bounded by four walls forming an arch at the top, the firmament—but regrettably little about his travels and the fact that he visited Abyssinia, India and Ceylon. He goes into detail only when he discusses the St. Thomas's Christians of Ceylon and India, obscure reports of whose existence had already found their way to Europe:

Even in Taprobanê [Ceylon], an island in Further India, where the Indian sea is, there is a Church of Christians, with clergy and a body of believers, but I know not whether there be any Christians in the parts beyond it. In the country called Malê [Malabar], where the pepper grows, there is also a church, and at another place called Calliana [Kalyana, near Bombay] there is moreover a bishop, who is appointed from Persia. In the island, again, which is called the Island of Dioscoridês [Socotra] which is situated in the same Indian sea, and where the inhabitants speak Greek, having been originally colonists sent thither by the Ptolemies who succeeded Alexander the Macedonian, there are clergy who receive their ordination in Persia, and are sent on to the island, and there is also a multitude of Christians. I sailed along the coast of this island, but did not land upon it. I met, however, with some of its Greek-speaking people who had come over into Ethiopia. And so likewise among the Bactrians and Huns and Persians, and the rest of the Indians, Persarmenians, and Medes and Elamites, and throughout the whole land of Persia there is no limit to the number of churches with bishops and very large communities of Christian people, as well as many martyrs, and monks also living as hermits. (*The Christian Topography of Cosmas,* translated by J. W. McCrindle, London: The Hakluyt Society, 1897, pp. 118 f.)

Elsewhere he notes a few facts about the island of Ceylon which clearly show the commercial interest of the former merchant getting the better of the pious monk:

The island being, as it is, in a central position, is much frequented by ships from all parts of India and from Persia and Ethiopia, and it likewise sends out many of its own. And from the remotest countries, I mean Tzinista [China] and other trading places, it receives silk, aloes, cloves, sandalwood and other products, and these again are passed on to marts on this side, such as Malê, where pepper grows, and to Calliana which exports copper and sesame-logs, and cloth for making dresses, for it is also a great place of business. (*The Christian Topography of Cosmas,* translated by J. W. McCrindle, London: The Hakluyt Society, 1897, pp. 365 f.)

He also tells us a little about east Africa—once more in connection with costly merchandise, viz. gold and frankincense. But this is all in parentheses, and at bottom it interests only Cosmas himself. For his contemporaries, his travels, astonishing as they were, were manifestly of little importance. Apparently his book aroused interest mainly because it contained the first detailed information about the Indian Christians, who, although regarded as heretics, were none the less considered noteworthy.

For a long time the Middle Ages believed that Indian Christianity went back to the Three Wise Men from the East, who came to Bethlehem at the birth of Jesus and later returned to their Eastern homelands. This is, of course, a pious superstition. For in fact these alleged kings from the East, as already surmised by Kepler at the beginning of the seventeenth century, were Jewish astronomers from Babylon. There is known to have been an ancient school of astronomy at Sippar near Babylon, and a cuneiform text which chance has preserved records that the celebrated conjunction of Saturn and Jupiter in the year 7 B.C. was observed in Sippar. Now in Babylonian astronomy Saturn had been held since time immemorial to have a particular significance for the western lands of Syria and Palestine; this may have been connected with ancient Jewish traditions to the effect that Saturn was the star of Israel. The conjunction of such a fateful star with the royal planet Jupiter must have been regarded by the early astronomers as an event of the highest importance. It is therefore very understandable that a few Jewish astronomers, having observed the convergence of the two great planets on 12th April, 7 B.C., should have resolved to journey to Syria themselves. After the drawing together of the two stars on 12th April, they would have been visible again at the beginning of October and the beginning of December so close to one another as to have looked almost like *one* star. And so Matthew makes his Wise Men say: 'Where is he that is born King of the Jews? for we have seen his star in the east, and are come to worship him.'

This is the story of the Three Wise Men from the East, and in fact Asiatic Christianity has no connection whatsoever with them. Perhaps Jews first carried the idea of Christianity to the Orient, or perhaps it was brought by some of the many refugees who fled to the outskirts of the Roman Empire during the early persecution of the Christians. At all events, a 'well-organized Christian community' existed on the Tigris as early as 170, as Richard Hennig states, and on this sub-structure a proper Nestorian national Church was erected in Persia during the fifth century.

Indian Christianity, on the other hand, probably goes back to a Christian missionary named Pantænus of Alexandria, who visited India in *circa* A.D. 200. The story that the Apostle Thomas had managed to escape to India in A.D. 52, there finding the three Wise Men from the East and baptizing them into the Christian faith, arose in Europe only during the eighth century. After the death of St. Thomas, his companion, Jacob of Antioch, was supposed to have succeeded him as Patriarch of India. Malabar Christianity, however, is of much greater antiquity than this pious legend. In reality, the name 'St. Thomas's Christians' is probably derived from a wealthy Indian merchant called Mar Thomas, who is traditionally reputed to have endowed the Malabar Christian community with great possessions. As we know, they received their own metropolitan bishop (Friar Jordanus of Sévérac, Bishop of Kaulam) towards the end of the eighth century, and shortly afterwards a secular organization developed out of this hierarchical one: a Christian State with kings at its head, the so-called Tamutiri. The St. Thomas's Christians are Nestorian in doctrine and their liturgical language is Syriac. In the early years of the present century they still numbered something less than half a million in Cochin and Travancore.

Just as Cosmas was of importance to his contemporaries for quite special reasons and not simply because of his travels, so we hear too of another monk—the Irishman Fidelis, who travelled south two centuries later. We owe the extant accounts of this traveller to the Irish geographer Dicuilus, author of a comprehensive geography written in 825 whilst residing at the Court of Charlemagne. Therein he tells of a monk who, on the occasion of a pilgrimage to Jerusalem around 750, journeyed on to the Land of the Nile and then passed along a canal from the Nile into the Red Sea:

> Although I have never seen it stated by any chronicler that a branch of the Nile issues into the Red Sea, Friar Fidelis has related this and confirmed it in my presence. According to his account both clergy and laymen coming to Jerusalem as pilgrims have travelled on to the Nile, where they boarded ships and reached a mouth of the Nile in the Red Sea . . .

Dicuilus could not have known, as we do, that in fact this unknown mouth of the Nile in the Red Sea was a canal; nor could he have known how enormously this canal shortened the voyage to India. Actually the plan conceived in the middle of last century by Negrelli and Lesseps, the builders of the Suez Canal, was based on immensely ancient prototypes. For the first artificially constructed link between these two seas—originally following the detour taken by the Nile— goes back to Rameses II, the Great, in the thirteenth century B.C. The sand of the desert gradually gnawed away this huge piece of building-construction. Seven hundred years later, towards 600 B.C., Pharaoh Necho had the canal renewed. Herodotus writes of it as a marvellous and grandiose piece of building: 'This canal', he says, 'is so long that it takes four days to sail from one end to the other. And it is so wide that it can accommodate two triremes abreast. The water is drawn from the Nile; one hundred and twenty thousand Egyptians perished in the course of this work.'

A hundred years later the waterway was improved and widened by the Persian king, Darius. This is attested by a cuneiform inscription from the fifth century B.C. According to the extant remains the canal was 150 feet wide and about 20 feet deep. Its banks were walled with ashlars. Then there is silence. Half a millennium later we hear from Plutarch that after the battle of Actium Cleopatra tried to transport her fleet over the isthmus and assemble it in the Red Sea. The plan miscarried, however, obviously because only small sections of the canal were still usable. But the Roman geographers of the imperial period were well aware that a navigable link had once existed between the two seas. They called the Suez Canal *Amnis Trajanus*, the Trajan River, and from this it has been deduced that Trajan sought to render it navigable again. Since nothing more is said of it, however, we must assume that Trajan's efforts proved fruitless. Round the middle of the seventh century the canal was re-established by Caliph Omar after the conquest of Egypt, and for a hundred years thereafter it continued to be used by Arab ships, though still only as a link between the Nile and the Red Sea. No doubt it was mainly used by warships, since Caliph Omar's principal motive in creating rapid communications between Arabia and Egypt must have been military. But it also bore trading and passenger vessels; for it was at this period that Fidelis sailed down it. Around 770 the Abbaside Caliph Abu Jafar, whose capital was Bagdad, had long stretches of the canal filled in to deprive the southern Arabian rebels of the waterway to Egypt.

Another long silence falls. Towards the end of the fifteenth century, however, traces of the ancient canal were still clearly visible. When monks and lay brothers journeyed to Abyssinia at the bidding of the Pope round 1484/5, they saw with amazement the sand-covered remains.

'On the second day after our departure from Cairo,' reports one of these clerical gentlemen, a certain Battista d'Imola, 'we reached the Red Sea, and on the following day we walked across a broad moat. This was dug by Sesostris, King of Egypt, and after him by Darius of Persia and Ptolemy. It is a hundred feet wide, that is to say, fifty-three paces, and thirty feet deep and joined the Red Sea to the Mediterranean. But since the Indian Ocean has a higher surface level than the Mediterranean, these kings did not wish to complete the canal. For a connection between the two seas would have submerged the whole of Egypt under water. The remaining traces of it still induce a feeling of wonder, even though the sand borne by the simoom has half filled the moat at some places.'

Two hundred years later, in 1671, a document lay on the desk of Louis XIV of France. In decorative court script it bore on the front the strange title *Consilium Ægyptiacum*, 'Egyptian Advice'. Its author was Leibniz, the celebrated German mathematician and philosopher. And because the man in far-away Hanover was so famous that even the courtiers at Versailles had heard of him, they had not dared to withhold this document from the king, although it was as absolutely crazy as everything else concocted by those Germans:

Sire,

The reputation for wisdom enjoyed by Your Majesty encourages me to lay before you the outcome of my deliberations on a project which, in the judgment of many eminent men, may be numbered among the greatest conceivable and most easily realizable . . . I refer to the conquest of Egypt . . . Possession of Egypt would open to France a rapid connection with the wealthiest lands of the Orient. It would bind the trade of India to France and open the way to great leaders for further conquests worthy of an Alexander . . .

This is what we read in the *Consilium Ægyptiacum*. Not a word about a canal between the Mediterranean and the Red Sea, of course, and the great Hanoverian is certainly not to be ranged alongside Rameses II and Darius as one of the fathers of the Suez Canal. But it is also certain that France would have begun by establishing a navigable connection of this kind between the two seas—*if* she had gone to Egypt!

But she did not go to Egypt; she made a fruitless attack on the Low Countries, and Leibniz's memorandum was filed in Louis XIV's archives.

It was found there by Napoleon. The proposals of the great German philosopher won the approval of the great Corsican statesman. In 1799 he embarked on the conquest of Egypt, and a little later he stood himself before the still clearly recognizable relics of that ancient artificial waterway which had breached the 'wall between the Red Sea and the Mediterranean'. '*Messieurs, voilà le canal des Pharaons!*'

But his engineers, headed by chief designer Lepère, expressed serious misgivings. Like the masons of Rameses the Great two thousand years before them, like the scholars of the Middle Ages, they believed that the surface level of the Red Sea was higher than that of the Mediterranean, and since they estimated this difference of levels at four feet they were of the opinion that an artificial system of locks would be necessary to prevent the Indian Ocean from breaking over the land and inundating the whole of Egypt. They reported this to Bonaparte.

They communicated the same professional opinion to the Press. And the public was convinced by it. Napoleon too believed it. One man alone rejected it, and that was the great French physicist and mathematician Laplace, who proved in trenchant terms that the whole idea was nonsense and that there could not possibly be any difference in level between the seas. But nobody listened to him. For nearly two thousand five hundred years it had been 'known' that the level of the Red Sea was higher. No amount of logic and mathematical proof could avail against that!

So the Suez Canal was not built. Goethe, who told Eckermann in 1827 that 'it would be worth the trouble of living another fifty years' to see with one's own eyes the severing of the isthmus between the seas of Europe and Asia, had been dead a long time before the first spadeful of sand was lifted in the great undertaking. Even the all-powerful Austrian chancellor, Prince Metternich, whose energy was responsible for the founding of a society to study the problem of the Suez Canal in 1846, was dead when the Canal was opened. Dead too was the engineer Negrelli, whose calculations and technical proposals formed the basis of the great work of construction; and hundreds of thousands of Egyptian workmen who had perished in the desert were dead. But the Canal was there, and year after year the shareholders of the *Compagnie universelle du canal maritime de Suez* received enormous dividends—in some measure confirming that strange oracle announced by the priests to Pharaoh Necho: 'Cease, O Lord, from this plan. If thou puttest it into execution thou wilt not serve Egypt, but covetous barbarians!'

At the same time as Cosmas and Fidelis were travelling in the Middle East and India, journeys were being made on a scale far beyond that to which Europe was accustomed. It is recorded from the epoch of the Byzantine Emperor Justinian (A.D. 527–65) that two Christian monks arrived in Byzantium from the far-off Eastern country *Serinda*, bringing with them important secrets. And now the old books tell us of a nice little bit of commercial espionage, and of economic disputes between the great powers of the period, corresponding exactly to the disputes that rage today about oil and uranium.

Naturally they did not concern either of these inflammable substances, for which mankind at that time had no use, but silk. Kings, dukes, bishops, the rich merchants, the great scholars, were all clad in silk; their wives were decked in the finest silk stuffs, and there was no household with any pretensions to social distinction in which this wonderful fabric did not play an important role. In the Rome of the first emperor the intemperate demand for silk in the great cities had already seriously endangered the European balance of trade with the East. In the meantime the problem had merely grown more acute, because the Church had entered the market as a heavy buyer of silk. The Byzantine churches in particular were stiff with silk.

All this would not have been so bad if the silk road through Asia, originally established by the Chinese emperors, had remained open. But the Tarim basin had been seized in about A.D. 130 by savage Huno-Mongolian tribes, who cut the silk road at this point. The sea route for silk to the Western World, which was thereupon used instead, ended in the country of the Parthians and their successors in power and rights, the Persian Sassanids. Parthians and Persians at once realized what a monopoly this gave them; both peoples made every effort to squeeze the last ounce of profit from it, and whereas a pound of silk could be bought for about £180 in the time of the Roman Emperor

Aurelius, the same quantity cost nearly £500 under Justinian around A.D. 550.

This was a bitter blow. On top of it, there were many political disagreements between Byzantium and the Persians. If the Emperor took up arms to settle them, the supply of silk came to an immediate stop and Justinian's ears rang with the complaints not only of his wife and daughter, but also, which was much worse, of his bishops and patriarchs.

It was a difficult situation. Justinian sought to meet it by a grandiosely conceived commercial manœuvre. Ever since the early fourth century very close politico-diplomatic relations had existed between Byzantium and the Christian kingdom of Axum, which corresponded roughly to present-day northern Abyssinia. With acumen and energy the Christian kings of Axum had gradually extended their power to the Red Sea, and for a long time their port Adulis, the modern Zula south of Massawa, succeeded in dimming the brilliance and importance of the mighty and ancient Alexandria. The rulers of Axum had even crossed over to Arabia, and since about 520 the kingdom of the Himyarites, modern southern Arabia together with the Yemen, had belonged uncontested to the Axumitic sphere of power. Since time immemorial southern Arabia had produced the finest navigators and sailors on the Indian Ocean. How would it be, thought Justinian, to get the silk trade in his own hands with their help? If Byzantium were to send her own ships to Ceylon, at that time the world mart for silk, and leave the Parthians and the Persians to whistle for it? Of course, Justinian would have to pay a considerable commission to the Axumites and Himyarites. None the less it would be excellent business to squeeze the Persian mercantile firms, with their shameless lust for profit, out of the silk trade!

In 535 Justinian sent one of his best diplomats, Admiral Nonnosus, to Axum and the Yemen. On both sides of the Red Sea the proposed transaction met with approbation; after long haggling over the terms of commission the partners finally reached agreement, and all necessary preparations were made to sail to Ceylon with the next monsoon. And then it turned out that it was not the Persians, but Justinian and his business associates who had to whistle for it: somehow or other the Persians must have smuggled agents in amongst the shipowners, silk merchants, and financiers who were negotiating in Byzantium, Adulis and the Yemen. For when the ships of the Himyarites docked in Ceylon, there was not an ell of silk left. The Persians had beaten them to it, their agents had simply bought up the whole stock and taken over

49. Nordrsetur—the northern hunting-grounds of the Vikings in Greenland. This region is called by the Eskimos Umanak, 'The Place That Stills the Heart'.

50. Gold ornaments from Lake Hidden. These ornaments probably belonged to the Danish king Harald Bluetooth, d. 986 A.D. Their collective weight is about 17½ ounces. The cruciform pendants terminate in stylised representations of a falcon's head.

51. Gold ornaments from Wiskiauten, East Prussia. Six Persian gold coins hang from this Viking necklace dating from c.1000 A.D. From the burial-ground of Wiskiauten.

the storage facilities *en bloc*; the Yemenite skippers could do nothing but watch and curse as bale after bale of the costly fabric was stowed in foreign ships.

At just this juncture, as Procopius, the most celebrated historian of the early Byzantine era, records, two Christian monks who had lived for a long time in Serinda and knew the secret of silk arrived in Byzantium. 'After repeated questioning as to the true facts concerning silk, the monks told the Emperor that the producer of this stuff was a particular kind of worm, whose nature it was to devote itself unceasingly to the production of silk.' The two monks added that they saw no reason why these worms should not continue their activity in the Byzantine Empire. They had only to be fetched from Serinda. 'They could not be obtained alive. But the worms could soon be procured, for the eggs of each generation were numberless.'

Naturally, Justinian was much impressed by this report. He promptly sent the two monks back to Serinda—we do not know the exact position of this country, but it was probably the oasis of Khotan in southwest Sinkiang, to which silk cultivation had been introduced two hundred years earlier. A few years later the two clerical smugglers were back in Byzantium. Hidden in their hollow pilgrim's staves were innumerable silkworm's eggs. 'These were transformed', as Procopius relates, 'by a rebirth into worms, which lived on the leaves of mulberry trees. And thenceforth silk was manufactured in the Roman Empire.' This was done above all in Greece and especially on the Peloponnese. On account of its many silk farms with their mulberry trees it was known throughout the Middle Ages as Morea, after *Morus alba,* the mulberry-tree.

4

These accounts show that even without the stimulus of the crusades, pilgrims and others travelled to the East. Pilgrimages to the Holy Sepulchre at Jerusalem in particular were made at all periods, sporadically it is true, but none the less again and again. For many centuries, even under the dominion of the Arabs and the Turks, this journey was no more difficult or dangerous than others, apart from occasional attacks by robber bands and the usual trouble with customs officials. At the turn of the eighth to ninth centuries there was a regular exchange of ambassadors between Charlemagne and Haroun al Rashid and the beginning of friendly relations. Naturally enough, these diplomatic courtesies had their effect on everyday affairs. Travel to the Holy Land seems to have become so much easier as a result that it was worth while bringing out proper travellers' guides. The *Peregrinatores,* a body of writers concerned with the preparation of these 'Baedekers', originally confined themselves to bare statements of routes, distances, lodgings, tolls and taxes. Later these brief remarks were interspersed with short notes on countries and peoples, places of interest, curiosities and geographical peculiarities, and so works were produced bearing a very close resemblance to our guide-books.

58. *Greek mercenaries of Psameticho II scratched this clumsy inscription on the leg of one of the colossi of Abu Simbel in Nubia in* circa 590 *B.C.*

This may cause surprise. But actually it was merely a return to a very ancient custom. For travellers' guides—including one for the journey to China, though it has not been preserved and we know of it only from hearsay—already existed in antiquity. Apparently there was a great love of travel in the ancient world. Time after time, for example, the names of antique pleasure-travellers, who stood in amazement before the pyramids, have been found scratched on some block of stone in these tombs of the ancient Egyptian pharaohs. We know that there were guides for foreign visitors to Troy and Athens, and a flourishing memento industry. The big industrialist Flavius Zeuxis from the Phrygian city of Hierapolis, who lived at the time of the first Roman emperor, expressly announced in his tomb inscription that he had made twenty-one journeys to Italy. It was natural enough for someone with an inventive mind to conceive the idea of travellers' guides as long ago as two thousand years. The most famous of these ancient 'Baedekers' is the ten-volume guide to Greece written by Pausanias and published in *circa* A.D. 200. From it a long and never entirely broken chain of such works leads to the modern guide-book.

With the crusades the sphinx that was Asia grew gradually more familiar and more visible behind the sand-veils of her great deserts. This vast continent was already looked upon as the land of magic and the supernatural, of marvels inexplicable to Reason. The spread of Oriental, especially Indian, myths and legends in the poetry of the Occident, the appearance in it of lions, serpents, magicians, sages and seafarers who underwent fantastic adventures (modelled on Sinbad), which began with the crusades, clearly shows the European's attitude of fearful wonder towards this enigmatic and alien world. When the presence of strong Christian influences in Islam were observed, when

Christian pilgrims entered the Holy Land from India, Persia, Abyssinia and other far-off lands, it was only a step to the genesis of that half Christian, half pagan myth of a mysterious priest-king John living amongst the huge mountains and vast deserts of inner Asia. After the crucifixion of Christ, ran the legend, he 'who had not seen death' and who was linked in people's minds with both John the Baptist and the favourite disciple of Jesus, had made his way unrecognized to Asia and there, untouched by age and death, had founded an immense Christian kingdom, whose royal master and highest priest he was.

59. *The alleged banner of Prester John. After the* Libro del Conoscimiento, *or* Book of Knowledge, *a travel romance written by a Spanish monk in* circa 1350.

The first step in the emergence of this fable was the visit to Pope Calixtus II at Rome, in 1122, of an alleged Bishop John, Patriarch of India, who had many marvellous things to relate. The legend was brought into full prominence, however, by Bishop Otto of Freising, one of the most famous and learned historians of the Middle Ages. In autumn 1145 Otto of Freising was called to conference with Pope Eugenius III at Viterbo in Italy; during his stay at the Papal Court he made the acquaintance of the Bishop of Antioch in Syria. This prince of the Church, Otto of Freising has recorded for posterity, told him that a few years ago a certain John, who lived beyond Persia and Armenia in the farthest Orient, who was at the same time king and priest and belonged with his people to the Christian faith, had made war on the Kings of the Medes and Persians, and had taken Ecbatana their capital. This sounds fabulous in the extreme, yet a great battle fought in the east, and precisely in the year 536 by the Hejira (1141), is also recorded in Arab sources. We may, therefore, take it as proven that the major event recounted by Otto of Freising, the great battle in the

east, rests upon fact. It is fair to assume that the subsidiary statement—
that the leader of the victorious host was a Christian—also has some
foundation.

Who was Prester (or Presbyter) John? No final answer to this question has yet been found. It is possible that the priest-kings of the St.
Thomas's Christians were the prototypes for the Prester John myth;
it is possible that it referred to the Christian rulers of Abyssinia; it is
also possible, and this is the most likely explanation, that it relates to
Yeliu Tashi, the chief of the Kara Khitai, a Turki people living in the
north of Tien-shan at the beginning of the twelfth century. Part of the
Kara Khitai professed the Nestorian Christian faith, while part adhered
to Buddhism. King Yeliu Tashi, who built up a great empire between
1125 and 1144, is thought to have been a Nestorian.

In 1141 he inflicted a crushing defeat on the Mohammedan Seljuks
near Samarkand. The whole of Turkestan was now under the suzerainty
of the Kara Khitai and Yeliu Tashi is believed to have been on the
point of advancing westward, as the Huns before him and Genghis
Khan after him. For some reason unknown to us, he never put this
plan into action. Yeliu Tashi died in 1144, and with his death the vast
empire he had created collapsed without a sound.

As we have said, it is by no means sure that this allegedly Christian,
but possibly Buddhist, Khitan king was really the original of the
Prester John legend. Certain circumstances speak in favour of this
theory, however. The news of a shattering defeat of Moslem forces at
the hands of a Christian king reached Europe at a time when the Arabs,
following the successes of the first crusade, had launched a series of
devastating counter-blows against the invading European troops. On
the first day of Christmas 1144 Edessa was recaptured by the Mohammedans. This was a painful loss and in view of the disheartening situation in the Holy Land it looked like being the prelude to further re-
verses. When first vague rumours and then more definite reports of the
battle of Samarkand reached Europe a little later, the supposition that
a Christian ruler in distant Asia had inflicted an overwhelming defeat
on the awe-inspiring followers of the Prophet naturally made a deep
impression. The strange and far-away potentate who had emerged
victorious from this battle seemed as though sent by God, and so the
Prester John legend may have sprung up out of mingled despair and
hope.

Into this situation, rendered even more dismal by the failure of the
second crusade of 1147/8, there burst a sensation of the first magnitude which set the chancelleries of Europe buzzing: the Greek Emperor

Manuel, the Roman Emperor Frederick, the Pope, and other Christian sovereigns received a letter from the priest-king John! An exceedingly imperious, exceedingly arrogant letter. For the supreme representatives of the three great powers of the day were given to understand in no uncertain terms that their power and their wealth were as nothing in comparison with the absolute perfection of Prester John:

> If Thou, Manuel, wilt discern My greatness and My excellence and if Thou wilt know where upon earth Our omnipotence reigneth, Thou shalt admit and believe without doubting that I, Prester John, am the Lord of Lords and that I surpass all the kings of the whole earth in riches, mercy and omnipotence. Seventy-two kings pay tribute to Us alone.

The letter continues in this style for several pages. Prester John portrays in detail the wonders of his country, the vast quantities of gold and precious stones in the rives, the magnificence of his palace, the fertility of his fields and gardens—but he also relates that in his kingdom there is no war, no private property and hence no poverty, and finally he stresses that despite his infinite perfection he is only a simple, humble priest before God:

> Wherefore it will not astonish Thy sagacity that Our venerable person may not be named by any worthier name than that of Prester [presbyter or priest]. We have at Our court many ministers possessing higher spiritual offices and dignities. Our Lord High Steward, for example, is a Primate and King, Our cupbearer a King and Archbishop, Our Chamberlain a Bishop and King, Our Marshal a King and Archimandrite, Our Master of Our Kitchens a King and Abbot. And therefore it doth not beseem Our Highness to be named by the same names and bear the same ranks as those with which Our palace overflows. Our Eminence therefore prefers out of humility to be designated with a lesser name and office.

This letter is patently spurious, but there seems to have been a very good reason behind its circulation. It outlines a political Utopia intended to throw into relief the injustices and abuses of the day. Both the fantastic descriptions and the haughty tone were adopted to secure for the letter the maximum publicity.

This alleged letter from Prester John was, in fact, translated into many European languages and the unknown author undoubtedly succeeded in bringing his conception of a natural democracy, very similar to that expounded two centuries later by Nicholas of Cusa, before a wide audience. The contrast between conditions in Europe and those in the ideal State of Prester John were glaring. Whereas the medieval emperors continued to have themselves designated and revered as divine, the incomparably more powerful priest-king declared that he was and remained a mortal man and was content, despite his almost divine omnipotence, to be a simple priest. And whereas the nascent monetary economy in Europe was beginning to make the 'God-given' antithesis between noble and burgher on the one hand and the oppressed peasant and disenfranchised day-labourer on the other painfully evident, the Christian Communist author of Prester John's letter laid emphasis on the fact that in the immeasurably wide and wealthy Eastern wonderland there was no private property, because everything belonged to God and his high priest. And finally, whereas war, faction, dissension, envy, murder and violence were rampant in twelfth-century Europe, the lands of Prester John lived in a state of perpetual peace and tranquillity, safeguarded by law and free from all fear save that of Almighty God.

Thus the unknown author of this mysterious epistle was able to project into the bloody and turbulent arena of his epoch the image of an ideal ruler such as the Middle Ages longed for and awaited. If the thesis briefly outlined here is correct, we can understand why the letter was addressed to the three antagonists of the twelfth century: Frederick Barbarossa, the Byzantine Emperor and the Pope, and why only the last named of these three felt any inclination to reply to it. For the two greatest secular potentates of Europe left the *soi-disant* Prester John's letter unanswered. The Pope might have done the same; the fact that, on the contrary, he answered the letter at great length, seems to suggest that he recognized its character as a Utopian political programme.

In 1177 Pope Alexander III wrote a long letter to the '*Magnificus Rex Indorum, Sacerdotum sanctissimus,* Prester John', although he did not know the latter's address and no one could tell it him. The Pope had to write this letter, because the tremendous circulation of the priest-king's manifesto compelled him to state the basic principles which had governed the Christian West for nearly twelve hundred years. Even the Vatican, however, does not appear to have attached much diplomatic importance to its letter. It is couched in pretty blunt terms and leaves the distant Prester John in no doubt that there is only *one* successor to St. Peter, namely the Roman Pope, and that he, Prester John, can expect friendly treatment from Rome only if he takes this fact to heart. This was rather rough language for a potentate who had boasted that seventy-two kings paid tribute to him and that kings, dukes and earls waited on him at table. Nevertheless, the letter was entrusted to the Pope's personal physician, Magister Philippus, who had just returned from a journey to the Middle East, to deliver to Prester John.

Master Philip did, in fact, set out on his diplomatic mission. Needless to say, he was never seen again, nor was anything further heard from Priest John.

The wide impression made by the self-styled Prester John's open letter to the rulers of Europe is reflected in the many languages into which it was translated. One of the most striking of these translations was that into German by Otto of Diemeringen, Canon of Metz, which appeared in the early fourteenth century and expanded the original text into a kind of folk-book. Four extracts from this are given herewith, since, apart from anything else, they afford a very clear picture of the geographical conceptions of a fourteenth-century European scholar.

First, there is the far-away wonderland of India, of which the crusaders back from Jerusalem had heard and repeated so much:

India is a great wide country, and there is more land in India than in all the rest of the world. The Kings of Babylonia as well as Yerses of Persia and Allexander and the Romans made their way thither.

Then there is the story of the wonderful *sidicus* bird, of which the crusaders related that it could speak like a human being. This was the parrot, unknown in the West till then, of which Otto of Diemeringen writes:

There all kinds of merchandise are found and there too is found the sidicus, which is a beautiful kind of bird. And it understands human speech: these birds talk to one another and answer correctly like humans, so learned are they . . . The bird is green all over its body, save only its feet and its beak, which are red; and the bird has a long tail and has a red band round its neck, and has a tongue like that of a man and is long and thin, not much bigger than a woodpecker . . .

After this and similar amusing anecdotes in the introductory chapters, Diemeringen comes to the theme proper:

Priest John has under him some 72 kingdoms, ruled over by great lords, each of whom has several other kings under him; . . . Priest John has his dwelling in the land of Pentexoria just like the Great Khan at Cathay, and always has the Great Khan's daughter as his wife . . . He dwells for the most part in a city called Susa, and always has by him some 12 archbishops and some 20 other bishops, which are all mighty lords, all kings and princes. And there are many good Christians among his courtiers and in his country, who believe in the Holy Trinity, although they do not believe in many articles which we have. They also do not know much about Christendom nor about our creed nor about our pope . . . They have a patriarch there as we have a pope; and him they obey and likewise Priest John . . . And if

Priest John goes to war, nothing but a cross made of wood is borne before him; this he does from reverent humility and also has a golden basin full of earth carried before him at all times . . . in recognition of the fact that his dominion is earthly and that his body must moulder in the earth, however great a lord he is. And that is very wise.

After this description of Prester John himself and a lengthy portrayal of the precious things contained in his palace, Otto of Diemeringen tells us a little more about the wonders of Asia. There is a heartwarming naivety about the Canon of Metz's account:

In Priest John's country there are many strange lands with many strange customs of men and beasts, and at one end of his country there is a sand-sea; that is, a sea covered all over with flowing sand, and there is so much sand and the sand is so deep that it is not known for sure whether there is water underneath or not. At both ends animals like fish come out of it; but they are not like proper fish. And they are good to eat . . . The sea stretches as far as the deserts of India, so that no man may come thither. About three days' journey from the sea in the wilderness and in the desert lies a range of mountains, and out of the mountains flows the water in which grow precious stones, as has been described. And beyond the water is a great broad plain, entirely of sand. This is of such a nature that every day, as soon as the sun rises, small young trees spring up out of the ground and grow up out of the earth with the sun every day, and when the sun sinks and sets they too disappear beneath the earth until the next morning, when they come back again and so on . . . There are also many wonders of the same kind in the desert. For there are also very many wild people who have horns on their heads and do not know any language, they yelp and grunt like pigs. There are also many Sydicus, that is to say, parrots, in the same region, which fly to the people in the fields and speak to them and greet them with proper speech, as though they spoke the tongue of men. Priest John also has mountains of gold and other metal; there mice and ants and other animals dig out the gold, so that it is found beautiful and pure, which is not such hard work as here in our country . . .

With this we will conclude Otto of Diemeringen's account. It may be seen that all sorts of matter from antique legend, such as the tale of the gold-digging 'mice and ants', is mingled here with modern elements like the statement that Prester John has the daughter of the Great Khan as his wife. The account contains observations in natural history, geomorphological reports like that of the Indian sand-sea—the first glimpses of the central Asian deserts with their swelling sand-dunes— and over it all lies Diemeringen's view that the kings and potentates of this world are only mortal men: an essentially democratic idea which clearly prefigures the future with its concepts of the Rights of Man.

The bias of his narrative is quite different from that which characterizes Cosmas Indicopleustes or the monk Fidelis. To Otto of Diemeringen the earth itself with its wonders and its boundlessness, and the adventures which befall the traveller passing through it, are in themselves astonishing and worthy of relation. This outlook is inseparable from the democratic thread that runs through his account. For a new type of man and a new spiritual attitude were beginning to show themselves in Europe. And yet Otto of Diemeringen belongs entirely to the Middle Ages. For alongside these few episodes, which stand out from the bulk of his narrative, there are long passages such as might have come from any medieval romance of magic and are therefore of no interest to us here.

In spite of all the disappointements inflicted upon waiting Europe by the legendary Prester John, the hope that a mighty Christian potentate was reigning somewhere in Asia remained alive for a long time. Even after the publication of Marco Polo's travel narrative relating that the ruler who bore the name of Prester John had died long ago, hope of Christian aid from the Far Orient flared up again and again. The Occident continued to await the great Eastern king until well into the fifteenth century. And then Prester John too found rest at last.

5

All the bells are tolling.

Their plangent voices are ringing through the high noon far across the land. Avignon is tolling its bells. Avignon, the papal city, is calling the faithful to prayer on this July day in 1338.

And everywhere, as far as the voice of Avignon reaches, men doff their caps and women and children fold their hands in prayer.

A miracle has happened! An incredible miracle! And like wildfire the news has run from out of the tortuous streets of the ancient city into the villages round about: the Great Khan of China has sent the Pope an embassy consisting of Friar Andrew and fifteen Tartar princes. And now that the bells are tolling, the deep-voiced bell of Notre Dame du Dôme, the silvery bell of Santa Maria, and the rather cracked bell of the Hôtel de Ville, they are entering the city.

First comes the municipal guard, then the guards of the Pope, Benedict XII, then, beneath a silken canopy, the high clergy—thus the long procession winds its way slowly through the streets; haltingly it crosses the narrow bridge of Saint-Bénézet to the Papal Palace. And there they are: Friar Andrew in a hair shirt, with humbly bowed head and bearing a candle in his hand, and behind him in a long line the Tartars, all of them wondrously clad in heavy silk strewn with precious stones and gems. Beneath their tall, pointed helmets they have broad foreheads, prominent cheekbones set far apart, and narrow, slanting eyes from which an occasional glance darts over the waiting multitude, over the foaming river, over the battlemented ramparts of the city.

At the forecourt, in front of the entrance to the palace, the procession divides. The clergy turn inward, the glittering, gleaming guards of the Pope fringe the semi-circle, the bells are still. The monk Andrew steps forward, and in the deep, solemn silence that now envelops the city his voice rings up to the palace, requesting entry:

In the power of Almighty God! This is the command of the Emperor of Emperors:

We send Our ambassador, Andrew the Frank, with fifteen companions across the seven seas to the Pope, the Lord of Christendom, in the country of the Franks, where the sun sets, to open a way that We may often send the Pope embassies and that the Pope may often send embassies to Us, and that We Ourselves may ask the Pope to send Us his blessing and always to remember Us in his holy prayers. And We recommend to him the Alans, Our servants, Christian sons of the Pope!

Here Friar Andrew pauses. For the next passage in the letter from the Great Khan Shun-ti (Mongolian Togan Timur, 1332–70) is not for public declamation, but for the Pope's private eye. It concerns, as he knows, the potentate's very ardent personal wish. 'May we also be sent from the Land of the Sunset horses and other wonderful things', Shun-ti had quickly added to the completed document. The sentence stands a little cramped in the space between the solemn text of the letter proper and the subscription to the whole document: 'Given at Cambaluc in the year of Rati, in the 6th month, on the 3rd day of the new moon.'

This was written in July 1336, two years ago. Friar Andrew remembers it well. So now he is in Avignon, and in a moment he will see the Pope. And then, behind these high, forbidding walls, he will also read out the second letter which he still carries in his pocket, the letter from the four Alans, as the Christian Mongolian princes are called:

In the power of Almighty God and in the honour of the Emperor, our lord!

We, Futim Yuens, Caticen Tungii, Gemboga Evenzi and John Yuckoy with forehead to the earth and kissing his feet present our greeting to the Holy Father, our Lord Pope! We beseech his blessing and his grace and that he will remember us and never forget us in his holy prayers. Let Your Holiness know that we were for a long time instructed in the Catholic faith and that we were salutarily guided and greatly consoled by Your legate, Brother John [John of Monte Corvino, Archbishop of Cambaluc], a strong, saintly and patient man. But he died eight years ago, and since that time we have been without a shepherd and without spiritual comfort. We should have been glad to hear that You had made arrangements to send us another legate. But he has not yet come. Therefore we beseech Your Holiness that You should send us a good, patient and wise legate, who will take care for the salvation of our souls. And that he should come quickly, because we are in a sorry plight without a supreme head and without consolation. At the same time we beseech Your Wisdom to return a friendly answer to the Lord our Emperor, because thus, as he himself wishes, the way will be opened and free and agreeable for embassies to be sent frequently from You to him and from him to You, so that friendship may be established between You and him. Therefore may Your Holiness take care that he receive a definite answer and an embassy, as becomes Your Holiness, because the Christians in these parts enjoy great honour, even if lies and deceit are sometimes to be met there.

Written in Cambaluc in the year of Rati, in the 6th month, on the 3rd day of the new moon [July 1336].

They were two grandly naive letters which Friar Andrew delivered. He was certainly no confidence trickster, and his yellow-skinned Chinese companions were certainly not Chinese merchants seeking to gain entry to Benedict XII under false pretences. Shun-ti's hastily interpolated note that he would very much like to have a few horses and other wonderful things from the Land of the Sunset—Arab thoroughbreds, of course, for there were plenty of shaggy little Mongolian ponies in Cambaluc—is the obviously genuine expression of a keen desire on the part of a man with a passion for horses; it must have been added by the Great Khan's own hand.

And the submissive diction of the Alan princes' letter, unmistakably influenced by their own experience of the omnipotence of the State, likewise points strongly to the Mongol potentate having been the author of this mission.

This embassy from the Tartars was not altogether unexpected. Ever since the emergence of the Prester John myth, i.e., since 1150, every pope in turn had endeavoured to trace the alleged Christian sovereign in the Far East. In the middle of the twelfth century Asia was, so to speak, 'the fashion' in Europe, just as China was at the end of the eighteenth century, or Japan at the end of the nineteenth and beginning of the twentieth. All the same, the Vatican's decision to enter into relations with the Oriental powers was due neither to a passing vogue nor to chance, but to far-sighted political calculation. It was this which prompted the Vatican to employ one of its best men for the task, the Franciscan John of Plano Carpini. In spring 1245 Plano Carpini received instructions to lead an embassy from the Pope to the Great Khan of the Tartars and establish friendly relations with the Mongols.

It is not known whether or how far the fundamental aims of this mission were disclosed to Carpini. But since he was a perceptive diplomat of great experience, they can scarcely have remained hidden from him. In the summer of the previous year, in the middle of August 1244, Jerusalem had fallen once more into the hands of the infidels. Things were going badly for the cause of Christendom in the Holy Land, and in central Europe too the Pope had serious worries. He therefore had good reason to put out feelers to extra-European powers. One factor in this decision was doubtless the hope of being able to stir up the Mongols, bitter foes of Islam, against the followers of Mahomet and so relieve the situation in the Middle East. It was not many years since an army of Teutonic Knights had been annihilated by the cavalry and artillery of the Mongols far north of the Alps in the lands of the east, which had just been colonized. Suppose the Mongols could now be sent against Bagdad?

This was the position when the decision was taken in the Curia at the beginning of 1245 to establish contact with the Mongol rulers. This action was manifestly regarded as very important. Four separate groups were dispatched to work on parallel lines. The first was led by Plano Carpini. Its task was entirely political and its goal Caracorum, the summer capital of the Mongols and the residence of the Great Khan himself. Group two was headed by Laurentius of Portugal. It too was to make straight for Caracorum, but its tasks were of a purely missionary nature. There is no record of its fate. The third group of the eastern Asia expedition, under Friar Anselm, was delegated to the first Tartar general it could find anywhere in the vast expanse of the Orient. It was to obtain from him by negotiation an undertaking that he would conduct no further campaigns against Europe. Finally, the fourth group under Andrew of Longjumeau had instructions, like group two, to carry on missionary work among the heathen. Its destination was not Caracorum, however, but, like group three, the first Mongolian army camp it could find.

The first to set out on his long jurney was John of Plano Carpini who left on Easter Sunday 1245. Carpini, one of the pupils and closest associates of St. Francis of Assisi, was no longer a young man. When he received the Pope's instructions to embark on this undertaking, which was not without hazards, he was already in his sixties. But he had travelled much and was used to hardships. He had served the Order of St. Francis successively in Saxony, Bohemia, Hungary, Lorraine, Norway and Spain, and was rich in experience. He seemed,

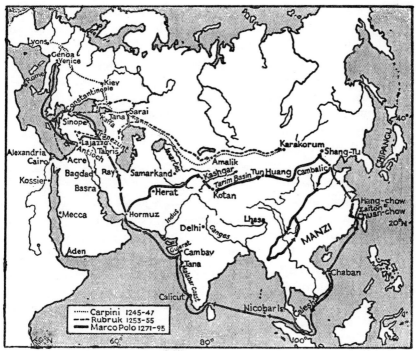

XXX. *Land and sea traffic to eastern Asia during the Mongol period.*

therefore, predestined for this new perilous and responsible task. He crossed Bohemia and Poland to Kiev and passed from there over the Don and Volga to Saratov. There he learnt that the Great Khan Kuyuk, the grandson of Genghis Khan, was staying at Caracorum, a City south-west of the modern Urga on the mountain slopes of the upper Orkhon. As fast as he could go, following the route of the Mongol State Post—by which, if one possessed the necessary documents, it was possible to travel in one seat from Kiev to Canton—Carpini trotted on perpetually renewed stage horses across Asia, round the north of the Aral Sea and through the Dzungarian Gate to the summer capital of the Great Khan in a bare four months. There, at the end of August 1246, he witnessed the coronation of Kuyuk as the new Mongol Emperor and was at last able to deliver the Pope's message.

In some respects conditions for his mission were not at all unfavourable. Kuyuk's closest collaborator Cadac, several of his physicians, and one of the ruler's generals were Christians, the Mongols themselves were indifferent or even tolerant in matters of religion. To this was added the fact that, in the course of its conquests during the last few decades, the Mongol Empire had spread its boundaries to include many Christian peoples and had carried off thousands of Christian captives into the interior of Asia. Thus, for instance, the papal envoys met in Talas in the Altai Mountains of Dzungaria a large number of Germans engaged in gold-mining and arms-manufacture for the Mongols— apparently a Transylvanian mining village transported *en bloc*. And Caracorum itself was positively teeming with Frenchmen, Flemings, Englishmen and Germans, who lived there in their own caravanserais and were there for purposes of trade.

Hence Christianity was well known to the Tartars. Kuyuk had ordered 'that in the law of God there shall be no difference between a Latin, a Greek, an Armenian, a Nestorian, a Jacobin and all who worship the cross. For among us all are one.' None the less, the world looked quite different from Caracorum than from Rome, and amongst the several thousand high dignitaries who had converged upon the capital of the Great Khan—including Russian grand-dukes, emissaries from the Caliph of Bagdad, Turks, Persians, Koreans, Chinese and many great lords from the Middle East—Carpini was only one of many, and the Pope's message was greeted and understood as one of the usual declarations of homage. Hence Kuyuk replied:

> Therefore you must come yourself at the head of all your kings and prove to Us your fealty and allegiance. And if you disregard the command of God and disobey our instructions, We shall look upon you as Our enemy. Whoever recognizes and submits to the Son of God and Lord of the World, the Great Khan, will be saved, whoever refuses submission shall be wiped out.

This struck a familiar note. But Kuyuk continued:

> You inhabitants of the western lands consider yourselves alone to be Christians and despise others. How then do you know who is worthy in the sight of God to partake of His mercy? When you say to yourselves, 'I am a Christian, I pray to God and serve Him, and I hate the others', how do you know whom God considers righteous and to whom He will show His mercy?

There may be an echo here of the type of philosophical reflection characteristic of Asia. But the letter also has an almost nationalistic ring, or at least a ring of outspoken opposition to the arrogant West, such as has been heard from the East many and many a time since then. In the face of this attitude Carpini's mission was doomed to failure, and as regards its original political and theological aims it did indeed fail. But it was successful inasmuch as it revealed that, with reasonable good fortune, such long journeys could be made—in other words, that even by land the Arab blockade of the road to India could be turned.

After a very difficult winter journey Carpini returned safe and sound to Europe. He must have arrived at the Papal Court at Lyons in November 1247. In the light of his impressions and the reports which he brought back with him and set down very vividly in his *Historia Mongolorum*, it must have appeared to the Vatican very dubious whether attempts to establish a link with the new Great Power in central Asia enjoyed any prospect of success. Other Western rulers sprang into the gap left by the Vatican, however. Six years later, in the winter of 1253, King Louis IX of France also sent an embassy to the Great Khan at Caracorum—perhaps unconsciously pursuing the Franks' age-old striving to enlarge their sphere of influence by winning friends far to the east and maintaining good relations with them however alien their ways might be; in Charlemagne's day it was Haroun al Rashid, now it was the Great Khan!

This mission was led by the Flemish Franciscan William of Ruysbroek, a cool-headed character whom one cannot imagine to have been pleased with his task—especially as he was personally acquainted with Andrew of Longjumeau, the Pope's missionary to the heathen whom we mentioned above, and must have learnt from him the true situation at Caracorum. On the other hand, fairly well authenticated reports were for ever coming in from Asia to the effect that some Mongolian prince or other was a Christian.

It does appear that various members of the Mongolian ruling class had been baptized. But these 'Christians' patently regarded baptism as a new kind of prophylaxis against evil spirits, without having grasped any of the inner meaning of this elevated religious philosophy. In other cases these 'Christians' were in reality Buddhists, and superficial observers from the West had been deceived by the many points of contact between this doctrine and Christianity.

Anyhow, William of Ruysbroek set out for the Orient in 1253. He too travelled across the region of the Aral Sea and through the Dzungarian Gate, i.e. along the northern caravan route. His original goal was the pastureland on the lower Volga, where the ostensibly Christian Mongol prince Sartak was said to reside. Ruysbroek reached Sartak, but was passed on by him to his father, Prince Batu, at Saratov, who in turn passed him on to the Great Khan at Caracorum, both Sartak and Batu saying the matter was outside their authority. The former made no very agreeable impression on Ruysbroek. In his travel report he remarks:

I do not know whether Sartak believes in Christ or not. I do know, however, that he does not wish to be called a Christian. It seems to me that he is ridiculing the Christians . . .

Ruysbroek confirms, however, that there were many Christians in central Asia. On St. Andrew's Day, 30th November 1253, he relates, he came to a village near Cailac (Kopal in Semiretchinsk) where there was a Nestorian church. 'We entered and sang joyfully, as loud as we could, *Salve regina*, for it was a long time since we last saw a church.' But he has the good sense not to draw any general conclusions from this, and he does not take the view that Asia is fundamentally a Christian province. At the end of December 1253 he reached the court of Mangu Khan, grandson of Temujin, the ruling Great Khan, who received the Western delegation in a not unfriendly manner. In May 1254 long discussions took place between the various creeds represented at Caracorum; in the course of these Mangu condescended to receive the Flemish monk for a lengthy private talk on matters of religion. But all this remained without any palpable result; and Ruysbroek's account occasionally leaves the reader with the impression that he could well understand a ruler of the Mongol Khan's omnipotence considering the religious differences between Catholics and Nestorian Christians, between Jews, Mohammedans and Buddhists, matters of little consequence. At least he saw that in the endless distances of Asia things must be measured with other yardsticks than those employed in Europe, which even in those days was already constricted and oppressed by a multitude of historical memories. Anyhow, Ruysbroek concludes his account with the cool and objective statement:

It seems to me useless for a Brother to journey to the Mongols again, as I and the Dominicans journeyed to them.

The gift of calm observation that characterizes William of Ruysbroek in matters of religion did not abandon him in other domains, which were doubtless less familiar to him. It was natural for him to disapprove of the, by Christian standards, loose way of life of the Nestorian Christions, because the central Asian custom of polygamy—which had been established in the Middle Kingdom since time immemorial—was strange to him. In view of the spirit of his age, it was natural that he should not have a single good word to say for the Mohammedans.

But in spite of these things, which must have distressed him considerably, he did not fail to notice what a well-ordered kingdom he was in. He was particularly struck by the punctuality and speed of the traffic on the great imperial roads of the Mongol rulers. Unlike many other Western travellers, however, he did not feel entirely at ease in the country of the Great Khan. On the subject of his first meeting with Tartars, for instance, he notes: '*Invenimus Tartaros, inter quos, cum intravi, visum fuit mihi recte quod ingrederer quoddam aliud sæculum.*' (We met Tartars. It seemed to me, as soon as I found myself amongst them, that I had stepped into a different century.) And when he had got safely past the first staring horde of Tartars, he sighed with relief: '*Visum fuit mihi, quod evasissem de manibus dæmonum.*' (I felt as though I had escaped from the hands of demons.) We can judge from this that it took a good deal of personal courage voluntarily to place himself in the power of the Tartars, even if he were an envoy of the Pope and under diplomatic protection. A large number of travellers, many of them Christian missionaries, paid for their boldness with their lives. None the less, William of Ruysbroek brought back much valuable information, for instance that there was paper money in China, that the Caspian Sea was not a bay of the Southern Ocean, but an enormous inland sea, that the Chinese alphabet consisted not of letters, but of symbols, and a great deal more besides.

William of Ruysbroek's true missionary aims were in no way fulfilled, however. On the contrary, Mangu Khan gave the 'Western devil' to understand in no uncertain terms that the quicker he went back home the better. Thus the French king's delegation achieved no more than the emissaries sent to the Far East by the Pope. For a time, therefore, the idea of any extensive missionary work in far-away Asia was abandoned.

6

One important success all these otherwise rather unproductive enterprises did achieve: western and central Asia became increasingly well known in Europe and gradually entered the range of operations of big merchants. Ahead of everyone else in this respect was Venice.

The beautiful city on the lagoon was at this time, round the middle of the thirteenth century, at the peak of her power. She had begun as a fishing village that was not even distinguished by a particularly favourable position. During the Hun and Lombard invasions of the fifth and sixth centuries A.D. it became a place of refuge for the largely urban population of Venetia, so that a superstructure of well-to-do burghers was now erected on the substratum of primitive fishermen. The wars between Byzantium and the Lombards left Venice to laugh up her sleeve and draw the profits. As early as the seventh century she built a fleet, which soon developed into a factor of considerable power. It was inevitable that the Mediterranean trade should fall into her hands; skilful negotiations with Charlemagne soon secured for her a predominant influence on the overland trade of central and western Europe as well.

The crusades increased Venice's influence still further and rendered her the undisputed 'Mistress of the Adriatic'. The never-ending conflict between Emperor and Pope gave the city of the lagoon, with its superior diplomacy, an opportunity to strengthen its sovereign position, as had happened five hundred years before during the disputes between Byzantium and the Lombards. Her influence soon extended to Egypt as well as to the Black Sea and southern Russia, the two focal points of medieval trade with Asia. Venetian merchants were stationed both on the Crimea and in Tana on the Don estuary—the first for the sake of south Russian grain, the second on account of the ancient trade route which, as we have heard, ran from here to the Russian interior and Siberia; but Venetians had also settled in Sinope and Trebizond on the Asia Minor coast of the Black Sea. For a number of major caravan routes from central Asia to the West ended here, while a considerable part of the stream of goods from the Persian Gulf to the north-west flowed in this direction. Venice was the great mart of world trade. For what came to her from the East was distributed and passed on to north and west from the counting-houses of the city on the Lido. If the housewife of Augsburg or Nuremberg, or of Stockholm, was able at this time to buy from her grocer Malabar pepper, Arabian spices and myrrh, Chinese rice, Spanish or Italian saffron, cinnamon from Ceylon, southern Asian galingale and ginger from India, as well as 'grains of paradise' from west Africa, she owed no small part of these exotic things to Venice.

It was only to be expected that representatives of this first city of world trade should now swell the stream of travellers to Asia. Competition with other Italian cities compelled her to remain active. Nevertheless the brothers Nicolo and Maffeo Polo, who owned a factory in the Crimea, set out for Asia for purely private commercial reasons, not under instructions from the State. When they began their journey in 1255, they had no intention whatever of going to China. They were seeking a meeting with the Mongol prince Barca, who varied his capital between Bulghar and Sarai, two great cities on the Volga. They did in fact succeed in reaching Barca's court, but when they wished to return home Fate took a hand. War had broken out between Barca and another Mongol prince, and since travel on the roads to the south-west had become unsafe the two Venetians journeyed to the south-east, came to Bokhara and there joined forces with an embassy that was on its way to the new Great Khan, Kublai.

Nicolo and Maffeo Polo were in Bokhara round about 1260; one to two years later they arrived in Cambaluc, the modern Peking, to which Kublai Khan had transferred his capital. They began the return journey in about 1265, reaching Acre in spring 1269. They carried with them a message from Kublai Khan to the Pope asking the spiritual head of Western Christendom to send him a hundred pious monks.

The golden tablet which Kublai had given his two Venetian guests ensured them preferential treatment all over Asia. No doubt it also served them in Europe as proof of their good relations with the Great Khan. None the less, the Curia could not make up its mind to send the hundred clerics requested. And there were good reasons for this. For prior to the Polo brothers' departure, the Great Khan had called them to him and declared:

How would you have me to become a Christian? You see that the Christians of these parts are so ignorant that they achieve nothing and can achieve nothing, whilst you see the Idolaters can do anything they please, insomuch that when I sit at table the cups from the middle of the hall come to me full of wine or other liquor, without being touched by anybody, and I drink from them. They control storms, causing them to pass in whatever direction they please, and do many other marvels; whilst, as you know, their idols speak and give them predictions on whatever subjects they choose. But if I were to turn to the faith of Christ and become a Christian, then my barons and others who are not converted would say: 'What has moved you to be baptized and to take up the faith of Christ? What powers or miracles have you witnessed on His part?' (You know that the Idolaters here say that their wonders are performed by the sanctity and power of their idols.) Well, I should not know what answer to make; so they would only be confirmed in their errors, and the Idolaters who are adepts in such surprising arts, would easily compass my death. But now you shall go to your Pope, and pray him on my part to send hither an hundred men skilled in your law, who shall be capable of rebuking the practices of the Idolaters to their faces, and of telling them that they too know how to do such things but will not, because they are done by the help of the devil and other evil spirits, and shall so control the Idolaters that these shall have no power to perform such things in their presence. When we shall witness this we will denounce the Idolaters and their religion, and then I will receive baptism; and when I shall have been baptized, then all my barons and chiefs shall be baptized also, and their followers shall do the like, and thus in the end there will be more Christians here than exist in your part of the world! (*The Book of Ser Marco Polo,* translated by Henry Yule, London: John Murray, 1874, 2nd edition, Vol. I, pp. 339 f.)

The Curia obviously could not accede to these conditions, and when the two Venetians set out for China again in 1274—this time with Nicolo's seventeen-year-old son Marco—they received from Pope Gregory X a spiritual escort of two monks, Nicholas of Vicenza and William of Tripolis. But these two missionaries feared the road to their yellow-faced, slit-eyed and pigtailed flock. No sooner did they reach the Gulf of Alexandretta in Armenia, than they turned back— without, of course, informing the Pope. Marco Polo is of the opinion that this timorous desertion prevented the conversion of Kublai, which would have changed the whole history of the world. Whether this is correct is another question. True, the Great Khan, a grandson of Genghis Khan born in 1214, was a man of real greatness and un- doubtedly one of the most outstanding of all the Mongol rulers. Whereas Genghis Khan's immediate successors were swashbuckling warriors with little interest in the things of the spirit, Kublai, who was made Emperor in 1256, was a very intelligent and cultivated man with strong scholarly interests. And doubtless Marco Polo knew his friend the Emperor as well as a European can know an Asian. But it must not be forgotten that at all times Asia has reckoned in other terms than Europe. We have already heard that many influential persons in the entourage of the Mongol emperors were baptized Christians. But this had no perceptible influence on the policy of the great Asian power.

Anyhow, after the desertion of the two clerics, our three Venetians had to journey on alone. Their precise route is uncertain, whether via Mossul and Bagdad or farther north in the direction of Erzrum. They definitely passed through Hormuz and also Kashgar. From there they took the southern route via Yarkand, Khotan and Charcham to Shachau (Sachiu), where they were already in the true realm of the Great Khan. In Kan-chou, capital of the western province of Tangut, they were met by a guard of honour from Kublai which conducted them first along the Hwang-ho, through the north of the province of Cathay, to Chandu (Coleridge's Xanadu), the summer capital of the Emperor, where they arrived about May 1275.

The Great Khan received the three Italians with great cordiality and honour. The young Marco Polo, who was born shortly after his father left on his first trip to Asia, soon enjoyed the Emperor's particular trust and friendship. He became the latter's private secretary and finally the Great Khan's governor in Yang-chou, capital of the southern province of Manzi, which Kublai had just taken from the Sung Dynasty. Thus Marco was able to make good use of the seventeen years he passed at the court of Kublai, looking round him with open eyes. Whereas neither Carpini nor Ruysbroek penetrated into China proper, he had every opportunity of getting to know it thoroughly. He did not know Chinese, but he spoke Mongolian as well as Persian and Arabic, and the accuracy and vividness of the accounts which he later wrote show that his ignorance of the language did not inhibit his observations in China.

Marco Polo begins his narrative with the impressions and experiences he underwent on the journey. He tells of the Tartars and their *yourtas*, felt tents which folded into the smallest possible space; he reports on their mode of life, their food, their women, horses and dogs. Then he speaks of the march over the Plateau of Pamir:

> The region is so lofty and cold that you do not even see any birds flying. And I must notice also that becouse of this great cold, fire does not burn so brightly, nor give out so much heat as usual, nor does it cook food so effectually. (*The Book of Ser Marco Polo,* Vol. I, p. 181.)

As we know, both observations are entirely correct. With very few exceptions, no birds are to be found at high altitudes, and at heights at which the air has a low oxygen content fires do not give out anything like the same heat as nearer sea level. Marco Polo's knowledge of physics did not, of course, suffice to explain these phenomena, and he contents himself with noting them and then passes on to describe the highly civilized, densely populated land of China, which is of more interest to him than the wastes of Pamir. He writes at length of the great city of Canpchu (Kan-chou in Kansu) with its three Nestorian churches; he tells of the old imperial silk road along which they marched; he speaks at length about the Hwang-ho, the huge river which they followed in a north-easterly direction. Not far from the Hwang-ho they entered the province of Tenduc, the modern T'ien-te, a region which, Marco Polo believes, was once the home of Prester John.

> Tenduc is a province which lies towards the east, and contains numerous towns and villages; among which is the chief city, also called Tenduc. The king of the province is of the lineage of Prester John, George by name, and

he holds the land under the Great Kaan; not that he holds anything like the whole of what Prester John possessed. It is a custom, I may tell you, that these kings of the lineage of Prester John always obtain to wife either daughters of the Great Kaan or other princesses of his family.

In this province is found the stone from which Azure is made. It is obtained from a kind of vein in the earth, and is of very fine quality. There is also a great manufacture of fine camlets of different colours from camel's hair. The people get their living by their cattle and tillage, as well as by trade and handicraft.

The rule of the province is in the hands of the Christians as I have told you; but there are also plenty of Idolaters and worshippers of Mahommet. And there is also here a class of people called *Argons*, which is as much as to say in French *Guasmul*, or, in other words, sprung from two different races: to wit, of the race of the Idolaters of Tenduc and of that of the worshippers of Mahommet. They are handsomer men than the other natives of the country, and having more ability they come to have authority; and they are also capital merchants. (*The Book of Ser Marco Polo*, Vol. I, p. 275.)

When Marco Polo comes to speak of the Emperor Kublai, his description sounds at the outset like an extract from Prester John's letter to the potentates of Europe. But a different note soon creeps in, revealing Marco's close personal friendship for the Great Khan:

Now am I come to that part of our Book in which I shall tell you of the great and wonderful magnificence of the Great Kaan now reigning, by name Cublay Kaan; *Kaan* being a title which signifyeth 'The Great Lord of Lords', or Emperor. And of a surety he hath good right to such a title, for all men know for a certain truth that he is the most potent man, as regards forces and lands and treasure, that existeth in the world, or ever hath existed from the time of our First Father Adam until this day. (*The Book of Ser Marco Polo,* Vol. I, p. 323.)

The personal appearance of the Great Kaan, Lord of Lords, whose name is Cublay, is such as I shall now tell you. He is of a good stature, neither tall nor short, but of a middle height. He has a becoming amount of flesh, and is very shapely in all his limbs. His complexion is white and red, the eyes black and fine, the nose well formed and well set on. (*The Book of Ser Marco Polo,* Vol. I, p. 348.)

Now this Cublay Kaan is of the right Imperial lineage, being descended from Chinghis [Genghis] Kaan, the first sovereign of all the Tartars. And he is the sixth Lord in that succession, as I have already told you in this book. He came to the throne in the year of Christ 1256, and the Empire fell to him because of his ability and valour and great worth, as was right and reason. (*The Book of Ser Marco Polo,* Vol. I, p. 324.)

The Venetian depicts the Great Khan's surroundings with equal clarity: Kublai's Summer Palace at Chandu (Shangtu north-east of

Kalgan), which must have been as striking as any of the châteaux of rococo Europe, and his Winter Palace in the great city of Cambaluc (Peking). As a citizen of Venice, one of the best-governed administrative units in Europe, Marco Polo was particularly impressed by the efficiency of the Great Khan's administration, which he describes at great length. This chapter of his book aroused tremendous interest in the West, which was at that time striving to rid itself of obsolete and unserviceable forms of government. It was this aspect of Marco Polo's account, in particular, which inspired such a widespread desire amongst European travellers to visit the land of the Great Khan.

You must know that the Great Kaan hath chosen twelve great Barons to whom he hath committed all the necessary affairs of thirty-four great provinces; and now I will tell you particulars about them and their establishments.

You must know that these twelve Barons reside all together in a very rich and handsome palace, which is inside the city of Cambaluc, and consists of a variety of edifices, with many suites of apartments. To every province is assigned a judge and several clerks, and all reside in this palace, where each has his separate quarters. These judges and clerks administer all the affairs of the provinces to which they are attached, under the direction of the twelve Barons. Howbeit, when an affair is of very great importance, the twelve Barons lay it before the Emperor, and he decides as he thinks best. But the power of those twelve Barons is so great that they choose the governors for all those 34 great provinces that I have mentioned, and only after they have chosen do they inform the Emperor of their choice. This he confirms, and grants to the person nominated a tablet of gold such as is appropriate to the rank of his government.

Those twelve Barons also have such authority that they can dispose of the movements of the forces, and send them whither, and in such strength as, they please. This is done indeed with the Emperor's cognizance, but still the orders are issued on their authority. They are styled *Shieng,* which is as much as to say 'The Supreme Court', and the palace where they abide is also called *Shieng.* This body forms the highest authority at the Court of the Great Kaan; and indeed they can favour and advance whom they will. (*The Book of Ser Marco Polo,* Vol. I, p. 417.)

The Emperor's Mint is in the City of Cambaluc, and the way it is wrought is such that you might say he hath the Secret of Alchemy in perfection, and you would be right!

He makes them take the bark of a certain tree, in fact of the Mulberry Tree, the leaves of which are the food of the silkworms—these trees being so numerous that whole districts are full of them. What they take is a certain fine white bast or skin which lies between the wood of the tree and the thick outer bark, and this they make into something resembling sheets of paper, but black. When these sheets have been prepared they are cut up into pieces of different sizes. The smallest of these sizes is worth half a tornesel; the next, a little larger, one tornesel; one, a little larger still, is worth half a silver groat of Venice; another a whole groat; others yet two groats, five groats, and ten groats. There is also a kind worth one Bezant of gold, and others of three bezants, and so up to ten. All these pieces of paper are issued with as much solemnity and authority as if they were of pure gold or silver; and on every piece a variety of officials, whose duty it is, have to write their names, and to put their seals. And when all is prepared duly, the chief officer deputed by the Kaan smears the Seal entrusted to him with vermilion, and impresses it on the paper, so that the form of the Seal remains printed upon it in red; the Money is then authentic. Any one forging it would be punished with death. And the Kaan causes every year to be made such a vast quantity of this money, which costs him nothing, that it must equal in amount all the treasure in the world.

With these pieces of paper, made as I have described, he causes all payments on his own account to be made; and he makes them to pass current universally over all his kingdoms and provinces and territories, and whithersoever his power and sovereignty extends. And nobody, however important he may think himself, dares to refuse them on pain of death. And indeed everybody takes them readily, for wheresoever a person may go throughout the Great Kaan's dominions he shall find these pieces of paper current, and shall be able to transact all sales and purchases of goods by means of them just as well as if they were coins of pure gold. (*The Book of Ser Marco Polo,* Vol. I, pp. 409 f.)

Marco Polo also writes with enthusiasm of the Great Khan's State Post:

Now you must know that from this city of Cambaluc proceed many roads and highways leading to a variety of provinces, one to one province, another to another; and each road receives the name of the province to which it leads; and it is a very sensible plan. And the messengers of the Emperor in travelling from Cambaluc, be the road whichsoever they will, find at every 25 miles of the journey a station which they call *Yamb,* or, as we should say, the 'Horse-Post-House'. And at each of those stations used by the messengers there is a large and handsome building for them to put up at, in which they find all the rooms furnished with fine beds and all other necessary articles in rich silk, and where they are provided with everything they can want. If even a king were to arrive at one of these, he would find himself well lodged.

At some of these stations, moreover, there shall be posted some 400 horses standing ready for the use of the messengers; at others there shall be 200, according to the requirements, and to what the Emperor has established in each case. (*The Book of Ser Marco Polo,* Vol. I, pp. 419 f.)

The Venetian goes on to explain that much of the power and efficiency of Kublai's realm is due to its enormous population, which in turn is the result of two factors: the large families arising out of the heathen practice of polygamy, and the ability of the inhabitants to live on an almost exclusive diet of rice, buckwheat and millet, which the country produces in large quantities. He also tells how, when bad weather has spoilt the crops, the Khan not only relieves the peasants from the payment of taxes, but, through his officials, supplies them with grain for their food and for the next year's planting. This grain is drawn from supplies stored in the State granaries during years of exceptionally good harvest, which is sold in time of need at a quarter of the normal price. The Great Khan renders similar assistance when a farmer's herds have suffered from disease, supplying him with beasts from the State herds.

As an example of Kublai's thought for his subjects, Marco Polo is particularly impressed by his practice of planting trees by the wayside, of which he writes:

The Emperor moreover hath taken order that all the highways travelled by his messengers and the people generally should be planted with rows of great trees a few paces apart; and thus these trees are visible a long way off, and no one can miss the way by day or night. Even the roads through uninhabited tracts are thus planted, and it is the greatest possible solace to travellers. And this is done on all the ways where it can be of service. The Great Kaan plants these trees all the more readily, because his astrologers and diviners tell him that he who plants trees lives long.

But where the ground is so sandy and desert that trees will not grow, he causes other landmarks, pillars or stones, to be set up to show the way. (*The Book of Ser Marco Polo*, Vol. I, p. 426.)

The tremendous effect made on Europe by Marco Polo's report has already been mentioned. It influenced not only geographical knowledge, but the actual course of cultural evolution. These accounts of the dominion of the Great Khan may well have provided the first incentive to both the planting of trees along the highways and to the use of paper money in Europe. Another point in his narrative that must have aroused great interest is a reference to a 'black stone' which is dug from the mountains and burns like charcoal. Europe too knew the 'black stone'—pit-coal is mentioned in England at the beginning of the ninth century, and it was definitely mined here from the thirteenth century onwards. On this subject the Venetian says:

It is a fact that all over the country of Cathay there is a kind of black stones existing in beds in the mountains, which they dig out and burn like firewood. If you supply the fire with them at night, and see that they are well kindled, you will find them still alight in the morning; and they make such capital fuel that no other is used throughout the country. (*The Book of Ser Marco Polo,* Vol. I, p. 428.)

Marco Polo naturally took a particular interest in the religious notions of the Chinese. He was the first to acquaint Europe with the doctrine of the transmigration of souls and to outline a religion which, like the teachings of Confucius, was based on ancestor worship.

Their view of the immortality of the soul is after this fashion. They believe that as soon as a man dies, his soul enters into another body, going from a good one to a better, or from a bad to a worse, according as he hath conducted himself well or ill. That is to say, a poor man, if he has passed through life good and sober, shall be born again of a gentlewoman, and shall be a gentleman; and on a second occasion shall be born of a princess and shall be a prince, and so on, always rising, till he be absorbed into the Deity. But if he has borne himself ill, he who was the son of a gentleman shall be reborn as the son of a peasant, and from a peasant shall become a dog, always going down lower and lower.

. . . They show great respect to their parents; and should there be any son who offends his parents, or fails to minister to their necessities, there is a public office which has no other charge but that of punishing unnatural children, who are proved to have acted with ingratitude towards their parents. (*The Book of Ser Marco Polo,* Vol. I, p. 438.)

These brief quotations from Marco Polo's travel-narrative reveal the warmth and vigour of his descriptions. As may be seen, his notes go far beyond the sphere of geography and contain much valuable information on almost every domain of life. The Middle Ages possessed no other equally full account of China.

In addition, Marco Polo travelled widely outside China on behalf of Kublai Khan. One of his first journeys took him to Tibet, over which the Great Khan had recently extended his sway. From there the Venetian travelled to Burma, whose wonders he describes at length; then, with a wide sweep to the east, he returned northwards to the Great Khan's Residence. On another long journey, likewise to the south, Marco Polo came to Kinsay, the southern Chinese city of Hang-chou in Che-kiang. This former capital of the Sung Dynasty, the hereditary ruling house of the southern Chinese, had been a centre of culture since time out of mind and was much more cultivated and infinitely richer in tradition than the fundamentally somewhat barbaric Cambaluc. Understandably enough, Marco Polo, whose standards of judgment were derived from conditions in Venice, felt more at home here than in the Great Khan's northern capital. He could not even live in Milan; he was accustomed to the wide vision and whirling tempo of a cosmopolitan city, and the way of looking at things in terms of a single continent, which naturally prevailed at Cambaluc, remained all his life alien and uncongenial to him.

Here in Kinsay, the 'City of Heaven' as he calls it, one could really smell the salty tang of the broad ocean. Sailors of all nations sauntered through the streets; all races, the brown and black as well as the yellow, were represented. Thousands upon thousands of masts stretched skyward in the harbour. Alongside the great seagoing freighters which made the runs to India, Persia and the island-dotted sea around Java, lay innumerable junks that plied the south China coast, and the boats that sailed the inland canals. A colourful picture! And then there was the enormous number of the city's inhabitants. In Marco Polo's day the imperial tax-collectors reckoned that about one million six hundred thousand families were resident here, i.e. considerably more than five million individuals. Naturally, Kinsay was also an immensely wealthy city. For it manufactured salt, and from this alone, as Marco Polo states, the Emperor derived an annual revenue of six million Venetian ducats; on top of this, commerce and other industries were also taxed, so that huge sums poured into the imperial coffers from Kinsay.

During his stay in south China, Marco Polo heard for the first time that, far to the east of this most easterly shore in the world, a large, immeasurably rich island lay in the middle of the vast ocean—the land of Chipangu, our Japan. In the imagination of the Chinese, Chipangu seems to have been a kind of fairy-tale island. It was only fifteen hundred miles off the Chinese coast, yet few travellers had ever succeeded in reaching Chipangu. Nor had the Great Khan been able to conquer it. And yet the island was immensely wealthy. The royal palace, for example, is 'entirely roofed with fine gold, just as our churches are roofed with lead'; while 'all the pavement of the palace, and the floors of its chambers, are entirely of gold, in plates like slabs of stone, a good two fingers thick; and the windows also are of gold'. Moreover they have fine pearls in abundance and quantities of other precious stones.

As may be imagined, reports like this roused the West to the highest pitch of attention. They were very largely responsible for the efforts made by the navigators of every civilized nation to find the shortest route to this land of abundant riches. Marco Polo's lucid and precise account stood out from amongst the many vague and obscure rumours. Yet it was pure chance that led Marco Polo to write his narrative at all.

He did so while a prisoner of war. In 1298, three years after his safe return from China, he took part in a naval battle between Venice and Genoa, during which he fell into the hands of the Genoese. He employed his captivity, which lasted about ten months, in writing his book. Besides much respect and admiration, due in no small part to his having returned to Venice laden with treasure, he also reaped a rich harvest of mockery. Because of his frequent allusions to numbers of a magnitude to which Europe was unaccustomed, he received during his lifetime the nickname *Messer Marco Milione*, Master Marco Million. No doubt he often made mistakes in his figures; perhaps, too, he occasionally exaggerated in order to impress the Venetians, who were used to big numbers. Marco Polo's travel-narrative contains a hard core of truth, however, and the report of an old Italian chronicle that on his deathbed in 1324 the Venetian firmly refused to retract anything of what he had written is entirely credible. He is reputed to have said that he had not told the half of his amazing experiences!

## 7

While the three Polos were returning by sea to India via Indo-China, Sumatra and Ceylon on their way back to Europe, a Westerner sailed past them eastward who was to remain in China for almost forty years. This was the Franciscan monk John of Monte Corvino, one of the greatest pastors and missionaries produced by the Christian Church. We recall that the two elder Polos returned home from their first visit to China in 1270 with the Great Khan's request that the Pope should send him a hundred Christian missionaries. We also heard that two monks were sent with the two Venetians when they left for China again, but that these monks turned back as soon as they reached Asia Minor. Now Gregory X's successor, the energetic Pope Nicholas IV, took up the old plan afresh. John of Monte Corvino set out for Asia in 1288 with letters from the Pope to Kublai Khan. His first stop was Persia, whose Mongolian King Aboga, a nephew of Kublai Khan, was at that time threatened by the Arabs in their advance towards the east, and hence was no doubt very willing to establish contact with Europe— another enemy of the Arabs.

From Persia Monte Corvino journeyed, probably in 1290, to India, where he spent nearly a year among the St. Thomas's Christians of the Coromandel coast. Then he travelled by the sea route to Kublai Khan at Peking. And here in Peking he closed his eyes thirty-six years later,

rich in years and after a life of undisputable successes. In 1310 he even
succeeded in persuading the ruling Great Khan Haichan (Wu-tsung),
the successor of Timur and grandson of Kublai Khan, to undergo
baptism. The way was prepared for the striking act of conversion—
which remained without any general effect owing to the early death of
Wu-tsung—by Monte Corvino's nomination as Archbishop of Cathay
in 1307 and the dispatch to China of nine bishops (only three or four
of whom ever reached their Far Eastern destination however). It
looked for a time as though Christianity was on the brink of greatly
increased influence in China.

A round millennium earlier, as we know, there had already been a
period in which the Christian faith had become quite widely diffused
in the Middle Kingdom. Favoured by Emperor Tai-tsung and his successors, Nestorianism had won many adherents; it might have been
elevated to the State religion, if one of the emperors had allowed himself to be baptized. But everything that had been built up collapsed and
Christianity disappeared from sight. For many centuries every foreign
religion that reached China was ruthlessly suppressed. Yet many traces
of Nestorianism remained, and we have heard on several occasions how
European travellers on their way to Caracorum or Peking came upon
Christian churches and Nestorian communities.

With this early Christian epoch in mind, and above all in view of
Kublai Khan's sympathetic attitude to Christianity, the fact that Monte
Corvino did not reach Peking until after the Polos had left it and that
by this time Kublai Khan, who was almost eighty, was too old to give
active support to the new doctrine, has been deplored as a disastrous
blunder of Fate. The most audacious vistas have been sketched of what
might have happened if Monte Corvino had got there earlier. If a
younger Kublai Khan had gone over to Christianity and carried his
people with him by the force of his personality, it has been said, history
would have been different. It is always idle to contemplate the might-
have-been, but in this particular case the chances that any radical
change in the course of events would have been brought about are
really not as great as they might seem. Modern studies on the cultural
relations between East and West reveal the complexity of problems
such as this. It is very questionable whether even the entirely spon-
taneous adoption of European forms of thought and moral values really
changes, or can change, the Asian outlook. Anyhow, just as Alexander
the Great did not go to Chandragupta, the brilliant ruler of India, so
the Pope and the Great Khan did not meet now. Even in later centuries,
despite repeated incipient attempts to draw together, there has never

been any real union between the two hemispheres. Perhaps the time for mutual comprehension has still not come.

For just this reason, we are all the more deeply moved by a letter written by one of Europe's spiritual emissaries to the Orient. The letter was addressed by the Franciscan Andrew of Perugia, Bishop of Zayton, in the winter of 1326 to the 'Reverend Father of the Friars and Prior of the Monastery at Perugia'. This letter runs:

Friar Andrew of Perugia of the Order of the Minorites, by divine leave nominated Bishop, to the Reverend Father of the Friars and Prior of the monastery of Perugia greetings and everlasting peace.

On account of the enormous distance by land and sea between me and you, I can scarcely hope that this my letter will come into your hands.

You have learnt that I, and with me Friar Peregrinus, my fellow bishop of blessed memory, the sole companion of my wanderings, after overcoming much toil and exhaustion, hunger and the most various torments on land and water, where we were robbed of everything, even our cowls and under garments, finally came with God's help to Cambaliech [Peking], where the Great Khan and Emperor has his Court. This, I believe, was in 1308 after the incarnation of Our Lord. There, after we had been ordained Archbishop according to the instructions given us by the Apostolic See, we remained for almost five years. During this time we received from the magnanimous Emperor an *alafa* for the feeding and clothing of eight persons. This *alafa* is an allowance which the Emperor makes to the emissaries of great lords, to orators, generals, artists in the various arts, spear-throwers, the poor and the most various persons for greatly varying reasons, allowances which exceed the expenditure of the majority of Roman kings.

Of the wealth, generosity and fame of this great emperor, of the prodigious extent of his realm, of the multitude of his peoples, of the number and size of the cities, and of the regulations laid down by the Emperor in consequence of which no one dares to raise his sword against his neighbour, I shall say nothing, because I have not space to write of them and because the reader would find them incredible. For even I, who am in the land, hear many things that I can scarce believe.

There is a great city on the shores of the Ocean Sea, which is called in the Persian tongue Zayton [Chuan-Chow], and in this city a rich Armenian lady did build a large and fine enough church, which was erected into a cathedral by the Archbishop and given during his lifetime to the Friar Bishop Gerard and the friars who were with him. When this bishop died and was interred in his church, the Archbishop wished to make me his successor there, but since neither the place nor the succession pleased me, he transferred them to the aforementioned Friar Peregrinus, who went thither at the first opportunity and, after fulfilling this office for a few years, died there in 1322, nine days after St. Peter and St. Paul. Some four years after his demise, not receiving proper encouragement at Cambaliech, I succeeded in arranging for the aforesaid *alafa* or imperial alms to be paid to me in the city of Zayton, which lies nearly three months' journey from Cambaliech.

Since then I have lived here permanently and defray my expenses from the aforesaid imperial alms, which, according to the currency of the merchants of Genoa, amounts to about one hundred gold florins yearly. Of this I have used a great part for the erection of a monastery church. I do not know of any other monastery in the whole of our province that can be compared with it for beauty and general amenity. Finally, not long after the death of Brother Peregrinus, I received an order from the Archbishop appointing me to this See. For good reasons I agreed to this and now pass my time, entirely in accordance with my wishes, either in the church of the said city or in the monastery. And since I am in good health, I may well be able to labour for several more years in this field, as long as the span of life allotted to me allows. Of course, partly as the result of physical injuries and partly because of my age, I am grown grey.

In this vast empire there are people belonging to every race under the sun and men of every sect. And it is permitted to all of them, one community like another, to live according to their faith. For here they hold the opinion, or rather the erroneous opinion, that every man may be saved after his own creed. Hence we can live freely and preach without danger; but no one of the Jews or Mohammedans is ever converted. Many of the Idolaters are baptized, though many of those baptized do not walk in the true way of Christianity.

Four of our Brothers were martyred by the Mohammedans in India. One of them emerged unscathed after being thrown twice into a huge fire. And in spite of this amazing miracle, not one of the Mohammedans was turned from his unbelief.

All the foregoing I have written briefly to Your Reverence that you may bring it to the knowledge of others. I do not write to my brothers in Christ nor to my particular friends, because I do not know which of them have gone to their rest and which still live. Wherefore I beg their forgiveness. I send my most heartfelt greetings to all.

Given in Zayton in the year of Our Lord 1326, in the month of January.

Zayton was one of the bishoprics founded by Monte Corvino round 1313, after the arrival of the survivors from amongst the nine monks sent to him by the Curia. From Andrew of Perugia's reference to the fine church and excellent monastery in Zayton, it may be concluded that his work in this open-minded and intellectually wide-awake seaport bore fruit. And yet there is no mention of Christians in any contemporary Chinese account. Even when one of the Great Khan's vassals, King George of Tenduc, allegedly a descendant of Prester John, went over to Christianity with the major part of his people—

a really important occurrence which Monte Corvino himself was able
to report to Rome in 1305—no Chinese recorded this event. It is quite
patent that in medieval China, Christianity led only an esoteric existence,
in the margin, as it were, and unregarded. This outward insignificance
casts into even stronger relief the glorious figure of John of Monte
Corvino, who held undeviatingly to his faith and his mission in the face
of incomprehension or outright hostility and amidst an environment
which, though highly civilized, was so alien to him.

'I myself have grown grey and look like an old man,' he wrote rather
resignedly to Rome in 1305, 'although I am no more than fifty-nine. I speak
and write Tartar with perfect fluency. I have translated into this tongue
both the New Testament and the Psalter, and I have seen to it that they were
translated as beautifully as possible. In writing, reading and prayer I bear
public witness to Christ's doctrine of salvation . . .'

The Archbishop's activity in China was not entirely without effect,
however. In addition to the Great Khan himself, he was able, as he
states in his letters, to baptize and save for Christianity some five
thousand souls. In comparison with the huge population which China
already had in the Middle Ages this was few enough, and when George
of Tenduc died Monte Corvino had to watch his subjects gradually
abandon Christianity. Nevertheless, at his own death in *circa* 1330,
there were three Franciscan monasteries in Peking and one each in
Zayton, Kinsay, and Yang-sho-fu on the Yangtse Kiang. It is possible
that the number of converts amounted at this time to several hundred
thousand souls. None the less, Monte Corvino must have wondered
with concern what would become of his missionary work after his death.

After Monte Corvino, one further high Catholic cleric went to
China: the papal legate John of Marignola, who set out for the East
in 1338 and did not return to Europe till 1353, fifteen years later.
Then, in 1368, the nationalistic, xenophobe, and anti-ecclesiastical
Ming Dynasty came to power in China. With this, all possibility of
Western influence on the Middle Kingdom ended for a full three
hundred years.

John of Marignola left for China in December 1338, six months after
the arrival in Avignon of the embassy from Shun-ti described above.
He carried gifts for the Great Khan and an autograph letter from
Benedict XII. The Pope was clever enough to return a cordial answer
to the Great Khan's naive but honest epistle, though he made a point
of emphasizing his own dignity and high position. We may suppose
that, in writing his reply, the Pope was not uninfluenced by the entreaty

52.  Magic of the desert. A Mongolian camel-rider in the deathly solitude of the Gobi Desert.

53. In the desert of the Tarim Basin. Travellers on the old silk roads along the mountains visible in the background looked down with a shudder on this ocean of sand.

54. When Allah is angry he sends the simoom. Here it is breaking over the little oasis with gigantic clouds of sand-dust. In a moment darkness will fall upon the oasis. In a moment the scorching hot simoom will force its way in through the closed windows, clutching at the throats of the inhabitants with its strangling claws.

to avoid angering the Great Khan which can be read between the lines of the letter of Futim Yuens and his fellow princes.

So John of Marignola travelled to China. He has left a detailed and not uninteresting account of this journey in which, amongst other things, he writes:

We, Brother John of Florence of the Order of the Minorites, unworthy Bishop of Bysinia, were sent in the year of Our Lord 1338 by the Holy Father Benedict XII with letters and gifts from the Apostolic See, as legate to the Kaam, Great Emperor of all Tartars, whose dominion and power extends over almost half the Orient and a quite incredible multitude of countries, cities, peoples, tongues, and wealth. We left Avignon in the month of December [1338], came at the beginning of the season of fasting to Naples, and there awaited until Easter, which fell at the end of March, the arrival of a Genoese ship with the envoys from the Tartars, whom the Kaam of Cambalec, the greatest city of this people, had sent to the Pope to ask for legates to open the road and conclude an alliance with the Christians, for he loves and honours our faith.

Three years after our departure from the Papal Court we came to the borders of Armalec and to the Cyolloskagon, i.e. to the sand-mountains, which are formed by the wind and beyond which, before the Tartars, the land was not thought to be habitable, indeed it was not even believed that there was any land beyond. But the Tartars crossed them by the will of God and thereupon found themselves in a vast plain, which is called by the philosophers the hot terrestrial belt and is considered impassable. Nevertheless, the Tartars crossed it and I have also done so twice.

When the Great Khan saw our palfreys and other gifts together with the papal bulls and ourself, he evinced great joy, found everything good, or rather excellent, and showed us all possible honour. I appeared in priestly vestments with a very beautiful cross, which I caused to be borne before me with candles and incense, before the Kaam, who was seated in a splendid palace. I commenced to sing 'I believe in one God', and when the chant was at an end I gave him an ample blessing, which he received humbly. Hereupon we were conducted to an extremely well-furnished apartment in the Imperial Court, and two princes were allotted to us, who amply supplied us through servants of the Emperor with food and drink and every necessity, even including papyrus for lamps. For nearly four years these princes showed us all possible honour, provided both ourself and our servants with costly raiment, so that we, together with thirty-two persons, reckoning everything exactly, cost more than £400. Many religious disputations were held with Jews and others, but also many souls harvested. The Minorites also have a cathedral in Cambalec immediately next to the Palace, a splendid archbishopric, and several churches with bells, in the city, and all live from the Emperor's table in high honour.

The Emperor agreed very unwillingly to my departure and only when he saw that I was absolutely determined upon it; then, however, he gave me the expenses for three years and very important gifts to the Pope—but on condition that either myself or some other cardinal with appropriate authority should come back to Cambalec and be Bishop in the land, a dignity for which all the inhabitants of the Orient, whether Christians or not, have the greatest respect; the Bishop should also be of the Order of the Minorites. For these are the only clerics known to them . . .

Marignola goes on to describe the difficulties and dangers of his return (begun in 1345), mainly to give prominence to his own person and achievements. This renders his account a trifle repellent. All the same, his descriptions—e.g. of the Yangtse Kiang, the cities of Hang-chow (Kinsay), Zayton, where there were still three Christian churches in his day, or Columbum (Quilon), one of the centres of Indian pepper cultivation and trade, and of the flora of Ceylon with the Indian bread-tree, coconuts and bananas—are not without charm. Thus, for instance he relates of the Yangtse Kiang:

I have crossed it, and on its banks lie very large, splendid cities, especially rich in gold; on the river itself, however, the most skilful artists live permanently in wooden houses—principally weavers of silken and golden stuffs—in such numbers as are not to be found in the whole of Italy; they travel on the river with their houses, without changing them in any way, and taking their families with them, in order to work the silk, of which more grows on these banks than in the whole world. This I have seen . . .

Of Columbum, Marignola says:

On Palm Sunday 1357 I entered Columbum, the most famous city in the whole of India, where all the pepper in the world grows. It grows on creepers, which are planted exactly like vines and first produce wild grapes of a green colour. Thereupon a kind of grape forms containing red wine, which I have squeezed out on to the plate with my own hand as a condiment. Thereafter they ripen and dry on the trees. And when the immoderate heat of the sun has dried them hard, they are struck down with staves and collected on linen cloths spread out beneath. This I have seen with my own eyes and felt with my own hands throughout fourteen months. Pepper is not burnt, as has been erroneously stated, nor does it grow in deserts, but in gardens. And the owners thereof are not Saracens, but St. Thomas's Christians, who deduct from every pound which they send out into the world a tribute from which I, in accordance with my office as papal legate, drew every month a hundred, and at the end a thousand, *fan* of gold. There is in Columbum a Latin church of St. George, where I stayed and which I decorated with beautiful pictures and where I dispensed Christian instruction . . .

But despite his well-observed and often charmingly told accounts, and many indisputable personal merits, Marignola lacked the human qualities which enabled John of Monte Corvino to achieve such successes. At the same time it must be noted that the Emperor Shun-ti, a weak and feeble descendant of Kublai Khan, was manifestly not capable of giving the Curia's emissary any assistance. Things did not go well with China during his reign. There was a succession of droughts and poor harvests, and when some ten million Chinese died as the result of a terrible famine in 1334, Shun-ti could think of no other remedy than the issue of more and more paper money.

Even in his day this was patently an utterly inappropriate method of pacifying a despairing people and convincing it of the administrative ability of its leaders. Scarcely had Marignola left the Middle Kingdom when a revolt broke out against Shun-ti and the Mongols. In the endeavour to drive these dangerous foreigners from the land, everything that was not Chinese was indiscriminately destroyed or cast out. In the course of this rising, the Christian communities in China were exterminated, and various legates sent to China by Pope Urban V in 1370 and 1371 disappeared without a sound. Some relics of the Western religious tradition seem, however, to have survived the holocaust. For instance, Richard Hennig relates that a Jesuit Father working in China during the seventeenth century found a Bible written in Gothic script on parchment in the possession of a Chinese mandarin.

8

Here we must add an appendix concerning one of the most tormented personalities of the late Middle Ages: the Bavarian Hans Schiltberger from Frisingen near Munich, who took the field against the infidels as squire to the knight Leinhart Richartinger under King Sigmund in 1394, was taken prisoner by the enemy and returned home in 1427 after thirty-two years of captivity. Soon after his return, he wrote a brief account of his experiences in the distant Orient.

His adventures began at the battle of Nicopolis, 28th September 1396, between King Sigmund and Sultan Bajazet, in the course of which, according to Schiltberger, the Duke of Burgundy launched an untimely cavalry attack that carried him into the third line of the Turks, from which he could not extricate himself. The Christians suffered a crushing defeat, and the following day Sultan Bajazet had all the prisoners beheaded. Schiltberger was one of the few to survive, because the Sultan's son interposed on behalf of the sixteen-year-old lad. Schiltberger came to the Sultan's court, where he acted first as a running footman and later as an outrider.

I was taken to the palace of the Turkish king; there for six years I was obliged to run on my feet with the others, wherever he went, it being the custom that the lords have people to run before them. After six years I deserved to be allowed to ride, and I rode six years with him, so that I was twelve years with him. (*Travels of Johann Schiltberger*, translated by J. Buchan Telfer, The Hakluyt Society, 1879, p. 7.)

After relating an unsuccessful escape attempt and other events at the court of the Turkish ruler, Schiltberger goes on to describe the great battle at Angora on 20th July 1402 between the Mongol Timur Beg (Tamburlaine) and Bajazet I, in which the latter lost both land and life to Tamburlaine, while Schiltberger became a prisoner of the Mongols in place of the Turks.

Schiltberger had no doubt become hardened to grim sights during the past years. But Tamburlaine's hideous brutality still shocked him. Years later he described a scene which was typical of the Mongol Khan. Timur had taken the capital of Ispahan and occupied the town with a garrison. No sooner had he departed than the citizens rose against the foreign mercenaries and slew them. Timur halted his march and swept down on the rebellious city like a storm. And then began a gruesome slaughter.

He assembled all the citizens, and ordered all those over fourteen years to be beheaded, and the boys under fourteen years he ordered to be spared, and with the heads was constructed a tower in the centre of the city; then he ordered the women and children to be taken to a plain outside the city, and ordered the children under seven years of age to be placed apart, and ordered his people to ride over these same children. When his counsellors and the mothers of the children saw this, they fell at his feet, and begged that he would not kill them. He got angry, and rode himself amongst them and said: 'Now I should like to see who will not ride after me?' Then they were all obliged to ride over the children, and they were all trampled upon. There were seven thousand. Then he set fire to the city, and took the other women and children into his own city; and then went to his capital called Semerchant [Samarkand], where he had not been for twelve years. (*Travels of Johann Schiltberger*, translated by J. Buchan Telfer, The Hakluyt Society, 1879, pp. 27 f.)

This ghastly act of cruelty is imputed to Tamburlaine by several Oriental authors. Only Schiltberger mentions any unwillingness on the part of his followers to carry out his order; from what we know of them any such hesitation is unlikely!

After Tamburlaine's death Schiltberger came into the hands of his son, Shah Rokh, who lived at Herat in the kingdom of Khorasan. When a young Tartar prince residing at the court of Shah Rokh was recalled to his country to assume its sovereignty, Schiltberger was ordered to accompany him. After a long journey to Siberia he returned to Caffa (Feodosia in the Crimea). From here, he and four other Christian prisoners succeeded in fleeing to the sea, where they boarded a European ship; and after various further adventures he finally returned to Munich in 1427, aged almost fifty.

As this quick glance at Schiltberger's wanderings shows, he did not enter any country totally unknown in his day. He cannot, therefore, be looked upon as a discoverer. None the less, Hans Schiltberger could not be omitted from our narrative. For the account of his adventures, like Marco Polo's, found its way to a wide public with geographical interests during the late Middle Ages, and helped to prepare the West for the epoch of great discoveries that was soon to dawn. Schiltberger was not a personality of Marco Polo's calibre. But perhaps he should be appraised not according to his individual powers, but as a sign and symbol of those unnumbered thousands who were swept to and fro in the Orient as long as the crusades lasted, who somehow managed to get back to Europe in their old age, and here—most of them being unable to write—regaled any audience they could find with their adventures.

What a change took place in men during the period we have been discussing! At the outset the breadth of the world meant nothing to them. The narratives of Cosmas Indicopleustes and Fidelis lay unheeded in some monastery library; Ibn Batuta's reports were forgotten, and Marco Polo's scoffed at. Now people everywhere sat on the village greens or in the inns and taverns of the towns and listened open-mouthed to the travellers' tales. What new spirit had entered into them?

The spirit of *our* time was beginning to appear and making these men, a bare twenty generations before us, our true forebears. The Middle Ages were drawing to a close, the modern era was dawning.

With the story of the seaway to India—first sailed in search of an entry into Paradise, which was believed still to exist as a physical reality somewhere in the wastes of Asia, a story that now remains for us to tell—we enter into the no-man's-land of morning twilight between two epochs. Our narrative ends at the daybreak of a new age.

## PART ELEVEN

# THE PORTUGUESE AND AFRICA

*The first German menu card and old German recipes · Salt meat every day · Cold war against the West · Is Paradise in Abyssinia? · Europe's trade deficit with the East · Who were the Guanches and where did they come from? · Gold from Sofala · Malays discover Madagascar · Prince Henry the Navigator and Africa · Jean Mermoz flies through the Pot-au-Noir · Negro slaves, a sensation in Europe · Is the Senegal a tributary of the Nile? · The Portuguese and Prester John · Diego Cão stakes everything · Martin Behaim and the astrolabe · New directions for the voyage to Africa · Benedetto Dei in Timbuctoo · European inflation, the Centurione bank, and the gold standard · Antonio Malfante in the Sahara · Portugal plays two aces · The* Cabo Tormentoso *and Pedro de Covilhao's expedition · From the* Ploughman of Saaz *to the new era.*

# I

MOST of the previous chapters began with an ancient stone bearing runes or some other inscription; this time we start with a menu card. It is the first menu card mentioned in any European country, and the dishes listed on it are some centuries older than the card itself.

The first German menu card lay, during one of the many banquets at the Imperial Diet of 1555, beside Duke Henry of Brunswick, an enormously fat man and a gourmet. It was obviously Duke Henry's private invention, the outcome of a prudent agreement between himself and the Head Cook who had arranged this banquet.

All this was recorded by Henry's table-companion, Count Haug of Zimmern. He saw that the Duke of Brunswick had beside his plate a long card, which he continually consulted. So he asked Henry what this meant, and as the story appeared to him important he related it in his family annals, the *Zimmerian Chronicle*:

Duke Henry had a long card lying beside him on the table, which he frequently looked at. Count Haug sat opposite him and wondered why the Duke looked so often at the card; finally he plucked up courage and asked him. Then the Duke showed him the card. The Head Cook had written thereon all the foods and drinks in order. And Duke Henry was able to arrange his eating accordingly and save himself for the best dishes.

What a sly dog, thought Count Haug of Zimmern. But he too made diligent use of the Head Cook's card, and saved his appetite for the 'best dishes'.

What was written on this menu? Unfortunately, the chronicle does not tell us this. But we do know what dishes the people of the period found appetizing. For it is recorded in an old German cookery-book dating from the mid-fourteenth century, whose hundred or so recipes show the close attention paid to food in the Germany of that day. This cookery-book, published by the Stuttgart Literary Society in 1844 under the title *A Book of Good Food*, is a mine of terrestrial delights to the epicure. And yet it can be used only with the greatest caution. For its recipes are so strongly flavoured, so full of pepper, ginger, mint, cardamom, galingale, nutmeg, sage, parsley, caraway seed, saffron, aniseed, garlic, almonds, cloves, onions etc., that they would take our breath away and bring tears to our eyes.

Dishes like the ones in this cookery-book were certainly on Duke Henry's card, and we will give two of the most popular herewith:

*Fish Pasty.* To make a fish pasty, first scale the fish and skin them when they come to the boil. Chop them into small pieces, mix in chopped parsley and sage, and add plenty of pepper and ginger, mint and saffron. Moisten the whole mixture with wine. Make a thin, stiff dough and put the fish in it, pour the wine over them, and cover them with a thin layer of dough all over. Make a hole in the top and place a lid of dough over this hole. Then bake. The same can be done with chicken, as well as meat or game, eels or birds.

This must certainly have been one of the 'best dishes' for which Brunswick and the Count of Zimmern saved up their appetites. Another was very probably Stuffed Eels, an indispensable adjunct to the flowing bowl:

*Stuffed Eels.* Take fresh eels and clean the slime off with ashes. Loosen the skin at the head and pull it back to the tail. Chop sage and parsley and add plenty of ground ginger, pepper, aniseed and salt. Throw this over the eels and pull up the skin again. Sprinkle the eels with salt, roast thoroughly on a wooden spit, and serve.

This was no doubt a favourite dish. We should have found it absolutely uneatable, however, because we could never deal with such masses of pepper, ginger, salt and aniseed. We also make use of tart sauces, trimmings and condiments. But we exercise some moderation. In the recipes of five hundred years ago, on the other hand, the words 'take plenty' occur with unfailing regularity. The cooks of the day were manifestly wildly liberal with every kind of spice.

This did not spring from any inherent tendency to excess, but had a simple agrarian explanation. Before the introduction of root crops and the rotation of crops, European agriculture was not capable of providing sufficient winter fodder to sustain any number of beasts. Consequently, at the onset of the cold season, particularly in northern Europe, all livestock anything like ready for slaughter were slaughtered and salted down. To render this monotonous diet of salt meat palatable, it was enlivened with large quantities of spices. It must be remembered that the Middle Ages were unacquainted with either the potato or vegetables as we know them; all they had were a few types of cabbage.

It was the same with beverages. Coffee and tea were as unknown as cocoa. Wine was the drink of the rich. The middle classes drank small beer and more or less alcoholic fruit cordials that were turned into a kind of dubious punch by the addition of Oriental spices.

Thus every fairly well-to-do household used huge quantities of spices, which, in view of their prices, constituted a heavy financial burden. In addition, medicine at that time made copious use of spices. Each of the frequent epidemics was first combated by burning incense; when that failed, pills and electuaries were prescribed whose alleged curative properties were thought to be so much the greater the hotter and more nauseous they tasted, the more expensive they were, and the greater the distance from which their ingredients came. As a result of the number of middlemen involved in transporting these goods from the country of origin to the country of consumption, their prices were enormous. Whereas, for instance, 2 cwt. of pepper cost £50 in Marseilles in the thirteenth century, the same quantity cost £70 to £80 in England. This was an impossible state of affairs, and since there was no means of reducing Europe's predilection for Oriental and African commodities, the need to establish some direct connection with the producing countries to the south and east grew to such an extent that, by the end of the fifteenth century, the discovery of direct routes to these countries had become an urgent necessity for European States.

To this economic exigency was added an immediately political one. Not even the issue of edicts by the highest spiritual authority, the Papacy, had proved sufficient to break the Egyptian and Ottoman grip on overseas trade. Unless it were broken, however, Europe was permanently susceptible to an economic blockade. True, there could be no real threat to her basic food supply. But the Turks and Egyptians would have had no difficulty in cutting off her supply of spices, and this alone would have had incalculable consequences. After the fall of Constantinople in 1453, the Black Sea, one of the great gates to Asia, was closed. And after the Turks had conquered Egypt as well in 1517, Ottoman warships patrolled the whole of the Mediterranean. Something had to happen; some measures had to be taken by the State itself. Little Portugal was the first European State to recognize the necessity and shoulder the burden.

This was no easy matter for the poor, mainly agricultural State on the west coast of the Iberian peninsula. Whereas Aragon and Castile had long ago taken to sea and sent their ships on the Mediterranean and Flanders runs, Portugal had remained spiritually landlocked until the end of the fourteenth century, when, with English support, she achieved complete independence from Castile. And now a totally new development began. In 1415 the Portuguese captured the Arab city of Ceuta, one of the Pillars of Hercules, thereby gaining a springboard for the expeditions to Africa which they now undertook.

The desire to reduce the price of imported spices was, of course, only one of the causes of the sudden centring of universal interest on the Dark Continent towards the end of the Middle Ages. To begin with, indeed, religious motives were much more in the foreground. For when the rise of the Ming Dynasty in China put an end to Christian hopes of an Asian ally against Islam, when no 'Prester John' could be found in Asia, Europe's geographical interest quite logically switched to Africa, and the Vatican turned its attention to Abyssinia, whose king was, in fact, a Christian.

Abyssinia, the famous and mighty kingdom of Axum of the early Middle Ages, whose influence for a long time extended as far as southern Arabia, had become Christian as early as the fourth century of our era. This was no coincidence. For centuries the interest of the world had been concentrated on Abyssinia as the 'production centre' for war elephants, and when the Romans conquered Egypt they too began to pay heed to the southern highland. First came surveyors, who mapped the strange country. They were followed by merchants and traders. The latter gradually grouped themselves in Christian communities and so initiated the Christianization of Abyssinia during the third century. According to legend, the word of Christ was already brought to Abyssinia by St. Matthew, who died there a martyr's death. But it was only in 350 that Christianity was elevated to the State religion—about the same time as Arabia too was converted to Christianity. But whereas in the latter country the Christian doctrine gained only a temporary foothold and did not survive the appearance of Mahomet, Abyssinia remained loyal to Christianity, though in the, to us, alien form of the Coptic Church. It is one of the few regions of Africa and Asia that has adhered to the Christian doctrine for more than a millennium and a half.

The link between Europe and Abyssinia was not broken until the rise of Mahomet and the conquest of Egypt by the Arabs in the middle of the seventh century. Then, however, the strange land became almost inaccessible and the subject of a luxuriant crop of legends. True, direct connections between Abyssinia and the Vatican appear to have persisted even then, despite all dangers—in 1267, indeed, the Dominicans were explicitly requested by the Pope to send missionaries to Abyssinia. None the less, the mystery surrounding the country made it the obvious place to site the enigmatic realm of Prester John, now that Asia was out of the running. By the end of the fourteenth century, even the Curia seems to have adopted this view. It was now considered definite that Prester John and the ancient Paradise of the Bible, placed under his administration by God and believed by medieval man to be an existent physical reality, must be located in Abyssinia and nowhere else.

Since it soon became impossible to get to Abyssinia by way of Egypt, because of the hostility of the Arabs, it was logical to ask whether it might not be possible to reach Prester John from north of West Africa. This was an additional reason for the interest in the Dark Continent which began to be felt in Europe during the late Middle Ages. The third reason was once more of an economic character—gold!

After North Africa went over to Islam, a state of perpetual war at first prevailed between the two opposing shores of the Mediterranean, which led to predatory incursions and raids on both sides. But the two continents were so economically complementary to one another and Africa's interest in the enormously lucrative market of densely-populated Europe so direct and so pressing, that after the eleventh century a complex system of agreements existed between the Tunisian and Moroccan Sultanates on the one hand and the Sicilian Norsemen and the Spanish and Italian mercantile cities on the other, which almost completely eliminated military disturbances. And now trade started to flow. It is true that exports from Africa were not nearly so manifold and colourful as those from Asia: they were confined in the main to gold, ivory, Negro slaves, pepper and ebony. Quantitatively, however, they certainly surpassed the latter, while in value they at least equalled them. Gold came principally from the Senegal and the Niger. It was taken first to Timbuctoo on the southern fringe of the Sahara and went from here by one of two caravan routes to Marrakesh. A third route, which forked at Tuat with branches to Oran and Constantine, afforded a direct link between Timbuctoo and the Mediterranean littoral.

The market for Oriental and African goods in Europe was considerably greater than the capacity of Africa and the East to absorb European exports, so that the possibility of trade by barter was soon exhausted. Hence there was no alternative but to pay for Oriental imports with precious metal. This led, just as it had in Diocletian's day, to a severe drain on Europe's gold reserves, and during the fourteenth and fifteenth centuries the point was reached when the gold- and silver-mines of the Old World were no longer capable of replacing its annual monetary losses to the Orient. At this period three hundred thousand ducats of gold a year, an enormous sum, were shipped to Alexandria by Venetian galliasses alone. This resulted in the doubling of the value of gold as compared with corn in Europe. What this meant for the broad mass of peasants, craftsmen and day-labourers is shown by the fact, disclosed by the German mineralogist Heinrich Quiring, that at this period a miner in the gold-mines of Reichenstein in the Glatz highlands had to work fifty shifts to earn one gold piece. This was naturally a further incentive to European interest in Africa.

As we know from records, many voyages were made along the East and West African coasts. But none of them brought any extensive knowledge of the Dark Continent. Without the lure of gold they would never have been undertaken. The waterless seaboard of North Africa was too inhospitable to invite geographical investigation, so that the geographic importance of these voyages was small. One piece of success, however, the skippers who made these voyages did achieve: the rediscovery of the Canary Islands. Previous sections of this narrative have told us that the Canaries were already known to early antiquity. In particular, they were frequently visited by the Phœnicians, who obtained from them the 'dragon's blood' and dyer's lichen (litmus) used in the production of Tyrian purple. No doubt the Greeks too knew these islands in the Ocean. But then oblivion descended on the blossoming, fruitful isles. Throughout the Middle Ages they seem to have been totally unknown. This is hardly credible. The Peak of Tenerife is visible from a great distance and the smoke billowing from its crater can be seen from the West African coast. The Arabian geographer Idrisi refers to it, and one would have expected some ship or other to have sailed far enough westward to see where the smoke was coming from. Since, however, there is no record of any such reconnaissance, we are left to assume from the sudden appearance of the Canaries on charts of the early fourteenth century that this group of islands was first rediscovered in the late Middle Ages.

When this took place the Canaries were inhabited by a scarcely civilized, fair, blue-eyed, manifestly Nordic people, the Guanches, who died out during the seventeenth century. When and how these people came to the island remains unexplained. It is possible that the Guanches were an offshoot of the wave of Indo-European peoples which seems to have swamped Europe in the third century B.C.; it is possible that they were Goths or Vandals cast up on the Canaries by accident, who then deteriorated into the tribe of naked savages described in the earliest reports from the mid-fourteenth century.

Madeira was probably also rediscovered round this time. Scholars are not yet able to tell us who made the discovery or when it took place. Here too we can only infer from the inclusion of Madeira in early maps that it must have been round about 1350. Beyond this we are completely in the dark.

The finding of Madeira and the Canaries at the beginning of the fourteenth century was followed by numerous voyages to these groups of islands, in the course of which geographical knowledge of the north-west African coasts was undoubtedly deepened. It is unlikely, however, that they extended beyond Cape Bojador on latitude 26° N. Anyhow, nothing of the coastal regions south of this point is shown on the maps of the period.

The Middle Ages possessed a clearer picture of the eastern than of the western seaboard of Africa. For one thing the East African coast was not nearly so dangerous to navigate as that of the West, for another the area as far as Cape Corrientes on latitude 27° S. had been sailed since early times. The Mozambique Current between Madagascar and the African coast long constituted an insuperable obstacle. Ships wishing to return northwards had to describe a wide arc down to the south and up past the east of Madagascar. The Arabs seem to have been the first, a great deal later, to cope with the swift Mozambique Current. Even then, they cannot have got much beyond Sofala on latitude 20° S., and certainly no farther than Cape Corrientes. Sofala itself, however, was of great importance to the Arabs, for it was here that the *Zandj*, as the Arabs called the Negroes, used to bring the gold from the deep hinterland. At Sofala it was taken over by the Arabs and transported north. Naturally, this was common knowledge in the West—all the more so since the gold ingots of Sofala were universally renowned for their purity. There was no need to treat them with mercury, as had to be done with the less-pure West African gold. It is not impossible that some European made a personal visit to Sofala; Jews in particular were great travellers at this period. There is, however, no record of any European expedition into these waters until a good two hundred years later, when the first Europeans succeeded in circumnavigating Africa as the Phœnicians had done under Pharaoh Necho in *circa* 600 B.C.

Here we must briefly consider a geographical and navigational feat that was launched not from Europe and its sphere of culture, but from Malayo-Polynesia: the discovery of Madagascar, to which allusion has already been made. This island, despite its considerable size, remained unknown to Europe until the beginning of the sixteenth century, when the Portuguese skippers Coutinho and Lopes landed there by chance.

It had been discovered and peopled something like a millennium and a half earlier, however, round about the time of the birth of Christ—and right across the vast expanse of the Indian Ocean. At about this period a Greek navigator and adventurer came to Madagascar and found there a highly civilized population of manifestly Malayan origin. Admittedly, we have no other documentary evidence, and it was not until much later, in the twelfth century, that Idrisi described the trade relations and travel between Java and Madagascar as follows:

The people of Madagascar possess no ocean-going vessels; ships come to them from Oman and elsewhere. They then sail on to the islands of Dja-vaga [Java], which form part of the isles of India. The foreign seafarers exchange their wares for those of the Malagasies. The people of the islands of Djavaga come to them on barques and large ships and export their wares, for they understand one another's languages.

This account by Idrisi dates from 1144. Its meaning is clear: Direct trade was still carried on between Java and Madagascar in Idrisi's day; both peoples spoke the same language; both peoples were in contact with Sofala and East Africa, but the Malagasies did not make long voyages because they possessed no large ships. The original clothing of the Malagasies consisted of sarong and *lamba*; their weapon was the blowpipe; the outrigger canoe was their seagoing craft as in Malayo-Polynesia; rice and sugar-canes were cultivated in Madagascar as in Indonesia; and as in Indonesia, social life was hedged about by taboos, fixed and inviolable religious prohibitions. And Ibn Said, an Arab geographer who lived before Idrisi, states explicitly that the Malagasies once immigrated from Indonesia.

It may, therefore, be assumed that a considerable proportion of the population of Madagascar originally came to this island all the way across the sea from Indonesia. If ethnographic and linguistic evidence did not unanimously support this hypothesis, it would certainly be dismissed as fallacious. But there are still nearly a million brown people living in Madagascar whose close kinship with the Malays is indisputable. How their forebears, who came to the island in successive waves of immigration from the first century A.D. to the tenth or eleventh, managed to cross the enormous stretch of water between Java and Madagascar in primitive and, in our judgment, unseaworthy craft is a complete enigma. But they did. Not once and by chance, but in many scores of journeys. And these were no audacious ventures carried out by some bold ship's crew, but expeditions involving numbers of boats laden with women and children and household paraphernalia. If anything is calculated to show that various parts of the world were settled by people who sailed immense distances to reach their new home, it is the story of the colonization of Madagascar. In most cases, unfortunately, the tracks have been so much obliterated that, although we suspect these migrations of having taken place, they cannot be proved with certainty.

2

The various voyagers to Africa would have produced little tangible or lasting result had it not been for the intervention of the Portuguese government in the person of the Infante, Prince Henry of Portugal, whom history honoured with the title 'Henry the Navigator'.

In 1415, at the age of twenty-one, he played a decisive part in the capture of Ceuta. This set the key for the rest of his career. Portugal's development into a maritime nation was entirely his handiwork.

At the outset, like a true child of the Middle Ages, he pinned his faith to the legend of Prester John and the pious fairy-tale that the Paradise of the Bible still existed somewhere in the remote wastelands of the earth. The prodigious treasures which fell into his hands after the capture of Ceuta seem to have inspired in him the wish to reach the lands of their origin. It was altogether in keeping with his epoch that this automatically conjured up the shadowy figure of the legendary priest-king. Political conditions ruled out any possibility of reaching him via the Nile and the Red Sea. The Mohammedan blockade of the eastern route had long since become impassable. An organized advance along the caravan trails of the Sahara seemed, according to Prince Henry's reports, to offer equally little prospect of success, since the losses of men and beasts were likely to approach 90 per cent. Hence there was no alternative but to reconnoitre the third way—out on to the sea and along the coasts of Africa to the south.

The first of Prince Henry's voyages of exploration did not achieve any particular fame and gained little fresh information. But in 1432 the Infante dispatched an expedition of several caravels with instructions to find out whether there was any land in the western ocean. It is possible that this expedition was prompted by obscure rumours put about by unknown seafarers to the effect that they had seen land in the ocean; it is possible that Prince Henry was incited by the imaginative mapmakers who dotted the Atlantic with a multitude of islands; it is possible that he was so gripped by the idea of the earth's spherical shape that he too was beginning to feel his way towards the west.

Whatever the motive, however, the Azores were discovered—or rediscovered, since Carthaginian ships almost certainly landed on the Azores as early as 320 B.C.—by Portuguese ships in 1432.

It is easy to imagine the stir caused in Portugal by this voyage of discovery; its encouraging psychological effect may well have contributed to the circumnavigation two years later (1434) of the notorious Cape Bojador. The ancient legend, transmitted by the Arabs, that the Sea of Darkness, the end of the world, began immediately south of this clearly defined point was probably more of an obstacle to passing it than the strong current and the heavy surge which pours foaming and thundering over the reefs and banks that jut far out into the sea in this area. Anyone reading the ancient descriptions of this gloomy region in the tranquillity of his study, or remembering them as he steams calmly southwards far to the west of the shore on one of our great passenger liners, will be inclined to dismiss all this with a smile. But the man who, rather like the first European seafarers to pass this spot, flew by on his way to South America in one of the fragile aeroplanes of the thirties, must have remembered the 'Sea of Darkness' with a shudder. We owe to the biographer of the French ocean-flier Jean Mermoz, who in 1935, after many successful flights, disappeared in the lowering cloud-bank of the *Pot-au-Noir* on his way back from South America, a very striking description of this infernal region:

In the last shimmer of daylight Mermoz saw a huge black wall rise up in front of him out of the red and green glitter of the sea. The funereal blackness of the cloudbank of the 'Pot-au-Noir' seemed to merge with the surface of the ocean. But as he drew closer Mermoz thought he could make out a narrow break between the dark surface of the ocean and the beginning of the cloud. He headed his plane towards this break. He soon realized that to slip through here would be the most difficult thing he had to do in all this witches' sabbath of swirling darkness into which his wings cut like a sword. In the depths of this world without light he could distinguish columns of water, sombre masses that took on the shape of gigantic beasts, monstrous castles and infernal abysses. All these intangible black shapes whirled round in an endless gyration, as though seized by a perpetual and senseless haste. It was like a tornado without wind. Bottomless craters yawned, filled up with cloud and a few seconds later spewed fresh avalanches from their sides in horrible silence.

The plane had been flying for hours through this darkness split with fiery flashes, when all of a sudden a shower of boiling hot water streamed into the machine. Threatened from all sides, Mermoz had been unable to avoid flying into a burst of torrential rain that felt like molten lava. The cockpit was inundated. Suffocating steam caught the three men by the throat. They were tormented by thirst. Mermoz, who was the first to be struck and who had been subjected to enormous physical strain, suffered more than his companions. Yet the safety of all of them depended upon his every manœuvre. The machine vibrated, shook, fell and slipped into unseen traps. At the price of three human lives he must not lose control of it for a single second. A second stream of water broke over them, forced its way into the engine, strangled and drowned it.

Sea and cloud must have offered very much the same appearance to the skippers who sought to circumnavigate Cape Bojador five hundred years ago. After several attempts the Portuguese succeeded in rounding this cape, and to their astonishment they found that south of this danger spot there was neither a gelatinous, congealed sea in which they stuck fast, nor did loathsome sea monsters drag their ships down into the depths, nor were any of them turned black by the scorching rays of the sun. But so deep-rooted were all these nightmare tales, very largely inherited from antiquity, that Prince Henry had to exercise direct personal pressure before his captains would obey him and sail round the frightful cape.

This great achievement, though its actual results were very modest, broke the ice. Seven years later the Portuguese got as far as Cape Blanco. And this expedition brought back Negroes, who caused a sensation because although Europe was familiar with brown-skinned Arabs and Indians, it knew nothing of really black-skinned peoples. It is true that Negroes had occasionally cropped up in the European slave-trade; there is even a record of a respectable French colonial pioneer who brought a black wife and black servants back from Africa with him. Apparently, however, the Negroes were regarded as merely dark 'sports' of brown ethnic groups. Only now did Europe realize that there was a genuinely black race in Africa. This was an extremely sensational discovery, and there was no dearth of voices to declare that these thick-lipped, woolly-haired bipeds were animals. The view won no general acceptance, however, and so trade in 'black ivory' began. Only if they were human could these creatures be saved from everlasting damnation and converted to Christianity, thus making it a Christian act to bring Negro slaves from Africa. This does not imply that there was no trade in slaves before this moral double-somersault was devised. Nor did every Negro taken as a slave have a bad time. Since slaves represented a capital investment and perhaps considerable profits, both slave-dealer and slave-keeper had every interest in treating their property as well as possible. None the less, the slave-trade, which was for many centuries an inseparable concomitant of the white man's discovery

of the earth, is a highly unpleasant chapter of history. Anyone wishing
to set a date to its commencement would not be wrong in noting this
year 1441.

Four years later, in 1445, another sensation followed. A Portuguese
ship discovered the Senegal, whereupon it was universally assumed
that the western branch-estuary of the Nile, whose existence had been
repeatedly conjectured by the ancient world, had at last been reached.
To navigators who had set out in quest of a waterway to Prester John,
this discovery was naturally of prime importance, particularly as Prince
Henry had predicted to his skippers that they would find the western
estuary of the Nile south of the desert region. The Senegal, or at least
the fact that there was a big river in north-west Africa, was known in
Europe in the circles of learned cartographers through the reports of
Arab travellers. Hence there is nothing surprising about Prince Henry's
prediction. Oddly enough, however, the Portuguese do not seem at
first to have made any serious attempt to penetrate the African interior
along the Senegal or the Gambia, which was discovered shortly after.
Not until ten years later do we hear that a Genoese captain in the
service of Portugal, Antonio Usodimare, sailed up the Gambia.

In 1446 the Portuguese reached Cape Verde, the 'green' cape. This
expedition too caused a sensation. While the desolate sandy coasts
hitherto encountered bore out the statements of the ancient geographers
that sun-scorched, sterile and uninhabitable zones lay south of the
temperate latitudes, there now appeared traces of vegetation which
increased in luxuriance the farther south they went. Hence a contemporary observer of the Infante's enterprises, the Portuguese Diego
Gomez, governor of the castle of Cintra, was able to write on hearing
of this discovery:

Ptolemy divided the world into three parts, to wit an inhabited part in
the centre of the world, a northern part which was not inhabited on account
of the excessive cold, and a part on the equator which was uninhabitable
because of the excessive heat. We have now found the situation to be quite
the reverse. For we have seen that the northern zone is inhabited right up to
the Pole, while on the equator there live Negroes, the number of whose
tribes is almost past believing. And the southern part is full of trees and
fruits, of course of strange kinds, and the trees are of almost incredible girth
and height . . .

On top of this was the fact that the coast turned from its original
south-westerly direction and began to run south-east. From this it was
hopefully inferred that the southern tip of the Dark Continent would
soon be reached.

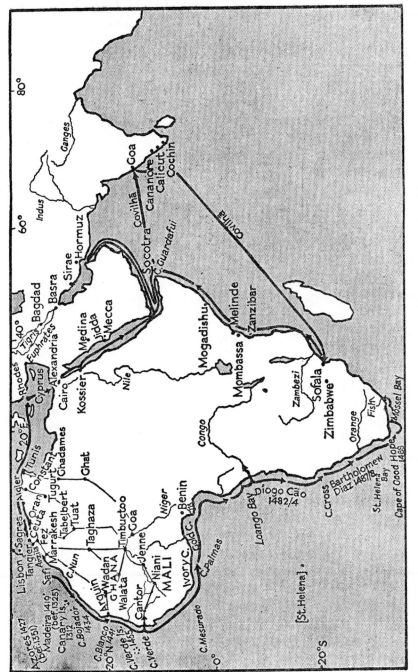

XXXI. *Portuguese voyages of discovery round Africa.*

Up to 1446 Prince Henry had dispatched and financed more than fifty ships on voyages to the south. But apart from a few scientific sensations nothing had been gained thereby, and it is understandable that at this period the Infante enjoyed more notoriety than renown amongst his countrymen. True, he had succeeded in flattering Portuguese national pride, and it must have suited his book that Danes, Germans and Italians applied to him for permission to serve in his exploration fleet. But this did not alter the fact that by the end of the 1450's the Prince was head over ears in debt. Moreover, his expeditions had caused friction with Castile, who also laid claim to the West African coast—friction which led ultimately to a three years' war between Portugal and Castile. This dispute was terminated in 1455 by a decision on the part of Pope Nicholas V, whom the two parties had called in as arbitrator. He awarded the African discoveries to the Portuguese, and therewith the door to fresh ventures was opened to Henry the Navigator.

In the same year, therefore, a caravel put out for Africa under the command of the Genoese Antonio Usodimare. Prince Henry seems to have needed a widely visible, directly practical success. Hence he gave the Genoese instructions to sail up the Gambia, so as at last to reach Abyssinia and Prester John. Apparently Usodimare actually did sail up the Gambia, though of course in vain. He got to within a mere three hundred miles of Prester John's kingdom, he declared somewhat boastfully and quite inaccurately. Unfortunately he could not proceed any farther owing to the hostility of the natives, who peppered his ship with poisoned arrows. So he had to turn back. It appears that Usodimare himself firmly believed he was only a short distance from Abyssinia. He even gave the name of the reigning priest-king. He was called John V, reported Usodimare, and since he claimed to have spoken to soldiers of this John V, his statement must have sounded quite convincing to people at home. Usodimare cannot have penetrated very far up the Gambia. At all events, he says nothing of the celebrated city of Cantor in the neighbourhood of the Barracunda Rapids, from which point on the Gambia, then as now, becomes impassable to vessels of any size.

Two years later, in 1457, Cantor was reached by another Portuguese expedition. At Cantor the Portuguese heard about Timbuctoo, whose name was continually in the mouths of Arab caravan leaders from the Sahara, and learnt that numerous merchants from Fez, Tunis, Cairo and other towns on the North African coast went there to purchase gold.

The Portuguese were now more convinced than ever that they were close to the land of Prester John.

Prince Henry the Navigator did not live to see any further expeditions to Africa. First his hands were tied by lack of money, then he was occupied by a fresh war with the Moors. He had no further opportunity of putting his plans into execution before his sudden death in 1460 at the age of sixty-six.

Now followed a long interruption in Portugal's maritime development. Although Prince Henry had established a school of navigation at Lagos, equipped with all the nautical aids of the period, where a race of tough, bold and well-trained navigators was produced, the brain of the African expeditions was missing and Portugal vacillated irresolutely, unable to make up her mind what to do. This uncertainty seems to have led the Portuguese to inquire from the leading scientific authority of the late fifteenth century, the Florentine geographer and physician Toscanelli, whether it would not be possible to reach India by sailing west across the Atlantic Ocean. There is unfortunately no record of the wording of this inquiry. But Toscanelli's reply is extant. It states quite definitely that a ship sailing across the western ocean would quite soon come to land and that this land would be the east coast of Asia. Since the earth was a sphere it was certainly possible to reach Asia by crossing the great sea.

This was the period when Portugal made her attempt to get to Asia via the far north, along the old Viking routes. We have already heard of Corte Real, who accompanied the Pining-Pothorst expedition. But his reports on the new lands west of the ocean cannot have sounded very promising; moreover, at just this juncture, 1473, all profits from trade with West Africa, in particular those accruing from pepper, slaves, ivory and gold, were assigned to the Portuguese heir apparent (who later became King John II) as his personal property. Hence he had a direct interest in seeing that some mercantile utility was at last derived from the expeditions to Africa initiated by the Infante Henry.

In the middle of December 1481, therefore, a fleet of several ships commanded by his trusted captain Diego Cão set sail for Africa. Four weeks later, this expedition landed on the Gold Coast somewhat to the east of the present Cape Three Points and there founded the fort and town of Elmina. After completing this task, Diego Cão sailed on southwards to Cape Santa Maria almost on latitude 14° S. We can follow his journey exactly because Cão marked it himself. Since 1467 all Portuguese skippers entering unexplored areas had instructions to set up wooden crosses at prominent positions along the coast, with inscriptions recording their presence. Wooden crosses soon proved inadequate in the humid heat of the tropics. Cão therefore carried marble crosses on board. Three of these crosses were found in the course of the nineteenth century. One was immediately south of the Congo estuary, another on Cape Santa Maria in Benguela in Portuguese West Africa, the last, set up during a second voyage by Diego Cão in 1485–6, on Cape Cross at 22° S., slightly north of the Swakop estuary.

All the inscriptions on these crosses, which bore the arms of the King of Portugal, were heavily weathered; but that on the Cape Cross stone could be deciphered. It reads:

6685 years had passed since the creation of the world, 1485 since the birth of Christ, when His Most Illustrious and Serene Highness King John of Portugal ordered this pillar to be erected here by his knight Diego Cão.

A further piece of evidence for this voyage to the far south we owe to the Nuremberg patrician Martin Behaim of Schwarzbach, who, as a young merchant, happened to pass through Lisbon on a commercial trip in the summer of 1484. Behaim's real province was the Flanders trade; he had been to sea on several occasions himself, so that he was extremely interested when the Nuremberg mathematician Regiomontanus, who may have been a friend of the family, demonstrated to him the use of the astrolabe. This very important precursor of the sextant was not yet very widely known at the end of the fifteenth century. It was totally unfamiliar to the Portuguese. They naturally realized the value of an instrument that made it possible to calculate a ship's position, and when King John of Portugal heard that the young German merchant knew how to use an astrolabe he quickly invited him to join his *Junta dos matemáticos,* an astronomico-nautical learned society. And when Cão returned successfully from his first expedition, Behaim offered his services as nautical adviser on any further voyage.

The famous navigator's second voyage began in 1485 and ended nineteen months later in 1486; it took him at least as far as Cape Cross, where the aforesaid column was found. Of this expedition a short inscription on the terrestrial globe made later by Martin Behaim states:

When 1484 years were numbered since the birth of Christ Our Lord, His Serene Highness King John II had two ships, called caravels, fitted out in Portugal with a crew, victuals and arms sufficient for three years. The men and ships were given in the King's name the order to sail out beyond the pillars which Hercules set in Africa, always towards the south and towards the rising sun, as far as they could. The said King also supplied the ships with all kinds of goods and merchandise for buying and selling.

The most striking point in this report is the statement that Cão's second expedition had orders to sail always towards the south and, if possible, towards the rising sun, to the east. Hitherto the instructions given to the leaders of expeditions had doubtless been to seek a route to Prester John, i.e. to get to Abyssinia along the alleged western arm of the Nile. There is no further mention of this here. The expedition is to head south and east, it says, and the only possible interpretation of Martin Behaim's text is that the sole and unequivocal aim of the Portuguese expedition was now the circumnavigation of Africa.

What can have caused this change of objective? Why does all mention of the famous priest-king's name suddenly cease? Was he no longer necessary as an aid to propaganda? Perhaps the solution to this problem is to be found in the simple fact of Cão's having reached such high southerly latitudes (for despite their primitive means of measuring the altitude of the sun, the Portuguese can have been in no doubt that they had come farther south than, to their knowledge any European before them). Under no circumstances could Prester John be found here; in Africa as in Asia he vanished like a puff of smoke. He was no further use, and this veil which Henry the Navigator had wrapped round his first African ventures fell empty to the ground. Cão was well aware of this, and the fact that his second expedition was pushed a full eight degrees farther south than his first allows us to surmise that, at this second attempt, he aimed to circumnavigate Africa. Since his fleet was equipped for a three years' voyage, there was every possibility that the fame of being the first to round the Cape of Good Hope would fall to Cão. Why this expedition was broken off after only nineteen months is unknown. Probably, as is now supposed, he fell ill, or even died, on the voyage. He is never alluded to again, even by Martin Behaim.

3

Here we must digress for a moment. Our narrative up to now may have given the impression that the exploration of Africa by the white man was confined exclusively to the sea. As far as the Portuguese are concerned this is perfectly correct. As they proceeded entirely systematically and for reasons of State, they were clear from the outset that Africa could never be mastered along the land route, and that the belt of the Sahara was an utterly impassable barrier to enterprises on any scale.

This does not mean, however, that North Africa was a totally unknown and untrodden area. In the high Middle Ages, North Africa,
like Siberia or central Asia, was regularly crossed by caravans and also
accessible to white travellers and merchants. We should know nothing
of this were it not for the chance survival of a private letter from the
otherwise unknown Florentine merchant, Benedetto Dei, dating from
the 1470's and stating quite casually that in 1470 he travelled to Timbuctoo, 'a city in the kingdom of the Berbers'. This is all the more
astonishing as there is no further mention of any European journeying
to Timbuctoo, the 'Queen of the Sahara', until four centuries later,
when the Hamburg explorer Heinrich Barth reached the city in 1853.
Until then this great desert city of caravans had remained as inaccessible to all *giaour*, or Christians, as Mecca. In Benedetto's day there seem
to have been no difficulties. The Florentine patently did not consider
his journey anything remarkable. He was certainly not impelled to
make it by any interest in geography. Instead of relating how and by
what route he traversed the sand-sea of the Sahara, all he actually tells
us is that there was a trade in thick Lombardy cloths in Timbuctoo.
Since Benedetto Dei shows no particular restraint in the rest of his
letter, but cheerfully boasts of his other achievements, the casual way
in which he speaks of what one would have thought to be his really
great feat of travel leaves one to infer that in his day Timbuctoo was
a well-known centre frequently visited by caravans and not worth
talking about at any length. We may safely assume that in North Africa
too, despite the difficulties and dangers, trade and traffic were much
more widespread than we know for sure.

Whereas Benedetto Dei was purely a merchant with no concern for
the country and its people, but only interested in disposing of his
goods, a man of quite a different stamp was in the Sahara in 1450,
twenty years before him: the banking expert and prospector Antonio
Malfante of Genoa. He did not go as far as Timbuctoo, but only to the
oasis of Tuat. There was no need for him to go farther to learn what
he wanted—namely that there was no gold in the Sahara and that the
Arab gold-caravans arriving at the North African seaboard came from
territories very far to the south.

Malfante did not travel on his own account, but on behalf of the
Genoese banking and mercantile firm of Centurione, which, with its
branches in Genoa, Caffa in the Crimea, Mallorca, Lisbon, Rouen,
Antwerp, Bruges and Bristol, was of world-wide importance in the
mid-fifteenth century. The business of this firm was hard hit by the
rapid flow of precious metals to the Middle and Far East and by the

political upheavals brought by the fifteenth century—the Hundred Years War between France and England, the turmoil in Germany, and the collapse of the Eastern Roman (Byzantine) Empire, which led to the capture of Constantinople by the Turks. For the shortage of money, which was becoming increasingly apparent, resulted in every Elector and King striking new coins the moment he came to power, and these new coins were invariably of less intrinsic worth than their predecessors although bearing the same face value. European currency relationships were everywhere in confusion, the value of money was falling everywhere, interest was everywhere centred on 'real values', supra-national trade relations were maintained with difficulty by clearing-house agreements—in short, inflationary tendencies were making themselves felt with ominous force.

These currency disturbances may have been very advantageous for the development of European art; there is much to be said for the thesis sometimes advanced that these inflationary phenomena led to capital going into 'real values', i.e. to the building of showy houses and the purchase of paintings, sculpture and expensive jewellery, which were regarded as 'investments'. This condition of scarcely veiled inflation was, in the long run, as vexatious for the great banking houses of the period as it was dangerous for the kings and emperors, who were threatened by the drop in the real income of their subjects and their own mounting bank-debts. Displeasure at the universal situation seems to have made itself most strongly felt in highly capitalistic northern Italy. Anyhow, it was decided in Genoa in 1447 by a committee of experts under the ægis of the Centurione to introduce the gold standard. And as a logical sequel to this measure the Centurione dispatched its delegate, Antonio Malfante, to the Sahara the same year to ascertain what part of the African interior the gold exported to Europe really came from and whether there was any chance of taking a direct hand in the sale of production of gold.

Malfante was, therefore, a kind of prospector, though not an adventurer of the type we are familiar with from stories of the Sacramento or Klondyke gold rushes. Naturally, this Genoese was not without an adventurous streak. But he was an aristocrat; hence his Sahara expedition, which took him to the Tuat oasis, had a chivalrous rather than a purely commercial tinge. Malfante has left us a very vivid description of his journey in a letter to his friend Giovanni Marioni of Genoa. He writes:

As soon as we had left the sea behind us at Honein [probably the port of Tlemcen in Algeria], we set off to the south and rode for some twelve days. For seven days on end we saw no dwellings. Everything was sandy plains, like the sea; by day we took our direction from the sun, by night from the stars. When these seven days were passed, we found a fortified settlement [the oasis of Tabalbert]. Its inhabitants are very poor; their sole nourishment consists of water and the few products of their barren soil. They do not sow much, but they have enough dates to keep them alive.

So we came via the aforesaid fortified village to Tuat. Tuat consists of eighteen oligarchically ruled settlements surrounded by one wall. And the head of each settlement defends its interests whether or not right is on his side; for although they all border upon one another, each one seeks to win for itself as much credit as possible. And if any traveller comes here, one of the heads of the settlements immediately becomes his protector and will defend him to death. Thus merchants are in perfect safety here, I should say much safer than in the kingdoms of Tlemcen or Tunis.

I am a Christian, yet no one has spoken ill to me, and they say they have never seen a Christian before. It is true that at the beginning, when I first arrived, I was much irritated by the fact that everyone wanted to look at me and cried out in surprise: 'This Christian has a face just like us!' For they believed that Christians had deformed faces. Their curiosity was quickly assuaged, and I walk about everywhere without anyone speaking ill to me.

There are many Jews here. They live a good life, for they enjoy the protection of the heads of the settlements, and each of the latter actively supports his protégés. And so they have a peaceful existence. Trade here is in their hands and a great many of them are trusted by everyone.

This place is a stage on the way to the land of the Moors, to which merchants travel with their wares to sell them. They bring gold here, which they sell to those who come from the coast. The place here is called De Amamento [Tamentit], and there are many wealthy people here. Nevertheless, the mass of the people are extremely poor, because nothing can be sown and nothing is reaped except dates, on which they live. The only meat is that of gelded camels. It is very rare but of excellent flavour.

The Arabs, with whom we journeyed hither from the coast, bring corn and barley to Tamentit and they sell it throughout the year at the price of five florins in Saracen currency.

It never rains here. If it did, the people's houses would be destroyed, for they consist of a framework of salt and reeds. It never freezes here either. In summer it becomes so exceedingly hot that the people here are almost black. The children of both sexes go naked until their fifteenth year. The natives here profess the Mohammedan faith. Round about there are a hundred and fifty to two hundred oases.

Through the countries in the south there flows a very big river, which at certain times of the year floods those regions. This river goes past Tambet [Timbuctoo] and comes from Egypt. It is the river which flows into the sea at Cairo. There are many barks on it with which they trade. It is said that it would be possible to travel down to Egypt on this river, if there were not one point at which it drops down 300 ells deep over a cliff. No ship can pass this waterfall either up or down. From here to this river is twenty days' journey on horseback.

The people here, if I have heard aright, are neighbors of the Indians. Indian merchants come here and make themselves understood by means of interpreters. These Indians are Christians and worshippers of the cross.

I have asked often enough where the gold is found and collected. My protector answered me: 'I spent fourteen years amongst the Negroes and always kept my ears open. But I never found anyone who could state from certain knowledge, "I have seen it thus, or it is found and collected so." Therefore it must be assumed that it comes from far away and, I believe, from one specific district.' At the same time, he told me he had been in territories where silver was worth as much as gold . . .

One can see that the author of this letter looked round with open eyes in the strange environment in which he found himself. He very soon knew that no gold was produced in the Sahara, and it was also quite clear to him why a high proportion of the gold from the African interior accumulated at this particular spot. There was salt here, a mineral which wide areas of tropical Africa lacked and which they purchased with gold. This gold came from the deep south; it was not to be found either in the Sahara or on the coasts, but unattainably far away.

Malfante's report to the Centurione was therefore not very encouraging. For he also knew that the gold trade was in firm hands. True, in spite of being a Christian and a European he had encountered no hostility in the Tuat oasis—surprisingly, it must be added. But there can be little doubt from the tenor of his letter to Giovanni Marioni that the Arabs engaged in the gold trade watched jealously over their interests, and that there would have been little point in establishing a branch of the Centurione in Tuat. The statement that it would be possible to get to Egypt by the river which flowed past Timbuctoo, which he must also have included in his report to the Centurione, was undoubtedly deemed in Europe to confirm the information handed down from antiquity—a view fully endorsed by Malfante himself. It is not certain whether his report concerning Indian merchants in the Tuat oases really referred to Indians or to Abyssinians. It is perfectly possible that they were actually Indians; since Timbuctoo carried on a brisk trade with Egypt and Asia Minor during the fourteenth and fifteenth centuries, Indian traders might well have found their way into the region.

4

Although Malfante's journey was certainly only one of many expeditions into the African interior launched by Europe—just as Carpini's and Ruysbroek's travels in the interior of Asia were not isolated feats—the geographical significance of the advances made by sea greatly exceeded that of the possibly far more numerous land journeys. For it is generally more important to find out the extent and shape of an unknown country than the nature of its hinterland; exploration of the interior is usually a sequel to the charting of its coasts.

For this reason the Portuguese again and again renewed their southward advance. When Cão reached 22° S. on his second voyage, he probably heard rumours from the natives that it *was* possible to circumnavigate Africa. For whereas European geography in the late Middle Ages doubted whether Africa was circumnavigable, holding the Indian Ocean to be an inland sea, the majority of Arab geographers took the view that it was possible to sail round the Dark Continent—especially those who had themselves been to Arab East Africa. They had good reason for this belief. Not only did the east coast of South Africa run in a gentle curve to the west—which completely contradicted the antique conviction that Africa was joined to India—but there is also no doubt that from time to time some Arab skipper sailed far past Cape Corrientes, the southern limit of the Arab sphere of interest in Africa. Probably even, there is substance in the old Arab tradition that an Arab vessel rounded the Cape of Good Hope as early as 1420. It is by no means impossible that Cão also knew of this.

When his ships returned to Lisbon unsuccessfully, however, doubts seem to have been again raised as to the feasibility of reaching the Indian Ocean by sea. These doubts were all the more cogent because, towards the end of the fifteenth century, many voices were raised in Europe to demand a resumption of the ancient Asiatic trade route up the Indus and down the Amur Darya. Amongst other arguments in favour of this difficult route one was very important: even if there were a seaway to India round the southern tip of Africa, it would take a very long time and lead to the costly Indian spices being exposed for weeks and months to blazing heat. This would have a deleterious effect on their aroma, and there was cause to fear that the deterioration in flavour would reduce the profits, which had to be high to counterbalance the great element of risk.

It was evidently decided in Lisbon at this period to seek a final clarification of the situation. In 1487 the Portuguese crown threw two trump cards into the game at once: it dispatched a group of trusted nobles to India and Abyssinia along the land route, and in the same year sent out Bartholomew Diaz with two 50-ton caravels and an escort ship to complete the circumnavigation of Africa and open up the seaway to India.

The overland expedition left Portugal in May 1487, and Bartholomew Diaz weighed anchor for his great voyage in August. At the commencement it was under a lucky star. Northerly winds drove the little fleet rapidly southwards. The fearsome Cape Bojador was rounded at the first attempt. One after another the forts and strong-points established by the Portuguese appeared along the coast: the burgeoning Arguyn at Cape Blanco in North-west Africa, terminus of the old caravan routes over the Sahara, which later fell into the possession first of Brandenburg and then of France: after this the equally flourishing Elmina near Three Points on the Gold Coast. Then followed Diego Cão's marble crosses: at the estuary of the Congo, at Santa Maria in Benguela, and finally that at Cape Cross on the Swakop.

Now the Portuguese were confronted by virgin territory: a difficult coast, broken by reefs and sandbanks, pitilessly scorched by the sun, with barren, inhospitable mountain-sides. On Christmas 1487 they landed in Angra Pequena Bay at 26° 35' S., to celebrate the Nativity and get a little rest. Far and wide this bay was the only sheltered haven. Bartholomew Diaz's heart missed a beat when he thought how vulnerable to storms his fleet was. When he set sail again after the feast-days he would stand well out to sea. God help anyone who foundered here, or even ran aground on a sandbank! No water, no people, not a trace of vegetation anywhere. And this pitiless sun day after day. But he had made one encouraging observation: the rivers that flowed down from the land were mere trickles compared with the Congo which they had passed a few weeks back. This could only mean that these rivers had no hinterland in which to swell their waters. So the land here must be narrow; it must have got narrower and narrower since they passed the Congo; it must run to a point in the south. Again and again he went over in his mind what Martin Behaim had told him and Diego Cão confirmed: that the coast of east Africa seemed to recede in the south, that it seemed to withdraw to the west. And this coast here, on which he was celebrating Christmas—didn't it turn to the east? Didn't he have to veer a few points to larboard every few days?

They listened to Mass, there were extra portions of rum, there was fresh water, they larked about the ship and in the rigging. Christmas passed, and one day the mates' whistles trilled. The sails ran up the masts, and in the teeth of a fresh north-wester the three caravels heaved and set as they headed for the open sea. The north-wester held, it grew continually stiffer; Diaz thought with concern of the dangerous coast. The north-wester blew up to a gale. Away from land, God preserve us! 'Due south,' he bellowed to the helmsman through the howling of the gale, 'Due south,' came back the echo from the helm; the three ships heeled more sharply to leeward, and the shore sank beneath the jagged skyline. The gale held. With tautly braced yards they ran swiftly south —away from the land, only away from the land!

In the middle of January 1488 the storm at last died down. The wind hauled forward, then blew steadily from the west; Diaz sailed due east. Where could the land be? A day passed, and another. No sign of land. Trouble was brewing among the crew. The lads were scared. There was no denying that the supply position was bad. The salt meat hadn't kept. It lay grey and green on the tin plates, and the stores stank like a knacker's yard. 'Due north,' ordered Diaz, and the tubby craft swung clumsily into the new direction.

The third day was sinking into evening when there was a yell from the crow's nest, from the fore lookout: Tierra! Tierra! Land ahoy! There was still nothing to be seen from the fo'c's'le but sea, a long, rolling swell. No, there it was! A thin grey streak that gradually became heavier, darker, more distinct. No doubt about it, that was land!

It was the beginning of February 1488. Diaz had no idea where he was, and nor have we. He probably stood two hundred miles east of the Cape of Good Hope in the area of Mossel Bay. Perhaps he had a presentiment that he had rounded Africa during these days of storm. But he wanted certainty. So he followed the coast northwards for a few days. Then he knew he had done it. He had finally completed what Henry the Navigator had begun at the start of the century. Africa had been circumnavigated, the seaway to India found!

At the Great Fish River, between Port Elizabeth and East London, his mutinying crews forced Diaz to put about. He cruised cautiously westward against perpetual winds. And as he passed the Cape of Good Hope there was such a storm that he called it *Cabo Tormentoso*, Stormy Cape. This name did not please John II of Portugal. He changed it to the Cape of Good Hope, because the existence of a sea route to India had at last been proved.

Bartholomew Diaz was not able to realize the hope of getting to India this way, to which he himself doubtless also clung. The equip-

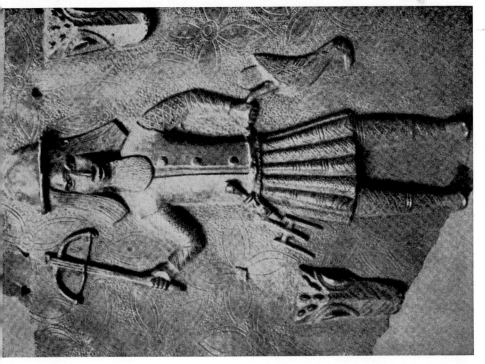

56. Portuguese seaman from the end of the 15th century. Negro sculpture from Benin, West Africa.

55. Prince Henry of Portugal, the Navigator. Late 15th-century miniature.

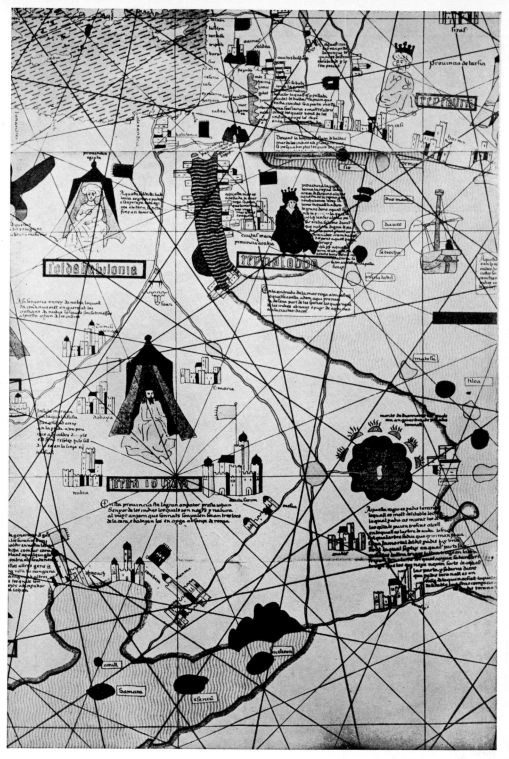

**57.** East Africa according to the 15th century Catalan map of the world. Although by this time people had been sailing down the east coast of Africa as far as Sofala for some 4,500 years, the late Middle Ages were still full of misconceptions about it.

ment of his ships would hardly have sufficed for the voyage. In any case, there was still a gap in the geographical picture of the seaway to India which had been gradually emerging since Prince Henry founded his school of navigation. This gap was filled in by the land expedition which left for India in the same years as Diaz and his little fleet. Its leading member, the knight Pedro de Covilhao, journeyed first via Aden to the Malabar coast of India, and on his return explored

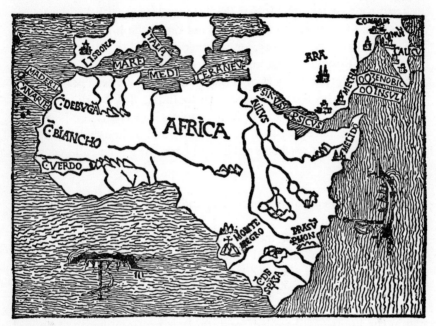

60. *Italian map of Africa. This map, made in Milan in 1508, the so-called* Itinerarium Portugallensium *or* Voyages of the Portu-guese, *reproduces the ideas about the shape of Africa current in Italy at the beginning of the modern era. C. Debuga corresponds to Cape Bojador, C. Biancho is Cape Blanco, C. Verdo is Cape Verde, Monte Negro is an eminence on which Diego Cão erected a stone pillar in 1486. The Persian Gulf is displaced into the Red Sea; Mecha (Mecca) is in quite the wrong position. The identity of Zenobic Insul is dubious. Compan in India represents Cambay; the other two towns in Hither India are Cananore and Calicut.*

east Africa as far as the Zambesi and the port of Sofala. His observa-tions, linked to those of Bartholomew Diaz, made it finally clear that the Atlantic and the Indian Ocean joined and that it was undoubtedly possible to reach India by sea.

This year, 1488, also fills in the last gap in our chapter on Africa and the Portuguese. At its beginning stands the impressive figure of Henry the Navigator, at its end the opening of the seaway to India by the Portuguese. This achievement was entirely the work of the Infante, who was alone responsible for Portugal's development into a seafaring nation, of which—in spite of her geographical situation on the ocean, her broken coastline and excellent harbours, and her population largely engaged in fishing and therefore used to coastal sailing—she had hitherto showed no sign. It was the Infante Henry with his mania for navigation who drove the Portuguese out on to the high seas. Whether the individual makes history, or whether a man like Henry is merely the medium through which impersonal historical forces find expression, one thing is certain: it was not the Portuguese squires, peasants and working men who opened the seaway to India, despite all those who gave their blood and their lives in the process, but Henry the Navigator —although he never went to sea himself, and although the Cape of Good Hope was not reached until he had been lying for a full generation in his grave.

We are at the end of our narrative, and at the same time at the gateway to a new era.

This era was not new merely because the seaway had opened eastward to the Indian fairyland and westward to the New World, and that consequently all the wonders of the earth were poured out over Europe. It was new because it gave birth to new men.

The emergence of a new type of man took place almost in a flash, within the limits of a bare half century. Its representatives in the world of outward, tangible achievement were men like Columbus, Cortés and Pizarro. In the world of the spirit, personalities such as Copernicus, Erasmus of Rotterdam, Dürer and Ulrich von Hutten—to name but four—made their appearance.

Before their advent there was wailing and gnashing of teeth. It seemed to the people of the day that bewilderment, unbelief, disloyalty and doubt had never reached such proportions; never, they thought, had wars been so bloody, murder so frequent, poison, the dagger and every kind of dastardly act so widespread; never had men believed the end of the world so imminent as in the last decades of the fifteenth century.

It was an ancient dread that stalked abroad. The sacred prophetesses of the old Teutons had already prophesied the ghastly Last Battle thousands of years ago. These images were now half obscured beneath a Christo-Oriental overlay. The mystic poem on the End of the World written by Methodius of Patara in A.D. 800 was reprinted in Cologne in 1475. Twenty years earlier, the Turks had overrun Byzantium, the holy city, with fearful slaughter, and Methodius's warning sent a shudder through the listening world:

The time will come when the Agareni will gather again in German lands and go forth out of the wilderness. They will take possession of the world for eight years. And they will pervert cities and kingdoms, they will strangle the priests in the holy places. They will lie with the women and they will drink from the sacred vessels. And they will tether their beasts to the hallowed graves.

An Apocalyptic note already rang in the mystical letter of Prester John to the three protagonists of the high Middle Ages, the Pope and the two Emperors. Now fear of the cataclysm rose to a horrifying certainty. And when, in 1485, a total eclipse of the sun visible to all Europe followed the conjunction of two such powerful and baleful planets as Jupiter and Saturn, it was clear to all who possessed understanding:

The signs and wonders brought by this eclipse and darkness are horrible and almost terrifying. And much more ghastly if any man has experienced and seen them. So much so that horror prevents me from declaring their import.

This was written in 1488 by the Alsatian scholar and astrologer, Johann Lichtenberger, in a widely distributed tract. W. E. Peukert has written of this at length in his interesting book *The Great Turning-point* (see Bibliography), leaving no doubt that Johann Lichtenberger was merely expressing the opinion of everyone: of the peasant trembling before the large-scale capitalism of the departing Middle Ages, of the burgher menaced by unceasing plundering and perpetual deeds of violence, of the kings and great lords in everlasting feuds with one another, of the monks and popes full of sins and transgressions.

But everyone sought to lay the blame for this 'eclipse and darkness' on someone else's shoulders. Peasants in debt to the Jews massacred them all over the country; Huss and Wycliffe inveighed against the sinful lives of the papists; emperors and princes blamed the corruption on each other; sick brains gave birth to the idea of the witches' hammer, the *malleus maleficarum*—and the most profound and poignant inner distress caused Josephus Grünpeck, historian to the Emperor Frederick III, to cry out to the impassive heavens:

It is true that when you perceive the miserable corruption of the whole of Christendom, of all praiseworthy customs, rules and laws, the wretchedness of all classes, the many pestilences, the changes in this epoch and all the strange happenings, you know that the End of the World is near. And the waters of affliction will flow over the whole of Christendom.

This cry rings familiar in our ears, as though it were our own lament, our own call for help.

But as heaven remained dumb, the chasms opened. Flowers no longer faded, they decayed. Death was no longer the calm close of a declining summer day; it was a grinning skeleton with bared teeth, indifferently swinging its scythe. Everything fell beneath its strokes: the grass, the flowers, the ripening corn, the young shoot, the withering leaf. Death was merry over his harvest: he was painted for the first time in joyful dance on the walls of the Cemetery of the Innocents in Paris in 1424. He has been depicted thus a thousand times since then, in woodcuts, sculptures and relief, culminating in the ghastly irony of Dürer's *danse macabre* in Hartmann Schedel's *World Chronicle* of 1493.

This is the background to the despairing dialogue between Death and the 'Ploughman of Saaz', Peter Kettenfeier, whose young wife, Mistress Margaret, the Great Reaper swept off into the Dark Kingdom in 1400. Most of us today have seen plenty of the handiwork of the great dark lord who says:

You ask whence we come: we come from the earthly paradise. There God created us. And named us with our true name, as he said: In the day that thou eatest thereof thou shalt surely die thy death. Therefore we sign ourselves: We, Death, Lord and Powerful One on Earth, in the Air and in the Waters of the Sea.

But this was also the background to the desperate attempt to forget everything in pathological intemperance, in wine, music, dicing, the harlotry of the bagnios, and naked dances. The *Zimmerian Chronicle* relates not infrequently that some woman 'danced quite naked with wanton persons, to the accompaniment of unspeakable lechery'. Cut yourself another thick slice and stuff it in quickly, for tomorrow everything may have come to a terrible end—this too was one of the signs of the times.

How familiar it all is! We have experienced it all ourselves, and how deep our own gods lie buried.

And yet humanity will no more perish today than it did five hundred years ago! For while the whole world was staring fascinated into the abyss of the Last Things, overcome by horror and delighting in it, the gates of a new age were slowly opening. Imperceptibly at first, growing gradually brighter and brighter, and finally dazzling and sparkling, light flooded into the prison gloom. Sails sped through the blue day, and as if by magic new shores rose up out of the void. A few decades later, Ulrich von Hutten, tormented by a loathsome disease and racked by festering sores, exclaimed with glowing enthusiasm: 'The spirits are awake, it is joy to be alive!'

Is this message perhaps directed to us as well? Have we not always recognized ourselves in the portrayal of men and events which has unrolled before our eyes? Are we, who have already been summoned by the Last Trump, perhaps standing beside a door that is slowly beginning to open?

We do not know. But we should like to believe so, we must believe so, and we have good cause to. For time and again, as long as there have been men on the earth, the old prophecy of Dr. Faustus has proved true: 'We to new shores are called by a new day.'

# BIBLIOGRAPHY

# BIBLIOGRAPHY

BERTHOLD ALTANER: *Die Dominikanermissionen des 13. Jahrunderts*, Habelschwerdt, 1924.

JULIUS ANDREE: *Bergbau in der Vorzeit*, Leipzig, 1922.

FRIEDRICH BEHN: *Kultur der Urzeit*, Berlin, 1950.

HELMUT BERVE: *Gestaltende Kräfte der Antike*, Munich, 1949.

E. BORCHARDT: *Das Grabdenkmal des König Sahure*, Stuttgart, 1912.

A. BRAGHINE: *A Shadow of Atlantis*, London, 1937.

J. H. BREASTED: *A History of Egypt*, New York: Scribner, 1905.

ADAM OF BREMEN: *Hamburgische Kirchengeschichte*, publ. by Schmeidler-Steinberg, Leipzig, 1926.

A. BREUSING: *Die Nautik der Alten*, Bremen, 1886.

A. W. BRÖGGER: *Vinlandsferdene*, Oslo, 1937.

PETER H. BUCK: *Vikings of the Sunrise*, New York, 1938.

F. CALLEJA: 'Note sur une stèle phénicienne trouvée en Brésil', in *Bulletin de la Société de Géographie d'Alger*, Paris, 1899.

J. CARCOPINO: *Daily Life in Ancient Rome*, translated by E. O. Lorimer, London: Routledge, 1941.

LAS CASAS: *Historia de las Indias*, in *Coleccion de documentos para la historia de España*, Madrid, 1875/6.

GEORGE CATLIN: *The North American Indians. Being letters and notes on their manners, customs, and conditions, written during eight years travel amongst the wildest tribes of Indians in North America, 1832–1839*, Edinburgh: John Grant, 1926.

A. V. CHAMISSO: *Reise um die Welt in den Jahren 1815 bis 1818*, Leipzig, 1842.

E. CHAVANNES: *Les Pays à l'Occident d'après le Heou-han-chou*, Paris, 1907.

HYDE CLARK: 'Examination of the Legend of Atlantis', in *Transactions of the Royal Historical Society*, London, 1885.

CONDAMINE: 'Rapport sur les monuments du Péru en temps des Inkas', in *Schriften der Perussischen Akademie der Wissenschaften*, Berlin, 1746.

RUDOLF CRONAU: *Amerika. Die Geschichte seiner Entdeckung von der ältesten bis auf die neueste Zeit*, Leipzig, 1892.

CHARLES T. CURRELLY: 'Viking weapons found near Beardmore', in *Canadian Historical Review*, March, 1939.

ERNST CURTIUS: *Griechische Geschichte*, Vienna, 1935.

TH. W. DANZEL: *Handbuch der präkolumbischen Kulturen in Latein-amerika*, Hamburg, 1927.

DEFREMERY-SAUGUINETTE: *Voyages d'Ibn Batoutah*, Paris, 1848.

H. DINER: *Seide. Eine kleine Kulturgeschichte*, Meisenheim a. Gl., 1949.

R. B. DIXON: 'The problem of the sweet potato in Polynesia', in *American Anthropoligst*, Vol. 34, No. 1, 1932.

MAX EBERT: *Südrussland im Altertum*, Bonn and Leipzig, 1921.

CAMILLE ENLART: 'Le Problème de la vieille tour de Newport', in *Revue de l'art chrétien*, Vol. 60, Paris, 1910.

CARL ERDMANN: *Die Entstehung des Kreuzzugsgedankens*, Stuttgart, 1935.

GABRIEL FERRAND: 'Le K'ouen-Louen et les anciennes navigations dans les mers du Sud', in *Journal Asiatique*, Paris, 1919.

FRANZ M. FELDHAUS: *Die Technik der Antike und des Mittelalters*, Leipzig, 1931.

B. FIMMEN: *Die kretisch-mykenische Kultur*, Leipzig, 1924.

O. FINSCH: *Südseearbeiten*, Hamburg, 1914.

JOHN FISKE: *The discovery of America*, London, 1892.

FR. FRAHM: 'Grabungen und Forschungen aus der Wikingerzeit der Schleswiger Landenge', in *Historische Zeitschrift, Bd. 151*, Berlin, 1933.

GEORG FRÖLEN: *Nordens Befästa Rundkirkor*, Stockholm, 1911.

GEORG FRIDERICI: 'Die vorkolumbischen Verbindungen der Südsee-völker mit Amerika', in *Mitteilungen aus den deutschen Schutzge-bieten, Bd. 36, Heft 1*, Berlin, 1928.

E. FRIEDELL: *Kulturgeschichte Ägyptens und des alten Orients*, Munich, 1951.

*Kulturgeschichte Griechenlands*, Munich, 1949.

KARL FROMME: *Die nordgermanische Kolonisation im atlantischen, Raum*, Kiel, 1939.

P. GAFFAREL: *Les Irlandais en Amérique avant Colomb*, Paris, 1890.

G. M. GATHORNE-HARDY: *The Norse Discoverers of America*, Oxford University Press, 1921.

'A recent journey in Northern Labrador', in *Geographical Journal*, Vol. 59, London, 1922.

K. GEISELER: *Die Osterinsel. Eine Stätte prähistorischer Kultur in der Südsee*, Berlin, 1883.

EUGENE GELCICH: 'Der Fischfang der Gascogner und die Entdeckung von Neufundland', in *Zeitschrift der Gesellschaft für Erdkunde,* Berlin, 1883.

GEORG GERLAND: *Der Mythus der Sintflut*, Bonn, 1912.

H. A. R. GIBB: *Selections from the Travels of Ibn Batuta*, London: Routledge, 1929.

FRANCESCO LOPES DE GOMARA: *Historia de las Indias*, Venice, 1564.

E. F. GRAY: *Leif Eriksson, discoverer of America*, New York, 1930.

SIEGMUND GÜNTHER: *Das Zeitalter der Entdeckungen*, Leipzig, 1901.

J. DE GUIGNES: *Histoire générale des Huns, des Turcs, des Mongols et des autres Tartares occidentaux*, Paris, 1736.

ERICH HAENICH: 'Kulturbilder aus Chinas Mongolenzeit', in *Historische Zeitschrift, Bd.* 164, Berlin, 1911.

R. HAMANN: *Ägyptische Kunst*, Berlin, 1944.
   *Grieschische Kunst*, Munich, 1949.

HENRI HARISSE: *Jeanet Sebastian Cabot*, Paris, 1882.

MASUKICHI HASHIMOTO: 'Origins of the Compass', in *Memoirs of the Research Dep. 37 the Toyo Bunko No. 1.*

ROBERT HEINE-GELDERN: *Die Megalithen Südostasiens und ihre Bedeutung für die Klärung der Megalithenfrage in Europe und Polynesien. Authropos XXIII*, Vienna, 1928.

R. HENNIG: 'Die Fruhkenntnis der magnetischen Nordweisung', in *Beiträge zur Geschichte der Technik und Industrie, Bd.* 21, 1931.
   'Das Christentum im mittelalterlichen Asien und sein Einfluss auf die Sage vom Priester Johannes', in *Historische Vierteljahresschrift, XXIX Jahrg.*, Dresden, 1934.
   *Terrae incognitae I–IV*, Leiden, 1936.
   *Wo lag das Paradies?*, Berlin, 1950.

H. HERBST: *Wilhelm von Rubruks Reisebericht an König Ludwig IX*, Leipzig, 1925.

ALBERT HERRMANN: *Die Erdkarte der Urbibel*, Brunswick, 1931.
   *Marco Polo am Hofe des Grosskhans*, Leipzig, 1949.
   *Die alten Seidenstrassen zwischen China und Syrien*, Berlin, 1910.

E. HERRMANN: *Das Nordpolarmeer*, Berlin, 1949.

P. HERRMANN: *Saxo Grammaticus gesta Danorum*, Leipzig, 1901.
   *Das grosse Wagnis*, Berlin, 1936.

THOR HEYERDAHL: *The Kon-Tiki Expedition. By raft across the South Seas,* translated by F. H. Lyon, London: Allen and Unwin, 1950.

I. C. HEYWOOD: *Documenta selecta a tabulario secreto Vaticano*, Rome, 1893.

FR. HIRTH: *China and the Roman Orient*, Leipzig, 1885.

HJALMAR R. HOLAND: *The Kensington Stone: a study in pre-Columbian American history*, Ephraim, Wisconsin, 1932.
*Westward from Vinland*, New York, 1940 (2nd edition 1942).
*America 1355–1364*, New York, 1946.

ALFRED HOLDER: *Altkeltischer Sprachschatz*, Leipzig, 1904.

A. HOOPS: *Reallexikon der germanischen Altertumskunde*, Leipzig, 1923.

SIEGFRIED HUBER: *Im Reich der Inkas*, Olten, 1951.

A. V. HUMBOLDT: *L'examen critique de l'histoire de la géographie*, Paris, 1836.
*Ansichten der Natur*, Stuttgart, 1851.
*Kritische Untersuchungen*, Berlin, 1852.

GUNNAR ISACHSEN: 'Hvor langt mot nord kom de norröne Groenlandinger paa sine Fangstaerder', in *Norsk Geografisk Tidsskrift*, *IV*, Oslo, 1932.

J. IVERSEHEN: 'Moorgeologische Untersuchungen auf Grönland', in *Mitteilungen der Dänischen Geologischen Gesellschaft*, *VIII*, Copenhagen, 1934.

HERBERT JAHNKUHN: *Haithabu*, Leipzig, 1937.

GEORG JAKOB: *Arabische Berichte von Gesandten an germanischen Fürstenhöfen aus dem 9. und 10. Jahrhundert*, Berlin, 1927.

L. JELIC: 'L'évangélisation de l'Amérique avant Chr. Colomb', in *Compte rendu du quatrième congrès scientifique international des catholiques, Section V*, Brussels, 1895.

J. JOHNSTON: 'Account of the present state of the Indian Tribes inhabiting Ohio', in *Archæologia Americana*, Boston, 1819.

PETER KALM: *Travels in North America*, translated into English by J. R. Forster, London, 1771.

RAFAEL KARSTEN: *Das altperuanische Inkareich*, Leipzig, 1949.

RICHARD KATZ: *Auf dem Amazonas*, Zurich, 1946.

C. M. KAUFMANN: *Amerika und das Urchristentum*, Munich, 1924.

JOSEPH KESSEL: *Mermoz*, Freudenstadt, 1948.

HEINRICH KIEPERT: *Lehrbuch der alten Geographie*, Berlin, 1878.

H. L. KLAPROTH: *Tableaux historiques de l'Asie*, Paris, 1824.

WALTER KNOCHE: *Die Osterinsel*, Concepcion, Chile, 1923.

AUGUST KÖSTER: *Schiffahrt und Handelsverkehr des östlichen Mittelmeers im 3. und 2. Jahrtausend v. Chr.*, Leipzig, 1924.
*Studien zur Geschichte des antiken Seewesens*, Berlin, 1934.

## Bibliography 437

H. Kühn: *Auf den Spuren des Eiszeitmenschen*, Wiesbaden, 1950.

Walter Krickeberg: *Märchen der Azteken, Inka, Maya und Muiska*, Jena, 1928.

J. M. Lappenburg: *Hamburgische Urkunden in niedersächsischer Sprache*, Hamburg, 1861.

*Hamburgische Chroniken in niedersächsischer Sprache*, Hamburg, 1860.

Lechler-Gray: *Die Entdecker Amerikas vor Columbus*, Leipzig, 1939.

Walter Lehmann: 'Uber das Alter der amerikanischen Kulturen', in *Ibero-Amerikanisches Archiv, XVII*, Berlin, 1943/4.

'Die Bedeutung der altamerikanischen Hochkulturen für die allgemeine Geschichte der Menschheit', in *Ibero-Amerikanisches Archiv, XVII*, Berlin, 1943/4.

A. Lesky: *Thalatta. Der Weg der Griechen zum Meer*, Vienna, 1947.

Lester-Millot: *Grundriss der Anthropologie*, Lahr, 1948.

Cl. Chr. Lyschander: *Grönlandska Chronica*, 1608.

J. W. McCrindle: *The Christian Topography of Cosmas* (Indicopleustes), London: The Hakluyt Society, 1897.

F. Markwart: 'Ein arabischer Bericht über die arktischen Länder aus dem 10. Jahrhundert', in *Ungarische Jahrbücher 1924, Jahrgang 4.*

John Marshall: *Mohenjo-daro and the Indus Culture*, London, 1931.

A. Martin: *Tartessos*, Seville, 1940.

F. G. Meinert: *Johann von Marignolas Reise in das Morgenland vom Jahre 1339 bis 1353*, Prague, 1820.

Rudolf Meissner: *Der Königsspiegel*, Halle, 1944.

Merian: *The Natives of the Tonga Islands*, London, 1818.

Samuel E. Morison: *Admiral of the Ocean Sea. A Life of Christopher Columbus*, Boston, 1942.

Alfred Métraux: *Easter Island*, Bulletin 16 of the Bishop Museum, Honolulu, 1938.

Eduard Meyer: *Geschichte des Altertums*, Stuttgart, 1901.

Heinz Michaelis: 'Riesenschiffe', in *Meereskunde, VIII, Heft 3*, Berlin, 1914.

M. Mjelde: 'Eyktarstadproblemer og vinlandsreisene', in *Norsk Historisk Tidsskrift, V*, Oslo, 1927.

C. v. Moeller: 'Die Osterinsel und Peru', in *Zeitschrift für Ethnologie, Heft 1/3*, 1937.

Oskar Montelius: 'Der Handel in der Vorzeit', in *Prähistorische Zeitschrift*, 1910.

G. de Mertillet: *Origine de la pêche*, Paris, 1890.

Fritjof Nansen: *In Northern Mists*, London, 1911.

I. NASMYTH: *Itineraria Symonis Simeonis et Willelmi de Worcester,* Cambridge, 1778.

GUSTAV NECKEL: *Die erste Entdeckung Amerikas durch die Nordgermanen,* Leipzig, 1934.

PAUL NÖRLUND: *Wikingersiedlungen in Grönland. Ihre Entstehung und ihr Schicksal,* Leipzig, 1937.

ERLAND NORDENSKIÖLD: *Origin of the Indian civilisations in South America,* Göteborg, 1931.

LEONARDO OLSCHKI: 'Der Brief des Predigers Johannes', in *Historische Zeitschrift, Bd.* 144, Munich, 1931.

GUSTAVE OPPERT: 'Der Presbyter Johannes', in *Sage und Geschichte,* Berlin, 1864.

KARL PAGEL: *Die Hanse,* Oldenberg, 1942.

O. PARET: *Das neue Bild der Vorgeschichte,* Stuttgart, 1948.

S. PASSARGE: *Geographische Völkerkunde,* Berlin, 1951.

E. PASTOR: 'Die Germanen kannten die Kugelgestalt der Erde', in *Wacht im Osten,* Danzig, 1938.

OTTO PELKA: *Bernstein,* Berlin, 1920.

O. PESCHEL: *Geschichte der Erdkunde,* Munich, 1877.

ALFRED PETRAU: *Schrift und Schriften im Leben der Völker,* Berlin (no date).

W. E. PEUKERT: *Die grosse Wende,* Hamburg, 1948.

GERTRUD GRÄFIN VON PODEWILS-DÜRNITZ: *Legenden der Chibcha,* Stuttgart, 1930.

ED. POEPPIG: *Im Schatten der Cordillere. Reisen in Chile,* Stuttgart, 1927.

ARTHUR POSNANSKY: *Precursores de Colon. Las Perlas Agri Nosotros,* 1933.

HANS PRUTZ: *Kulturgeschichte der Kreuzzüge,* Berlin, 1883.

HEINRICH QUIRING: *Geschichte des Goldes,* Stuttgart, 1950.

BERNARDO RAMOS: *Inscripcões e Tradiciões da America prehistorica,* Rio de Janeiro, 1932.

C. CHR. RAFN: *Antiquitates Americanæ,* Copenhagen, 1837.

O. S. REUTER: *Germanische Himmelskunde,* Munich, 1934.

F. V. RICHTHOFEN: *China,* Berlin, 1878.

CH. DE LA RONCIÈRE: *La découverte de l'Afrique au moyen âge,* Cairo, 1927.

FRITZ RÖCK: 'Sternglaube und Weltbild der Tolteken als Zeugen verschollener Kulturbeziehungen zur Alten Welt', in *Mitteilungen der Anthropologischen Gesellschaft,* Vienna, 1922.

E. D. Ross: 'Marco Polo and his book', in *Proceedings of the Royal British Academy*, XX, London, 1933.

Sophus Ruge: *Columbus*, Berlin, 1902.

Hans Schaal: *Vom Tauschhandel zum Welthandel*, Leipzig, 1931.

R. Scheppig: 'Die Cão-Säule von Kap Cross', in *Wissenschaftliche Beilage zum Programm 340 des Reform-Realgymnasiums*, Kiel, 1903.

Henry Schoolcraft: *Historical and statistical information respecting the history, condition and prospects of the Indian tribes of the U.S.*, Philadelphia, 1851–7.

W. H. Schoof: *Periplous maris Erythraei*, Stuttgart, 1912.

Percy E. Schramm: *Kaiser, Rom und Renovatio*, Leipzig, 1929.

Fr. Schulze-Maizier: *Die Osterinsel*, Leipzig (no date).

Adolf Schulten: *Tartessos*, Hamburg, 1922/51.

Oskar Schumann: 'Islands Siedlungsgebiete während der Landnahmezeit', in *Mitteilungen des Vereins für Erdkunde*, Leipzig, 1899.

G. Schwantes: 'Die Vorgeschichte Schleswig-Holsteins', in *Geschichte Schleswig-Holsteins*, Kiel, 1934.

J. Sefton: 'Eirik the Red's Saga', *Proceedings of the Literary and Philosophical Society of Liverpool, No. XXXIV*, 1880.

Alexander Seipel: *Rerum Normannicarum Fontes Arabici*, Oslo, 1896.

Freya Stark: *The Southern Gates of Arabia: a journey in the Hadhramaut*, London, 1946.

Theodor Steche: *Wikinger entdecken Amerika*, Hamburg, 1934.
'Die nordgermanischen Fahrten nach Vinland und ihre Nachwirkungen', in *Zeitschrift für Deutsche Philologie*, Halle, 1935.

Eberhard Stechow: 'Geographisch-historische Probleme aus antiker Zeit', in *Naturwissenschaftliche Rundschau, Heft 11*, 1950.
'Santorin-Katastrophe und Ägyptische Finsternis', in *Forschungen und Fortschritte*, Berlin, 1950.
'Kannte das Altertum die Insel Madagaskar?', in *Petermanns Geographische Mitteilungen, Heft 3–4*, Gotha, 1944.
'Wann kamen die Malaien zuerst nach Madagaskar?', in *Forschungen und Fortischritte, Nr. 18*, 1944.
'Der Umkehrpunkt der Fahrt im "Periplus Hannonis" ', in *Forschungen und Fortschritte, 21.–23. Jahrg., Nr. 10–12*, Berlin, 1947.

Vilhjalmur Stefansson: *Das Geheimnis der Eskimos*, Leipzig, 1920.

F. Storbeck: *Berichte der arabischen Geographen des Mittelalters über Ostafrika*, Tübingen, 1912.

Gustav Storm: *Annales Reseniani ad annum 1121*, Christiania, 1888.

440        *Bibliography*

'Om Biskop Oddsons Annaler', in *Archiv für nordische Philologie, IV*, Lund, 1890, Christiania, 1888.

ED. STUCKEN: 'Polynesisches Sprachgut in Amerika und in Sumer', in *Mitteilungen der Vorderasiatisch-Ägyptischen Gesellschaft*, Berlin, 1926.

SNORRE STURLASON (1178–1241): *Heimskringla or the Lives of the Norse Kings*, translated into English by Erling Monsen and A. H. Smith, Cambridge: W. Heffer, 1932.

JOHN R. SWANTON: *The Wineland Voyages*, Smithsonian Miscellaneous Collections, Vol. 116, No. 3: Washington, 1947.

J. BUCHAN TELFER: *The Bondage and Travels of Johann Schiltberger in Europe, Asia, and Africa, 1396–1427*, London: The Hakluyt Society, 1879.

WILLIAM THALBITZER: *Two Runic Stones from Greenland and Minnesota*, Smithsonian Miscellaneous Collections, Vol. 116, No. 3: Washington 1951.

KARL THORNBERG: *Omde i Svensk jord funna österländska mynt*, Stockholm, 1857.

J. TOBLER: *Biblica Geographia Palæstinæ*, Leipzig, 1867.

W. TREUE: *Die Eroberung der Erde*, Berlin, 1939.

JUAN DE TORQUEMADA: *Los veinte y un libros rituales y monarchia Indiana*, Madrid, 1723.

LUKA WADDING: *Annales Minorum Fratrum*, Quaracchi, 1932.

ANNE TERRY WHITE: *Lost Worlds. Adventures in Archaeology*, London: Harrap, 1943.

VON WILAMOWITZ-MÖLLENDORF: *Homerische Untersuchungen*, Berlin, 1884.

HEINRICH WINTER: *Die Nautik der Wikinger und ihre Bedeutung für die Entwicklung der europäischen Seefahrt*, Danzig, 1938.

N. WINTHER: *Färöernes Oldtidhistorie*, Copenhagen, 1857.

WILHELM WITTER: *Wörtherbuch der Antike*, Stuttgart, 1950.

HENRY YULE: *Cathay and the Way Thither*, London: The Hakluyt Society, 1866.

    *The Book of Ser Marco Polo, the Venetian*, London: John Murray, 1874 (2nd revised edition 1875).

FRIEDRICH ZARNCKE: 'Der Priester Johannes', in *Abhandlungen der Königlich Sächsischen Akademie der Wissenschaften, Phil.-Hist. Klasse, VII*, Leipzig, 1879/83.

EGMONT ZECHLIN: *Maritime Weltgeschichte*, Hamburg, 1947.

E. ZYHLARS: 'Das Land Punt', in *Zeitschrift für Eingeborenensprachen*, Leipzig, 1941/2.

# INDEX